The *Zorro* Television Companion

The *Zorro*
Television Companion

A Critical Appreciation

GERRY DOOLEY

McFarland & Company, Inc., Publishers
Jefferson, North Carolina, and London

Library of Congress Cataloguing-in-Publication Data

Dooley, Gerry, 1954–
The *Zorro* television companion : a critical appreciation / Gerry Dooley.
p.   cm.
Includes bibliographical references and index.

ISBN 0-7864-2058-8 (softcover : 50# alkaline paper) ∞

1. Zorro (Television program)   I. Title.
PN1992.77.Z67D66   2005   791.45'72 — dc22   2005009057

British Library cataloguing data are available

Cover design by Mark Durr

Manufactured in the United States of America

*McFarland & Company, Inc., Publishers
Box 611, Jefferson, North Carolina 28640
www.mcfarlandpub.com*

To Mom and Dad
and Suzie

Acknowledgments

Many people helped in the writing of this book. Here are a few: Andy Shepherd, who helped get the ball rolling. Pete Poplaski for his knowledge and encouragement; he's a good man with a sword too. Kathy Gregory for always being a Zorro fan and a great collector. A.G. Lane for her information on the Argentina period. David Cook for his interesting discussions and merchandise information. Kris Stacey, who arrived at the last moment to do more typing than anybody should ever have to. Roberto Herrscher, my man in Argentina. Fernando Lupiz for being a good friend to Guy Williams. Jan Williams, Steve Catalano and Toni Williams for sharing invaluable information. I can't forget Buddy Van Horn, Britt Lomond, David Miller, and Peggy Sheldon. Thanks to Joanna Pasquale for her typing, and to Dave Smith at the Disney Archives.

Table of Contents

Oppression — by its very nature — creates the power that crushes it. A champion arises— a champion of the oppressed whether it be a Cromwell or someone unrecorded, he will be there.

He is born.

The Mark of Zorro, 1920

Introduction

I think I was three years old when I had my first brush with *Zorro*. I can still remember the episode to this day. I've had other heroes in my life—Roy Rogers, the Lone Ranger, etc.—but when all is said and done, it always comes back to Zorro. I'm not quite sure what it was: the costume, the sword fighting, the comedy, the theme song, or the fact that anything produced by Walt Disney was good.

I had seen other versions of *Zorro*, but it really came down to Guy Williams. *He was Zorro.* There was something about him that made you feel good. He exuded charm and cool. He seemed to be very sincere and just a nice guy. He also looked great in that costume.

In 1965, when *Zorro* went into syndication, I was in heaven. For the first time, I was able to see the entire series and my interest in a character that had been gone forever (four years, actually) was renewed. A lot of the merchandise was released again and my folks were understanding enough to buy a lot of it again. Most of my Zorro toys had either disappeared or been played with into extinction. I took a lot better care of them this time and I still have quite a few items to this day.

Fast forward to 1984 and the cable era. The Disney Channel was broadcasting *Zorro* five days a week. I happened to catch an episode during a free weekend of cable and I was hooked again. I quickly subscribed to the Disney Channel and was in heaven all over again. I also brought a VCR so I could watch episodes over and over.

As I watched the episodes through the eyes of a so-called adult, I became interested in how the shows were produced. It was at this point that the idea for a book came to me. Andy Shepherd, a friend who was a teacher in Taiwan, and I began to write letters to the various people involved with the show. What we determined is that I should have started this project about ten years earlier. Writer/director Norman Foster had passed away in the 1970s and both Zorro actors Henry Calvin and Gene Sheldon were also long since gone. Then I got perhaps the worst news of all, just as I was about to start this project: I learned from a friend that Guy Williams had died in Argentina. Some of the other folks involved with the series were up there in years and really couldn't remember all that much about the show.

I considered shelving the project but after some thought, I felt there was enough material out there to proceed. After a number of trips to the Disney Archives and innumerable telephone interviews (some good—Britt Lomond, Jan Williams, Ron Miller, Buddy Van Horn, Lowell Hawley, Bill Witney, Tony Russel, Bill Anderson,

Guy Williams: Zorro Forever (courtesy Walt Disney Productions).

etc.—and some bad—an actor who shall remain nameless) I set out to write the story of Walt Disney's Zorro. Much of the quoted material in the book comes from those interviews.

It really has been a great experience. I've had the opportunity to talk to the family and friends of one of my all-time heroes, visit the Disney Studios, and share it all with whoever might be interested. So saddle your horse, tie on your cape and strap on your sword as we gallop back to the '50s to the land of black and white where good always won, the body count was low and nobody ever recognized you with your mask on.

1

Presenting Señor Zorro
"Welcome to the TV Airways, Walt Disney"

Long before the familiar strains of the *Zorro* theme song could be heard, and long before the proliferation of television, a rather anonymous writer named Johnston McCulley created one of pop culture's most enduring heroes ... Zorro.

Zorro made his first appearance on August 9, 1919, in the pulp magazine *All-Story Weekly*. The first adventure and origin of the character played out through five weekly installments titled *The Curse of Capistrano.* The plot had Zorro fighting an evil military regime in the Pueblo de Los Angeles and in the process becomes the champion of the people. It was in these stories that the archetype for the dual identity "crime fighter" was born.

McCulley's basic premise was this: By day, Don Diego Vega, a wealthy young aristocrat, pretended to be a limp-wristed, ineffectual fop, uninterested in the hardships and problems of others. By night, he became Zorro, a masked avenging angel striking terror into the hearts of evildoers. This is a formula that has subsequently been used countless times in the pulps, comics and movie serials and on television.

Zorro himself can be traced back to two primary sources: Alexandre Dumas' *The Three Musketeers* and Baroness Orczy's *The Scarlet Pimpernel.* It wouldn't be an overstatement to say that Dumas created the swashbuckling tradition when he wrote *The Three Musketeers* and *The Count of Monte Cristo* in the 1800s. McCulley's masked swordsman owes much to the adventure and romance of the Dumas novels. The combination of the Musketeers and the Count established two of the basic motifs of the genre: gentlemen adventurers pledging their swords to defend the reputation of a lady and the honor of the country (*Musketeers*); and aristocratic avengers, assuming a disguise, to right wrongs done to them or their families (*Monte Cristo*).

The Scarlet Pimpernel, a novel and play published in 1905, introduced Sir Percy Blakeney, an English aristocrat, fighting to save innocent members of the French upper class from the guillotine of Robespierre. Blakeney pretends to be an insufferable fop, spouting poetry whenever the mood suits him. It is with a series of disguises that he becomes a man of action and a savior of the aristocracy. McCulley simply took the elements he needed from both these authors to create *Zorro.*

Zorro, the man of action, is a close cousin to the musketeer D'Artagnan. Both are master swordsmen with a desire to see justice done. D'Artagnan, however, operates in the interests of the rightful governing powers of the state while Zorro fights against a corrupt military government. It is here that Zorro is closer to the Pimpernel in the fight against oppression.

What McCulley really borrowed from Orczy was Percy Blakeney. Transformed from eighteenth century France to late eighteenth century Spanish California, Blakeney became Don Diego Vega. These are almost identical characters and serve as perfect disguises for their more action-oriented alter egos.

Zorro's own impact can be seen on almost all modern crime fighters and superheroes. Bob Kane, creator of *Batman*, talked about the Zorro kinship regarding his character. "My second influence in creating Batman was *The Mark of Zorro*, a movie starring Douglas Fairbanks, Sr. I was a member of a club called the Zorros, and we wore black masks and tried to emulate Fairbanks' swashbuckling acrobatics. Zorro's use of a mask to conceal his identity as Don Diego gave me the idea of giving Batman a secret identity. Like the foppish and wealthy Spanish count, Bruce Wayne would be a man of means who put on a façade of being effete. Zorro rode a black horse called Tornado and would enter a cave and exit from a grandfather clock in the living room. The Bat Cave was inspired by this cave in Zorro."[1]

Another somewhat unlikely hero was also influenced by McCulley's creation. In his book *The Great Radio Heroes,* author Jim Harmon recalls the creation of another pop icon, the Lone Ranger: "...[W]hat would make WXYZ's western hero different, distinctive, successful? The staff of WXYZ discussed the matter around Christmas of 1932. [George] Trendle told them he pictured the hero as being dashing and heroic, like Douglas Fairbanks, Sr., in *The Mark of Zorro.* His reference to the masked avenger of old California struck a responsive cord. Someone suggested the hero be given a mask, to be a romantic figure of mystery, a Robin Hood of the Old West." Harmon continues, "[Fran] Striker's first script had the Lone Ranger as a laughing swashbuckler, no doubt fulfilling the original inspiration of Fairbanks' Zorro."[2]

Less than a year after *Zorro* first appeared, Douglas Fairbanks, Sr., brought to the screen *The Mark of Zorro* and it was very successful. It was his first swashbuckler and it changed his career forever. According to Tony Thomas in "The Great Adventure Films," "The idea of making *The Mark of Zorro* grew from Fairbanks' assessment of the changes in public taste following World War I. He sensed the need for a new image, something more substantial than his former comedic boyishness, and it seemed to him that there might be a market for romantic, fanciful escapism."[3]

With this film, Fairbanks transformed Zorro into a laughing, acrobatic daredevil, something he wasn't in the pulp stories. In a sense, Fairbanks is something of a co-creator of Zorro. It was the attitude created by Fairbanks' Zorro that would be copied for years to come. It was also the beginning of the swashbuckler film genre.

Fairbanks' movie proved so popular that when *The Curse of Capistrano* was republished in the form of a novel in 1924, the title was changed to *The Mark of Zorro.* In 1925, Fairbanks produced and starred in something of a sequel to *The Mark of Zorro* titled, *Don Q., Son of Zorro. Don Q* was not based on any particular McCulley story, but one written by K. and Hesketh Prichard. Fairbanks gave it the full swashbuckler treatment and he had another hit on his hands.

Zorro slipped from the realm of "A" pictures down to "B" when Republic Pictures purchased the rights to the character. Republic was largely renowned for making inexpensive Westerns and serials, short on plot and long on action. They brought *Zorro* to the screen in 1937 in *The Bold Caballero*, filmed in "natural color." This was the first sound feature based on McCulley's hero. Zorro was played by Robert Livingston, who had already played a Zorro-like character in the Republic serial *The Vigilantes Are Coming* (1936) and who went on to play the Lone Ranger in a 1939 Republic serial. Not a memorable film, *The Bold Caballero* has the hero appearing in drag during the climax. Various elements of the character were also changed (such as the social standing of Don Diego) as well as the locale.

That same year, Republic began to put Zorro to work in a 12-chapter serial titled *Zorro Rides Again*, this time starring John Carroll. The serial was an updated Western which included automobiles as well as horses and some period singing. It was directed by the team of John English and William Witney. In this collaboration, English would direct the dramatic scenes while Witney handled the action. The saving grace of all the Republic serials was the action scenes and nobody was better than Witney when it came to directing them. He practically invented the art of screen fight choreography. Twenty-one years after *Zorro Rides Again,* Witney would direct a number of *Zorro* episodes for Disney.

In 1939, Republic released yet another serial, *Zorro's Fighting Legion* with Reed Hadley assuming the title role. Once again, English and Witney directed and again the film's chief attribute is the action. The granddaddy of modern stuntmen, Yakima Canutt, doubled as Zorro in both serials. Like Witney, Canutt also worked the Disney series.

These chapterplays proved to be popular so Republic followed up with *Zorro's Black Whip*, a 1944 serial starring Linda Stirling as a female Zorro (no mention is ever made of Zorro in the 12 chapters). George Turner portrayed Zorro in the 1947 serial *Son of Zorro* and Clayton Moore, later television's Lone Ranger, played the lead in *Ghost of Zorro* in 1949. Both *Zorro Rides Again* and *Ghost of Zorro* would be edited and released as features in the late 1950s in an attempt to cash in on the popularity of the Disney series.

The main problem with all the *Zorro* Republic serials was that they were bastardized versions of the original pulp stories. The fact of the matter is that these serials were merely an excuse to do another Western, using the familiar Zorro name for marquee value. The studio made some fundamental changes to the character as well. Republic felt the need to change the color of Zorro's horse from black to white, and to make the pistol his main weapon rather than the sword. In *Zorro's Fighting Legion* the few dueling scenes there were came across more like sword sharpening than competent swordplay. The studio also felt it was necessary to remove Zorro's cape and to give him a band of followers. (With the exception of occasional help from his manservant Bernardo, Zorro was actually a loner.) Taking liberties with established characters was nothing new to Republic. Similar changes also occurred with their production of *The Lone Ranger* and *Captain America*, to name just a few. Republic certainly got their money's worth out of *Zorro*, producing *Zorro* knock-offs such as *Don Daredevil Rides Again* (1951) and *Man with the Steel Whip* (1954).

The cinematic landscape improved dramatically in 1940 when 20th Century–Fox released what is probably the best *Zorro* feature, *The Mark of Zorro,* featuring Tyrone Power and Basil Rathbone. Stylishly directed by Rouben Mamoulian with an exciting score by Alfred Newman, this film established Power as a swashbuckler of the first order. The climactic fencing scene between Power and Rathbone was choreographed by fencing master extraordinaire Fred Cavens. Cavens's son Albert doubled Power in one of the best fencing scenes on film. Seventeen years later, the Cavens would lend their services to Disney's *Zorro.*

In the late 1940s, things were changing in America: G.I.s were returning from the war, getting married and purchasing homes in what was to become known as the suburbs. There was another invasion taking place there, one that would forever change American culture — an electronic piece of furniture called the television set.

Nobody had any idea what television was and this included the Hollywood studios. Certainly no one could envision its potential. But the television people didn't care about potential, what they needed was product to fill up the daytime hours and they felt that Walt Disney's brand of entertainment would be perfect for the small screen. They approached him about the possibility of purchasing his library of cartoon shorts; Disney, believing that the cartoons still had great value in theaters, turned them down. He was still uncertain about the value of television, but he caught on quicker than the other studios and he realized that TV could be a great vehicle in promoting his feature films. Bill Walsh, a long-time producer and writer (*The Mickey Mouse Club, Davy Crockett, The Absent Minded Professor, Son of Flubber, Mary Poppins, That Darn Cat,* etc.) at the studio and a close friend of Walt's, reveals what changed his boss' mind about television: "An agency man from St. Louis appeared on the scene, a salesman-type fellow, who thought it would be useful to get Walt involved in the new medium. He had an essay written on what television really was. The essay helped convince Walt that he should do a Christmas show and do it on TV, and that's what he did."[4] His first *two* excursions into television were Christmas specials. *One Hour in Wonderland,* a promo for *Alice in Wonderland* (1951), aired in 1950. The second was *The Walt Disney Christmas Show,* airing in 1951.

The timing was perfect when, in 1952, theatrical agent Mitchell Gertz came to Disney with the rights to *Zorro,* which he had purchased five years earlier from Johnston McCulley's agent. Disney remembered what a fan he had been of Fairbanks' *Zorro* and the fun Fairbanks had with the character. With an eye on the new television medium, Disney felt it was time to get thoroughly involved in the live-action genre. He wasted no time purchasing the property for WED Enterprises.*

Because Disney himself was under contract to the Walt Disney Studios to produce films and was prevented from said activities with WED, he chose a WED associate, Bill Cottrell, to produce the series. By 1953, Cottrell had begun casting for *Zorro* and scripts were being drafted. Props and furnishings were purchased at a cost of $65,000. The complete cost just to prepare for the series rose to $208,000. Cottrell recalled what happened next: "Walt and I personally took a *Zorro* brochure and all the other material we had to the top men of the two networks. (ABC was not yet

WED, an acronym for Walt Elias Disney, was a private corporation that Disney set up for himself so that he could do business on his own without the interference of the studio.

This is the only Zorro-related ad that Guy Williams ever appeared in.

a major network.) They said that it looks interesting, but you'll have to make a pilot. Walt said, 'I don't know why you'd expect us to make a pilot. I've been making films for years.' We went back to the studio and contemplated our next move which happened to be Disneyland. Walt said, 'Let's put *Zorro* aside and put our energy into the leisure park.'"

Disney had become obsessed with the idea of a theme park. But he needed money and he felt that television was a way to help make his vision a reality. Undaunted by his failure to interest the networks in *Zorro* without a pilot, he made a simple proclamation to CBS and NBC: "You back my leisure park and I'll give you a TV series you can announce as *Walt Disney Presents*, with all the prestige and public interest the name will stimulate for you." After long negotiations, neither network was willing to come up with the needed funds. Then "...one morning in the spring of 1953, the telephone rang and a voice said, "Walt, I hear you need money to build your fairground. If you will agree to put Mickey Mouse on our network, my directors are ready to advance you $250,000 for it. Furthermore, we're willing to come in on a joint venture with you and guarantee loans up to three million dollars."

"For God's sake, how many times do I have to tell people it's a leisure park, not a fairground! Who is this anyway?" Walt asked.

"My name's Kintner," the voice said, "and I'm an executive vice president of the American Broadcasting Corporation, otherwise known as ABC."

"The peanuts network!" Walt said. "What the hell good would it do me to work with you? You're the Little Orphan Annie of the TV airways, with hardly a station to call your own."

"Give us Mickey Mouse, Walt, plus the Disney name," the voice said, "and I guarantee that within two years we'll be one of the big three." A pause. "I hear you need the money real bad. A quarter of a million and a three million guarantee could be a great help, I figure. Is it a deal?"

"Make it half a million in cash and a $4,500,000 guarantee and Mickey is yours," Walt said.

"Done," Kintner said. Then in a mock announcer's voice, "And, welcome to the TV airways, Walt Disney."[5]

Because WED was now involved with the architectural design of Disneyland for an indefinite time, they sold their rights to *Zorro* to the Disney Studios.

Between 1954 and 1957, the studio's impressive track record at ABC was established. The *Disneyland* show was the first ABC series to crack the Nielsen Top 20, finishing in sixth and fourth place in its first two years. After the success of this show and the enormous popularity of *The Mickey Mouse Club*, it was clear the studio knew what the public wanted. A pilot for *Zorro* was now unnecessary. With the aid of storyboards, script outlines and Disney's unique ability to tell a story and convey his enthusiasm, the studio was given the go-ahead to produce 39 half-hour episodes for the 1957-58 television season.

The television landscape that *Zorro* was entering in the late 1950s was a mixture of variety shows, crime dramas, sitcoms and the relatively new "adult Western." Although *Zorro* itself was technically not a Western (it was jokingly referred to by cast and crew as a "southwestern"), anything with horses was thrown into that ever-expanding category. By 1959, there were 27 Westerns in prime time with *Gunsmoke*, *Tales of Wells Fargo*, *Have Gun Will Travel* and *Wagon Train* being some of the more popular.

Part of ABC's task was to interest sponsors in the show, but with the Disney name as an enticement they had little trouble. The 7-Up Company signed on as a chief sponsor and remained with the show for its entire run. The company poured an unprecedented amount of money into television, magazine and newspaper advertising for *Zorro* in the period before the show premiered. They wanted to make sure that anyone with a TV set would be familiar with the show before it aired. They went to far as to publish a monthly *Zorro News Letter*, which was sent out to 7-Up® bottlers all over the country. In New York, Chicago and Los Angeles, the company went all out,

"Fresh up Freddie" became a very popular spokescritter for Zorro's sponsor, 7-Up.

sending costumed "Lady Zorros" to all the major newspapers where they bestowed gifts of *Zorro* hats, buttons and six-packs of 7-Up. All were intended to remind the media of the impending "Z-day" (October 10, the series premiere).

The most potent salesman 7-Up® had for its product was a character called Fresh-Up Freddie. Freddie was the brainchild of the J. Walter Thompson advertising firm and the Disney animation department (and it should be noted, bore a great resemblance to another feathered character, Panchito from Disney's 1945 feature *The Three Caballeros*). Through a collaborative effort, 12 one-minute mini-cartoons were created for the first season of *Zorro*. What impressed and surprised the Thompson advertising firm was that the same people who were working on *Sleeping Beauty* were creating Fresh-Up Freddie. With the slogan "Nothing does it like 7-Up®," the rooster salesman became very popular, urging one television columnist to write, "Some television commercials are poor. Some are mediocre. Some are entertaining. In the latter category, we would have to include the 7-Up® plugs on ABC's *Zorro* show. They are about as cleanly executed as any we have seen in a long time."[6] Paul Frees, a character actor and voice animation veteran, supplied the voice of Freddie.

AC Sparkplug, the electronic division of General Motors, was the alternative advertiser, staying with the show for the length of its run. AC introduced the animated characters Alan Cranbroke and Cynthia Aldrich as a pair of TV talking heads. Live actor Gordon Mills, acting as a spokesman, often participated in these commercials. Later on, two more animated characters were added, Trapper, a St. Bernard dog, and Sparky, a white horse. None of these characters had the popularity of 7-Up's Freddie.

In an effort to give *Zorro* every chance of success, 7-Up® and AC joined Disney and ABC to create the largest advertising budget ever established for promotion of a network television program: $175,000 was budgeted for a print campaign in the nation's newspapers and TV publications to be concentrated between October 6 and November 14. This much was certain: If people didn't watch *Zorro*, it wasn't because they hadn't heard of the new show.

'ZORRO' SET AS ROSE FESTIVAL PARADE STAR

Visits Portland for June Event

Hundreds of thousands of youngsters and adults in the Pacific Northwest will get their first in-person glimpse of "Zorro"—the new national TV hero—when dashing Guy Williams visits Portland, Ore., June 12-14 to serve as Grand Marshal of the famous Portland Rose Festival.

Through arrangements just completed by Portland 7-Up Developer W. R. Moore and the Walt Disney Studios, Williams was announced for the coveted Grand Marshal role in the "Junior Rose Festival Parade" on June 13 and the "Grand Floral Parade" June 14.

* * *

Staged by 10,000 youths, the junior event is unique in the nation and is seen each year by some 200,000 children and parents.

Saturday's climaxing "Grand Floral Parade"—five miles of spectacular beauty—is viewed by three-quarters of a million people.

The year 1958 celebrates the 50th anniversary of the renowned Portland Rose Festival. It is staged annually to celebrate the height of the rose season in the city where, it is said, roses bloom in more profusion than any spot on earth.

* * *

The week-long festival concentrates in 13 blocks of downtown Portland and features every conceivable kind of event, including the coronation of the Rose Queen and two outdoor "spectacular" shows in Multnomah stadium and the 70th Rose Show itself which attracts rose fanciers from all over the world.

In addition to his Friday and Saturday activities as Grand Marshal, 7-Up's ZORRO star is scheduled for appearances each of the three evenings of the stadium show, titled "Fifty (continued on page 3)

'Fresh Up' Freddie" Is Named for Public

Seven-Up's brisk, unique TV salesman—"Fresh Up' Freddie" —will be identified by that name in the high-rated cartoon commercials within the ZORRO show beginning June 5 or 12.

An opening caption in the June spot, and in subsequent "Freddie" messages this summer and fall, will declare, "Here's Fresh Up Freddie."

Announcing parent company plans for insertion of "showcard" introductions of the 7-Up rooster character, J. M. Thul, advertising manager, said that all evidence points to the fact that (continued on page 3)

The **ZORRO** News Letter

7up

VOL. 2 — MAY 1958 — NO. 5

'ZORRO' AND 'BERNARDO' AT DISNEYLAND — They appear again with Henry Calvin and Britt Lomond over Memorial Day.

TV CAST 'DUELS' AT DISNEYLAND

Special performances by the ZORRO cast principals — Guy Williams, Gene Sheldon, Henry Calvin and Britt Lomond — again will be staged at Disneyland park in California over Memorial Day weekend, following a "complete smash" debut by the foursome there in late April.

Some of the biggest crowds in history stormed over Disneyland grounds April 26 and 27 to see the ZORRO stars in their first public appearance. Studio officials quickly re-booked the cast for the three-day holiday period, May 30-June 1.

"Zorro" again will "fight it out" in sword duels with "Sgt. Garcia" and "Monastario." Seconding the masked avenger is his devoted associate, "Bernardo." (continued on page 3)

CHORDETTES' 'ZORRO' RECORD A SMASH HIT

In Baltimore May 6, a costumed "Zorro" joined the Chordettes, famed pop singing group, for a parade through downtown streets . . .

In Cleveland last week, a radio disc jockey was reported to have parachuted into Lake Erie after scattering autographed record-sleeves from a plane over the city . . .

The two stunts "plugged" the Chordettes' new smash-hit recording, "Zorro," on the Cadence label. It's the title music from 7-Up's ZORRO series and threatens to top the million mark in sales, Cadence officials say.

The record "attracts the young 'uns the way 'Davy Crockett' did a few years back," according to one trade review.

Touring Baltimore in a convertible with a soundtruck and the Zorro-garbed figure, the Chordettes (Jinny, Carol, Janet, Lynn) later promoted their ZORRO tune on WJZ-TV's "Buddy Green Show," a teenage favorite. (continued on page 3)

"THE CHORDETTES," Cadence Recording Stars

VACATION'S OVER, so Guy Williams goes back to work at Disney Studios this month. He confers with director Charles Lamont.

The *Zorro News Letter* was sent out to 7-Up developers as a way to promote 7-Up and *Zorro*. They are highly sought after by collectors today (courtesy 7-Up and Walt Disney Productions).

To assist with the production of *Zorro*, Walt Disney turned to associate producer William H. Anderson. Anderson, who had been at the studio since 1943, recalled his early days: "I had been in the finance business and sales but that went to pot. I had always admired Walt so I went to the studio to help them during the World War II period when they were turning out animation shorts for the war effort. However, they seemed to be having trouble getting them out. So I went in as a part of a team to help keep track of that work and also to help management expedite it.

"I was there only a few months or so and they tapped me to manage the ink and paint department, which was an area that we all found was a problem as far as moving the product through. We got that straightened out and Walt approached me and said, 'When the war is over, I want you to come upstairs and start working with me.' That was around 1945.

"I then became manager of the animation department and worked with Walt on the first two or three animated features after the war. Following that, I became cartoon production manager and finally I ended up by working on live features with Walt." Anderson remembered his old boss with affection. "He was a marvelous person but he wasn't all fun and games. He was very tough and very demanding and yet he was a very fair man. As long as you could help, he enjoyed working with you. If you couldn't, he'd get rid of you. We got along very well."

The man Disney chose to help bring *Zorro* to life was writer-director Norman Foster. Foster was born in Richmond, Indiana, and began his career as an actor, appearing in the movies *Gentlemen of the Press, It Pays to Advertise* and *Orient Express*, among others. While Foster was at 20th Century–Fox, he became known as an easygoing, likable leading man. Unfortunately for him, another affable fellow named Henry Fonda began getting all the roles he felt suited for.

With his career stalled, Foster wasted no time in accepting the role of both star and director of the 1936 feature *I Cover Chinatown*. This began a long string of directorial jobs that included some of the better Charlie Chan and Mr. Moto films. In 1943 Foster directed what was perhaps his best film, *Journey Into Fear* with Orson Welles. It was on this film that Welles took note of Foster's techniques of storyboarding (the process of using drawings to plot out a scene, not unlike the comic strip).

In their book *American Directors Volume I*, Jean Pierre Coursodon and Pierre Sauvage wrote about Foster:

> Although many of Welles' admirers may frown upon the notion of a director of "B" films influencing a personality of Welles' stature, it is a fact that the Boy Wonder absorbed a considerable amount of cinematic technique, tricks and devices while systematically viewing movies, among them some directed by Foster, in preparation for *Citizen Kane*. Welles was impressed enough by Foster's work to hire him later to direct a segment of his aborted epic *It's All True*, then *Journey Into Fear*. The choice may be surprising, but it is understandable. Welles needed someone talented and sympathetic to his views in a situation where he found himself unable to meet all of his film commitments, someone who could do a job in the Welles vein without clashing with, or overshadowing the master. Foster fit the requirements rather well. There are affinities between his visual style and Welles', and it may be noted that Foster's direction in his late thirties mysteries to a certain extent anticipate the low-key, highly atmospheric style of the "film noir," a genre whose aesthetics were influenced by Welles' early films.[7]

Foster moved to Mexico in the mid–1940s where he directed several Mexican-produced films such as *Santa* (1944) with Ricardo Montalban, *La Fuga* (1945) and *La Hora De La Verdad* (1946). His 1952 Mexican docu-feature *Navajo: Sky Full of*

Moon, which he wrote and directed, was nominated for two Academy Awards. Foster followed with *Sombrero,* a 1953 love story set in his beloved Mexico, once again with Ricardo Montalban.

As television came onto the American scene, Foster reluctantly moved into the new medium. Although he disliked most of what he saw on the small screen, he did find something to enjoy in such series as *The Jack Benny Program* and *Your Show of Shows.* In 1953, he was lured to television by Loretta Young, who he had directed in 1948's *Rachel and the Stranger.* He had a great respect for Young as an actress and he also happened to be married to her sister, actress Sally Blane. Foster directed a number of episodes of Young's popular dramatic anthology series. The irony of Foster's move to television may be underscored by his son Robert's comment, "I could be wrong, but I think we were probably the last family in America to get a television set."

The Disney Studios, always on the lookout for talent, signed Foster to direct a new project they had in the works, *Davy Crockett.* The plan was to do a series about legendary Americans, the first of whom happened to be Crockett, who was chosen at random. Walt Disney wasn't too keen on the idea at first, but when *Davy Crockett, Indian Fighter* hit the airwaves on December 15, 1954, it had an enormous impact on kids across the country. Coonskin caps were everywhere, plus anything and everything else the merchandisers could fit the frontiersman's moniker on. Foster's enthusiasm for the subject matter and good direction was a major reason for the show's success.

Taking advantage of the popularity of *Davy Crockett,* the studio produced two more one-hour episodes featuring the Indian fighter a year later, *Davy Crockett's Keel Boat Race* and *Davy Crockett and the River Pirates,* again directed by Foster (and this time co-written by him). One of the reasons Disney liked Foster was because he wasn't a yes man. He spoke his mind and this earned him respect and a fair amount of enemies in Hollywood. Robert Foster recalls when his father sent two stagehands home from a *Davy Crockett* location because they weren't doing their job. "They were members of the union and this was the sort of thing that just wasn't done. The men arrived back at the studio and began to spread rumors but my father couldn't care less, he was intent on directing his movie and refused to play games."

Given the success of *Crockett,* it's easy to see why, when production began on *Zorro,* Disney put the series into the capable hands of Foster. Bill Anderson remembered him as a "high-keyed" but very talented guy. "He was very opinionated and sometimes difficult with actors; he drove them. He had a good story sense and a flair for action. He also loved Mexico and that culture, and he was very enthusiastic. Norman was also the kind of guy who would say 'Yes' to you and then pretty much do what he wanted." Although it should be stated that any product coming out of the Disney Studios ultimately reflected the taste of Walt Disney, it was Foster more than anyone else working on *Zorro* who really shaped the character and set the tone for the show. He directed 13 of the first 39 shows, writing five scripts and co-writing two more in the first season. When Disney wanted to inject comedy into the series, it was Foster's job to find just the right balance between the comedy and the action without crossing the line into farce.

As scripts* and sets were being readied, the following item appeared in the March 19, 1957, *Daily Variety:* "Norman Foster has been set to direct *Zorro* TV series for Walt Disney. He is auditioning actors for the title role." Not only for the title role, but the call also went out for four other actors who would portray the principal supporting characters. All of these characters would be taken directly from the Johnston McCulley stories with the exception of the commandante, Capitan Monastario. He was actually a composite of various evil military officers who appeared in the pulps.

The dual role of Don Diego/Zorro would have to be handled by someone who could convincingly portray both the mild-mannered scholar as well as the dashing swordsman. The role of Capitan Monastario would require a suave villain who was almost Zorro's equal with a sword. The oafish Sgt. Garcia, a likable buffoon, would provide comic relief. For the role of Bernardo, Zorro's mute confidante, an amusing and cunning sidekick, they required someone able to play the fool yet who could ably assist Zorro. Like Sgt. Garcia, he would play scenes for laughs. Wisdom, dignity and a fiery temper best describe Don Alejandro, Don Diego's father.

This much was certain: Disney wanted an unknown for the role of Zorro. In April, Disney casting directors Lee Traver and Jack Lavin sent 20 "Zorro hopefuls" to Norman Foster, and sometime-model and actor Guy Williams proved to be a standout. In a publicity release, Foster said, "We had checked every studio in town for film footage on our candidates. I was immediately impressed with Guy's looks. But I wanted to be sure he could handle a sword. So, the first day, I had him do three fencing scenes. From that film, Guy appeared to have been born with a foil in his hand. As far as I was concerned, Guy fit Zorro to a T. From the beginning I knew he was the fellow I wanted to play the part." According to Guy's wife Jan, Foster "felt so strongly about Guy that he wouldn't do the show without him." Walt Disney agreed and Williams was signed to a one-year contract with a seven-year option.

In a 1983 interview, Williams remembered the excitement concerning the *Zorro* series: "Every once in a while there was a role in town that everybody was talking about and *Zorro* was one of them. The fact that it was Disney and *Zorro* together made it very exciting. When you coupled those two names together it was a wanted job; it was careersville all the way if you got that. So everybody in town that could possibly qualify in any way showed up for that role and I was one of them."[8]

"I must say that in my wildest dreams I never expected to get a break as a Latin. I had gone on many interviews before where a Latin-type was needed. The casting directors took one look at me and just laughed, said I was too American and all that. Consequently, when I got the call to go to Disney's to be interviewed for *Zorro,* I had little hope. I was especially sure I'd not be considered because I had just finished some *Annapolis* TV shows and had my hair in a crew cut. But much to my surprise, Lee Traver said to me, 'I think you could look Latin all right.' I just about flipped."[9]

Guy Williams was born Joseph Armand Catalano (Armando to his family and friends) in the Bronx, New York, in 1924. The son of Attillio and Clare, Williams described himself as an indifferent student who excelled in math and loved to read.

---

*The scripts written in 1953 were discarded.

Guy Williams' April 1957 screen test for Zorro. Note Britt Lomond (right) is without his beard (courtesy Walt Disney Productions).

As a young boy Williams first learned about fencing from his father and uncle, both of whom served in the Italian Army. Williams spent some of his formative years at the Peekskill Military Academy before attending and graduating form George Washington High.

After high school, Williams sailed through a series of inconsequential jobs (welder, cost accountant, aircraft parts inspector). While working as a salesman in a department store, he put his good looks to use and took his first steps toward fame: "I was a salesman in the luggage department at Wanamaker's and Hope Lange's sister, Minelda, was a photographer. She took pictures of me and told me to take them to a male modeling agency; I didn't know there was such a business, but I brought the pictures over and was sent out on jobs. The pay was better than anything I had been earning up till then," Williams recounted.[10]

It was during this period that Armand Catalano had his ethnicity toned down and he became a "Guy." According to Williams, "In the 1940s if you had any foreign name outside of standard American type name, you were typed physically." Williams' wife Jan recalled it was Pat Allen of the Pat Allen Agency who came up with the name. "They had a call for someone to do a job and Pat said, 'All right, I'll send him over right away, his name is Armand Catalano.' The client said, 'No, don't send him over, we want an All-American type!," They quickly thought up a name for him and sent over Guy Williams, All-American. Williams himself said the name was along the lines of Rock Hudson, Tab Hunter, etc., "the most insipid, the most master-key as possible."

Williams was making a profitable living modeling for such magazines as *Ladies Home Journal*, *True Romance* (he appeared on the cover with Grace Kelly) and the Sears catalog. He was given the opportunity to appear in a March of Time short and was spotted by a Hollywood talent scout who arranged for a screen test. This brought Williams to the attention of MGM, who signed him to what Williams later described as "a short contract," and sent him to California. His first screen role was a bit part portraying a member of the bomber crew who dropped the first atomic bomb in *The Beginning of the End* (1947). Nothing much happened professionally following his film debut so Williams returned to New York and modeling. It was here that he met his future wife, Janice Cooper, on a modeling assignment. After a quick courtship, the two married.

As a result of his stint at MGM, Williams' interest in acting was piqued and he auditioned for and was accepted to the prestigious Neighborhood Playhouse where

An early modeling shot from the mid–1940s (courtesy of the Academy of Motion Pictures and K. Gregory).

he studied under legendary acting coach Sanford Meisner. Williams said, "It was not so much the text that was taken into account as the physical moves and diction. Believe me, when you come from a Martha Graham class, you know how to go down the street, you know how to walk." Because of his connection with the Playhouse, Williams became involved in summer stock in Pennsylvania grabbing small parts in productions of *Pal Joey*, *Rain* and *Fledermaus*.

After returning to New York, Williams appeared on local live television shows such as *Studio One*. With his confidence and experience growing, he was tested by Hollywood coach, Sophie Rosenstein, who saw Williams as a "Jeffrey Hunter type." On the strength of her recommendation, Universal–International

Pictures tested Williams and signed him in 1952. They quickly put him to work giving him a bit part in the forgettable *Bonzo Goes to College* (1952). Small parts in better films ensued: *All I Desire, The Man from the Alamo, The Mississippi Gambler, Take Me to Town* and *The Golden Blade* (all 1953).

While at Universal, Williams was injured, separating his shoulder and breaking his arm in two places when he fell off a horse. In an effort to recover and improve his basic body movement and coordination, Williams began to study fencing. While his recovery was progressing nicely, his movie career wasn't and he was dropped from his Universal contract. "You're in tough shape if they regard you as a leading man type. The role always goes to someone better know, and you're never considered for charac-ter parts, even if you can do them," Williams complained.[11]

In the mid–50s, Williams free-lanced, appearing in *Seven Angry Men* (1955) and *Sincerely Yours* (1955). He

When Williams signed with the Powers Modeling Agency, photographs such as these were sent out to prospective clients (cour-tesy of the Academy of Motion Pictures and K. Gregory).

then traveled south of the border to Mexico to play a cavalry officer in *The Last Fron-tier* (1956) with Robert Preston and Victor Mature.

When his film career stalled, Williams picked up some steady employment in television, working on such popular shows as *The Lone Ranger, Sergeant Preston, Highway Patrol, Four-Star Playhouse, Damon Runyon Theater* and Mickey Rooney's *Hey Mulligan.* He also appeared in a Pepsi commercial to help pay the bills and turned up in the camp classic *I Was a Teenage Werewolf* (1957) with future *Bonanza* star Michael Landon.

When the *Zorro* audition materialized, Williams was ready. So was every other tall, dark, handsome leading man type in town. Most of them were making their way to the Disney Studios in the hopes that they, like Fess Parker (Disney's Davy Crock-ett), would become overnight stars.

Jan Williams recalled her husband's optimism regarding the Disney series: "He felt very confident, he felt as though he was absolutely right for the role. As a mat-ter of fact, after he had tested and was waiting to hear, he and I used to drive over and park in the hills overlooking the Disney Studios and watch as the *Zorro* set was being built on the back lot and he would say, 'I'm going to do that show.'"

Tony Russo, an actor who later co-starred in three episodes of *Zorro*, also audi-tioned for the *Zorro* role. He says, "I went in and tested and I also watched Guy's test.

My confidence was up because I was a good fencer and a Pasadena Playhouse graduate and I could do all the dialects, so there was no problem there. I figured I had a really good shot at it and then one day I was walking down Sunset Boulevard about a week after the test and I ran into a friend of mine, Dick Norris, and he said, 'I hear you tested for *Zorro*, I don't think you're going to get it.' I said, 'Jeez, why not?' He said, 'If you go across the street to Frascati's [restaurant] Guy Williams and his agent are having lunch with Norman Foster.' I said, laughing, 'Gee, thanks a lot!' The ironic thing was when they needed a good fencer for later episodes they said, 'Get Tony Russo.'"

Britt Lomond auditioned for both the Zorro and Monastario roles and was signed on as Zorro's antagonist, Capitan Enrique Sanchez Monastario. Lomond, whose real first name was Glase, was an expert fencer, and at one time rated in the top 25 in the country. His theatrical career began in 1947 with a Connecticut stock company and he appeared in 50 stage plays and 25 movies, including *Scaramouche*, *The Purple Mask*, *Captain Scarlett* and *The Highwayman*.

Lomond remembered, "Like Guy, I also studied under Aldo Nadi and that's how we met. He had been there for a few weeks but I had been fencing for a year with Nadi and others. Guy asked me to help him in his fencing and I worked with him a little bit and we realized we were both going to test for the same roles. Actually, we each tested for both parts [Zorro and Monastario]. During the audition, we had to fence one another, taking turns as the commandante and Zorro. Now, Guy was not a competitive fencer so I said to him, 'Let's reduce the fencing to something very rudimentary.' So when the camera was on my back and looking at him I said, 'Guy, watch my hand' and I pointed to the next move and that's how we got through it.

"The Disney Studios took a while before they made a decision. Finally I got the lead heavy and Guy got the lead. It wasn't until about a year or two later that I found out why. Norman Foster and I became good friends during my run with the show and he and I were having dinner and he said, 'Britt, you may kill me, I probably cost you a lot of money. Walt wanted you as the lead and I wanted you as the heavy. I told Walt, I feel Britt can help Guy carry the show in the early going in the sense that he has more experience as an actor and is an expert fencer.' Walt thought about it a while and agreed." According to associate producer Bill Anderson, "Guy had a certain flair and a niceness about him; he had a nice easy smile. He also was very cooperative and worked very hard at the fencing. One good thing about Guy, he would try anything. I really don't think Britt had the right personality to play Zorro." Foster allowed Lomond a certain amount of freedom regarding his interpretation of the commandante. "They let me play the part the way I wanted to do it. I said, 'Look, this isn't serious acting. This is a caricature and I'm going to play it that way with the reactions and everything ... but play it straight and there will be an ingenuous fun with that character and with the show."

With the two leads chosen, the remainder of the supporting cast had to be selected. For the role of the bumbling Sgt. Dimetrio Lopez Garcia, a prime prerequisite was someone with ample girth. The actor who fit the bill perfectly was the multi-talented Henry Calvin. Born Wimberley Calvin Goodman and raised in Dallas, Texas, he studied journalism at SMU. While in college, he won a few parts in a

The Zorro screen test, April 1957, with Britt Lomond (left) and Guy Williams (courtesy of Walt Disney Productions).

local stock company production as a result of his singing in local Dallas churches. Calvin said, "I guess that's where it all started. All of a sudden, I decided I really wanted to go into show business and give up newspaper reporting so that's exactly what I did."[12] Calvin went to New York in 1939 and earned a position as the bass baritone soloist at Radio City Music Hall. After he returned from military service in

World War II, he appeared in a variety of Broadway plays including *The Chocolate Soldier, Sally* and *Happy at Larry.*

In 1948 he made a decision to switch to more dramatic roles and appeared in such films as *Crime Against Joe* and *The Broken Star.* Calvin also had his own radio show in 1950 and turned up in almost every major television show of the 1950s. It was in the Broadway hit *Kismet* that Calvin came to the attention of Disney casting directors. Bill Anderson stated, "Henry had a great sense of being a buffoon and being likable." Calvin was called upon a number of times to use his operatic singing voice on the *Zorro* series. He brought a touch of Oliver Hardy to the role which the McCulley stories never envisioned. Alan Reed was among the other actors who tested for the role of Garcia but the expansive talents of Calvin were too great to be overlooked. A few years later, Reed went on to certain immortality as the voice of Fred Flintstone.

For the demanding role of Bernardo, Zorro's mute manservant and the only one who knows Zorro's true identity, the versatile Gene Sheldon (formerly Eugene Search) was cast. Sheldon was born in Columbus, Ohio, the son of amateur entertainer Earl Search. According to Sheldon, "My father was chiefly remembered on the stage for having invented one of the versions of the now famous trick of sawing a woman in half. In this particular act, I was the girl who was sawed in half." As a boy, Sheldon spent much of his time mastering magic tricks and learning to play the banjo and guitar. His first professional job in show business was on radio in 1925 in Toledo, Ohio. After that he traveled throughout the country working the vaudeville and nightclub circuit, doing a musical comedy act which consisted of pantomime and banjo playing. Sheldon then sailed to Europe, where he performed his act to great success. He returned to the States and appeared on the stage in *Take a Bow* and *Priorities.* Sheldon headed west to Hollywood where his film career included *Where Do We Go from Here?*, *The Dolly Sisters, Golden Girl* and Martin and Lewis' *Three Ring Circus.* He was most widely known for his television appearances on the shows of Jackie Gleason, Julius LaRosa and Ed Sullivan.

Sheldon accepted the role of Bernardo even though it paid him less money than he was making in his nightclub act. But Sheldon and his wife, Peggy, had recently adopted a son and he felt it was time to settle down. The *Zorro* series came along at just the right time.

Regarding his role, Sheldon said, "If facial expression is the number one prerequisite for an actor, then this part of Bernardo surely is going to prove to me just how much this is really true."[13] Concerning the frustration of playing a mute, Sheldon complained, "Sometimes I want to talk on the show so badly that I can almost hear myself speaking out loud."[14] (Sheldon did kid Guy Williams about the pages of dialogue the star of the series had to memorize.) Nick Cravat, an outstanding acrobat who portrayed a mute in Burt Lancaster films such as *The Flame and the Arrow* and *The Crimson Pirate*, also tested for the role, but Sheldon's comedic experience and his past work as a mime won out.

George J. Lewis, a screen veteran of over 30 years, was signed on to play the role of Diego's father, Don Alejandro. Lewis, the only member of the cast to boast a Spanish heritage, was born in Guadalajara, Mexico, in 1903 of a Welsh father and Spanish mother. The family fled Mexico during the Mexican Revolution and settled in Coronado, California. Lewis caught the acting bug in high school while appearing in plays and headed for Hollywood soon after graduation. His big break came in the 1926 film *His People*, where he played a prizefighter. On the strength of his performance he was signed to a contract at Universal, where he starred in entries in the *Collegians* series in 1927.

With the advent of talking pictures, Lewis felt he needed more experience, so he headed for the New York stage where he stayed employed for four years. He then returned to California where he was in constant demand at Republic playing heavies in serials. His initial brush with Zorro came at Republic when he co-starred in *Zorro's Black Whip* and *Ghost of Zorro*. Lewis was very busy in television in the 1950s and came to the attention of Disney when he appeared in *Davy Crockett and the River Pirates*. Bill Anderson commented, "We knew enough about him and his career so he didn't have to audition. He did a fine job with the role." Although Lewis' Don Alejandro was an integral part of the series, he appeared in little over half the episodes filmed. For all the principals involved (Williams, Calvin, Sheldon, Lewis and Lomond), *Zorro* would be a career high point. With the exception of Williams, they would never again have the audience exposure or consistent opportunity to display their talents.

A number of continuing supporting characters also appeared in the initial episodes, portrayed by such veteran character actors as Jan Arvan (rancher Don Nacho Torres), Nestor Paiva (Tio or later Pacheco, the innkeeper), Romney Brent (Padre Felipe), Pat Hogan (Benito, the de la Vega head vaquero) and Than Wyenn (Piña, the lawyer). These characters helped give the series a feeling of continuity, at least for the first 13 episodes. Jan Arvan had been a member of the Pasadena Playhouse and appeared in over 40 films. Throughout the 1950s and '60s he was a regular on *The Red Skelton Show.* It was on Don Nacho Torres behalf that Don Diego first adopted the guise of Zorro. Nacho Torres would find himself in six of the first 13 episodes. Nestor Paiva appeared sporadically throughout the entire run of the series. His character of the innkeeper was mainly relegated to that of atmosphere. Occasionally he did engage is some comedy with Sgt. Garcia, usually trying to keep the Sergeant out of the wine cellar. Paiva is probably best remembered as an actor who played tough guy gangsters in "B" pictures.

Romney Brent had also been around for years when he stepped into the role of Padre Felipe. Born in Mexico City as Romulo Larrade, he was largely a stage actor who appeared in over 35 Broadway plays. He also collaborated with Cole Porter on *The Nymph Errant* in 1932. In the early going, the padre was sort of the moral conscience of the show, actually bringing Catholic beliefs into play in his dealings with the commandante. The character was taken directly from the McCulley short stories. (Fray Felipe, as he was known in the pulps, knew the identity of Zorro while Padre Felipe of the TV series did not.) The Padre appeared in four of the first 13 episodes and then mysteriously disappeared from the series. Other priests would pass through Los Angeles but never remain for more than one or two episodes. Pat Hogan (Benito), a relative newcomer, was half–Irish and half–Oneida Indian. He played Indians in a number of other Disney features including *Davy Crockett, Daniel Boone,*

Savage Sam and *Ten Who Dared*. He was seen in three episodes of *Zorro* and, like Padre Felipe, disappeared without a trace. Than Wyenn, who portrayed Monastario's cohort Licenciado Piña, may have been the most versatile actor in the cast. He had studied modern dance, ballet and acting under Lee Strasberg. He also appeared in the chorus of *The Merry Widow* singing and dancing. At the age of 18 he toured all over the country with a Shakespearean troupe. When television became a force, he moved to Los Angeles and became something of a stock player on *Dragnet*. He has appeared in hundreds of television shows and over 60 motion pictures.

2

"The Bold Renegade Carves a Z with His Blade"

Of Swords and Stunts

We did outrageous things, but in good style, Disney saw to that.
Guy Williams, 1986

In 1983, an interviewer asked Guy Williams if he did any of that "dangerous sword business." With a smile the actor proclaimed, "Oh I did it all. But it wasn't so dangerous when we got it all worked out in the routines that we used."[1] To devise those elaborate routines and to help Williams do it all, Disney hired 74-year-old Fred Cavens to coach the new Zorro in the fine art of fencing. There were other, very capable fencing masters in Hollywood, (Henry Uyttenhove, Ralph Faulkner and Jean Heremans), but when it came to fencing choreography, Fred Cavens was in a class by himself. Born in Belgium of French parents, he was 12 when he was sent to military school, where he was forced to take up fencing. Four years later he entered the Belgian army and then was sent to the Royal Fencing College of Brussels. He clearly took to the sport and was a professor of fencing at age 21. He soon emigrated to the United States where he choreographed his first film in 1922, *The Three Must-Get-Theres,* a comic parody of *The Three Musketeers.* In 1923 Cavens met Douglas Fairbanks, Sr., during the filming of the Cavens' choreographed *Dorothy Vernon of Haddon Hall.* From here Cavens' career took off. He worked for Fairbanks on *Don Q, Son of Zorro* (1925), *The Black Pirate* (1926) and *The Iron Mask* (1929). When sound films came in, Cavens staged the duels for some all-time classics: *Captain Blood, The Adventures of Robin Hood, The Sea Hawk, The Mark of Zorro, The Corsican Brothers, The Adventures of Don Juan, Cyrano de Bergerac,* and numerous other swashbucklers.

It was Cavens' contention that "skilled fencers were too fast for the camera because of their natural reflexes. Actors, on the other hand, were not burdened by such training and besides they remembered to act. To be a good screen fencer, an actor has to believe he is better than he is."[2] Cavens' philosophy of screen-duel staging was well thought out and refined over a 35-year period. He said, "All movements, instead of being as small as possible, as in competition fencing, must be large but nevertheless correct. Magnified is the word. The routine should contain the most spectacular attacks and parries it is possible to execute while remaining logical to the situation. In other words, the duel should be a fight and not a fencing exhibition, and should disregard at times classically correct guards and lunges. The attitudes arising naturally out of a fighting instinct should predominate. When this occurs, the whole performance will leave an impression of strength, skill and manly grace."[3] George Barrows, a fencing double who worked with other prominent fencing masters in many of his pictures, compared them to his mentor Cavens: "They didn't have the knowledge that Fred had of motion picture fencing. They were mostly strip [Olympic] fencers. They didn't have the flair or romantic look to their routines that Fred did. He knew more than anyone in the business."

Cavens believed that "if an actor is in good physical condition, has sound legs and wind, and a good head, I can make a fencer of sorts out of him in four weeks!"[4] Guy Williams had those requirements and, according to Disney Studio press releases, the actor believed the reason he was cast as Zorro was because of his fencing experience. As a boy, Williams had been coached by his father, Atillio, a captain in the Italian army. Williams said, "My dad taught me the principles." He also claimed half-seriously that "fencing was in the Catalano blood."[5] Perhaps more importantly, when Williams was injured at Universal and he began to take up fencing again, he studied under Aldo Nadi, considered by many fencing experts to be the greatest fencer of the Twentieth Century. "While I was at Universal I always passed in front of this dance studio where the Nadi brothers had their fencing school. I started fencing really seriously with Aldo Nadi."[6]

Williams' prior experience may have complicated Cavens' job. "Guy was my most difficult pupil. He knew too much. I had to make him forget before I could teach him the special unique thrusts and parries demanded in film work for dramatic effect. Guy was as fine a fencer as I have encountered on a movie set, he's best of all the Zorros,"[7] enthused the fencing master.

Williams began training under Cavens in mid–May of 1957, the actor working tirelessly to develop his technique as a screen fencer. With his exaggerated sword movements, charging balestras and great smile, he proved to have a charismatic style and a flair for swashbuckling. Considering some of the excellent actor-fencers Fred Cavens worked with (including Basil Rathbone, José Ferrer, and Olympian Cornel Wilde), Cavens' praise is impressive.

Even with his past fencing experience, Williams was really learning on the job — not an easy feat for someone carrying the weight of a series on his shoulders for the first time. Not only did Williams have to learn fencing routines (consisting of approximately 50 different fencing moves) every other episode but he also had to learn pages upon pages of dialogue as he appeared in almost every scene of every episode. He was also learning to play the guitar and brushing up on his horseback riding. It's a credit to Guy Williams that he never used a fencing double. This is something that great screen swashbucklers as Flynn, Fairbanks, Power, Wilde, etc., cannot claim. Williams' fencing contributed greatly to the credibility of the Zorro character. If Williams is not regularly mentioned alongside those sword-wielding actors, it's not for lack of skill or charisma, but rather because he worked in television, not movies.

On *Zorro* it was Fred Cavens' job to choreograph the fencing scenes and then

Fred Cavens (right) instructs Williams in a fencing scene for "The Man from Spain" (courtesy of Walt Disney Productions).

coach the actors through them. The style of fencing chosen by Cavens for the series was a mixture of foil, saber and épée. Saber by itself, which consists of exaggerated, slashing movements, looks dramatic but is relatively uncomplicated. However, when it is combined with the intricate point moves of foil, as it was with Cavens, the results can be mesmerizing.

The weapon Cavens chose was the épée blade with a saber hand guard and grip. The épée was picked over the saber blade for a number of reasons: It photographed better, it had a more impressive sound when the two blades met and, more importantly, the swordsmen had better control of their weapons. The competition saber blade was too flexible and therefore had a tendency to bend and whip too much. The épée blade was stiffer, and although there was always a risk, this helped to prevent anybody from taking a blade in the face. However, the tip of the blade was dulled to lessen the severity of injury in case someone was accidentally hit.

Cavens employed three fencing doubles on the series. One of the doubles was his son Albert, who had been fencing since the age of four and had worked with his father since the 1930s. Albert was the best screen fencer in Hollywood and appeared as Zorro's antagonist more than any other fencing double. He also worked closely with his father in choreographing the duels. Al had appeared in such films as *The Mark of Zorro, The Black Swan, Adventures of Don Juan* and *Cyrano de Bergerac.*

Stuntman Wayne "Buddy" Van Horn, who was hired primarily as Guy Williams' double, took up fencing at Britt Lomond's urging. He practiced with Fred Cavens for approximately three months before he did his first fencing routine on the show.

Van Horn recalled, "They would cast a villain who was my size so that I could double him and fence with Guy. He and I worked well together. I would occasionally go up to his house in Hollywood and we would practice our routines on the front lawn." His first extensive fencing appearance is in *Horse of Another Color,* three episodes into the second season. Van Horn appeared in approximately ten episodes as a fencing double.

Victor Paul, who first worked with Cavens in *Adventures of Don Juan* and who had been Pacific Coast Champion in three weapons and a winner of the individual Greco Award, began doubling on *Zorro* early in the first season. Paul explained how Fred Cavens would go about setting up a fencing scene: "Fred would look over the situation, find out what the story was about and go on the set and create a routine between Zorro and the villain. He'd look around the set at the tables and chairs and staircase and he would proceed from there and dream up a routine. Guy and I would write the names of the various fencing moves down on paper that Fred wanted to use. Then we would rehearse it over and over and over again. You have to work together — you have to have rhythm, it's like a dance. Rhythm is what sells it. If it hasn't got rhythm, it stinks!

"It was all rehearsed in phrases. If an entire routine consisted of 50 moves and each camera shot contained seven or eight moves, that's how we rehearsed it. Do the eight moves, stop and then do the next seven or eight moves. You can only fence for a few minutes at a time. You could have four, five or six different phrases; up the stairs, across the balcony and back down the stairs again.

"The actual filming of the fencing action was usually done in half a day or less depending upon how complicated it was and Fred's stuff wasn't easy. It wasn't like a feature film where you have all kinds of time to rehearse; this was television. You always felt as though you were a little bit under the gun because you're fighting a schedule. But I think we did a lot of nice stuff on *Zorro* considering it was television." Paul remembered Guy Williams as "a very good fencer. He took to it very well and enjoyed it so he worked hard at it. He was tremendously easy to work with and had a great sense of humor. We were always joking and kidding around together."

Britt Lomond, who handled his own swordplay in the first 13 episodes, elaborated on Paul's explanation. "Off the set we would work out the various fencing moves, then we would polish it by blocking it around the furniture on the set. We would walk through the scene three or four times. We'd block it out for ourselves slowly at quarter speed, and then we'd pick up the tempo to half speed while the camera crew watched us. Then we'd do it full speed one time to check and see how the camera would see it and what the problems were. Then, okay, let's try one, roll it, and we'd do it. Each shot was rehearsed three or four times and done once. Disney wanted the television audience to see the fencing moves so we had to bastardize a lot of our fencing because the normal doublé de doublé [the feint of a compound attack] is so fast it can't be seen."

Williams commented that "all of the sword work was done on Friday which was referred to as 'Fight Day.' Then if an injury occurred you would have a whole weekend to recover. The whole studio would stop on Friday and everyone would come over to the set, sit down and have coffee and wait to see what would happen."[8] Actor

Than Wyenn concurred with Williams: "They had to rehearse on areas where the footing was not the greatest, balconies, steps, etc., so we always came to see that because we knew it was like going into the gladiator ring in terms of the danger involved. You never knew what would happen."

Lomond exclaimed, "Fencing scenes were shot early in the morning because it was cooler then. It was very hot in those costumes and after five minutes of sword play you're soaking wet." Of Cavens, Victor Paul contended, "He was the greatest of all time, a great master. When you worked with Fred, you worked with him as one of the guys. He took you in as one of the family. It was a good relationship."

Stunts

Buddy Van Horn, fencing double and Williams' stunt double, was also the show's stunt coordinator. Any action, other than fencing, was choreographed by Van Horn. Although Williams was proficient as a horseman, Van Horn's primary responsibility was to double the star as Zorro on horseback and stand-in on any scenes that required dangerous leaping off of walls, running across rooftops, swinging on ropes, etc. Van Horn was used so much in the action sequences that the studio, believing that the public wouldn't know the difference, actually released a number of publicity stills with him as Zorro. Director Charles Barton used to kid Guy Williams by saying, "You better get a move on, Guy, because we can put a mask on Buddy and we won't even need you."

According to sources on the set, Williams had moments when grace and coordination seemed to desert him completely, but he made no apologies. He once confessed, "I didn't do any of the great falls. That was Buddy's department. If I came down wrong on my ankle, then I don't work for a week and that meant the show would be stopped. But we really did have some good stunt people on that show. We did outrageous things on *Zorro* but we did it in style, first class."[9]

Along with Van Horn, a core group of stunt people were assembled who worked the series so often they were on a weekly salary. They portrayed everyone from soldiers to townspeople. Regulars included Phil Schumaker who doubled as Henry Calvin (Sgt. Garcia), Lou Roberson and Charlie Sullivan, who sometimes stood in for Gene Sheldon (Bernardo), and Carl Pitti, who handled most of Zorro's bullwhip work with an occasional assist from Dave Kashner. Valley Kean, the only stuntwoman to work the show, doubled for Annette Funicello and any other woman who appeared in the series. Other stunt regulars included Bob Terhune, Charly Quirt and Joe Phillips.

Jack Lilley, another stunt man who was with the show from start to finish, recalled with amusement his hiring on *Zorro*: "They were casting [the Disney movie] *The Light in the Forest* and I went on an interview and they wanted to shave all our heads to play Indians and I said, 'I think I'll pass.' As I was walking out I went past the casting office and Lee Traver, the casting agent said, 'I think we've got a show you would be perfect for.' And of course, that was *Zorro*." Lilley can often be seen in the background portraying a lancer.

Many of the early action location scenes were filmed in August of 1957. They were shot by a second unit team headed by the dean of all stuntmen, Yakima Canutt. After years of performing stunts, Canutt chose the less painful path of second unit director. He came to the studio in 1956 to work on *Westward Ho the Wagons!* and *Old Yeller.* While under his short-term contract he also directed many of the dangerous stunts on *Zorro.* The segments handled by Canutt were the very same he had been performing years earlier at Monogram and Republic. The action consisted of bullwhip fights on horseback and horse and stagecoach chases. It also included a number of scenes such as Zorro riding across the countryside, riding out of his secret cave and galloping to the top of a hill, rearing his horse and waving. These Zorro scenes were used as stock footage throughout the entire run of the series.*

Use of stock footage is simply a cost-saving device in films and television. For *Zorro,* the footage usually consisted of action such as Zorro riding, running, leaping and swinging. These scenes were the most expensive to shoot so they were re-used whenever possible. Close-up facial reactions of Zorro were also used, but to a lesser degree.

The next order of business for Zorro was a mode of transportation. While not as fancy or memorable as Roy Rogers' Trigger or the Lone Ranger's Silver, Tornado, Zorro's black stallion, was always up to the task. Tornado was actually a beautiful seven-year-old quarter horse named Diamond Decorator. Purchased by the studio from the Double Diamond Ranch in Nevada, it had won the Grand Nationals Medal Class in the 1950s with 14 consecutive show wins. Decorator also had a very impressive pedigree. His maternal grandsire was quarter horse racing legend Joe Hancock. His paternal grandsire was foundation sire Old Sorrel. As with any movie or TV show that features animals, a number of doubles are always necessary. Buddy Van Horn had horses of his own that he used for such specialties as jumping, rearing and galloping across the countryside. His favorite Tornado was Ribbon. "He could do transfers and he could run. I could about outrun a camera car with him," laughed Van Horn. On the rare occasions when Guy Williams would mount Tornado for a brief trot or for publicity shots, Diamond Decorator was used. Williams also rode Decorator in public appearances at Disneyland and the Rose Parade. Glen "Corky" Randall, who along with Buddy Davenport was the wrangler and trainer on *Zorro,* said that Decorator was Williams' favorite mount.

As far as training the black stallion, Randall said, "Decorator was what we call 'whip broke.' You could call him and send him. He could whinny and pick up things with his mouth. He also did a lot of galloping." Randall, the son of legendary horse trainer, Glen Randall, Sr., stated that another double horse, Midnight, was so close in appearance to Decorator that in photographs even Randall could not tell them apart. Diamond Decorator was the only horse on the series owned by Disney. He was not used in any other movies or television series. After *Zorro* was over, Decorator was retired to Disney's Golden Oak Ranch in Newhall. He passed away in the 1980s.

Most of the scenes were filmed at Bell Ranch, Iverson's Ranch and Corriganville in Chatsworth. These locations were utilized by all of the TV Westerns in the 1950s. Once Canutt completed his stint at the Disney Studios, he continued to be much in demand and found himself directing the classic chariot race for Ben-Hur *and the memorable battle scenes in* El Cid *and* Spartacus, *among other things.*

3

"This Shall Be the Disguise of El Zorro"

Behind the Scenes — Costumes, Sets, Crew, Music

Costumes

Once Guy Williams was chosen for the dual role of Zorro and Don Diego, one of the first orders of business was costume fittings. The basic idea for the Zorro costume had more or less been established in the pulps and previous movies. The Disney version of the costume was closest to the 1940 Tyrone Power (*The Mark of Zorro*) outfit. Chuck Keehne, head costumer for Disney, remembered, "We ran the Power film to look at the outfits but we changed the costume slightly. It was simply our version of what we thought Zorro should look like."

Although Zorro wore a cape in the pulp stories, it was not a prominent costume accessory in the two film versions of *The Mark of Zorro* nor in the Republic serials. The most outstanding feature of the Disney costume was, however, a long black satin cape. There were two unusual characteristics to the cape: It had arm slits on the sides affording Guy Williams freedom of movement in the fencing scenes. It was also extremely wide in the back, giving it a draping effect. This width was used to dramatic effect by Williams when he would twirl part of his cape over his left forearm before crossing blades with an adversary. A lighter weight and slightly longer cape was used for riding sequences, adding to Zorro's dashing appearance.

The rest of the costume was relatively close to the 1940 version, the black dull silk shirt with large sleeves and the black wool elastic pants. The sash was made of black satin to match the cape. The traditional Spanish sash was wound around the waist several times and then tucked underneath in the back. Because of the action involved, costumer Keehne was concerned that the sash might frequently unravel. To prevent this, a modified version of the sash was made. Based upon the design of the cummerbund, it was hooked in the back. This gave the appearance of being an authentic sash, which was the general idea.

The Disney mask was similar in style to the version worn by Douglas Fairbanks, Sr. It covered the upper portion of the face and was separate from the black kerchief worn over his head. It differs slightly from the 1940 Tyrone Power model. Power's mask and head covering was one piece and could be worn in different styles. The distinctive feature of the Disney mask was the shape of the eyeholes. Instead of large, round ones, like Fairbanks, they were cut in an almond shape, giving it a cat's eye look. A Lone Ranger–style mask was used as interfacing underneath to help hold it in place.

Because Zorro was dressed all in black, it was necessary to add contrasting trim for highlighting purposes so that he could be seen on the screen. The hat was flat-brimmed and gaucho-style, and had a silver band around the base of the crown. The gauntlets, which were polished black leather, had white piping bordering the cuffs, once again for highlighting. Because Disney lacked the facilities of the larger studios and because they were so busy during this period, the only parts of the Zorro costume made there was the mask and head kerchief. The shirt, cape and pants were put together by Western Costume in Los Angeles. Church Keehne estimated that through the course of the show, as a result of wear and tear and outfitting doubles, approximately two dozen Zorro costumes were made. The hat, boots and gloves held up longer than the cloth articles and were not replaced as often. Keehne estimated that the entire Zorro outfit cost approximately $600.

Certain aspects of the costume were still being ironed out during the first dozen or so episodes. At times, the hat brim was crooked and bent and the sash looked too narrow; the forehead between the hat and mask was visible. These may seem to be minor details, but when a character is almost solely identified by the costume he wears, these particulars take on an importance of their own. One of the costume inconsistencies concerned how the cape was worn. In "Presenting Señor Zorro," the premiere episode, there were some scenes in which Zorro did not use one or both of the arm slits and other scenes in which he did. The same was true in Episode #2, "Zorro's Secret Passage;" during a fencing scene, Zorro is wearing his cape in the more traditional style, over the shoulders without using the arm slits. In Episode #9, "A Fair Trial," Zorro wears his cape without using the arm slits for the entire time he is on the screen. After this segment, Zorro would use both arm slits in every subsequent episode save for one. When the first 13 episodes were completed, only one costume change of note occurred. In Episode #14, "Shadow of Doubt," Zorro's forehead was covered up for the first time with the mask and the head kerchief overlapping. Finally, by Episode #20, "Agent of the Eagle," any and all costume inconsistencies were overcome and Zorro looked well-tailored each week.

Interestingly, some of the earliest publicity photos taken by the Hesse Studios of Guy Williams show a slightly different Zorro costume. In these photos, one of which appeared in a *TV Guide* ad the week of the premiere, the hat has no silver band and the gloves are also a dull black with no white piping. These are minor aberrations but worth noting because this version of the costume appeared only in very early publicity shots, not the actual television series.

The Dons

Some historical research was done for the dons' costumes. However, like the Zorro costume, they too were largely based upon the outfits worn in previous Zorro

An early Disney photograph (courtesy of Walt Disney Productions).

films. They were all of a basic style with white ruffled shirts, vests and waistcoats. The jackets and pants were usually decorated with intricate braiding. Scarf-like ties were tied with a bow at the neck with a matching sash worn around the waist. Over the course of the series, the Don Diego character had eight different outfits to choose from, all made from a durable elastic material. Usually three copies of each costume were produced to compensate for wear and tear and for the use of doubles.

Because relatively few color photos of the show exist, we do not know the colors of all the Don Diego's outfits. However, based on existing color photos, there was a navy blue suit for formal occasions (fiestas, etc.). The navy blue outfit used for the *most* formal occasions was adorned with intricate and elaborate gold braid. This is the suit that Diego wears upon his return to Los Angeles. He refers to it as "my fanciest jacket, the one with the gold braid." This outfit establishes him as something of a dandy and a fop in the eyes of the commandante.* The maroon suit, the light gray suit and the beige suit were used more or less for everyday affairs but were still rather fancy befitting the life of a young don. There was a tan suede suit that was probably used more than any other suit. It had some modest gold trim, but no vest, and was worn when Diego would go riding and attend to normal business.

Bernardo's suit was a simple olive green with no decorative braiding. It was worn with a matching vest, a plain collarless white shirt and dark sash.

The uniform worn by the commandante, Capitan Monastario, was almost an exact copy of the one worn by Basil Rathbone's character, Capitan Esteban, in the 1940 *The Mark of Zorro*. The differences are the red around the sleeves of the Disney version and some medals and braided rope worn over the shoulder. Likewise, the uniforms of the soldiers in the Disney series were very similar to the ones worn by the soldiers in the 1940 film.

Recalling the tight pants he was required to wear for his role as the commandante, Lomond recounts, "Guy and I were always playing practical jokes on each other because I always wanted to relax him; he was very uptight at times. Anyway, we both wore these skin-tight pants, so one day Guy comes out and he's taken a small towel and rolled it up and put it down the front of his pants. So I say, 'That S.O.B., I'll fix him.' I rushed to my dressing room and took a bigger towel and folded it up and put it in my pants. We shot the whole scene and we hear this tittering offstage when the director says 'cut.' And there were 25 nuns standing there watching. We got our asses chewed out for that one."

The Set

Art director Marvin Davis recalled with amusement how he was called upon to recreate the look and feel of Old California for *Zorro*. "One day I went to the men's room and there was Walt Disney standing beside me and he says to me, 'Hey Marv, how would like to do the *Zorro* series?' I said, 'Sure, I'm your man.'" Davis had worked at many of the major studios in town before he came to the Disney Studio in 1953. Along with Dick Irvine, he was one of the major architects of Disneyland. Davis also worked on *Davy Crockett* and *Westward Ho the Wagons!* before moving to *Zorro*.

About his initial preparation for the exterior *Zorro* set, Davis remarked, "I looked at all the things that were necessary like the church, cuartel, tavern and the Alcalde's

---

Chuck Keehne felt that "Zorro would've been a beautiful show in color. The dons' costumes were really attractive but you obviously couldn't bring the color out because it was a black and white show."

house and I'd find out how Norman [Foster] wanted things set up. I'd have meetings with him as I was designing it and I'd show him my drawings. After that, he'd leave it up to me as to the design of the architecture.

"The Pueblo de Los Angeles, which took up several acres on the east end of the Disney back lot, was the first big set at the studio. At a cost of approximately $500,000 and taking six to seven months to build, the set was a study in detail. The church was an exact replica of the original pueblo church which is located downtown in Los Angeles. The hinges on the huge hand-hewn doors were actual wrought iron. Windows of hand-pounded iron were carefully cast out of special prop materials and painted to reveal facets which might have been produced by hammers. Many of the intricate wooden windows were genuine, having been purchased from early Spanish building which had been recently dismantled. Every adobe brick was carefully antiqued with paint and putty to give the pueblo an aged and weathered appearance."[1]

The *Zorro* Plaza, as it was called, consisted of four main structures: the cuartel, the church, the tavern and the Magistrado's house. Most of the action took place near and around these buildings. Less prominent in the episodes were the blacksmith's shop, the winery warehouse and a few other smaller shops. In the first 13 episodes, a great deal of filming took place inside the cuartel, which consisted of the commandante's office, the jail, the stables and the soldiers' barracks.

A number of the larger buildings on the *Zorro* set were waterproofed and used as storage for props. A multitude of trees, market stands, a well and animals adorned the plaza, which gave the series a realistic feel, at least in the first season. The back lot also included the Alameda and Riverside berms. These were wooded areas where filming could be done in privacy. The berms also made it appear as though the action was taking place out of the country. Their names were derived from the streets which bordered the studio, Alameda and Riverside.

The bulk of the interior sets could be found on Soundstage 3 on the Disney lot. The de la Vega patio, sala and library, along with Diego's room and secret passage, were affixed to Soundstage 3. The interior of the tavern and the commandante's office were found there as well. Modifications were made on these existing sets to create whatever temporary setting the script required. If for any reason a set had to be dismantled, it would be photographed and then indexed and placed on wall jacks in the scene docks, which was in a large covered shed. When a set piece was needed again, it was located by its number in the card file. Scenes set in the secret cave where Diego kept his horse Tornado were actually filmed at two different locations. In the very early episodes it was an actual outdoor location at the Iverson Ranch. This was later recreated on a soundstage. All of the cave scenes which were shot during the first 13 episodes were used as stock film footage throughout the entire run of the show.

When the cast and crew went on location to the Mission of San Luis Rey, certain preparations had to be taken to give the mission an even more rustic look than it already had. The blacktop parking lot in front of the church had to be covered with dirt, and some papier maché boulders were added, giving it more of a period look as the lancers rode up on their horses. Two gates leading to the cemetery were also accented with ornate artwork. The doors remained that way until they fell into disrepair and were replaced with a less elaborate pair in the mid–1980s.

Marvin Davis worked very closely with set director Hal Gausman, whose job was to give life to the sets that Davis designed and built. Gausman, following in his father Russell's footsteps, began working in films for RKO at age 16. Six Academy Award nominations later, he started work at the Disney Studios in 1956. As a result of a union rule, he shared screen credit with department head Emil Kuri, but it was Gausman who found himself decorating the *Zorro* set on a regular basis.

He recalled, "I've done a lot of period films and my success has come through research. I'm a pretty good historian as a result of all the research that I've done. That seems to be the way I operate best." Describing a day on the set, Gausman said, "I would spend a lot of time on the set in the morning and get everything taken care of that needed to be done. I'd then go off and start building the sets for the next day."

All of the furniture, paintings, candle holders, curtains, bookcases, etc., were produced and put into place under the direction of Gausman. He also set up and designed the market stands in the Plaza. He had to be sure that everything was accurate for the 1820 period of Spanish California. It was really a "Disney-ized" version of the Pueblo de Los Angeles, cleaner and more romantic and certainly more compressed than it really was. Recalling Disney's benevolent dictatorship at the studio, Gausman said, "We had an old saying at the studio when somebody asked, 'Why are you doing that?' The answer was always, 'Because Walt says.' He knew what he wanted and there wasn't a helluva lot of vacillation."

Both the *Zorro* Plaza and the interior sets were also used a great deal by other Disney series such as *Swamp Fox*, *Elfego Baca* and *Texas John Slaughter*. *Swamp Fox* used the entire plaza and cuartel in an episode titled "Horses for Green." For that episode, Gausman tried to give the set a Carolina fishing village look by tossing some fishing nets around, but anyone who had ever seen the *Zorro* series would recognize the set immediately.

The exterior plaza was completely refurbished in 1967 to look like a contemporary French village for *Monkeys Go Home*. Parts of the *Zorro* Plaza were used continuously until most of the back lot was torn down in the mid–1980s to make room for office space. Britt Lomond remembers getting a call from the studio: "They asked if I would like to see the last of the *Zorro* set before they tore it down and I said, 'You bet your ass.' I went out and had lunch in the commissary and watched them tear down my old office, which was a little heart-tugging, I must say."

Matte Drawing

Tied in closely with set design and decoration was the matte drawing of Peter Ellenshaw and his first assistant, Academy Award winner Albert Whitlock. It was a staple of all Disney live-action features. Matte drawings were a way of saving money and making landscape shots look more impressive than they actually were. According to Ellenshaw, "Painting matte shots is a most tricky and meticulous art. Let us suppose we are on location and need a castle on a hill. We have the hill, but not the castle. On a large glass, about six feet in front of the camera, we paint the castle. Through the clear part of the glass, the characters go into action and are photographed at the same time as the background scene is recorded. This is a matte painting in its simplest form."[2]

The most impressive and cost-saving piece of matte work on *Zorro* was the exterior for the de la Vega hacienda. It was used as an establishing shot and it existed only as a matte painting done by Albert Whitlock. (Occasionally other exteriors on the back lot were used as part of the hacienda, such as the rear of the tavern which also doubled as the rear in the de la Vega house.) The majority of all the other mattes, such as chasms that Tornado would leap or trails on the sides of mountains, were painted by Peter Ellenshaw. According to Hal Gausman, "Because Albert and Peter did the same kind of thing, it became difficult for the two of them to work together and Albert eventually left and went to work at Universal where he continued his work as a matte artist. Sometimes I think that Albert was a little more versatile than Peter so it was too bad he left."

Directors

Although it has been said that the film is a director's medium and television is a producer's, all of the directors on *Zorro* seemed to have distinctive styles that contributed to the show's success. After Norman Foster (who was more than just a director) was chosen, it was the job of associate producer Bill Anderson to locate directors who were adept at both comedy and action. "I was watching a lot of television and films at that time, looking at various people's work and talking to people. I'd get an idea about someone and bring them in and interview them and try to get their concept of the show," Anderson commented.

Anderson chose Lewis Foster, Charles Barton and Charles Lamont who, along with Norman Foster, directed the bulk of the first season's episodes. In keeping with Walt Disney's desire to inject a certain amount of comedy (slapstick or subtle) in every episode, all three directors had their roots in comedy. Lew Foster had worked as a gag writer for Hal Roach, and also wrote and directed silent comedies. He went on to direct such features as *Captain China, Crashout* and *Dakota Incident.* Perhaps his greatest achievement was winning as Oscar for his original story *Mr. Smith Goes to Washington.* He also wrote the screenplay for *The Farmer's Daughter.* Along with directing, Lew Foster wrote a number of *Zorro* episodes.

The two Charlies, Barton and Lamont, had very similar careers. Lamont began his career directing two reel-comedies for Mack Sennett and went on to direct Abbott and Costello and Ma & Pa Kettle films. Barton started out as a prop man and "gofer" for director William Wellman. It was Wellman who first let Barton try his hand as an assistant director. Barton directed his first film, *Wagon Wheels,* when he was 32, and went on to direct some of the best Abbott and Costello films, such as *The Time of Their Lives* and *Abbott and Costello Meet Frankenstein.* Like Lamont, he also did time on the Ma & Pa Kettle series. Anderson remembered Barton as a director "who had a sense of humor, had a lot to offer and was a very clever guy."

The one common thread that runs through the résumés of all these directors is that they were B-directors, which was almost a necessity for working in television.

B-films were made cheaply and quickly. Although *Zorro* was on a five-day shooting schedule (lavish by television standards), it was still relatively similar to the pace these directors had worked in films. Put simply, they were required to work fast and turn out a quality product or they were fired.

The two aberrations in the directing corps were John Meredyth Lucas and Robert Stevenson. Each would direct only three episodes apiece and neither had a comedy nor a B-film background. Lucas was an appropriate choice because his mother Bess Meredyth adapted the screenplay for *The Mark of Zorro* (1940). It would be his first real directorial chore; he also wrote the episodes that he directed. Lucas, who had been with the studio for a few years before he worked on *Zorro*, amusingly recalled the unusual circumstances under which he was engaged: "I was hired to do a series of behind-the-scenes shorts of the filming of *20,000 Leagues Under the Sea*. I ended up with a cutter, cameraman, an editor; my own film unit. I said to a friend of mine on the lot, 'I don't see a lot of the producer who hired me, Card Walker.' My friend said, 'Card Walker is the head of publicity, not a producer.' So, I said [laughing], 'I wonder if I have a valid contract?' He said, 'Don't worry. That's the way they do things around here.' In those days Walt could hire a janitor to go out and do things. It was a big family atmosphere, like a small Midwestern campus and Walt was sole commander."

Englishman Robert Stevenson had directed such films as *Tom Brown's School Days, Joan of Paris* and the prestigious *Jane Eyre*. He came to the Disney Studios in 1957 and directed *Old Yeller* and *Johnny Tremain*. After *Zorro*, Stevenson stayed at the studio to direct over a dozen films, among them *The Absent Minded Professor, In Search of the Castaways, Son of Flubber, The Love Bug* and his greatest triumph, *Mary Poppins*. Ron Miller, one of the many assistant directors on *Zorro*, recalled, "Most of TV at that time was all dialogue with 10 to 15 pages a day to film and a whole episode was shot in five days. On *Zorro* we had one-quarter of a page of action in the form of a swordfight. It took at least half a day to film. It was a very stunt-oriented show and we would take five days to shoot one episode, about 40 scenes per day. It was very ambitious. Bob Stevenson had heard of the budget problems we had on *Zorro* and said, 'I'd love to take a crack at this.' He was very budget-conscious so he was given three shows to direct. The average price per show was about $78,000 and he told Walt 'I know I can do it for less than that.' When all was said and done, his average cost per episode was $105,000. He couldn't cope with it. When he got to the action, it was just too much."

Assistant Directors

Second season director and movie veteran Bill Witney declared, "A good assistant director is worth his weight in gold." Explaining an assistant director's duties further, Witney commented, "He comes in and breaks the picture down to a certain number of days. If you move onto a set and you have three sequences to shoot there, you go ahead and film these sequences even though they're out of continuity. You do this to save time and the assistant director is aware of all these things and sets them up for the director. He also sets the background action and if he's good you don't have to tell him because he knows the script. He gives out the calls, dismisses the people; he's a very important person."

The most often-used assistants on the *Zorro* series were Arthur Viteralli, Vincent McEveety and Russ Haverick. Viteralli, McEveety, and McEvetty's brother Joseph, who was also an assistant director, eventually became directors. Ron Miller, who worked as a second assistant in the first season and a first assistant in the second season, would go on to become a producer and finally president and CEO of the Walt Disney Studios in the 1970s. Bill Sheehan and Robert Shannon were also relatively active as assistants during *Zorro's* second season.

Film Editors

There were approximately six film editors who worked on *Zorro* throughout the entire run. These are men who work very closely with the director and piece together the film into a cohesive story. Fade-outs, fade-ins and camera cuts all come under the realm of the editor. Roy Livingston, Cotton Warburton and Hugh Chaloupka worked on *Zorro* more than any other editors (the entire run of the series). Warburton was an ex-football player and, according to Bill Anderson, "one of our best editors at that time and great fun to work with. When he wasn't working on *Zorro* it was because he was needed on a feature." Robert Stafford, George Gale and Ed Sampson would fill in when the other three were working on other studio projects.

Writers

Although the official credit read "Based on the Zorro stories by Johnston McCulley," that was only partially true. Obviously all of the main characters were taken from the McCulley pulps. Occasionally names from the pulp stories were used on the series as well. But by and large, the scripts on the television show were original and reflected the values and mores of the 1950s.

The two main writers on the series were Lowell Hawley and Bob Wehling. They were the closest thing to a writing staff that the show had. Both Hawley and Norman Foster had worked on *The Loretta Young Show* where Hawley had written over 30 scripts. It was Foster who recommended the writer to Walt Disney. Hawley, who was a published author, had also written for *My Friend Flicka*, *Jim Bowie* and *The Millionaire*. He had only scripted two of the first 13 episodes but Walt Disney liked them enough to make him head writer, a position he held for the remaining 65 episodes. Hawley would stay at the studio for many years writing such films as *Swiss Family Robinson*, *Babes in Toyland*, *A Tiger Walks* and *The Adventures of Bullwhip Griffin*.

Bob Wehling became interested in theater when he was growing up in South Dakota. After World War II (he was a member of the Signal Corps Counter Intelligence Team), he returned to school and got his Master's degree in drama from the University of South Dakota. He did some acting work and became a director of the

Hollywood School of Drama from 1951 to 1958. He too was brought to the Disney Studios by Norman Foster and the pair collaborated on the premiere episode.

Most *Zorro* episodes were not collaborations, but occasionally Hawley and Wehling got together to script an episode. Hawley commented, "Bob was easy for me to work with but he wasn't easy for a lot of people. He had very set ideas and felt that's the only way it could be. He believed very much in what he was writing. When we collaborated, we would both do a rough draft and then get together and confer. Bob was very good at dialogue and I would usually help chart out the story line." Wehling wrote a few things outside the studio such as *Sugarfoot* and *The Richard Boone Show.*

Anna Wehling, Bob's wife, recalled a bet between her husband and Lowell Hawley over something that Walt Disney did. Hawley lost the bet and paid off by drawing a mask and hat on some transparent tape and putting it over Lincoln's face on a $5 bill. He then framed it. It hangs on a wall in Wehling's dining room to this day.

N.B. Stone, Jr., contributed nine scripts to the series, many in the first season. He scripted six episodes of the Eagle saga, three of them being among the best in the series. Prior to *Zorro*, Stone had written for *Cheyenne* and *Celebrity Playhouse* and penned the 1955 film *Man with a Gun*. In 1962 he wrote the highly acclaimed *Ride the High Country* for Sam Peckinpah. A number of other writers also contributed to a lesser degree in the first season. Anthony Ellis, Malcolm Boylan, Joel Kane and Jackson Gillis were all freelance writers who came in and worked on the show briefly, usually with collaborators. Gillis, who had written many episodes of *The Adventures of Superman* series, co-wrote two episodes, then went on to become associate producer of *Perry Mason.*

Cameramen

The crew that worked behind the camera remained relatively consistent throughout the entire run of the series. Gordon Avil was the director of photography. There could be as many as four men working around one camera. Avil himself, after conferring with a director, lined up shots and planned all camera action, following the script. Travis Hill was the operator who actually pushed the camera button while first and second assistants like Bob McGowan and David Walsh loaded, focused and generally cared for the camera itself.

Sound

Robert O. Cook was head of the sound department and a Disney veteran of over 41 years. Cook's early life was spent as a radio operator aboard a ship followed by a stint at a California broadcast station that eventually went bankrupt. He caught on with Roy and Walt Disney just as sound pictures were coming in and stayed at the studio until 1971. Along the way, Cook worked on all the major features and was Oscar nominated numerous times.

Cook reminisced about his work on *Zorro*, "The sound crew consisted of three men, one runs the recorder, one operated the microphone boom, one fellow called a mixer monitors everything and makes sure that the dialogue doesn't overlap and that he gets a quality product. He's also trying to keep the sound of airplanes, trucks, etc., off the sound track. It was a bit of a problem on the back lot because the studio was near a busy traffic corner. Sometimes a siren would go past and we would end up having to loop the dialogue [a process where the actor re-records the dialogue on a soundstage so that it's free of background noise]. The looping was done quite often on *Zorro* because you're trying to do things quickly and you can't stop for every sound, you have to keep going." Regarding the fencing scenes, Cook commented, "The sound of the swords hitting together was usually live but sometimes it was added later. It was a difficult thing to synchronize so if you could get it live it was preferable."

When it was announced that the Disney Studios would be doing a weekly half-hour adventure show, some of the other studios were dubious of Disney, according to Cook. "They said that we couldn't do it because we had only three sound stages and we didn't have the capacity to record the orchestra, sound effects, dialogue and then mix it all together and get it to the laboratory and keep to the schedule. Walt loved a challenge and didn't know the meaning of the word no. Through hard work and determination, we did it. I never saw a studio that had the high morale or teamwork that the Disney Studios had. You didn't care how many hours you worked or if you got paid to do it," Cook declared.

Of his old boss, Cook said, "Walt was every kind of person wrapped in one. He could be a Perry Como, a soft and sweet guy, or he could go into a rage and really raise the roof. And he was everything in between. He worked harder than anybody in the studio. He was the first to get there and the last to leave."

Music

Music was an integral part of all Disney productions and *Zorro* was no exception. The man chosen to score the music for the *Zorro* series was William Lava. Lava was a conductor, composer and arranger and was among the most prolific composers in the history of movies, scoring over 200 Republic films, one of which was *Zorro's Fighting Legion*. Some of the musical passages he composed for Republic serials were passed on to *Lone Ranger* creator George Trendle and used on the *Ranger*'s radio program. Lava jokingly referred to this period of time as "turning out music by the yard."[3]

He moved to RKO where he worked on Westerns featuring such stars as Tim Holt and George O'Brien as well as the *Dr. Christian* series. In the 1940s he went to Warner Brothers where he worked for 15 years turning out background music for over 100 Warner features. In the 1950s he entered television co-composing the theme to the Warner western *Cheyenne*. The music he composed for the Disney film *The Littlest Outlaw* and the Hardy Boys serial on *The Mickey Mouse Club* brought him to the attention of writer-producer Bill Walsh. Music department head Bob Jackman recalled Walsh's enthusiasm about Lava: "[Walsh] had worked on *The Littlest Outlaw* and was very impressed with Bill Lava. He told me about him and I went in and listened to the score and he was right, it was great. On the strength of that, we hired him for *Zorro*."

It was decided that each character should have their own musical theme. This was a technique Disney used in the *Peter and the Wolf* segment of *Make Mine Music* (1946). Jackman continued, "We then had a meeting with Walt and he explained what he wanted and then Lava and I would talk it over and then proceed from there. The musical themes that we used for each character were discussed by all of us. The theme that we used for Bernardo was partially Walt's idea." The themes mentioned by Bob Jackman consisted of three different, distinct melodies for each of the main characters: The dashing brass section for Zorro, the playful, mischievous flute and piccolo for Bernardo and the lumbering tuba and drums for Sgt. Garcia. Garcia's vamp was very reminiscent of the march segment of Tchaikovsky's *Nutcracker Suite.*

Even Tornado had his own theme, a variation on Victor Herbert's March of the Wooden Soldiers in his *Babes in Toyland* operetta. It was used sparingly. Lava was really at his best scoring the swordfights and chase scenes. They are in the tradition of the great Wolfgang Korngold and Alfred Newman swashbuckling scores of the 1930s and '40s.

Buddy Baker; a music veteran of such Disney projects as *The Mickey Mouse Club*, *Davy Crockett*, *Swamp Fox* and *Elfego Baca,* explained Lava's method of working. "He would sit through a spotting session and look at film and spot where there is going to be music. A music editor then gives him a time sheet and he times out his musical numbers. Bill usually liked to work at home, he had a piano right next to his bed and it usually wouldn't take him more than three days per episode to write his score. Most episodes had about 15 minutes of music and he would write a formula, injecting his musical themes here and there. It was almost like putting a puzzle together. Although he wrote new music for every episode, he was always using snippets from other episodes. He would just make a note for the copyists; 'copy eight bars from cue 1A.'" [Each piece of music is called a cue; the #1 was the number of the reel of film that contained the cue and the A stood for the first cue of that reel].

Baker continued: "One interesting thing about Bill, and I've never noticed this about anybody else, was that all of his cues were always on the same click tract, a 17-frame click track, and he seldom varied from that. The click track ranges from six frames to 30 and he only used one out of the whole range. It was always the same tempo. I never did figure out why." After Lava had scored the episode, he would then record it, conducting the 22 to 35 piece orchestra himself. Each episode would usually be completed in a three-hour session.

In a 1986 interview, Guy Williams recalled the fun he had working with Lava: "Bill was terrific with the music. I would do things like move a certain way just to see if Bill would score it. I told him once, 'I'm gonna drop you one and see if you score it. I'm not going to tell you what it is I'm just gonna drop you one and watch what you do.' Bill said, 'Okay, I don't care, I'll score it.' I had a scene where I had to leave the living room in Alejandro's house, a Diego scene.' As I walked across the room to get to the door, I had to pass a long table. It occurred to me to take my two

Gene Sheldon (*left*) and Guy Williams pose with 7-Up star Fresh-up Freddie.

fingers and walk them down as I was walking; you'd never see it. I waited and waited and the show got on the air and as soon as that scene came up, Lava did a whole series of pizzicato violin as I moved my hand down there. I called him and said, 'Bill, you son of a gun, you really did it.' We used to live for stuff like that."[4]

Most 1950s adventure shows (i.e., Westerns, detective series, etc.) had theme songs that were sung by a male solo or vocal group and *Zorro* was no different. Probably the most recognizable aspect of the *Zorro* series was its theme song. The melody was written by the prolific George Bruns, whose first chore for the studio was composing the score for the *Davy Crockett* mini-series. He was also nominated for an Academy Award for his work on *Sleeping Beauty*. He went on to compose the music for *101 Dalmatians, The Absent Minded Professor, Babes in Toyland, The Sword in the Stone, The Jungle Book* and *Robin Hood,* among others.

The lyrics to the *Zorro* theme were penned by writer-director Norman Foster and it became very familiar to the kids of America. Played at the fast waltz temp, the theme was sung at the opening of every episode by an in-house studio quartet called the Mellomen (Jimmy Joyce, Max Smith, Bill Lee and Bob Stevens). At the end of every episode it was played as an instrumental over the credits. (The second stanza was not used on the TV series, but did turn up on several recordings released in connection with the show.)

During the course of the series, some 23 songs were inserted in various episodes, sung by Sgt. Garcia or Don Diego. Henry Calvin, who had a powerful operatic voice, performed all of his own vocals. Guy Williams, on the other hand, was dubbed by Melloman Bill Lee. The songs often gave the show a slight "Gilbert and Sullivan" feel which was unique for series television but was found quite often in Disney films and television shows. Contributors to the musical numbers included Buddy Baker, Gil George, Joe Dubin, Tom Adair and the Sherman Brothers.

4

"Out of the Night"
Overview of the First Season

The 1957–58 season of *Zorro* consisted of 39 half-hour black and white episodes. Those 39 can be divided into two parts: the first 13 (the Monastario chapters) and the Eagle Saga. The first 13 segments, based most heavily on Johnston McCulley's pulp stories, told the basic story of Zorro: A young don returns home to California from Spain at the behest of his father and when he arrives he learns that his pueblo is under the heel of a dictator. To fight the tyrant, he adopts the guise of a fop by day and a daring masked swordsman by night. In the first 13 installments, Zorro is seen attempting to rid the pueblo of Capitan Monastario and to protect his secret identity.

What was unique about the *Zorro* series was the almost serialization of the episodes, which was familiar to fans of the serials of the '30s and '40s. Some characters would last for two or three episodes and then be killed off or disappear. At one time the idea of making each episode a cliffhanger was discussed. Story editor Lowell Hawley recounted, "Although I was not there when the series began, I was told that they had planned the show as a serial without any real beginning, middle or end to each episode. There would be a cliffhanger each week. It was a fact that if they followed the serialization concept, they wouldn't have to pay the writers as much." This idea was abandoned in favor of episodes that were complete in and of themselves yet also related by a basic storyline and continuing guest stars.

When Walt Disney purchased the rights to *Zorro* in 1952, his original format for the show was different from what finally developed. Bill Cottrell, who was to be the original producer for *Zorro*, explains, "We thought it would've been interesting to recall the time when Zorro actually took place; to do a series that had some notable authenticity. Not quite a documentary, but a show that could teach people something, using realistic sets, furniture, clothing, food, etc." The original series was to be very close to the McCulley pulp stories.

What happened between 1953 and 1957 was the great success of *Davy Crockett*. Crockett was really the archetype for most of the Disney live-action films and TV shows of the 1950s. It contained what was to become the studio's formula for success: action, a sprinkling of broad comedy, a musical number or two, a historical setting and a catchy theme song. In this sense, *Davy Crockett* was really the father of *Zorro*.

And it was certainly Disney's desire to inject comedy into the script. Writer Lowell Hawley remembers being stopped numerous times in the hallway and being told by Walt, "We gotta get more comedy into it." The concept of humor coupled with swashbuckling action had its genesis in the films of Fairbanks and was established in the early episodes. Producer Bill Anderson remembered, "For the first 13 episodes, everybody was in on the act, Walt and myself, and Norman got a lot of help to flesh out those scripts. Walt personally had gotten his biggest kick out of the first 13. He enjoyed working with Guy and Britt Lomond and Henry Calvin. He felt that the real meat of *Zorro* was in the first 13 episodes."

The studio pulled out all the stops for the first 13, hoping to make a big impression and establish the series. In these initial episodes there was a good deal of location filming as well. Two entire episodes, "Zorro Rides to the Mission" and "The Ghost of the Mission," were filmed at the Mission of San Luis Rey in Oceanside, California. There also was a lot of action: swordfights, chases across the countryside, swinging over rooftops. The studio was attempting to do a mini-movie each week conjuring up memories of *The Adventures of Robin Hood* and *The Mark of Zorro.* Each episode was a struggle between good and evil, freedom vs. oppression embodied in the form of Zorro against the commandante. Assistant director Ron Miller recalled, "The whole appearance of the series was big, it was grand scale. When you look at those shows and you look at the amount of production, you realize that it was very ambitious and that's the way Walt was."

Zorro was a polished, quality production in the Disney tradition, light years ahead of what the other studios were turning out. The budget for the first season was $3,198,000, approximately $78,000 per episode. This was an impressive amount of money for a half-hour series in 1957 — and all the more impressive because it was aimed primarily at children. In comparison, the price of the average half-hour black-and-white action Western such as Warner Bros.' *Lawman* and *Colt .45* was $30,000 per episode. *The Lone Ranger* filmed 39 half-hour color episodes in 1956 for a cost of $25,000 per episode. Miller explained, "We were getting $40,000 per half hour from ABC but unfortunately it was costing us $35,000 more than that per episode. Walt spent a lot more money than he got back." Disney believed that "television makes lots of friends. It's just good policy. When four million people see your television show, they carry away with them an image of what we're doing."[1]

One of the main reasons for the large budget was the action, specifically the fencing. Miller reasoned that Disney "wanted to keep the action flowing to hold onto the younger audience." In the first 13 episodes there was approximately a total of eight minutes of fencing action. With a fencing scene lasting an average of 35 seconds on screen and taking anywhere from two to four hours to shoot, it becomes obvious as to why the budget was inflated. This doesn't even include the horse stunts which appeared in many episodes. Stunt coordinator Buddy Van Horn recalled, "The horse work meant a lot of difficult riding, jumping horses, rearing horses and jumps from rooftops onto horses. It was just general livestock kind of work which included a lot of action. There are so many variables when you are involved with livestock and wagons, it's not like automobiles. You couldn't depend on everything to be exactly as you planned it." Britt Lomond recounted, "Nothing was spared in terms of production for making that show. We had the best costumes and the best sets. If we needed more time on a scene, we got it. We did everything we could to make that show 'el perfecto.'"

Although very few series of that era were shot in color, the idea of filming *Zorro* in color was discussed and there were a number of different opinions as to why the show was finally done in black and white. Producer Bill Anderson said, "We talked about it but it would've been too expensive. We didn't think we would sustain the show [for syndication value] much over two years anyway." Ron Miller explained, "Walt did everything else in color but he thought that *Zorro* should be a black-and-white character. He just felt *Zorro* was the classic black-and-white hero. He felt very strongly about that. However, it did create some problems later on as far as trying to sell the show in syndication." Britt Lomond claims that Walt Disney told him, "I should've made the show in color, it was a mistake not to." Both Chuck Keehne (costumer) and Marvin Davis (art director) felt that the show would have been beautiful in color. The bottom line seems to indicate that even if Walt Disney did want to film the show in color, the cost would have been prohibitive.

One of the difficulties that can arise on a series like *Zorro* is that it takes place in a country where everyone is supposed to speak Spanish. The end result is American actors speaking English with Spanish accents with an occasional Spanish word gratuitously thrown in. Although all of the regulars affected Spanish accents, some of the guest stars did not, so there was a loss of authenticity and consistency. Guy Williams commented, "I had auditioned with a heavy Spanish accent knowing I could drop it instead of starting out light and adding on. For the first couple of weeks somebody would be tapping me on the shoulder as I'm walking around on the set, and it would be Walt. He would say, 'Can you bring it down a little, Guy?' He didn't know what he wanted so I kept bringing it down. One day I finished the show and Walt didn't tap me on the shoulder, and that was the accent I kept."[2]

Britt Lomond said, "I studied with a couple of Spanish people and I do speak a little bit of Spanish, so I was very conscious of authenticity. I worked for three or four months on the accent so that when I started filming I had it down pretty good. Guy was following my accent. When they were casting the show, they didn't want to cast Spanish actors in the parts. Walt and Norman Foster's reasoning was interesting. They said, 'If we get a Spanish actor, we can't control the accent. If we get an American actor and he puts on an accent, we can control it.'" Don Diamond, who played Corp. Reyes in over 50 episodes and is a veteran of 350 TV shows said, "I was annoyed at some actors who knew they were doing a Spanish dialect and instead of learning to say Señor they would say Seeñor which is Italian. If you're being paid a salary as an actor, it behooves you to do some investigation into the part you're playing. In a way, maybe we should have all kept our accents down."

It was during the first season and especially the first 13 episodes that some of the kinks were worked out — the first being how Guy Williams would portray the dual roles of Don Diego and Zorro. In the two earlier and best incarnations of Zorro, the Don Diego character was played as an exaggerated fop by Fairbanks and Power. It was the sort of character who carried a perfumed handkerchief and wielded a parasol to shield himself from the sun's harsh rays. These two early movies were only taking their cue from the Johnston McCulley pulps. By and large, this is how the Don Diego character was written.

This presented something of a problem for Disney and Guy Williams, who explained, "Tyrone Power played Don Diego as a sissy, a real gay caballero. It was okay for him to do that once in a movie, but I knew that wouldn't work every week on TV. I didn't want to do that and Walt agreed. It would get tiresome, not to mention this was the '50s and a show with an audience including kids. So, I had to play Don Diego 'neutral,' which is difficult because it means 'nothing.' How do I make 'nothing' interesting?"[3] Story editor Lowell Hawley said, "We tried not to stress the effeminate part when he was Diego because it was not appealing to some people — we played that part down."

In these early episodes, Williams' portrayal of Don Diego was simply non-violent and studious rather than outright cowardly or foppish. He was a man who enjoyed reading, fine wines, playing the guitar and receiving the attention of women, although (because of the show's audience) the romantic aspects were also played down. It wasn't until the second season that a continuing romantic interest was introduced — and even then, she was more interested in Zorro than Diego. Williams believed that "if Zorro got married, that would be the end of the show. You'd have a wife, then you'd have children and pretty soon you'd be working your way towards *Little House on the Prairie.*" After the first 13 episodes and especially into the second season, the Diego character became a little more aggressive, actually taking an interest in the workings of the rancho and in some episodes physically protecting both his father and Bernardo. (See Episode Guide.)

Williams' interpretation of the Zorro character in the early going leaned more toward the Douglas Fairbanks, Sr./Errol Flynn laughing, taunting, hands-on-the-hips swashbuckler minus the Fairbanks acrobatics. Although Williams was probably receiving advice from all corners, more than likely this was Walt Disney's decision. This portrayal is most evident in the first eight or nine episodes and at times it seems forced. In these episodes, Williams' Zorro would often mock his enemies after defeating them, the sort of rogue whom laughs in the face of danger. In episode 2, "Zorro's Secret Passage," Zorro laughs after almost being shot. In Episode 6, "Zorro Saves a Friend," a laughing Zorro throws adobe bricks at lancers who have him trapped atop a church scaffold.

One thing that didn't seem forced was Williams' penchant for flashing a big smile while wielding a sword. This may have been the influence of director Norman Foster and fencing master Fred Cavens, both of whom worked very closely with the new Zorro. Regardless, it worked perfectly and became something of a trademark. As the series progressed and Williams' confidence grew, he began injecting his own personality into the Zorro character. And Zorro became a little more suave and cool.

The relationship between Diego and his manservant, Bernardo, is one of true camaraderie. These two men share a secret and the bond between them is very strong. Although it is clear that Diego is the master and Bernardo his servant, it is an aspect of the relationship that is played down to a certain extent. It's almost as if they are playing the parts of master and servant for the outside world in order to sustain their masquerade — certainly far different than a real relationship of this kind would have been in Spanish California of 1820. However, this was 1950s Eisenhower America where all people are equal and a master-servant relationship would never do. As a matter of fact, all of the de la Vega servants were treated with a certain amount of respect reflecting the social climate of the 1950s rather than the 1820s. In this particular regard, the Disney show certainly differed from the McCulley short stories. In "Zorro Frees the Slaves," a 1946 short story, Diego agrees to intervene in the case of some debtor peons who are being worked like slaves. Before leaving for Los Angeles, "he clapped his hands and a house servant entered. 'Summon Bernardo,' Diego ordered. 'Tell him I walk to the Plaza. Have him fetch my hat and tell him to bring a sunshade to hold over me.'"[4] This is the sort of behavior that the series shied away from. It would have made the lead character too unattractive.

The interplay between Don Diego and Sgt. Garcia remained relatively the same throughout the entire run of the show. The Garcia character, which was introduced in the McCulley novels in the 1940s *West Magazine,* was fat, lazy, not too bright, but generally kind-hearted. It was Garcia who put a soft edge on the evil activity of the commandante. Diego basically used Garcia as a funnel for information to help him in his activities as Zorro. Garcia could be very easily bribed with wine and would usually reveal more than he realized. It was also clear that Diego genuinely liked Garcia and in the guise of Zorro actually fought side by side with him and rescued him from a number of precarious situations. Even so, Garcia constantly dreamed of capturing Zorro and collecting the 2,000 peso reward. Of course, the only way this would happen is if Zorro walked up to Garcia and gave himself up.

The relationship between Don Alejandro and Diego remained consistent throughout the first season. A proud man, Alejandro was often quick-tempered and exasperated over his son's lack of interest in anything except poetry and playing the guitar. In the early going, Don Alejandro's disappointment with Diego was much more apparent than in subsequent chapters. As a matter of fact, Alejandro's displeasure with Diego all but disappeared after the first 13 episodes. He simply accepted his son as he was. Actually, George Lewis' portrayal of Don Alejandro was not unlike that of Montagu Love in the 1940 *The Mark of Zorro*. Both were faithful to the McCulley stories.

Like most series of this type and especially one filmed in the 1950s, the characters remained consistent and two-dimensional. There was little or no evolution. Story editor Lowell Hawley explained, "Established characters were kept pretty much the same way. We'd bring in other characters that would be there briefly but the established characters really couldn't change. We were confined in terms of the formula of a TV series. It's almost like having a strait-jacket on and trying to wrestle."

For Britt Lomond (Capitan Monastario), certain things needed to be established, such as the motivation for his villainy. Lomond recounted the time he put this particular question to Walt Disney and his director, Norman Foster: "One of the things that bothered me was that I was putting women in prison, beating people, whipping Indians, etc. So I said to Norman and Walt, 'Why am I doing all these things? Can't we do something to give me a reason?' And so Norman said, 'You're the heavy, a heavy doesn't have to be explained.' He eventually came around to my way of thinking and so for the first episode (we were now shooting the second and third) we re-shot a scene in which my lawyer Piña [Than Wyenn] and I are talking and Norman says, 'Here's a line that will give you a reason.' And at the very end of the scene I almost look into the camera and I say to my lawyer friend, 'Nothing shall stop me from becoming the richest man in California.' Norman says *cut* and a grip, up on the catwalk, yells out, 'And that's how the Bank of America got started.'"

All in all, the first 13 episodes helped to re-establish the Zorro legend with a new generation of fans. Now those grandparents and parents who grew up with Douglas Fairbanks, Sr., and Tyrone Power finally had something in common with their children and grandkids.

In an effort to arouse interest, Guy Williams' first appearance on television as Zorro actually took place on September 11, a month before the premiere of the series. He appeared on the *Disneyland* television series, which was used by Walt Disney as an entertaining promo tool for the Disneyland Park as well as a vehicle to air films, short subjects and cartoons from the studio library. The episode featured Walt Disney describing the upcoming *Disneyland* TV season to the Mouseketeers. Filmed on one of the soundstages, it has a behind-the-scenes feel to it. As Disney is surrounded by the Mouseketeers, he attempts to rattle off the names of the upcoming events but is constantly interrupted by Moochie's, "What about Zorro?" Walt explains that he really shouldn't talk about Zorro because it's an entirely different show. The Mouseketeers insist and Walt begins to tell the story of Zorro, accompanied by slow, Spanish guitar.

"A long time ago there was a masked rider who rode the countryside. This was in old California, back in the days of high adventure and low Spanish guitar."

The Zorro opening complete with theme song plays across the screen. As it fades out, Walt states, "And that's the little bit I promised you." Moochie inquires, "Boy, oh, boy, was Zorro a real person?"

WALT: I'm afraid not, Moochie. You see Zorro was a mythical character. He's something of our imagination.
ZORRO: Ahaa!!
WALT: What's that?
MOOCHIE: That's your imagination.
From atop the balcony of the de la Vega patio, the camera pans to ... Zorro.
ZORRO: Señores y Señoritas
MOOCHIE: Zorro!
ZORRO: At your service. As you say, perhaps I am only part of the imagination. I remember that's what they said about me in California. Some would smile and say, "Zorro? Poof, he's a ghost, a dream, a myth, a something of the imagination."
Just then an armed shadow appears behind Zorro.
MOOCHIE: Look out!! Watch out, Zorro!
A brief fencing bout ensues in the shadows and Zorro quickly disarms his opponent.
ZORRO: Ha, ha, ha, ha, ha! So you see, my friends, it is entirely a matter of opinion.

This is a personal thing between you and me. Whether I am real or not is for you to decide. Each of you in your own mind and heart. Meantime, 'til we meet again.

Zorro then makes the sign of the Z and disappears.

MOOCHIE: The sign of Zorro!

This appearance is interesting for a number of reasons. The costume worn by Guy Williams is slightly different from what was seen in the series. There was no silver band around the crown of the hat, and the gloves were a dull black without the white piping on the cuff. The sash was dull black rather than satin. Zorro also appears without his sword scabbard and cape.

Finally, there was something of a mini-debate about the sound that would be heard when Zorro made the sign of the Z with his blade. There was a faction who supported a combination of Zorro's voice with the sound of the blade slicing through the air which came out something like "ha, ha, ha." This is what was heard in the promo spot. The other side won out, however, and what was used on the show was simply the sound of the blade cutting through the air. As a matter of fact, when studio personnel asked each other what show they were working on, one would simply reply by mouthing the swish-swish-swish sound, the universal code for *Zorro*.

A few weeks after the *Disneyland* show, on October 4, 7-Up® sponsored an exclusive *Zorro* showcase which was beamed to 29 ABC affiliate stations around the country. The closed-circuit telecast, which was filmed specifically for 7-Up® developers, included *Zorro's* premiere episode and appearances by Walt Disney and Guy Williams. Disney's portion of the program featured a behind-the-scenes look at the show, which included the Disney concept of *Zorro* for television. ABC president Leonard Goldenson and 7-Up® president Ham Grigg also put in appearances and outlined the unprecedented advertising and publicity used to help promote *Zorro* in its initial weeks.

Three days later, Disney held a conference to introduce his stars to the press. It was an exciting event which featured all the actors in costume. To set things off, Guy Williams swung off a balcony and crossed swords with Britt Lomond in what was described as a "duel to the death." No stone was left unturned in an effort to make Disney's swashbuckling hero a success.

5

The First Thirteen

Episode Guide, Part 1

EPISODE 1

"Presenting Señor Zorro"

Filmed: July 15–19, 22–26, 1957, August 15 & 26, 1957; *Air Date*: October 10 1957; *Director*: Norman Foster; *Writers*: Norman Foster, Bob Wehling; *Cast*: Britt Lomond (Capitan Monastario), Jan Arvan (Nacho Torres), George Lewis (Don Alejandro), Eumunio Blanco (Alcalde), Than Wyenn (Licenciado Piña).

In 1820, a ship is sailing to Spanish California bringing Don Diego de la Vega back to his home in Los Angeles. Don Diego is returning after spending three years at the University in Spain. Following a morning fencing bout with the ship's captain, Diego learns that many things have changed in California. Los Angeles is now run by a tyrannical commandante; military force has taken over.

Diego returns to his cabin and discusses the situation with his mute manservant, Bernardo. The information from the ship's captain, coupled with a letter Diego received from his father, convinces him that he must plan a course of action. He decides that he will take the advice of an old proverb, "When you cannot clothe yourself in the skin of a lion, put on that of the fox." For the time being, he will play the part of a scholar, caring only for books. All of his fencing trophies are tossed overboard. Bernardo will play the part of the fool and pretend to be deaf as well as mute. Diego believes that people will speak more freely in front of a deaf man.

While going through customs in Los Angeles, both Diego and Bernardo play their parts perfectly, easily convincing the bumbling Sgt. Garcia and the more devious Capitan Monastario that they are a harmless pair. While his luggage is searched, Diego sees his neighbor, Nacho Torres, being brought in under military guard. Diego, trying hard to restrain his anger, learns that Torres is accused of treason for speaking out against the tyranny of the commandante. The young don realizes that the time for action is fast approaching.

Don Diego returns home to his spacious hacienda and to the warm greeting of his father, Don Alejandro. With great difficulty, he continues to play the part of the frivolous scholar, not wanting to involve his father in his impending plan of action against Monastario. The next day, Diego takes Bernardo to a remote canyon and introduces him to Tornado, a beautiful black stallion. An old shepherd raised the

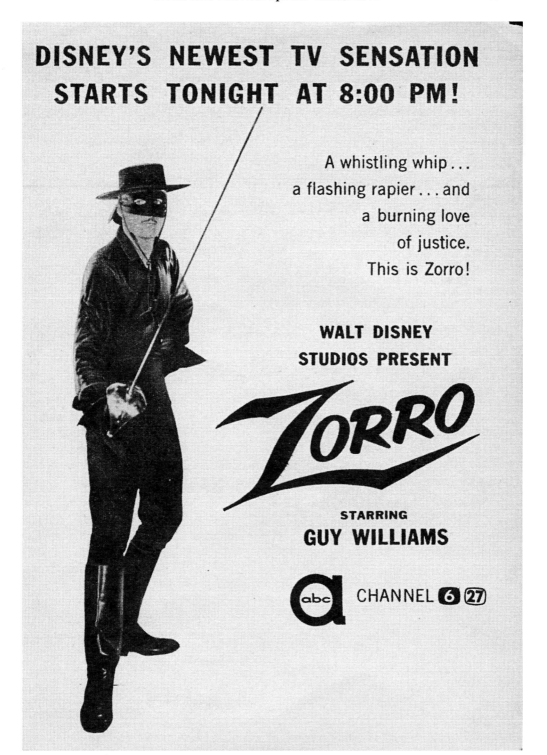

A *TV Guide* ad for Zorro's premiere episode (courtesy of P. Poplaski).

horse for Diego while he was away. He will be a valuable ally in their fight against Monastario.

Late that night, Diego decides to make his move. Dressed all in black with a mask to shield his identity, he rides to the cuartel. Scaling the side wall, he makes his way over the rooftops. Zorro's arrival is very timely. Monastario is planning to free Torres and then shoot him as if he is trying to escape. As Monastario's cohort Licenciado Piña, an unscrupulous lawyer, is about to free Torres, Zorro places a sword at the lawyer's back. Piña is bound and gagged and then Zorro helps Torres escape over the wall.

Monastario, sensing something has gone wrong, sprints from this office and fires a shot at a figure scaling the wall; he misses. The commandante races toward Zorro with drawn sword. Both are excellent swordsmen and the outcome is in doubt until Monastario lunges and Zorro steps aside. The capitan puts his sword through the cell wall and is unable to remove it. Zorro places him in the cell and makes his escape. He then meets with Torres and instructs him to head for the Mission of San Gabriel where he will find asylum. Torres is safe for the moment as Zorro rides off into the night, a wanted man.

Author's Notes

With "Presenting Señor Zorro," the series gets off to an impressive start. Beginning with announcer Dick Tufeld's intonation "The Walt Disney Studios Present Zorro," the silhouette of a fox appears on a wall. Zorro then appears in the shadows with his cape obscuring the lower part of his face. He lowers the cape and with a sweep of his sword cuts a Z in the air as Tufeld announces, "This week's adventure is brought to you by 7-Up®." A brief 7-Up® commercial plays and then a darkened sky appears as thunder cracks and lightning flashes a Z against the clouds. As the theme song begins, the silhouetted figure of Zorro (part live-action, part animation) rides into view and the moon breaks through the clouds.

While the theme continues to play, a montage of action clips runs across the screen. Most of these scenes were used for the opening and never appeared in an episode. One of the snippets of action has a knife with a note attached to it thrown into a door. The message reads, "My sword is a flame to right every wrong, so heed well my name ... Zorro." While this couplet never made it into an episode, it did turn up on the Disneyland LP *Four Adventures of Zorro* in the record adaptation of this premiere episode. The opening theme also contains a brief instrumental break which was eliminated in subsequent episodes. The show's opening was quite lavish compared to other series of the day.

As the episode begins, the format of the series, action-comedy is established quickly. The action on board ship, in the form of a fencing contest, greets the viewer. From this scene Diego's ability with the sword becomes apparent — and from his smile, it's obvious he's a bit of a rascal. When Diego returns to his cabin, Bernardo makes his first appearance. As Diego discusses the political situation in California with Bernardo, his manservant's hand gestures and facial expressions makes it obvious

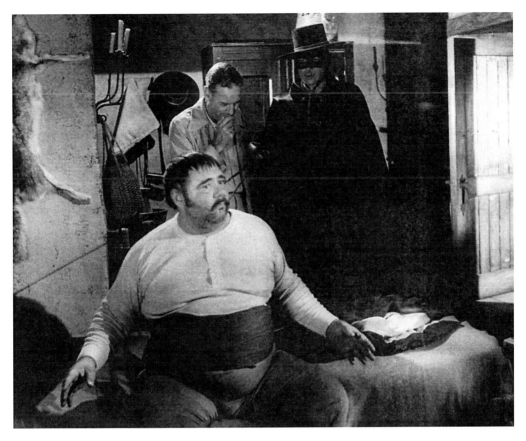

Director Norman Foster (*left*) ponders a scene in the premiere episode, "Presenting Señor Zorro" (courtesy of Walt Disney Productions).

that the series will also contain some light comedy. It is quickly apparent that Bernardo is not some bumbling sidekick, the kind that dominated B-Westerns of the 1940s and early '50s. It is Bernardo's idea that Diego portray himself as a studious bookworm. It is also his suggestion that he pretend to be deaf.

The dual between Zorro and Monastario is well choreographed by Fred Cavens but a disturbing precedent is set that continues throughout the series—the habit of cutting away from the swordplay to get a reaction shot, or to record some peripheral comedy bits. Although sometimes this is necessary for plot progression, more often than not it has a tendency to slow the momentum of the action. However, the scene still retains its excitement thanks to the score of William Lava and the able fencing of the two stars. Because both Williams and Lomond performed all their own sword work, they were able to inject their own personalities into the action, rather than have their physical idiosyncrasies disrupted by stunt doubles. As Lomond recalled, there is sometimes a price to pay when actors perform their own stunts. "When Guy and I fenced in the cuartel compound in front of the jail in the first routine we did together, Guy forgot a move and hit me just above the left eye. It wasn't bad, just a flick. I couldn't catch his blade in time. There was some blood, everyone went, 'Oh

God!' And it scared the hell out of me. But I said, 'Just cover it up with makeup and let's finish the scene.' I still have the scar." There is one incorrect insert during the fencing. A master shot shows Zorro and Monastario in profile fencing. A moment later, a one-shot insert of Zorro shows bales of hay behind him. According to the original master shot, the jail cell should be at his back.

The last scene of the episode featured Zorro riding to the top of a hill, rearing Tornado and waving. It would be used as stock footage and shown many times during the course of the series. Stuntman Tap Canutt, who occasionally doubled for Guy Williams, remembered some of the tricks used when rearing a horse. "The saddles we used had a slight cantle [an upward-projecting rear part of the saddle] in them. We had the wardrobe department all over us because the saddles were very slick so we'd take resin and put it on the saddle to prevent slippage but the seats of those black pants turned white. As a substitute for the resin, we'd get a cup of water and pour that on the saddle which also worked but then you've got the wranglers mad because you're putting water on their saddles."

The series employed a fair amount of day-for-night shooting which is a process that makes a scene that is filmed during daylight hours look like nighttime. It is used here when Zorro arrives at the cuartel to rescue Nacho Torres. The day-for-night

It was during this fencing scene for "Presenting Señor Zorro" that Britt Lomond (*right*) was injured (courtesy of Walt Disney Productions).

process requires the use of a special filter that is put over the camera lens to turn the sky dark. It can only be accomplished on a clear day because only a blue sky will turn dark on film. This was used on many series during this time simply because it's cheaper. *Zorro* would, on rare occasions, film at night but the majority of scenes that take place at night are being filmed under the sunny skies of Southern California.

Before Zorro can free Torres, there is a familiar scene in which he gets the drop on Sgt. Garica. Zorro blindfolds the Sergeant, stands him in a corner and angles the Sergeant's own sword against his back, telling him, "I'll be standing right behind you!" as he quietly exits. It's familiar because it is borrowed from *The Mark of Zorro* (1940) when Zorro pulls the same stunt on the evil Alcalde.

Finally, just a brief word about coming attractions shown at the end of each episode: They were sometimes better than the episodes they heralded. With hyperbolic narration read in a Saturday matinee, no-holds-barred fashion by Dick Tufeld and accompanied by action scenes from the upcoming teleplay, they made the viewer feel as though the last thing they would want to do is miss next week's episode.

Behind the Scenes

> The part of the ship's captain, Diego's fencing opponent, is played by Al Cavens [son of fencing master Fred Cavens].... The matte work of Albert Whitlock shows up twice: the L.A. pueblo from a distance and then the exterior of the de la Vega hacienda. The latter was used as an establishing shot time and time again throughout the series.... There is some impressive animation work from the special effects department when Diego makes the sign of the Z on a sheet of music paper. The tip of the sword is actually animated and gives the appearance of moving over the paper and making a Z.... One of the lighter moments has Zorro knocking Sgt. Garcia into a well that is near the jail cells. The well in question mysteriously disappears after this episode.... A scene which features Diego and Bernardo riding on horseback along a dirt road between two large boulders was filmed at Iverson's Ranch, at a site known as the Garden of the Gods. This was the first scene shot for the series.

EPISODE 2

"Zorro's Secret Passage"

Filmed: July 15–17, 22–26 & 31, 1957, August 2, 3, 7, 9, 19 & 26, 1957, September 4, 1957; *Air Date*: October 17, 1957; *Director*: Norman Foster; *Writer*: Anthony Ellis; *Cast*: Britt Lomond (Capitan Monasterio), Jan Arvan, (Nacho Torres), Romney Brent (Padre Felipe), Eugenia Paul (Elena Torres), Pat Hogan (Benito Avilla).

The following morning, posters are put up offering a reward for the capture of Nacho Torres and Zorro. Capitan Monastario believes that if he can capture Zorro, the apprehension of Torres will be a mere formality. He and his lancers ride out in search of "the fox."

At the de la Vega hacienda, Diego arrives from his night's activities to find a surprised Bernardo. "How did he get into his room without me seeing him?" wonders the bewildered manservant. Diego shows him a secret passage that he recalled from his childhood. He takes Bernardo on a tour of the underground hideaway.

After showing Bernardo how he will come and go as Zorro, Diego rides to the mission to pay his respects to Padre Felipe and to check on the welfare of Nacho Torres. At the mission, Diego feigns surprise at Nacho's appearance, and learns that Torres plans to head for Monterey to plead his case with the governor. Upon returning from the mission, Diego relays information to Torres' daughter Elena that her father is safe.

Diego arrives home to find trouble of his own in the guise of Capitan Monastario. In the commandante's possession is a Zorro costume. Diego tries to hide his surprise and is relieved to find that Monastario does not suspect him but is there to question the de la Vega vaqueros. Nonetheless, Diego insists on completely clearing his name. He does so by fencing with the commandante, so ineptly that he is entirely exonerated. At that moment, Sgt. Garcia arrives with Benito Avilla, the de la Vega head vaquero, and Monastario's number one suspect. During Monastario's questioning, it becomes apparent that Benito is trying to protect someone else. That someone is Elena Torres, whom Benito had seen the night before. He was trying to shield her from scandal, he being an Indian and she part of the upper class. Monastario forces him to don the Zorro costume and is now convinced that he is their man. To be positive, Benito is taken to the Torres hacienda where Elena is confronted.

Aware that Benito is in trouble, Diego decides that only the real Zorro can help him now. At the Torres hacienda, Elena admits that they were together; but for the final proof, Monastario must cross swords with his suspect. The vaquero is no match for the experienced commandante. As Monastario bears down on his opponent, Zorro strikes. The results are the same as the previous night; this time the capitan is left standing with a broken sword. Zorro escapes and the lancers give chase. They are no match for Tornado, who carries his master to safety. Monastario is outfoxed again.

Author's Notes

"Zorro's Secret Passage" is important if for no other reason than the viewer is given a guided tour of Zorro's secret passage. The passage is almost a character in itself, figuring prominently in many episodes. As Diego proclaims, it provides "all of the drama of a story book." By pressing a button under the fireplace mantle in his room, a panel swings open. A dark, dusty room with a table and trunk is revealed. It is in this secret room that Diego keeps his Zorro disguise. A stairwell leads to the first floor of the house. There are exits from the passage into both the sala and the library; however, neither will be used until later in the first season. Walking a short distance through a tunnel leads to a large, open cave area where Tornado is corralled. There is a running water spring and the opening to the cave is large enough for a horse and rider and obscured by thick vines and brush. Diego explains that the passage was built by his grandfather as protection against Indian raids and he discovered it as a boy. Why his father seems to have amnesia regarding the passage is never explained.

The fencing in "Zorro's Secret Passage" is not up to the standards that the series will set in episodes to come. It lacks fluidity because both Williams and Lomond are somewhat restricted inside the cluttered Torres hacienda set. Most of the camera shots are close-ups which prevent the entire scope of the fencing to be seen. It's useful for the entire body to be visible for the fencing to be effective.

The popular notion of Zorro being a creature of the night is touched on briefly. When it appears Zorro is needed, Diego exclaims to Bernardo, "I know its light but it shall be dark soon," as he runs to put on the disguise of Zorro. This concept really comes from the pulps where Zorro only prowled at night. However it becomes clear, early in the series, that Zorro will have to work days as well as nights if he is to keep up with the villainy of the commandante.

Behind the Scenes

> Coincidentally, the cave area where Tornado is corralled is an exterior location at Iverson's Ranch that was also used in the Republic serial *Zorro's Fighting Legion* (1939).... Some interesting location work was filmed for this episode and a few that follow. The Mission of San Luis Rey in Oceanside, California, served as the Mission of San Gabriel where Padre Felipe was stationed.... On the Disney back lot, the building used for the exterior of Nacho Torres' house was actually the rear of the tavern; the interior of the Torres hacienda is the interior of the tavern, redecorated.... A scene with Buddy Van Horn as Zorro has him mounting Tornado in the secret cave and riding out through the secret entrance. This became stock footage that was used quite often during the run of the series.... This is the only episode which features a shot of Zorro riding back into the secret cave.... The chase scene near the conclusion of this episode was filmed at the Iverson Ranch and directed by Yakima Canutt. It also contains the great gaffe in the series: high-tension poles can be seen in the background of the chase.... A matte drawing by Peter Ellenshaw helps create an exciting effect for a chasm that Tornado must leap.

EPISODE 3

"Zorro Rides to the Mission"

Filmed: July 16, 24, 29–31, 1957, August 1–3, 5, 6, 8, 26 & 28, 1957; *Air Date*: October 24, 1957; *Director*: Norman Foster; *Writers*: Jackson Gillis, Malcolm Boylan; *Cast*: Britt Lomond (Capitan Monastario), Jan Arvan (Nacho Torres), Romney Brent (Padre Felipe).

While searching for Nacho Torres, the commandante finally has some good fortune. A mission Indian sells him the information he is looking for: Don Nacho is hiding at the Mission of San Gabriel. Monastario and his lancers gallop for the mission with the hope of having Torres in their grasp before the day ends. Don Diego and Bernardo, also headed for the mission, are almost run off the road by the lancers. Diego realizes that trouble is brewing. Upon arrival, Monastrario has his men surround the church but they do not enter. Padre Felipe informs him that Torres is protected for 40 days by church sanctuary. Monastario is furious but he respects the Church's law.

Diego arrives and meets with Padre Felipe and Don Nacho. He realizes that at the moment there is little he can do to help. To coerce Don Nacho's surrender, Manastario takes all of the Padre's Indians and forces them into slave labor. The Padre needed them to help pick the orange crop but the commandante makes them move rocks for the construction of a new road. Don Nacho witnesses what is happening and wants to give himself up but Diego is able to dissuade him for the moment. Sensing trouble, Diego sends Bernardo to bring Tornado and his Zorro disguise.

While the Indians are worked mercilessly, Diego attempts to help Padre Felipe with the oranges. As he prays in the church, Torres is heartsick over the Indians' plight. The commandante wants Diego to try to convince Torres to give himself up. If he doesn't, the whip will be used on the Indians. Realizing that a climax is fast approaching, Diego attempts to stall until Bernardo arrives. He enters the church and begins to play the organ so loudly that the commandante, who is trying to convince Torres to give himself up, cannot be heard. Outside, the soldiers stop to listen to the beautiful music. Some of the Indians begin to slowly slip away as the soldiers drop their guard.

Bernardo has just returned and is carefully cutting loose the lancer's tethered horses. A shot is fired at one of the escaping Indians and Monastario races from the church. He orders his men to use the whip on the remaining prisoners. When Torres sees this, he can no longer bear the guilt and gives himself up. As a lancer drags him from the church, a black figure on horseback races to the scene. Zorro grabs the lancer's whip and turns it on the soldiers, who begin to run for the hills. Monastario mounts his horse and he and Zorro are quickly engaged in a deadly duel with whips. Zorro coils his whip around the commandante, who is now hopelessly bound, and sends him off into the night atop his galloping horse. Nacho Torres and Padre Felipe head back into the sanctuary of the church to give thanks for their black-garbed benefactor.

Author's Notes

"Zorro Rides to the Mission" was filmed almost entirely at the Mission of San Luis Rey in Oceanside, California, and uses the controversial Mission-Indian relationship in California as a plot device. The *Zorro* pulp stories and this series should not be looked to for historical accuracy and the situation set forth in this episode may be somewhat inaccurate depending upon which side of the issue one comes down on. The plot depicts an almost idyllic situation for the Indians as children of the Church. However, when the commandante forces them into torturous slave labor, that may be closer to the Church's actual treatment of them. At the very least, the Indians led a spartan and industrious existence at the missions. Considering the large part the Indians played in California history, they had a relatively small part in the series. Aside from a few early episodes, they were usually seen only as pueblo "atmosphere" along with other extras.

The plot moves slowly as the episode is long on talk and short on action. One of the difficulties in writing for *Zorro* was that, although the series was aimed primarily at children, adults could be brought in as viewers if the stories were plausible and the drama interesting. To further this end, sometimes a fair amount of exposition is necessary which usually limits the amount of action. The danger here is that the younger viewers may become bored. The series was usually able to walk that fine line with the promise that Zorro would always appear before the ending credits.

Filming at the Mission seemed to have a spiritual effect on Guy Williams as he recalled at the time, "You know, you can't help feeling the history of this place, and the peace of it. I know it sounds overly sentimental and maybe silly, but it's going to be hard to be quite the same after coming here. San Luis Rey rubs off on you."[1] A less spiritual moment for Williams occurred at the mission when, while filming a stunt, he fell and began cursing only to look up and see a group of nuns and children staring at him. An embarrassed Zorro quickly walked away in the opposite direction.

Britt Lomond recalled the extra pressure that filming on location brings: "There is a wonderful sequence at the San Luis Rey Mission which was a very tough location. It had very restrictive hours. We had to get in there, use just a specified area, shoot our scenes and get out. I had a scene, a long tracking shot with Romney Brent, a wonderful actor who played the priest. It's close to the end of the day, Norman Foster is directing and we have this three-page scene. So Norman says, 'We're going to do a dolly shot on this.' So he started the two of us walking and we stop and he keeps filming over my shoulder on Romney, then we walk a couple of more paces, stop, but this time with a different angle over Romney's shoulder on me and so on until I enter the front of the church. We did one complete rehearsal and then the whole thing without any intercutting with the two shots over the shoulder all worked into the scene. And we did it in 20 minutes! We wrapped at 4:15 and Norman let out a big sigh of relief."

The climactic bullwhip fight is something of a dichotomy. On one hand, it's exciting and well-choreographed. However, the use of doubles is very obvious. It was directed by Yakima Canutt, and both his son Tap and Carl Pitti are doubling Britt Lomond and Guy Williams. Lomond actually does some of his own whip work, but Guy Williams may not even have been on hand for the filming. Working in close with two horses and whips is very dangerous and best left to experts. Yakima Canutt preferred to shoot as many close-ups as possible and when the camera moves in, it's very clear that Williams is not behind the mask.

Behind the Scenes

> Britt Lomond recalled that Jan Arvan [Nacho Torres] was Jewish and was having trouble remembering how to make the sign of the cross. "Norman [Foster] took him aside and said, "Just remember it this way [*gesturing*], spectacle, testicles, wallet and watch.' He couldn't forget it after that!" ... The boulder-lined road that supposedly led to the mission was actually at the Iverson Ranch. Also shot there were the scenes with the Indians moving rocks and the bullwhip fight between Zorro and Monastario.... Charles Stevens, who had a bit part as the Indian who gives Monastario information, was a full-blooded Apache and

the grandson of Geronimo. Among his many films were *The Bold Caballero*, the first *Zorro* sound film, and *The Mark of Zorro* [1940].... A total of eight days was spent filming at the Mission in late July, 1957.... Zorro's double Buddy Van Horn has a small role as a lancer.... An early title for this episode was "Zorro Goes to Church."

EPISODE 4
"The Ghost of the Mission"

Filmed: July 22, 25, 29–31, 1957, August 1–3, 5–9, & 26, 1957; *Air Date*: October 31, 1957; *Director*: Norman Foster; *Writer*: Norman Foster; *Cast*: Britt Lomond (Capitan Monastario); Jan Arvan (Nacho Torres); George Lewis (Don Alejandro); Romney Brent (Padre Felipe).

Capitan Monastario has captured one of the Mission Indians and has him tied to the whipping post. He knows that the Indian would rather die than reveal the whereabouts of the remaining Indians but he has other plans for his captive. The commandante plans to tell Padre Felipe a "few harmless tales." He wants the Indian only to keep silent. If the Indian denies the stories, his family will be in danger.

Diego rides to the mission to check on Nacho Torres. He learns that Nacho plans to go to Monterey when conditions are safer. However, that may not be for some time as Monastario and his lancers arrive at the mission. The commandante has learned that the Indians are planning an uprising and the Padre's life is in danger. Therefore he is placing the mission under martial law. Padre Felipe realizes that this is merely a ruse to force Nacho out of the church. The Padre knows that without food or water, Torres may succumb to the commandante. Diego decides that Zorro would be of more help to the situation so he returns home, has Bernardo fill a saddlebag with food and returns to the mission in the guise of Zorro. He steals into the church but is seen by one of the lancers before he can get the food to Torres. After a chase through the church, he exits by way of the bell tower, barely escaping with his life.

Returning home, Diego realizes that he must use his cunning if he is to defeat Monastario and save Nacho. With Bernardo's help he devises a plan. The next morning, Diego arrives at the mission with a manuscript for Padre Felipe. Before being allowed to see the Padre, he must first report to Sgt. Garcia, who asks to see the Latin manuscript. It tells the tale of the Ghost of the Mad Monk, a priest (tortured and killed by Indians) whose ghost still haunts this mission. The tale is full of clanking chains, mission bells ringing for no reason and a robed figure with no face rising up in the cemetery. Diego swears Garcia to secrecy, knowing that this is the best way to get Garcia to spread the tale to anyone who will listen.

Late that night, Zorro and Bernardo put their plan into action. Because Garcia has told Diego's tale to all the lancers, everyone is jumpy. With an assist from Bernardo's slingshot, the mission bell begins to ring. Moans and clanking chains begin emanating from the cemetery. Monastario and Garcia investigate. The Sergeant is petrified but the commandante thinks he knows who is behind the unusual happenings. They chase a robed figure into the lancers' barracks where the soldiers run for their horses in horror. As Monastario and Garcia continue their search for the "ghost," the commandante is knocked unconscious when a hanging plant basket falls on his head. This is all Garcia needs to see as he runs for his horse and heads back to Los Angeles. The robed figure removes his cowl to reveal himself as Zorro! He runs to a stone bodega and releases Innocente, the Indian whom Monastario forced into silence. Now with all the lancers gone and Padre Felipe having locked Monastario in his room for the evening, Don Nacho is free to nourish himself before the journey to Monterey.

Author's Notes

"The Ghost of the Mission," a perfect Halloween episode, was once again filmed entirely on location at San Luis Rey, and is actually two episodes in one. The first half which deals with Zorro's efforts to get food and water to Nacho Torres is straight action-adventure. The remainder of the episode, Zorro trying to frighten the lancers so that they will leave the mission, leans heavily on slapstick comedy.

The first point of interest has Zorro failing in his first attempt to aid Torres. This is one of the very few times that one of Zorro's schemes fails and it's very refreshing to find that he is less than superhuman. The culmination of his failure is a spectacular scene where Zorro (stuntman Buddy Van Horn) is lowering himself from the bell tower by rope as Monastario is cutting it. Zorro comes crashing to the ground and barely escapes. Director Norman Foster films the scene from two angles. One is a master shot of Zorro's black form against the white adobe of the mission; the other is taken from Monastario's point of view looking down at Zorro from the top of the bell tower. Both shots establish the danger involved. Another interesting camera shot by Foster has Zorro (as the faceless "Mad Monk") walk right into the camera. All the camera picks up is the blackness inside the Franciscan hood. Foster uses this as an editing device to change scenes.

The first real interaction between Sgt. Garcia and Don Diego takes place; this is the first time that Diego actually uses Garcia's gullibility and innocence to aid Zorro. It occurs when Diego tells the fictitious tale of the Ghost of the Mad Monk to Garcia. Not surprisingly, the scene played more effectively on record than television. It appeared under the title *Zorro and the Ghost* on the LP *Four Adventures of Zorro*. Like in the days of old radio, the imagination is sometimes able to conjure up images that are more frightening than television can deliver. But, this episode did try hard and probably gave more than a few young viewers nightmares.

Zorro also received a lot of help from his sidekick Bernardo. He acts as a one-man Indian tribe, attacking the mission with bows and arrows, slingshot and playing the tom toms. Along with Zorro, he fires arrows that barely miss Monastario. The arrows land in the mission door and form the sign of the Z.

All of the night scenes were filmed using the day-for-night shooting process and it works very effectively. Seeing Zorro's black figure slip in and out of the shadows just out of view of a lancer's furtive glances creates a genuinely tense atmosphere. The images that director Foster creates last a long time after the episode ends.

Behind the Scenes

An early scene has Zorro riding up to the Mission without his mask and then dismounting and putting it on. It's unusual in that it's the only time it's ever done in the series.... The scene in which Diego tells Garcia the tale of the Mad Monk was filmed under the oldest pepper tree in California, located at the Mission of San Luis Rey.... Vincent McEveety, who went on to a distinguished career as a director, worked with Norman Foster as an assistant director on these episodes.... Zorro's ghoulish laugh, part of his mad monk character, is dubbed from the Disney feature *Ichabod & Mr. Toad*, 1949. The laugh was first used by the headless horseman in *The Legend of Sleepy Hollow* portion of the feature.

EPISODE 5

"Zorro's Romance"

Filmed: August 12–16, 19 & 27, 1957; September 4, 1957; *Air Date*: November 7, 1957; *Director*: Lewis R. Foster; *Writer*: John Meredyth Lucas; *Cast*: Britt Lomond (Capitan Monastario), Jan Arvan (Nacho Torres), Eugenia Paul (Elena Torres), Madeline Holmes (Doña Luisa Torres).

Suspecting that Nacho Torres has traveled from the mission to his home, Monastario and his lancers are en route to capture the fugitive. Within sight of the lavish hacienda, the commandante stops the patrol and muses with Garcia about the possibility of someday becoming Don Enrique Sanchez Monastario with the Torres hacienda as part of his domain. It seems that the capitan now has more on his mind than just capturing Don Nacho.

As fortune would have it, Don Diego and Bernardo are traveling in the vicinity. They see the patrol and ride ahead to warn the Torres family. Nacho is saying his goodbyes and preparing to leave for Monterey when Diego arrives with news of Monastario's impending arrival. Monastario has the lancers surround the hacienda at a discreet distance as he and Garcia approach. The capitan has decided to take the diplomatic approach as he discusses with Garcia the possibility of a romantic union with the lovely Elena, Nacho's daughter.

Monastario questions Nacho's wife, Doña Luisa, and she denies that Nacho is there; although from the saddled horse outside, Monastario believes otherwise. He and Garcia search the house with the Sergeant ordered to start in the wine cellar. Diego volunteers to assist the Sergeant and the pair descend to the cellar.

Monastario explains to the Torres women that the lands of a convicted traitor are subject to confiscation by the government. It becomes obvious that the sole reason for Monastrio's pursuit of Don Nacho is to gain possession of the land.

Diego attempts to steer Garcia away from Nacho, who has taken refuge in the wine cellar. It's a simple task: He simply engages the Sergeant in some wine tasting. Nacho slips out and takes refuge in another part of the hacienda. As Monastario searches upstairs, Nacho, with Diego's help, is able to stay one step ahead of the commandante. Diego realizes that for his friend to escape, he will have to take a more direct approach. With the help of Bernardo and a perfectly aimed potted plant, the commandante is knocked unconscious.

Diego carries him upstairs to Don Nacho's room, where he suggests someone wearing the commandante's uniform could probably leave the hacienda unmolested. Nacho heeds Diego's advice. By concealing his face at all times by his cape's collar, Nacho orders Garcia about and rides off in the capitan's carriage with a military escort. Diego realizes that the masquerade may not last long so he decides that Zorro should keep an eye on the situation. As the carriage travels away form Los Angeles, Garcia becomes suspicious. When he questions the capitan, he discovers to his surprise it is Nacho Torres. As the lancers are about to move in, Zorro strikes and holds the soldiers off long enough for Nacho to escape aboard Garcia's horse.

Sgt. Garcia leads the lancers back to the Torres hacienda where he finds his captain bound and gagged. When he is released, the commandante races through the house in search of Don Diego, who he now suspects of being Zorro. When he comes upon Diego and Bernardo in the wine cellar, the two are also bound and gagged. Monastario is now beside himself with laughter at the absurd thought he allowed himself only moments before.

Author's Notes

"Zorro's Romance" is something of a mistitled episode. There is very little Zorro and almost no romance. It's probably the least interesting and actionless tale in the entire series. It leans very heavily on comedy and endless dialogue. The main purpose of the segment appears to be to fully explain the motive for Capitan Monastario's evil activities against Nacho Torres. Writer John Meredyth Lucas, who went on to write five more *Zorro*'s and direct three of them, seems to have preferred the Don Diego character to Zorro. "I did find the Diego character more interesting because he's got the problems. When Zorro shows up it's straightforward, go save the world," he remembered. Lucas was true to his word: When Zorro finally does show up, he appears for less than a minute.

Britt Lomond, who was directed by both Norman and Lew Foster, felt that, "Norman was very punctilious, very careful and a very planned director. Lew, on the other hand, had a totally different directorial style. He would just say, 'Listen, fellas, here's what we're going to do now get in there and do it!' Norman was very good but I happened to like Lew's approach better."

Behind the Scenes

Some of the matte work of Albert Whitlock is on display as a master shot of the Torres rancho.... Don Diego sings a tune titled "Elena" [Joe Dubin, Gil George]. Guy Williams' voice is dubbed by Bill Lee. Incidentally, Gil George was the *nom de plume* of Hazel George, the studio nurse. George had a talent for lyrics and also contributed to the Disney films *Perri* and *Tonka*.... The final scene of the segment had Don Diego and Bernardo tied up and gagged, supposedly by Zorro, in the wine cellar. Exactly why Bernardo had to be gagged is a mystery to this day.... The location work was filmed at Albertson's Ranch and upper Iverson's.

EPISODE 6

"Zorro Saves a Friend"

Filmed: August 19–23 & 26, September 3, 4 & 23, 1957; *Air Date*: November 14, 1957; *Director*: Lewis R. Foster; *Writer*: John Meredyth Lucas; *Cast*: Britt Lomond (Capitan Monastario), Eugenia Paul (Elena Torres), George Lewis (Don Alejandro), Madeline Holmes (Doña Luisa Torres), Pat Hogan (Benito), Than Wyenn (Piña).

An angry mob has gathered outside the cuartel to protest the arrest of the Torres women. Even Piña, Monastario's legal counsel, protests this action. He fears that the dons will not sit still and allow this audacious act to stand unchecked. But Monastario will not relent. He is using the women as bait to capture Zorro. He knows that once he has this bandit behind bars, his plans to become the richest man in California can succeed.

Don Diego, who has heard of the women's imprisonment, prepares to travel to the cuartel and intercede on their behalf. Before he departs, his vaquero Benito expresses his concern for the Torres women. Benito, whose heart belongs to Elena Torres, also makes no attempt to hide his hate for the commandante. Diego tries to calm him and forbids him from taking any action against Monastario. When Diego arrives at the pueblo, he enlists the aid of Padre Felipe in trying to free the women. Upon entering the cuartel, Deigo pays his respects to Elena and Doña Luisa Torres. He learns that they have had neither food nor water. Diego and the Padre try to convince Monastario to free his prisoners but he refuses to give in unless he receives from the women a full confession "to the seditious acts and utterances of the traitor Nacho Torres." Benito, disobeying Diego's orders, bursts into the commandante's office and demands to see Elena. Outraged, Monastario refuses, and it is only the pleading of Diego and Padre Felipe that prevents Benito from being jailed. When

Diego inquires about bail for the Torres women, Monastario informs him "their bail will be nothing less than a full confession."

Late that night, a figure dressed in black makes his way over the cuartel wall and across the stable roof. He drops to the ground and knocks the guard unconscious. He attempts to free the jailed women but he is discovered by another guard who calls out an alarm. The masked figure fights gallantly but he is overcome by sheer numbers. A crowd of onlookers gathers, thinking that Zorro has been captured. Don Diego, part of the crowd, shows an unusual interest. When Monastario removes the mask, all are surprised to see the face of Benito. The commandante realizes that the vaquero could not be Zorro but plans to make an example of him.

A hangman's noose is set in place over the top of the cuartel entrance. An ox-cart is placed under it, to be used as a scaffold. The robed figure of a priest enters the cuartel to hear Benito's last confession. As the vaquero is placed atop the ox-cart, the priest stands at his side. As Monastario gives the order to start the wagon, the priest throws off his robes to reveal ... Zorro! With his sword he cuts the noose and grabs the reins to the cart. The pair race off to the shock of Monastario and his lancers. Charging through the cuartel, a wheel flies off. At Zorro's instruction, Benito leaps aboard the horse pulling the cart and gallops off to safety. As the soldiers close in, Zorro climbs atop the scaffolding of the plaza church. He fends off the attack of various lancers until Monastario himself climbs to face Zorro. Their sword fight moves back and forth until Zorro's blade cuts the thong that holds the scaffolding and Monastario goes crashing to the ground. Zorro leaps onto Tornado's back and the soldiers can only watch in frustration as he escapes.

Author's Notes

"Zorro Saves a Friend" is an excellent episode with a swashbuckling climax and a theme that touches on forbidden love between the classes. Benito returns and once again is in trouble over this love for Elena Torres. The problem; Benito is an Indian and Elena is the daughter of a wealthy landowner. Not a tremendously big deal is made over this, but it is clear that this is not acceptable.

Don Diego's feelings about Sgt. Garcia are made apparent for the first time. In a conversation with Padre Felipe, Diego says, "I have a genuine affection for Sgt. Garcia. At heart he is a good man." This comment is noteworthy because it establishes Garcia's character in relation to Diego. The fact is that Garcia may be a bumbling fool, but at least he's a decent fellow.

There is one scene which really encapsulated the Disney comedy formula for *Zorro* at its worst: Benito barges into the commandante's office demanding to see Elena. Needless to say, the capitan is furious but as a favor to Don Diego he agrees to forget Benito's intrusion. But the capitan tells him, "If ever an Indian such as you mentions the Señorita Elena with such ardor, you'd wish you'd been born without a tongue." After the lancers lead Benito out, Garcia turns and walks smack into the closed door. The serious, sometimes punctuated by the silly, seems to be the approach not only on *Zorro* but also on many other Disney live adventure TV shows and movies.

Director-writer John Meredyth Lucas recalled, "Disney was very, very basic and everything was largely black and white. All his comedy was drop the pants." This scene was also symbolic of the differences between Norman Foster and Lew Foster. Although Norman Foster did deal out his share of physical comedy, he would never dilute a serious scene this way.

The climax is reminiscent of the classic swashbuckling films of the 1930s and '40s. Zorro disguising himself as a robed priest and rescuing Benito in the nick of time is perfect. The duel between Zorro and Monastario and his lancers on the church scaffolding is a thrilling piece of choreography. The unusual aspect of this scene is that even the close-ups were filmed on the scaffolding on the back lot. Usually in a stunt like this, the master shots are filmed on the actual site using stunt men for safety reasons. The close-ups with the actors are shot on a sound stage mock-up. Director Lew Foster chose the more realistic approach but, according to Britt Lomond, the stunt doubles were less than enthusiastic. "There was a scene where Guy and I were supposed to fence on the scaffolding in front of the church. Disney was worried about this so they hired an ex-fencing master, Jean Heremans, to double me and Buddy Van Horn to double Guy in all the master shots. Heremans was the fencing coach at the Los Angeles Athletic Club. I had fenced under him there and worked with him on *Scaramouche*. Now, Guy and I had rehearsed the fencing moves on the ground and were going to do all the less dangerous close-ups. Jean took a look at this scaffolding bit and he told us, 'I won't do it. It's too dangerous.' I told Lew Foster, 'Give me the sword and roll the cameras!' And Guy and I did the entire scene. Afterwards, Heremans came up to me and said, 'You're an absolute goddamn fool!' I said, 'What do you expect? I'm an actor! Of course I'm a goddamn fool!' Heremans walked away and wouldn't talk to me the rest of the day."

Stuntman Tap Canutt, who doubled Lomond for the fall from the scaffold, recalled "I was in front of the other two lancers [stunt men] because I was doubling the commandante. The problem we had was if you were spaced the way we were then the first guy hits and then the second hits on top of him and so on. I ended up buried because I was the first one to hit."

Williams' portrayal of Zorro as the laughing, taunting rogue is very much in evidence in this episode. Even though he is trapped in what seems like an impossible situation, Zorro laughs and mocks the commandante from the church scaffold. This is very much the Fairbanks influence that would later be discarded.

The lancers as "Keystone Cops" is on display here as in no other episode and it tends to diminish the excitement a little. But the sight of Garcia and the lancers see-sawing up and down on a ladder is funny and probably appealing to a young audience. The final scene, which has Garcia attempting to explain how Zorro could escape and Monastario throwing his sword to the ground in exasperation, is one of the funnier moments in the series.

Capitan Monastario performs the sword and candle trick (using his blade to cut through a candle so quickly that the candle does not seem to move). It looks as though he has missed until he picks up the top half of the burning candle. This scene was lifted from *The Mark of Zorro* (1940).

Behind the Scenes

The title of this episode comes from a 1932 McCulley *Zorro* short story.... A brief song, titled "Noche Triste," is sung by Jaime Mendoza-Nava.... There is a very noticeable jump-cut edit when the lancers tumble off the ladder by the church scaffolding.... The original episode title was "Torres Family Imprisoned...." This script was revised by Lewis R. Foster.

EPISODE 7

"Monastario Sets a Trap"

Filmed: August 15, 16, 19 & 22–27, September 4 & 8, 1957; *Air Date*: November 21, 1957; *Director*: Lewis R. Foster; *Teleplay*: Lowell Hawley; *Story*: Joel Kane; *Cast*: Britt Lomond (Capitan Monastario), Than Wyenn (Piña), Edgar Barrier, (Don), Eugenia Paul (Elena), Madeline Holmes (Doña Luisa), George Lewis (Don Alejandro).

Don Alejandro rides to the cuartel and demands to see the Torres women. At first Monastario resists but his lawyer Piña convinces him it would be for the best. Monastario gives in while putting one of his devious plans into action. As Don Alejandro enters the women's cell and inquires about their welfare, his conversation is overheard by one of the soldiers. Alejandro tells them of a secret meeting of dons to be held at his hacienda that very day which will help to decide the women's fate.

At the meeting, the dons argue among themselves. Alejandro speaks for force, for mounting an attack on the cuartel. Diego tries to speak for logic and patience but the dons now have no use for those two attributes. They decide that Don Alejandro will lead them. When the gates of the cuartel are opened for Alejandro's visit, they will rush in. Once again Diego tries to warn them of the danger they will face but it goes unheeded. When Alejandro asks his son to join them, Diego refuses—he realizes that Zorro will be of far more use than Diego. He plans to beat the dons to the cuartel and lure the soldiers away to prevent the massacre of his father and companions.

However, Monastario has a plan of his own. When his spy returns with news of the don's attack, he sets up lancers all over the cuartel. Hidden from sight, they are not to move until all the dons are inside the cuartel and the gates are closed behind them.

As darkness closes in, Zorro scales a side wall at the cuartel and forces the commandante out of his office. The soldiers stay hidden as the two engage in a sword fight. The commandante is disarmed and yells for this lancers to attack. Zorro barely escapes on Tornado, hoping to lure the soldiers from the cuartel. Monastario is wise to his plan and instructs Garcia to take a few lancers and follow Zorro only so far and then return by the far side of the cuartel. The commandante hopes to trap the attacking dons between two forces. Then they will have no escape!

When Garcia and his small patrol end their pursuit of Zorro and head back to the pueblo, Zorro realizes what their game is. He wheels Tornado back toward Los Angeles hoping to beat the patrol. Zorro arrives just as the dons are rushing the cuartel. He warns the group off, but Don Alejandro is trapped along with Zorro inside the fortress. He helps his father over the wall but Monastario sees the elder don and fires a bullet into his shoulder. Zorro leaps over the wall and helps Alejandro onto Tornado; they gallop off with the soldiers in pursuit. Once they reach the countryside, they dismount and Zorro attends to his father's wound. They are safe for the moment but the lancers are closing in.

Author's Notes

"Monastario Sets a Trap" combines all the best elements of the series and is one of its most action-packed episodes. It has fast-paced thrills as well as a poignant scene between Zorro and his father. Don Diego is also seen involving himself more in the problems of the pueblo when he makes an impassioned plea to his father and the assembled dons not to use force in their dealing with Monastario. Here Diego is portrayed as a person who cares for justice as much as his alter ego. However his methods are more practical and stay within the bounds of the law. His is a non-violent and intellectual approach.

There is a very effective scene which takes place in Diego's room. Don Alejandro wants Diego to ride with him and the other rancheros to the cuartel to rescue the Torres women. Diego, realizing he must protect his identity, declines, much to his father's disappointment. After Don Alejandro leaves, Diego looks in the mirror and sees Bernardo's reflection. He nods to his master. Both men know there is work for Zorro. The scene is a perfect blend of camerawork, music, acting and writing.

The action which includes Zorro being chased across the length of the cuartel, up onto the balcony and over the roof, is top-notch. It's shot in a wide-angle movie style and although it seems as though there's no way for Zorro to escape, it's so well done that it's entirely plausible when he does. As usual, Buddy Van Horn handles most of the non-fencing action as Zorro. The duel between Zorro and Monastario, while it contains one complex exchange, is not quite as exciting as the previous episode; there's too much posturing, and it's rather slow to boot.

In a series not really known for its poignancy, there is a very touching scene between a badly wounded Alejandro and Zorro. He mutters to Zorro, "Strange, so strange. It's almost as if I have known you. You seem so much like someone I know. I am a foolish old man with foolish dreams. So often have I dreamed that my son would come back from Spain and he would be like you. Now that you're so close it is so much like my dreams that I feel I could almost pull aside the mask and there would be the face of my son Diego. I would not pull away the mask; I would not have the courage. An old man must cling to his dreams as desperately as he clings to life." It's very well done and one of the few times that the difficulty of Diego's secret identity is conveyed. The disappointment of his father is not overplayed and it is very real. This is also one of the few episodes that ends with a cliffhanger, as the series originally intended. When Zorro carries his father off, it's not clear if Alejandro is alive or dead. Tune in next week.

Behind the Scenes

Lowell Hawley made his *Zorro* writing debut with this episode. He went on to write 23 more and became the story editor. His script was revised by Lewis R. Foster.... The original title was "Alejandro Speaks Out...." The set for Zorro's secret cave was recreated on a soundstage. The original cave at Iverson's Ranch would now be seen only in stock footage.... Yak Canutt directed the location action filmed at upper Iverson's and Albertson's Ranch.... George DeNormand doubled for George Lewis in the chase scene.

EPISODE 8

"Zorro's Ride into Terror"

Filmed: August 16, 19 & 26–30, September 3, 18 & 24, 1957; *Air Date*: November 28, 1957; *Director*: Lewis R. Foster; *Writer*: John Meredyth Lucas; *Cast*: Britt Lomond (Capitan Monastario), George Lewis (Don Alejandro), Jan Arvan (Don Nacho), Don Diamond (Lancer Yvarro), Richard Wessell (Lancer Del Gato).

As Monastario and his lancers close in, Zorro leads his wounded father to his secret cave. As the soldiers continue to search, Sgt. Garcia finds Alejandro's jacket. This, coupled with the realization that they are on de la Vega land, leads Monastario to exclaim, "A wounded animal always crawls back to its own lair." The soldiers mount up and ride for the de la Vega hacienda.

Examining his father's wounds, Zorro realizes he will need medical supplies to stop the bleeding. He runs to his secret room, sheds his costume and searches his bedroom for the needed medical supplies. By this time, the lancers have begun to search the hacienda. Garcia hears a noise in Diego's room and he discovers the young don. Diego tries to excuse himself out of the situation but Monastario arrives and places Diego under house arrest to make sure that he cannot assist his father. Monastario leaves Garcia and two lancers in charge of the situation while he takes the remaining soldiers into the country to continue his search.

Diego, realizing that he must somehow return to his father, proceeds to get the soldiers drunk. By this time, Alejandro has turned delirious from fever and has wandered out of the cave in search of Monastario. During the drinking and merriment, Diego is able to slip out, don his Zorro disguise and return to the cave where he sees that his father is missing. He mounts Tornado and rides out in search of the wounded don.

Unfortunately for Alejandro, Monastario and his men have found him first. The old man tries to fight back but he is too weak. The commandante taunts him and attempts to stick him with a lance when Zorro attacks. He proceeds to knock the stunned capitan from his horse and then grabs Alejandro. The pair rides off with the soldiers in hot pursuit. As luck would have it, Nacho Torres, returning from a meeting with the Governor in Monterey, and protected by a special guard, intercepts Zorro and Don Alejandro. Zorro places his father in Torres' care and rides off, returning home before the drunken lancers realize he was ever gone.

Author's Notes

The seriousness of Don Alejandro's situation is offset with an episode that leans heavier than usual on comedy. Most of the humor derives from Diego's efforts to remove Garcia and his two lancers from the room so that he can return to aid his father. As in "Zorro's Romance," another comedy-laden episode, Diego uses Garcia's weakness for wine as an effective tool to incapacitate the Sergeant and the two guards. During the drinking bout, Garcia launches into a humorous song, "Here's to a Soldier of the King."

There is a neat bit of tension when Diego enters his room by way of his secret passage, and a moment later Garcia and two lancers enter followed by Monastario. Glancing about, Diego notices the panel that protects the hidden room has not closed completely. It's a sticky situation for Diego who eventually maneuvers the intruders out of the room with his secret intact.

The action consists of a joust on horseback between Zorro and Monastario. This was another attempt by the writers to find a way for Zorro to dispatch the villain without using his sword and it is fairly successful. The episode concludes with yet another chase scene ending when Tornado and his master leap across a canyon. The canyon comes courtesy of a matte painting by Albert Whitlock.

Behind the Scenes

"Here's to a Soldier of the King" was written by Gil George and Joe Dubin. The song is also heard on the LP *Songs About Zorro and Other TV Heroes*.... Don Diamond [*sans* moustache], who later became a semi-regular as Cpl. Reyes, makes his first appearance in the series as a lancer.... Yak Canutt once again directed the second unit with help from his son Tap. The location work was done at the Albertson, Bell and Iverson Ranches.... Some chase footage shown in the coming attraction did not appear in this or any other episode.... Tap Canutt and George DeNormand double Zorro and Don Alejandro respectively.

EPISODE 9

"A Fair Trial"

Filmed: September 24, 26, 27 & 30, October 1, 1957; *Air Date*: December 5, 1957; *Director*: Norman Foster; *Writers*: Jackson Gillis, Bob Wehling; *Cast*: Britt Lomond (Capitan Monastario), Sebastian Cabot (Judge Vasca), George Lewis (Don Alejandro), Jan Arvan (Nacho Torres), Than Wyenn (Piña), James Griffith & Carl Bensen (Lancers).

Don Nacho and Alejandro have turned themselves in, in the hope that they will receive a fair trial. They believe that Judge Vasca, known for his honesty, will treat them fairly. Capitan Monastario has other ideas. He sends Sgt. Garcia to San Pedro to intercept the judge so that Piña, Monastario's co-conspirator, will preside at the trial. Diego, learning of the plot, dons his Zorro disguise and heads for San Pedro with Bernardo to lend a hand to the judge.

At the Inn of the Golden Goose, Garcia tries to delay Judge Vasca, engaging him in an eating contest. The fat sergeant seems to have met his match in the equally rotund magistrate. Zorro, who has entered the inn from a rear window, is watching the proceedings from the upstairs balcony. During the gastronomic contest, Garcia slips the judge a sleeping potion and leads the sleepwalking magistrate to an upstairs bedroom to sleep it off. With some difficulty, Zorro and Bernardo are able to get the judge on his feet. By imitating the judge's voice, Zorro entices Garcia to the judge's room and forces the Sergeant to drink a second sleeping potion meant for Vasca. Garcia promptly passes out. Bernardo dons the Sergeant's uniform and leads the sleepwalking Vasca down into the tavern and out the door to a waiting coach.

In Los Angeles, the trial has begun with Judge Piña presiding. Just before he is about to render his verdict, Zorro enters through a back door. Unbeknownst to anyone in the courtroom, he places his sword at Piña's back and influences his decision. Piña declares Nacho and Alejandro innocent of all charges. When Monastario sees a look of discomfort on Piña's face, he rips aside the curtain and finds a poker sticking in Piña's back but no sign of Zorro.

Author's Notes

"A Fair Trial" is a light-hearted affair that leans more toward ingenuity and comedy rather than action. Zorro barely draws his sword in this particular teleplay. The judge is played with great comic effect by veteran actor Sebastian Cabot. A few years later, Cabot became well-known to the television-viewing public as the English butler Mr. French in *A Family Affair*. Judge Vasca was every bit the caloric equal of Sgt. Garcia, who finally meets his match in the judge.

In keeping with the Disney penchant for sound effects, William Lava had a habit of using musical sound effects. After a particularly harrowing incident, Bernardo shakes his head to remove the cobwebs. As he does, the sound of maracas is heard on the sound track.

Behind the Scenes

Some additional chase footage, which included Zorro pretending to be shot and then scattering the lancers' horses, was filmed but not used.... On a fashion note, Zorro wears his cape in the more traditional style, without putting his arms through the arm slits.... The Spanish guitar music written by Bill Lava for the cantina scene is quite beautiful as well as contemporary sounding.... In an uncredited part, actor William Schallert plays the role of the innkeeper. Schallert is probably best remembered as the father on *The Patty Duke Show*.... Yak Canutt directed the second unit at Bell Ranch with son Tap Canutt and Joe Yrigoyen doubling Zorro and Bernardo, respectively.

6

The First Thirteen

Episode Guide, Part 2

EPISODE 10

"Garcia's Secret Mission"

Filmed: September 4–6, 9, 10, 13, 16 & 19 & October 2, 1957; *Air Date*: December 12, 1957; *Director*: Norman Foster; *Writer*: Anthony Ellis; *Cast*: Britt Lomond (Capitan Monastario), Frank Yaconelli (Pancho), Nick Moro (Pepe), Nestor Paiva (Tio).

The soldiers awaken to find a white flag with a black Z flying over the cuartel. Garcia and his men try in vain to remove the flag before Monastario sees it but it is too late. As the commandante watches the soldier's attempts, he sees two peons laughing. For punishment he orders the two to repair the stable roof with pitch. They must haul the pitch from the tar pits, miles from the cuartel. It's an impossible task but they must complete it before the next evening or their families will suffer.

While reprimanding Garcia for his ineffectual attempts to remove the flag, Monastario comes up with a plan to capture Zorro. He believes the reason he cannot capture Zorro is because the common people are hiding him. He decides to strip Garcia of his rank so the Sergeant can mingle with the people — the same people who may be protecting Zorro.

Don Diego learns what has occurred and meets with Garcia in the tavern. The ex-sergeant says he wants to join forces with Zorro. Later that night in the tavern, Zorro talks with Garcia and sets up a meeting for the next day. Garcia reports this news to the commandante as Zorro watches. A wild goose chase follows: While Zorro leads Garcia, Monastario and the lancers away from the cuartel, he has also changed the orders of the day in an effort to help the overburdened peons. The orders now instruct a soldier to bring Monastario's carriage to the tarpits and fill it with buckets of pitch. Monastario realizes they are being fooled and heads back to Los Angeles. Zorro taunts them from afar and leads them on a merry chase until Monastario and Garcia fall into Zorro's grasp and land headfirst in the tar pits. Meanwhile with the help of Zorro, the two peons have the last laugh and the stable roof is repaired.

Author's Notes

"Garcia's Secret Mission" is unusual for the first 13 because it is self-contained — unrelated by theme to the other episodes. This is another teleplay in which Zorro lives up to his name, the Fox. Like "A Fair Trial," the emphasis is on comedy rather than adventure. The entire stimulus for all the action concerns a prank that Zorro has played and the problems that it causes. This is the first of just a few times in the series that trouble comes as a result of an isolated, unprovoked act by Zorro. This is another nod to the Fairbanks-inspired Zorro.

Norman Foster can always be counted on to give the series a more realistic atmosphere regarding the use of extras and lending the pueblo a more cluttered and lively look. In later episodes, few extras were used and the pueblo looked as though it was vacuumed every night.

Behind the Scenes

> The location work was filmed at the Bell Ranch ... Nestor Pavia as the innkeeper, Tio, makes the first of many appearances ... Frank Yaconelli appeared in *The Mark of Zorro* [1940].

EPISODE 11

"Double Trouble for Zorro"

Filmed: September 5, 6, 10–13, 19 & 26 & October 2, 1957; *Air Date*: December 19, 1957; *Director-Writer:* Norman Foster; *Cast:* Britt Lomond (Capitan Monastario), Tony Russo (Martinez), George Lewis (Don Alejandro).

A stranger named Martinez has arrived in Los Angeles. While enjoying the talents of one of the tavern dancers, he clashes with another patron who is also interested. The two engage in a duel, but Martinez is an excellent swordsman and the other man is killed. The commandante puts him in custody and begins to hatch a plot to destroy Zorro. He tells Martinez that he will drop the charges against him if he will disguise himself as Zorro and rob the guests at the dinner party he is planning for the rancheros that evening. Monastario believes that if he can discredit Zorro with the wealthy as well as the poor, then they will cease to protect him.

When Don Alejandro receives his invitation to the dinner, he refuses to go. He sends Bernardo with a reply to the capitan. While performing this task, Bernardo learns of Monastario's plot to destroy Zorro. When he gives this information to Diego, the young don decides to represent his father at the dinner. That evening at the dinner party, in an attempt to throw any suspicion off himself, Monastario tries to mend fences with any of the landowners he has offended. Martinez, disguised as Zorro, arrives on the scene and proceeds to rob the guests at gunpoint. Diego slips outside to the stables where Bernardo waits with the Zorro disguise and returns in time to intercept the escaping Martinez. After quickly out-fencing the imposter,

Zorro turns his attention to Monastario, who meets the same fate as Martinez. The commandante feigns ignorance about the unmasked imposter and has him returned to jail, finding a way to blame the entire episode on Garcia. While all the commotion is taking place, Diego slips back into the tavern with his own secret identity intact.

Author's Notes

"Double Trouble for Zorro" is a bit of formula piece in the best sense. All costumed heroes have had their trouble with villains attempting to impersonate them. *Batman*, *Superman* and *The Lone Ranger* have aired episodes dealing with their evil doubles. It's a staple of the genre and *Zorro* was no exception. This episode benefited from the fact that actor Tony Russo portrayed the evil Zorro with a light touch. Russo, who had originally auditioned for the role of Zorro, was perfect as the arrogant swordsman, Martinez. He gives a relatively realistic performance and imbues the part with just the right humor and subtlety. He is a man who is more a victim of circumstance than anything else — somewhat unusual in a series with, essentially, two-dimensional characters.

Norman Foster, a fan of flamenco, opens with a rather seductive dance that gives the episode more of an adult flavor and works very well. Foster also tended to inject a little more violence than other directors who worked on the series. Here Martinez runs a man through in a duel over a woman. This is one of the few times in the entire run of the series that anyone is killed in such a manner.

One of the best scenes has Diego training Tornado for his work as Zorro's horse. This sequence is a great deal of fun because it's obvious that Diego must keep his horse in some kind of training to remain sharp and this all-too-brief scene shows how he does it. Coupled with this is the arrival of Sgt. Garcia and the lancers, who think they have discovered Zorro's hideout. As Diego takes Tornado to safety, Bernardo throws the lancers off the trail. Once again it is a great juxtaposition of comedy and tense action which Foster does better than other *Zorro* directors.

Another sequence which shows Foster's tight grasp of the Disney concept of *Zorro* has Bernardo playing musical ladders as he moves it back and forth between two balconies to deceive the imposter Zorro. As written by Foster, this scene once again displays a perfect balance between comedy and action, never sacrificing one for the other.

The duel between Zorro and Martinez is brief and unexciting. Señor Martinez is a master swordsman and proves himself to be Monastario's better in the next episode. The fencing scene between the two Zorros did not live up to its potential. However, the sword fight between Zorro and the commandante is the best of the series so far with Guy Williams looking more confident with the passing of each episode.

There is one miscue in the duel between Zorro and his double. When they are fencing at the top of the stairs, Zorro (Williams) is camera right. The camera cuts to a split second close-up of Williams and cuts back to find Zorro (Williams) camera left. It is the job of the assistant director, in this case, Vincent McEveety, to keep all actors in their proper place. It would seem he got his Zorros mixed up.

Behind the Scenes

> A minor mistake has actor Romney Brent [who portrays Padre Felipe] being given screen credit for an episode in which he did not appear…. The location work was filmed at Bell Ranch…. The original title for this episode was "Zorro with Two Zs."

EPISODE 12
"The Luckiest Swordman Alive"

Filmed: August 3, 5–7, 9, September 16, 18–20 & October 2, 1957; *Air Date*: December 26, 1957; *Director*: Norman Foster; *Writer*: Lowell Hawley; *Cast*: Britt Lomond (Capitan Monastario), George Lewis (Don Alejandro), Tony Russo (Martinez); Than Wyenn (Piña), Romney Brent (Padre Felipe), Pat Hogan (Benito), Roque Ybarra (Innocente).

A coffin is loaded on a cart under the watchful eye of the commandante. The capitan has Garcia spread the word that he, Garcia, has shot Martinez while trying to escape. This is all part of Monastario's new plan, for the coffin is filled with rocks and Martinez is still very much alive.

Monastario and the lawyer, Piña, take a ride out into the hills where Martinez is hiding. The commandante wants Martinez to continue his masquerade as Zorro. This time he even supplies him with a black horse. Monastario instructs Martinez to ride to the mission to steal the gem-filled crown of the Virgin. Not only will this theft give them a fortune in gems, but the people will be up in arms over this sacrilegious act — which is what Monastario wants. Once this is done, a ship will be waiting in San Pedro to take Martinez out of the country to safety. Martinez carries out Monastario's plan but in the process fatally wounds a mission Indian. Before the Indian dies, he identifies Zorro as the culprit.

At the de la Vega hacienda, Benito tells Diego that some Indians have reported seeing Zorro riding toward the mission. Obviously the young don is surprised by this since Martinez is supposed to be dead. As Zorro, he rides to the mission to investigate Benito's claim. While there, he is attacked by the angry mission Indians who feel that he has betrayed them. He barely escapes and returns home to learn that Padre Felipe is there with news that Zorro has stolen the Crown of the Virgin.

With Bernardo, Diego hatches a plot using some imitation gems of his own which he hopes will cause a falling-out among thieves. Diego arrives at the crowded tavern and sits with the lawyer Piña. Carefully he and Bernardo begin to plant the phony gems. Piña returns to the commandante with this information. Monastario believes that Martinez has broken up the stolen crown for its gems and is now acting on his own and therefore must be eliminated.

As Monastario heads for the hideout, Diego and Bernardo follow. At the campsite, the commandante and Martinez exchange accusations and then engage in a furious sword fight. Martinez disarms Monastario and prepares to escape. Diego realizes that he cannot let the imposter flee. At the risk of revealing his secret identity, he duels Martinez, disarming him in a clumsy fashion. As Martinez tries to escape, Monastario realizes that dead men tell no tales, so he shoots and kills him. Diego attempts to explain his being the "luckiest swordsman alive" but Monastario is becoming increasingly suspicious of Don Diego and his luck with a sword.

Author's Notes

"The Luckiest Swordsman Alive" is the conclusion of the two-parter that began with "Double Trouble for Zorro." Although it doesn't have much Zorro in it, it still makes for some interesting viewing. As directed by Norman Foster, it has a fast-paced plot as well as exciting location scenes filmed at the Bell Ranch. There is also another touch of the Foster penchant for violence with Martinez as Zorro stabbing and killing an Indian in the mission church. Incidentally, these scenes filmed at the mission provided a financial bonanza for actor Tony Russo.

Russo explains, "I was sitting around the set and I asked the assistant director when I was going to steal the jewels. And I was told that it had been done four weeks ago on location at the Mission. Buddy Van Horn did the scene. I thought, 'Good. That's something less I have to do.' Norman Foster was just going to shoot a close-up of me and insert it. Now an oldtimer on the set came up to me and said, 'Tony, did I hear that somebody did your character when they were on location? ... Was a stunt involved?' I said, 'No, just robbing the jewels.' Well, I found out that there is a rule called 'Right of Role' which means you have to do everything unless it is a stunt. I was new in the business and didn't know but it seems that I was under contract as of the time they shot that scene. I went to the union and, sure enough, Disney had to pay me for an extra four weeks. In 1957, $350 a week was a lot of money. It made my year. Then Disney combined the TV episodes and made a movie out of it called *The Sign of Zorro*. I went to see it in the movies and these scenes are in it. Disney had sent me some money for the amount of time I worked but they hadn't included the extra four weeks. So all in all I probably made $5,000 for that episode which is more than anyone ever made in the '50s as a supporting actor for two weeks work on a television show."

There is one obvious flaw in an otherwise excellent plot. When Diego sets up Monastario to lead him to Martinez's hideout, he doesn't bring his Zorro disguise. When it comes time to prevent Martinez from escaping, he must do so as Don Diego. Although he tries to hide his skill with a sword, he all but reveals his secret identity to the commandante. The fact that Diego must hold back makes the episode and subsequent situation more interesting, but logically it makes little sense.

Director Foster takes full advantage of the boulder-covered Bell Ranch terrain for the climactic fencing scene between Diego and Martinez. Foster uses long master shots of the two adversaries atop a rocky cliff as well as some more intimate low-angle camera shots. The climax to the scene is perfect: The tip of Diego's sword is stuck in a rock crevice. As Martinez is about to drive his sword point home, he exclaims, "You see, señor, luck is not enough." Just then, Diego frees his sword and with an uppercut motion sends the shocked Martinez's sword hurtling into the distance. This duel further illustrates Diego's superior abilities with a sword; he is able to defeat a professional swordsman while fighting in an awkward style.

For Tony Russo this particular fencing scene turned out to be as dangerous as it appeared on film. He said, "Instead of choreographing it, Norman Foster just said to Guy, 'In this scene you just swish the blade and go after Tony and Tony will back away a little bit....' And because it wasn't choreographed, I got poked in the eye. The top of the epée blade, which is flat, had lifted the dilation muscle in the pupil of my eye. They took me right to the hospital and for five days I lay in bed and I didn't know if I was going to lose my sight. The vision came back slowly. To this day my eye does not dilate or contract like it used to. The accident wasn't really anybody's fault. We were on the side of a mountain and hurrying up because the sun was going down. Norman was a good director but I sometimes think that his concern was more for budget than anything else."

One confusing note is the appearance of the de la Vega vaquero, Benito. When last seen in "Zorro Saves a Friend" he was being rescued from the hangman's noose by Zorro. Presumably he is still wanted by the commandante yet he appears in a brief scene at the de la Vega hacienda as if nothing has happened.

Behind the Scenes

There's an impressive stunt fall performed by Lou Roberson, while doubling for Tony Russo. Roberson tumbles from atop a boulder and lands on his back after being shot. It looks quite painful but Roberson survived intact.... Padre Felipe [Romney Brent] and Benito [Pat Hogan] make their last appearances in this episode. In 1969, Romney Brent returned to Mexico City to teach. He died in 1976. Pat Hogan continued to act but died in 1966 at the young age of 35.... Innocente the Indian (Roque Ybarra) makes his second and final appearance.... The *Zorro* theme song is expanded and included in the opening are five new film clips of Zorro in action.... In the early 1960s, Tony Russo changed his last name to Russel. He finally got to star as Zorro in a 1962 Italian film called *Il Guiramente di Zorro.*

EPISODE 13

"The Fall of Monastario"

Filmed: September 19, 20, 23 & 24, 1957; *Air Date*: January 2, 1958; *Director*: Norman Foster; *Writer*: John Meredyth Lucas; *Cast*: Britt Lomond (Capitan Monastario), John Dehner (Viceroy), Lisa Gaye (Constancia), Than Wyenn (Piña).

Largely as a result of Diego's duel with Martinez, Monastario is certain that Don Diego is Zorro, so he has him arrested and brought to the cuartel. As he is reading the charges against him, a courier arrives and explains that the Viceroy and his daughter are approaching the pueblo. A frantic Monastario has Garcia empty the jails and supply free wine to all in hope of presenting a picture of tranquility and happiness in the pueblo. When the Viceroy's carriage arrives at the pueblo, the people are cheering wildly as a result of the orders of the commandante. Monastario tells the Viceroy he has a celebration planned for that evening in the tavern where he has a special surprise in store.

At dinner, to the surprise of everyone, Monastario presents his prisoner: A man dressed as Zorro is led by soldiers and ceremoniously unmasked. The Viceroy and his daughter are surprised to see Don Diego, a friend of the family, standing before them. Diego asks the Viceroy to tell the commandante to step outside to "cool his befuddled mind." A short period of time passes and then Monastario is brought back in. The Viceroy asks the commandante to make one final, positive identification of the masked figure who stands before him. "Without a doubt this man is Zorro," exclaims the commandante. At that moment, from behind the bar steps Diego. It seems that while the commandante was cooling his heels outside, a lancer exchanged clothes with Diego at the Viceroy's command. Monastario realizes that he has been duped and in one final desperate act challenges Diego to a duel. Diego accepts and defends himself as best he can, careful not to expose his fencing expertise. Monastario disarms him and, as he presses his blade to Diego's throat, shots are heard outside the tavern. A masked rider on horseback throws a knife at the tavern door with a note attached. The Viceroy reads it aloud: "Sorry to have missed your fiesta. Zorro."

This is the last straw for the Viceroy. He explains to Monastario that he already had enough evidence against him and his cohort Piña before he came to Los Angeles. He has the two men taken into custody and led away. Diego breathes a sigh of relief and covertly thanks his servant Bernardo, who has just arrived, for donning mask and cape. Before the Viceroy departs, he appoints Sgt. Garcia acting commandante. It is a proud moment for the beaming sergeant and the future of Los Angeles is looking brighter indeed.

Author's Notes

"The Fall of Monastario" is a bit of an aberration. To begin with, there is technically no appearance by Zorro. Also, vehicles (comic books, pulps stories, etc.) that deal with a lead character with a secret identity (Superman comes to mind immediately) quite often use unbelievable excuses and explanations to fend off accusations about the hero's alter ego. This episode handles the situation a bit more realistically.

In "The Luckiest Swordsman Alive," Don Diego took the risk of exposing himself when he fought Martinez in front of Monastario. When Monastario asks Diego how he, one of the most inept swordsmen alive, could beat one of the best, Diego replies flippantly, "Perhaps Martinez was right. Maybe I am the luckiest swordsman alive." Usually, after a comment like that, the issue is dropped with little or no further accusations made by the antagonist. However, the result of Diego's action comes home to roost in this episode when Monastario brings formal charges against Diego and accuses him of being "the outlaw Zorro." The straw that broke the camel's back was seeing Diego out-duel Martinez. As clumsy as Diego pretended to be, it still served to confirm the capitan's growing suspicions.

The very idea that no one seemed to notice that Zorro arrived on the scene at the same time Diego returned home from Spain must be explained away to dramatic license. The same can be said for the fact that nobody recognizes Diego in his Zorro costume. With only a mask to cover the upper part of his face and a voice that is not disguised, it seems that eventually even the least observant of souls would recognize Diego to be Zorro. But, the fact that Monastario finally puts two and two together does add a touch of realism to a rather shaky premise.

The script is very good and funny, as evidenced by this exchange between Sgt. Garcia and the capitan, regarding the Viceroy's daughter.

MONASTARIO: You must have noticed that the Señorita seems quite smitten with me.
GARCIA: Oh, you think so?
MONASTARIO: Well, is this so difficult to understand? Look at me, Sergeant. You find me attractive?
GARCIA: No!
MONASTARIO: You idiot, I mean if you were a woman.
GARCIA: If I was a woman and fat like this, I wouldn't be particular.
MONASTARIO: Oh, a marriage between the Viceroy's daughter and I would be mutually advantageous. Don't you think so?
GARCIA: It would certainly be a quick way of becoming a colonel.

As in the previous episode, Diego is forced to duel clumsily to preserve his secret identity. There were only two episodes where Diego found himself pretending to be an inept swordsman and, coincidentally, they ran back to back. In this teleplay, his fencing looks a little too good. It seems unlikely that onlookers would be convinced that this "fop" had disdain for swordplay.

Obviously "The Fall of Monastario" is the conclusion of the commandante's reign and also the departure of actor Britt Lomond. Lomond claimed that there was talk about bringing him back to the show. "They talked about it many times but the problem was that every time they were going to bring me back, I was busy, tied up on something else, so I never came back. In fact, they had written about a dozen episodes for me to appear in but, unfortunately, I was under contract to Desilu so that was that." Associate producer Bill Anderson contends, "We were approached by [Lomond's] agent about his returning to the show, but how could you. The implication in his last episode was that he was done away with." (Lomond was seriously considered for the lead in the *Eltego Baca* series but lost out to Robert Loggia.)

In a sense, Lomond did stay with the show after his tenure was up. He appeared with Guy Williams making a number of personal appearances at Disneyland and other venues around the country. Both he and Williams appeared in costume, putting on fencing exhibitions. About his former co-stars, Lomond said, "One of the things that used to amaze all of us about the show was that we all liked each other and we all got along so well. I liked Guy very much; he was a wonderful human being. A nice fellow with a good sense of humor. Henry and Gene were two of the dearest people I knew. I stayed friends with these people and was involved socially with Henry and his wife. Gene was one of the funniest guys you would ever meet and talk to in your life. He would regale us with stories and pantomime and his banjo routine. George was also a wonderful guy."

As a result of the comic books, puzzles, games, etc., most of which were based on the first 13 episodes, the Monastario character became closely identified with the series. According to Lomond, he was receiving 80 percent of the fan mail that Guy Williams was. All in all, the commandante was the consummate villain and Zorro's most formidable rival.

Behind the Scenes

> Once again director Foster fills the episode with a large cast of extras. As a matter of fact, this episode boasts the largest cast [non-speaking roles] of any episode, forty four people in all.... Excellent character actor John Dehner, who plays the part of the Viceroy, played Paladin on radio in *Have Gun Will Travel*. Throughout the '50s, 60s and 70s, Dehner usually played villains on TV although he was cast against type in this episode. Dehner also worked as an animator at the Disney studios in the late '30s, working on *Bambi* and *Fantasia* ... Buddy Van Horn plays the part of the lancer who is forced to slip into the Zorro costume in order to fool the commandante.... Strangely, Don Alejandro does not appear in this episode. One would expect him to be on hand as his son is on trial accused of being Zorro.... One final footnote regarding Zorro and the commandante is that Zorro never actually disarmed Monastario in any of their duels together. More often than not Zorro sent his rival tripping over some furniture or hurtling from a scaffolding or standing with a broken sword. Technically the commandante was never disarmed.... The original title for this episode was "The King's Emissary." This title was used in the Dell Comics [#933] adaptation of this episode.... This script was revised by Norman Foster with additional dialogue by Malcom S. Boylan.

Most of the critics who reviewed *Zorro* did so during the first 13 and by and large they were very high on the series. Many felt that *Zorro* might even outdo *Davy Crockett*. Here's a sampling of what they wrote:

Richard Shepard, *The New York Times*:
  • "Youngsters and adults who crave dashing heroes, leering villains, the usual comic sidekicks and lots of flashy sword play will enjoy this polished production.... The show has the virtue of being honestly juvenile and does well at it."

Lawrence Laurent, *Washington Post and Times Herald*:
  • "*Zorro* combines action, an outsized hero and quality production.... It is a good show and should be a great favorite with children. If *Zorro* were not scheduled opposite Groucho Marx, I'd predict that it will be one of the big favorites of the new season. Even opposite Groucho, it has all the elements for a high rating."

The Disney studio saturated the public with information about their new star, Zorro.

Paul Molloy, *Chicago Sun-Times*:
- "Disney's latest TV contribution *Zorro* has unusually fine adventurous humor and a deft story line — both a relief from the monotonous clippity-clop of lookalike Westerns."

Variety:
- "Disney's new series is a well-produced, actionful entry which should capture a combined adult-juvenile following."

Erskine Johnson, Hollywood TV writer for NEA:
- "The *Davy Crockett* craze of 1954–55 will be mild compared to the *Zorro* craze of 1957; the new king of Disney's wild TV frontier is Guy Williams."

Philadelphia Inquirer TV Digest:
- "With his theme song resounding from their TV sets and mysterious Z's scrawled all over the house, millions of American parents have become acutely aware that a hero they knew in their youth is riding again. In the field of kid's idols there has been nothing like *Zorro* since *Davy Crockett* became a household problem three years ago."

TV Guide:
- "*Zorro* is an action-packed series that keeps children and their elders, too, close to their television sets.... Guy Williams is an acrobatic hero who can swash and buckle with the best."

Bob Williams Philadelphia Bulletin:
- "This will be the year of the Big Z, the year of Zorro.... It is the only new show we've seen this season that flashes the hit sign in blazing letters. It just can't miss."

With *Zorro's* popularity growing weekly, the masked hero was on his way to becoming the #1 bone fide craze of the 1957–58 TV season.

7

The Eagle's Brood
Episode Guide, Part 1

The most satisfaction Walt Disney had while running his studio was getting a new project off the ground and *Zorro* was no exception. He enjoyed working with Bill Anderson and Norman Foster on the first 13 episodes but the series was time-consuming and there were too many other projects at the studio that needed his attention. Realizing that he couldn't give *Zorro* the time it deserved, Disney turned more of the responsibility over to associate producer Anderson.

"When Walt started working with the writers on the next batch of shows, he found that he used the juiciest material in the first 13. The work became more difficult and he didn't have the time, so he started to shift me into it more and more. By the twentieth episode I became full producer and I couldn't even get him to read a script. I didn't want to grab the credit but he didn't want his name on it if he wasn't producing it. That's why it was titled *Walt Disney Studios Present Zorro* as opposed to *Walt Disney Presents Zorro*," said Anderson.

After the initial episodes, Disney felt it was vital to maintain the momentum the show had built. Writer Lowell Hawley explains his boss's strategy: "Originally I was called in to write a couple of the first 13. Walt liked the ones I had written so at the end of those he wanted an outline of where the series was going and he put me and director Bob Stevenson in charge of working out a program. For the next 13 episodes I did a lot of research and found that California was far removed from Spain so we decided to have an idea with somebody else trying to take over the government. We brought in a character called the Eagle. I conceived of the Eagle as a 'little' Mussolini. He would be capable, shrewd and entirely unscrupulous; a man whose natural leadership ability had somehow been twisted to a truly villainous purpose. As I was telling Walt about it, he wasn't buying it, so I began to explain everything visually. And all of a sudden Walt's eyes sparkled and he said, 'Yeah, you could take a feather and cut it and hold up in front of a candle or a lantern and have a shadow on the wall.' When he thought about it visually, he liked the idea of the Eagle."

The remainder of the first season's 26 episodes deals with Zorro's struggle against the Eagle. These can be divided into seven chapters which are delineated by directors and story theme. The first three episodes were handled by director Robert Stevenson, who helped chart the course of the remainder of the first season.

The look of Stevenson's episodes is very similar to those of Norman Foster: a touch of mystery, top-notch action, location filming and a serious tone. Stevenson, like Foster, was able to put together an impressive-looking episode.

EPISODE 14
"Shadow of Doubt"

Filmed: October 3, 7, 8–11, 14, 15, 17, 18, 24 & November 4, 1957; *Air Date*: January 9, 1958; *Director*: Robert Stevenson; *Writer*: Lowell Hawley; *Cast*: Vinton Hayworth (Magistrado), Robin Hughes (Esteban Rojas), Myrna Fahey (Maria Crespo), Jack Elam (Gomez), Charles Stevens (Josephat), George Lewis (Don Alejandro), Don Diamond (Cpl. Reyes), Peter Damon (Capitan Melendez).

All of Los Angeles is excited over the imminent arrival of the new commandante, Capitan Melendez. The people hope that the new capitan will be just and treat all in the pueblo fairly. Unnoticed amidst the activity is the arrival of Esteban Rojas, the "prodigal son" of Don Domico. When he threatens the innkeeper, Rojas runs afoul of the new Magistrado, Carlos Galindo. Rojas is asked to leave and will comply with the order the following dawn.

Amid much fanfare, the new commandante arrives. As he is giving a speech about law and order and equality for all, a shot rings out and kills him. Rojas is the secret assassin and he plants the murder weapon on Josephat, a mentally impaired beggar. Maria, a waitress, saw Rojas commit the crime. He takes her aside and convinces her that *he* is Zorro and that the commandante was a wicked man who had to die.

Don Diego, in town with his father to greet the new commandante, doubts that Josephat could have committed the murder. He passes his opinion along to Garcia and the pair begins to question witnesses. Rojas is secretly working in concert with the Magistrado. When they learn that Diego has been seen questioning Maria, they decide that she must be eliminated. Rojas and his accomplice Gomez kidnap the waitress and place her in his coach. Gomez then drives her out of the pueblo with plans to ensure she can never testify. Bernardo sees what has happened and relays the information to Diego.

Zorro pursues the coach and is able to save Maria just before the coach topples off a cliff. Zorro returns Maria to the pueblo where she is able to tell Garcia the truth and save Josephat. Before returning home, Zorro enters Rojas' room and begins to search. He finds Rojas dead with an eagle feather clutched in his hand.

Author's Notes

"Shadow of Doubt" is something of a minor milestone in the series because it introduced the Cpl. Reyes character to fill the comedic void left by the exit of Britt Lomond's commandante. Most of the humor up to this point came as a result of Garcia's ineptitude and Monastario's exasperated reaction to him. Don Diamond, who played the Corporal, spoke about his addition to the cast: "They needed a foil for Sgt. Garcia. They did a film test and I was advised to keep it down [not overplay it] which I did, so I got the job. They guaranteed me 10 out of 13 episodes and I eventually ended up doing about 50 episodes." Diamond was no stranger to playing Latin characters as he had portrayed "El Toro," the sidekick of *Kit Carson* (a 1951 TV series). Diamond added, "I was told they wanted the jokes to bounce off of me. I think Oliver Hardy was Henry's character. I don't think I consciously tried to do a Laurel and Hardy bit, but I think he did."

A new heavy joined the cast to fill the commandante's shoes. Vinton Hayworth plays the part of Carlos Galindo, the magistrado and chief agent of the Eagle in the Los Angeles pueblo. The character as played by Hayworth has a kind of reptilian quality. The main difference between Galindo and his predecessor is the Magistrado poses no threat to Zorro physically. He is an older man and not the master swordsman that Capitan Monastario was. Galindo simply hires henchmen to do his bidding, many of whom are killed along the way. While the Galindo character is almost entirely humorless, Hayworth seems to be having a great time engaging in a bit of overacting, doing everything but twirling his mustache. Hayworth will be best remembered by radio fans as the character Jack Arnold on the show *Myrt & Marge* which ran for six years. In the late 1930s he appeared in many pictures at Twentieth Century–Fox.

Robin Hughes, who was very convincing as Rojas, was an Englishman who had worked with the Old Vic prior to World War II. He came to America in the late '40s and appeared in such diverse films as *Cyrano de Bergerac*, *The Flame and the Arrow*, *Dial M for Murder*, *Auntie Mame*, and *The Thing That Couldn't Die*. He eventually appeared in more than 250 television roles.

Myrna Fahey, who appeared in four episodes as Maria Crespo, was very busy in television in the late 1950s. She acted in such shows as *Maverick, Bat Masterson, Bonanza* and *Perry Mason*. In 1961 she had her own series, an adaptation of the film *Father of the Bride* in which she recreated the part originally played by Elizabeth Taylor.

This episode contains a scene rare for its introspection when Diego discusses his private life for the first time. As he and Bernardo listen to the new commandante's pronouncements of "law and order ... and equality and justice for all," Diego muses wistfully, "Yes, Bernardo, I believe it is true, peace and tranquility in Los Angeles and ... goodbye to Zorro, eh? With a man like that in our midst, there's no need for Zorro. His mission is accomplished." Bernardo looks at him disappointedly. "No Bernardo, Zorro is dead. Now I'm free to do as I wish. Perhaps I shall get married. What do you think of that?"

The climactic stagecoach chase was directed by Yak Canutt using a stunt crew at the Iverson and Bell Ranches with Tap Canutt doubling as Zorro. The process shots were filmed using Guy Williams on a soundstage mock-up. The tension and excitement was aided by the matte work of Peter Ellenshaw, which gave the illusion that the coach was traveling along the edge of a steep cliff.

The last two scenes of "Shadow of Doubt" are heavy with mystery as Zorro searches Esteban Roja's darkened room looking for clues. The final scene included

Disney's vision for the use of mysterious shadows: While in his secret room with Bernardo, Zorro forms the silhouette of a Z on the wall using an eagle's feather and his hands against the candlelight. In a prophetic monologue he then reflects on the situation at hand. "It's something deep-seated and sinister, something that spreads a shadow over the future for all of us and may bring an even greater need for the work of ... Zorro."

Behind the Scenes

Director Stevenson uses an interesting special effect when Zorro must quietly walk Tornado into the cuartel to return the rescued Maria: He simply films it in slow motion so the horse appears to be moving delicately ... Charles Stevens returns to play the part of Josephat. He had a bit part in "Zorro Rides to the Mission...." Veteran heavy Jack Elam's appearances in "Shadow of Doubt" and the following two episodes were uncredited ... Nestor Paiva once again appears as the innkeeper.... There is also a minor costume adjustment: For the first time, Zorro's exposed forehead is covered by overlapping the headkerchief and mask.

EPISODE 15

"Garcia Stands Accused"

Filmed: September 30, October 4, 7–9, 14, 16–18 & 24, 1957; *Air Date*: January 16, 1958; *Director*: Robert Stevenson; *Writer*: Lowell Hawley; *Cast*: Vinton Hayworth (Magistrado), Henry Wills (King's Messenger), Mort Mills (Lancer), Don Diamond (Cpl. Reyes), Myrna Fahey (Maria), Jack Elam (Gomez), Lane Bradford (Zorro Imposter).

Garcia receives a late night visitor: Zorro. Zorro tells the Sergeant that if he comes to Cahuenga Pass alone, he will surrender to him. Without revealing all the details, Garcia discusses the matter with Don Diego and decides to meet with the Fox. He rides out at night and comes to Cahuenga Pass where a voice from behind a rock tells him that he must leave his sword behind if he wants to meet Zorro. He obeys and rides on, eventually realizing that he is on a wild goose chase and that his late night visitor was an imposter.

The next morning an injured rider comes into Los Angeles and falls from his horse. He reveals that he is the King's messenger from Monterey and he has been robbed of the Army payroll. He explains that a soldier robbed him and he has a broken military saber to prove it. The Magistrado lets the messenger look over the soldiers to see if he can identify his assailant. When Garcia arrives, he is immediately recognized by the injured messenger as the assailant.

The Sergeant is quickly tried, found guilty and sentenced to death at sunrise. Don Diego visits with Garcia, who tells him of Zorro's late night visit. The young don suspects that Garcia has been framed. When Diego asks the Magistrado about the messenger, he learns that he is on his way back to Monterey. Zorro springs into action and, after a chase along the King's highway, captures the messenger. He confesses to Zorro that the Magistrado is involved with him and surrenders his eagle feather. Zorro returns the criminal and the payroll to the pueblo just in time to save Garcia.

Author's Notes

"Garcia Stands Accused" begins in an unusual fashion when Zorro appears immediately, riding through the pueblo. Only three other episodes in the entire run of the series contained early appearances by Zorro. Although it turns out to be an imposter, it's refreshing to see things done a little differently. These scenes of Zorro riding through the pueblo were used as stock footage in many subsequent stories.

Diego has a chance to sing a song to Garcia as the Sergeant daydreams of being the heroic commandante who captures Zorro. It's an amusing dream sequence with Garcia atop a white steed as the señoritas swoon in his presence. When he locks Zorro in a cell, the throng of people cheer. In this scene, Buddy Van Horn portrays Zorro, brought in at the end of Garcia's rope.

The Sergeant also gets off some of the episode's funniest lines. When he is accused of stealing the soldier's payroll, he orders Cpl. Reyes to "put me in Cell #1 and post a double guard. I think I am a very dangerous man." Later, when he tells Diego that maybe someone has impersonated him, he says, "In the whole world there is only one person who looks like me, that is my cousin in Monterey. You could not tell us apart except for one little thing. He is skinny like a rail." When he is put in front of a firing squad, he is asked if he has any last words. In a very childlike way he exclaims, "Sí, I wish I never joined the Army."

The action gets going with a wild stunt directed by Yakima Canutt and his second unit team. Canutt's son Tap and Henry Wills perform a difficult horse-to-horse transfer. Tap Canutt explains how it was done: "As Zorro I would ride in and jump on the back of Henry's horse. I would fight my way around him and go into what is called a fender drag which is hanging upside down while holding onto the saddle. As I'm doing this, I'm kicking up at him. I had the cape shortened so the horse wouldn't step on it. I was using steel L steps for the stirrups so that I wouldn't get caught up in anything. I also put a saddle trip on the side of the saddle which trips the latigos. At the right moment I yell to Henry and pull the pin to the trip and we leave the horse, saddle and all." The action was shot at the Albertson Ranch in Newhall, California.

The last scene in the story once again takes place in Zorro's candlelit secret room as he takes an eagle's feather, daubs it in ink and slashes a Z over a piece of paper. These scenes, which are used as tags for all three of Robert Stevenson's episodes, work perfectly in maintaining an air of mystery and suspense.

Behind the Scenes

Character actors Lane Bradford and Mort Mills appear in small roles, uncredited.... The song "Garcia My Friend" was written by Gil George and Joe Dubin. Bill Lee dubs Guy Williams' singing.

EPISODE 16

"Slaves of the Eagle"

Filmed: September 7, 10, 11, 14–18, 24 & November 4, 1957; *Air Date*: January 23, 1958; *Director*: Robert Stevenson; *Writer*: Lowell Hawley; *Cast*: Vinton Hayworth (Magistrado), Jack Elam (Gomez), Ray Teal (Vasquez), John Doucette (Tax Collector), Anthony George (Elasavio Crespo), Myrna Fahey (Maria), Don Diamond (Cpl. Reyes), Robert Warwick (José Morales).

On his way to Los Angeles, the new tax collector is waylaid by bandits and has his papers confiscated. He is blackmailed into staying out of the pueblo and told to keep his mouth shut. One of the bandits poses as the new tax collector and imposes a heavy tax which many peons cannot pay. Those who cannot pay are thrown into jail. When Elasavio Crespo, the brother of Maria the barmaid, is jailed, she asks Don Diego to investigate.

Diego learns that the Magistrado has sold those who cannot pay into slavery as indentured peons. He also begins to suspect that the tax collector is an imposter and part of the "Eagle's brood." He proves his theory when, discussing the de la Vega tax with the collector, he flashes an eagle's feather and the collector immediately reduces his taxes.

Sgt. Garcia sympathizes with the peons and fears that Zorro will not rescue them before they are taken to the slave mines in Sonora. He decides to take matters into his own hands. Garcia disguises himself as Zorro and tries to free the peons but fails and is reprimanded by the Magistrado. In the process, he has upset the plans of the real Zorro to rescue the jailed men.

The next day, the peons are led out of Los Angeles in chains on their way to the mines. They are closely followed by Zorro and Bernardo, who also wears a Zorro disguise. From a distance, Zorro taunts the slave trader and his guards. They give chase and end up pursuing Bernardo as the real Zorro rides back to release the peons. After a brief struggle with the guards, Zorro frees the enslaved men. He concludes that someone is plotting not only against the Army but also against the people. Zorro must find out the significance of the eagle feather and who has started this "deliberate campaign of misery and suffering."

Author's Notes

"Slaves of the Eagle" is another strong entry from director Robert Stevenson. One of the more interesting scenes has Diego teaching Bernardo how to fence and ride so he can assist Zorro in his work when the situation arises. It's similar to "Double Trouble for Zorro" in which Diego is training Tornado. An amusing scene here has Bernardo leaping onto Tornado and landing backwards as the black stallion rides off. The tricky stunt was performed by Jerry Brown, who stood in for Gene Sheldon.

The comedy revolves around Sgt. Garcia when he disguises himself as Zorro in an attempt to rescue the prisoners. When he is captured by his own soldiers and questioned by the enraged Magistrado, he replies innocently, "How did you know it was me, Excellency? I'm wearing a mask."

When Zorro returns home after an aborted attempt at rescuing some prisoners, a new side of the character is shown. Angry that Garcia has botched his plans, he flies into a rage, some of which is directed at Bernardo. He quickly calms down and mends his friend's bruised feelings. It's a well-played scene that adds a touch of realism and emphasizes the desperate situation.

The action climax, once again directed by Yakima Canutt at the Bell Ranch, suffers from mismatched doubles. For this one episode, Republic Pictures veteran Dale Van Sickel doubled for Guy Williams as Zorro. Unfortunately Van Sickel, an All-American football star, was much too husky for the part. Although the stunt work is excellent with Zorro leaping off of boulders and jumping over horses, even the most casual viewer can tell that Guy Williams is nowhere in sight and the scene suffers because of that.

Behind the Scenes

> The opening of the show has some new action clips and the theme has been extended to include a brief instrumental break.... The coming attractions for this episode contain a scene from "Presenting Señor Zorro" which is not in the episode: a shot of Zorro moving stealthily across a rooftop.... Actors appearing uncredited include John Doucette and Ray Teal [who went on to play Sheriff Coffee in *Bonanza*]. The song "Zorro the Brave" was penned by Tom Adair and Joe Dubin.

EPISODE 17

"Sweet Face of Danger"

Filmed: November 1, 4, 5–8, 11 & December 13, 1957; *Air Date*: January 30, 1958; *Director-Writer*: John Meredyth Lucas; *Cast*: George Lewis (Don Alejandro), Vinton Hayworth (Magistrado), Julie Van Zandt (Magdalena), Edward Colmans (Don Francisco), Amzie Strickland (Doña Inez).

A secret messenger of the Eagle has arrived in Los Angeles by coach. The Magistrado learns that a spy for the Viceroy has arrived aboard the same coach. He instructs one of his henchmen to eliminate the spy and the man is killed in the town plaza by an arrow. Don Diego, who is involved in a conversation with Sgt. Garcia nearby, rushes to examine the body. He finds a small eagle's feather which he places in the inside pocket of his jacket. When Diego returns home, he compares it with the other feathers he has confiscated in hopes of finding some sort of code.

The de la Vegas are visited by Don Francisco and his daughter Magdalena, who arrived in the same coach as the man who was murdered. Don Alejandro would like nothing better than to see his only son marry and Diego does find Magdalena quite attractive. The next day they go for a carriage ride to a nearby lake and, while conversing, Diego learns that Magdalena traveled aboard the same ship that carried the murdered man. He begins to suspect that she may have had something to do with the murder.

That evening a party is held at the de la Vega hacienda in honor of Magdalena's return to Los Angeles. While Diego is keeping a close watch on her, he sees her slip an eagle feather to the Magistrado. Diego accidentally bumps into the Magistrado and lifts the feather. He takes it into the sala and clips a few of the feathers and, once again bumping into the Magistrado, returns the feather. As the party is ending, he sees the Magistrado talking to a dangerous looking man. It is then that he realizes that he has sealed the fate of Magdalena. Diego thought that his clipping of the feather would cause the death of the hired killer; instead it is about to spell the end for Magdalena.

Diego has trouble slipping away but with the help of Bernardo he is soon Zorro, pursuing Magdalena's carriage and the Magistrado's henchman who is following it. Zorro catches up with the carriage and wrestles with the killer, knocking him off and onto his own knife. After Zorro pulls the carriage to a halt, Magdalena explains that she didn't realize anyone would be killed. Zorro tells her in no uncertain terms that it would be best for all concerned if she returned to Mexico.

Author's Notes

"Sweet Face of Danger" is the first of three episodes written and directed by John Meredyth Lucas. Lucas, who wrote two of the first 13 episodes, is the only director other than Norman Foster to actually write the episodes he directed. His style is comparable to Foster and Bob Stevenson. As a matter of fact, the stunt at the end of this episode is very similar to the action scene at the conclusion of Stevenson's "Shadow of Doubt" right down to the matte painting by Peter Ellenshaw. The action here has Zorro (Tap Canutt) rescuing Magdalena and her father from a knife-wielding agent of the Eagle. It was directed by Yakima Canutt and filmed at Corriganville and Bell Ranch. This episode also begins with footage that opened "Shadow of Doubt"—a coach pulling into a crowded plaza.

Lucas has a way with dialogue and some of it is a bit more mature as evidenced by this flirtatious conversation between Don Diego and Magdalena.

DIEGO: I used to swim here when I was a child.
MAGDALENA: I would love to come out here sometimes and swim. Oh, but I'm afraid I would shock my father very much. Does it shock you?
DIEGO: Let us say I am not entirely unmoved by the idea.

Julie Van Zandt, the actress who played this scene, had fond memories of Guy Williams, "I've never had so much help from an actor. He was graceful, cooperative and unselfish. He was also a big tease. He kept telling me how great I was, but I couldn't decide whether or not he was serious."[1]

Like those that preceded it, the look of these episodes is first-class: daring stunts, location filming, etc. Lucas remembered what he perceived to be a casual attitude regarding money at the studio: "We had a production meeting and I said, 'I need a boom here and a Chapman crane.' And everything I asked for they said, 'Yeah, fine.' Finally they got a production man who had done some real live production work outside the studio and when I saw him I said, 'Thank God, now I feel like I'm making a movie.' Up until that point everything had been so casual. It reassured me that there was a real world out there."

Henry Wills must have had a sense of déjà vu while filming this segment. Just two episodes prior in "Garcia Stands Accused," the actor–stunt man, wearing a false mustache, played a similar part as one of the Eagle's henchmen. At the conclusion of both episodes he is called upon to use his stunt expertise for dangerous horse chase action.

Behind the Scenes

> Lucas tips his hat to the McCulley pulps when he has Diego exclaim to Bernardo, "Saddle the black horse." It was a phrase used quite often in the old *Zorro* short stories.

Episode 18

"Zorro Fights His Father"

Filmed: October 21–25, 28, November 1, 4 & 25, 1957; *Air Date*: February 6, 1958; *Director-Writer*: John Meredyth Lucas; *Cast*: Vinton Hayworth (Magistrado), George Lewis (Don Alejandro), Peter Brocco (Señor Barca), Don Diamond (Cpl. Reyes), Joan Shawlee (Clara), Julian Rivero (Tamayo).

An angry group of peons has gathered outside the Magistrado's office. They are protesting the fact that the illegally collected tax money has not yet been returned to the people. As the Magistrado addresses the crowd, one of his agents, who has been planted in the mob, attempts to start a riot by throwing a rock at the Magistrado. The crowd is ordered to disperse by Sgt. Garcia as the Magistrado discusses the people's unrest with some of the landowners. As a result of the near riot, the Magistrado tries to convince the rancheros that the peons are bent on anarchy. Don Alejandro remains unmoved until later that evening when a don and his wife are attacked by some of the Magistrado's henchmen posing as peons.

The landowners meet to discuss the problem and decide that Zorro has somehow sown the seeds of discontent. Diego tries to argue against this but is overruled. A Committee of Vigilance is formed with Don Alejandro as its head. Their first act is to arrest a young man named Paco, who they believe is the leader of the peons. Don Alejandro thinks that Paco has merely been brought in as a ruse to capture Zorro and that no harm will come to him. The Magistrado has other ideas and wants Paco executed because he is a troublemaker. Diego overhears this and decides that Zorro is better suited to solve this problem than he.

When Zorro shows himself outside the cuartel, Sgt. Garcia and a small contingent of soldiers gives chase. The Fox doubles back and frees Paco but in the process has to fight his father who is guarding the boy. Careful not to hurt him, Zorro forces Don Alejandro back into a cell and slams the door. Zorro and Paco escape on Tornado.

When Don Diego reappears, he proposes drinks with his good friend, the Sergeant, and his father. But Don Alejandro declines, admits it was wrong to take the law into his own hands and says that he is finished with the Committee of Vigilance.

Author's Notes

"Zorro Fights His Father" is another good episode as long as the viewer can get past the hard-to-accept plot. The very idea that Don Alejandro would want to capture Zorro is rather unbelievable considering the fact that Zorro saved Don Alejandro's life a few episodes back ("Monastario Sets a Trap" and "Zorro's Ride into Terror"). However, the irony of Zorro actually having to fight his own father makes for a dramatic story. John Meredyth Lucas, like Bob Wehling and Norman Foster, writes dialogue that's very clever. This conversation between the Magistrado and Diego is an example of Lucas at his most erudite:

MAGISTRADO: I hope you have not reconsidered and share your father's desire for order and justice.
DIEGO: Justice is blind, Your Excellency, and she can be led around by anyone.
MAGISTRADO: You are the one who is blind, Diego. You will find nothing in your books to compare with what you will see here where history is being made.
DIEGO: I have no quarrel with history but I am often appalled by the people who make it.

Buddy Van Horn, doubling as Zorro, engages in what is technically his first fencing scene. It's one of the very few times he had to double Guy Williams in a duel because it required Zorro to fence while on horseback. There wasn't any intricate sword work involved; it was Van Horn's expertise as a horseman that was required. The brief long shots are Van Horn while the close-ups are Williams. Lucas uses a very dramatic camera angle for this scene. The master shot is from up high looking down at the action. It was an angle of the cuartel that had never been seen before and would never be seen again.

Joan Shawlee, who plays the part of Clara the barmaid, appeared in five Billy Wilder films including *Some Like It Hot*, *The Apartment* and *Irma La Douce*. Wilder said she was "one of the best comediennes in America." Unfortunately she is wasted here where most of her activity takes the form of caustic barbs about Garcia's weight and drinking.

Behind the Scenes

The Committee of Vigilance was based upon actual vigilance committees that first formed in California in 1836.... Victor Paul doubles Peter Brocco in the sword fight with Zorro.... Scenes which have Don Alejandro trying to thwart a robbery and rounding up peons were filmed on the back lot in the woodland area during a rare night shoot. A number of these night shots were mixed with day-for-night scenes.

EPISODE 19

"Death Stacks the Deck"

Filmed: October 24, 25, 28–31, November 1, 4 & 11, 1957; *Air Date*: February 13, 1958; *Director-Writer*: John Meredyth Lucas; *Cast*: George Lewis (Don Alejandro), Don Diamond (Cpl. Reyes), Vinton Hayworth (Magistrado), Peter Brocco (Señor Barca), Miguel Landa (Don Ramon Santil), Jim Bannon (Carlos Urista), Joan Shawlee (Clara).

Ramon Santil's father has died. Before Ramon can finish mourning his father's death, the Magistrado has demanded the full tax due on the Santil rancho. As the funeral procession passes through the pueblo, Don Diego notices a stranger, Carlos Urista, with an eagle feather in his hat. Diego also observes that the Magistrado and the stranger seem to know one another.

After the funeral, Don Alejandro asks Diego to try to help Ramon. The two young dons attended the same university in Spain but Ramon was thrown out for gambling. Diego tries in vain, as Ramon sells all his cattle for 11,000 pesos and proceeds to lose that and his rancho in a card game to Carlos Urista.

Once in possession of the Santil rancho, Urista opens a tannery on the land. It quickly pollutes the spring of water that runs to all the other ranchos. Furthermore, it seems that Urista is willing to purchase land from any ranchero whose water he has polluted. The landowners are furious but the Magistrado, knowing that possession of the land would benefit the Eagle's cause, explains that the law is on Urista's side. Diego realizes that only Zorro can help Ramon now. As Urista prepares for a late night rendezvous with the Magistrado, Zorro intercepts the gambler and forces him into one last card game with Ramon Santil. Zorro tells Urista simply, "If you win, you die." As the game gets underway, Cpl. Reyes spies Zorro through the tavern window and alerts the Magistrado, who rallies the soldiers.

Before the lancers can break through the door, Ramon has won his land back. Zorro tells him that he is to work the rancho for one year and then exclaims, "If I find out you have gambled, it will be the last card you ever turn." The soldiers break in and after a brief struggle they pursue Zorro, up the stairs, out the window and onto the roof of the tavern, only to see him escape into the night.

Author's Notes

"Death Stacks the Deck" is John Meredyth Lucas' final contribution to the series and it's a fine way to go out. It contains one of the better action sequences of the series with Zorro fighting off a group of lancers in the tavern and in the process breaking his sword. Part of the action includes Zorro (Buddy Van Horn) riding the top of a ladder from one rooftop across to another. The stunt was performed with the help of a wire attached to a ladder rung.

The one problem with this episode is the relationship between Ramon and Diego, which has them attending the same university together. The story could have been more intriguing if Ramon's suspicion of Don Diego's personality change (man of action to man of letters) upon returning to California could have been raised. Unfortunately the real potential of the episode was left untapped.

This story also includes a look at the evolving comedic relationship between Sgt. Garcia and Cpl. Reyes. In a tavern scene, Reyes' pointed comments are aimed directly at the Sergeant.

> GARCIA: You know what they say. A fat man always has a good sense of humor.
> REYES: With a stomach like yours, you need a sense of humor.
> GARCIA: You are addressing your commandante.
> REYES: (Sarcastically) All right ... Sergeant.
> GARCIA: Sergeant? Don Diego, it's no use. To my own men I'm only a little sergeant.
> REYES: A big, fat sergeant!

In subsequent episodes, the banter between the two was toned down and was less acerbic.

Behind the Scenes

> For one of the exterior scenes, Jim Bannon's dialogue is dubbed by voice specialist Paul Frees.... Bannon was known largely for his Western roles. He starred as Red Ryder in a series of films in the late 1940s.... Peter Brocco and Joan Shawlee return for their final episode.... One song is performed, "Because I Think So," written by Tom Adair and Joe Dubin.

EPISODE 20
"Agent of the Eagle"

Filmed: November 19–22, 25–27, 29, December 2 & 3, 1957; *Air Date*: February 20, 1958; *Director*: Charles Barton; *Writer*: N.B. Stone, Jr.; *Cast*: Vinton Hayworth (Magistrado), Anthony Caruso (Don Juan Ortega), Sandy Livingston (Rosarita), George Lewis (Don Alejandro), George Keymas (Roberto), Henry Corden (Leon).

Juan Ortega, the new commandante, has arrived in Los Angeles with his aides Leon and Roberto. He quickly meets with the Magistrado and, using a feather as a calling card, establishes himself as an agent of the Eagle. It seems that the real Juan Ortega met with a fatal accident aboard the ship that brought the two men to Los Angeles. According to the Magistrado, it will be the new commandante's job to wring as much money as possible out of the people to support the Eagle's cause.

In the pueblo, Don Diego encounters a childhood friend, Rosarita Cortez. She has arrived aboard the same ship that brought the new commandante and is in Los Angeles to visit her aunt and uncle. As the old friends reminisce, Rosarita invites Diego to a party that evening and he gladly accepts.

At the fiesta, Diego introduces the Magistrado to Franco Barbarossa and his daughter. The Magistrado does not try to hide his disdain for Barbarossa, who is not of the upper class. Diego explains that Barbarossa is to be admired because he has worked hard and built his life from very little. Unwittingly, Diego gives the Magistrado information to use against Barbarossa.

The following day, the Magistrado uses an obscure law to confiscate Barbarossa's land unless he can pay 5,000 pesos in taxes. Barbarossa refuses and is sentenced to six months of hard labor. Diego learns of his plight and speaks on Barbarossa's behalf but the Magistrado will have none of it. Barbarossa is put to work in the grist mill where he is guarded at all times.

That evening, Sgt. Garcia, always looking for a free drink, encounters lancers Leon and Roberto in the tavern. In the course of their conversation, Garcia, believing that Zorro will try to rescue Barbarossa, unwittingly lets the two lancers in on his plan to capture Zorro. The two soldiers temporarily dispose of Garcia, and set their own trap for the Fox. As expected, Zorro appears and dispatches both soldiers, one of whom is killed in the struggle. When Capitan Ortega arrives, he too is disarmed after a brief duel. The helpless capitan is left with a Z on his tunic as Zorro helps Barbarossa to escape.

Author's Notes

Charles Barton's first entry, "Agent of the Eagle" is almost immediately different in tone from the previous six episodes that inaugurated the Eagle's saga. Given Barton's comedic background (Abbott & Costello, Ma & Pa Kettle), the emphasis is more humorous than dramatic as Sgt. Garcia rides out to greet the new commandante and his two aides. Explaining his disdain for the sea as the reason for not meeting the commandante's ship at San Pedro, the Sergeant is immediately teased by the commandante's aides. So much so that Garcia almost gets seasick on the spot. It's a theme that becomes an integral part of the plot later in the episode that leads to still more comedy at the Sergeant's expense.

Once again as a result of his dual identity, Diego has his own problems. When his attempts to reason with Magistrado regarding the harsh sentence of Franco Barbarossa fail, he is all but accused of being a coward by his childhood sweetheart.

Rosarita: Is that the best you can do?
Diego: Perhaps, if I write a letter to the Governor, he might...
Rosarita: Write a letter! If I was a man I would do something about this, and it wouldn't be writing a letter.
Diego: Rosarita, I know how you must feel and I...
Rosarita: What happened to you, Diego? When you were a boy, you wouldn't

have stood idly by while a man was tortured. You're not half the man you were when you were only ten years old!

The Eagle's goals for conquest of California are also clarified once and for all: The people must be demoralized, money must be extorted, and Zorro must be done away with. In the course of this dissertation, the Magistrado exclaims, "I've been cursed with a succession of incompetent commandantes." The only commandante that Galindo has had to deal with is Garcia, who has indeed been incompetent, but there have been no others (with the exception of Capitan Melendez who was assassinated immediately upon his arrival in "Shadow of Doubt"). This was writer N.B. Stone's first script and he may not have been sufficiently familiar with the history of the show.

Anthony Caruso, who plays the part of Ortega, is an imposing presence. Although he began his career playing Shakespeare with the Pasadena Playhouse, he made a reputation appearing as tough guys and gangsters. He appeared in over 150 films, among them *The Asphalt Jungle, Song of India* and *Never a Dull Moment.*

The concluding sword fight between Zorro and Capitan Ortega is simple but exciting, employing only the most basic of fencing moves. According to the production call sheet, Fred Cavens was supposed to double Anthony Caruso (Ortega) for this segment but from all appearances it seems as though Caruso performed most if not all of his own fencing. This may be the reason for the rudimentary nature of the swordplay. Caruso's fencing is something of a rarity in that most of the actors were doubled for the swordplay action. This was also the first extended fencing scene featuring Zorro in nine episodes.

During the sword fight, Zorro actually cuts the sign of the Z on a villain for the first time in the series. Before this he had left his mark on a jail cell wall, a sheet of music paper and a coach door. This practice of Zorro putting his mark on his adversary was actually started by Douglas Fairbanks, Sr., in *The Mark of Zorro* and adopted by Johnston McCulley for his pulp fiction stories. In those adventures Zorro applied his mark to the flesh. In the Disney series, the villains got off a little easier; Zorro would only cut his Z on their clothes.

One sad footnote in the plot, somewhat overlooked in all the concluding action: Although Franco Barbarossa has been rescued by Zorro he still has lost all he has worked for — his land and his home. Zorro's final words to Barbarossa are, "Get as far away from here as you can as fast as you can." His life has been spared, but unfortunately, the immediate future does not appear to be bright for Barbarossa and his daughter.

Behind the Scenes

> Bill Anderson receives his first credit as producer with this episode ... Nestor Paiva returns as the innkeeper ... Henry Corden, who appears as the soldier Leon, went on to supply the voice of Fred Flinstone after Alan Reed (the original Fred) died.... The grist mill which is used only in this episode was set up behind the tavern.... Diego plays the song "Elena" at the piano, a tune he first sang in "Zorro's Romance."

EPISODE 21

"Zorro Springs a Trap"

Filmed: November 11–15, 18–21 & 27, 1957; *Air Date*: February 27, 1958; *Director*: Charles Barton; *Writer*: Lewis Foster; *Cast*: Vinton Hayworth (Magistrado), Anthony Caruso (Capitan Ortega), Don Diamond (Cpl. Reyes), George Keymas (Roberto).

A cage, wheeled out into the plaza by the soldiers, contains a black-clothed figure that appears to be Zorro. Word of the legendary bandit's capture spreads quickly as Sgt. Garcia reads the proclamation that Zorro will be unmasked and then hung at noon. A surprised Don Diego tells Bernardo that the situation bears watching and he will need a change of clothes. Bernardo makes the sign of the Z and Diego nods. This is all part of Capitan Ortega's plan to capture any peons who try to rescue Zorro and make them talk — to tell him where the real Zorro is hiding.

Outside in the plaza, a crowd of angry peons is gathering in support of Zorro. They build a barricade between the gates of the cuartel and the caged Zorro. Diego tries to persuade these men to go home but they are determined. It is time for the real Zorro to step in. The peons try to release the masked figure, but the imposter calls for the lancers. As the commandante and his men ready their attack against the peons, a black-caped figure gallops into the plaza and proclaims that he is the real Zorro. The peons rip off the mask of the man in the cage to reveal Roberto the lancer.

The soldiers charge out of the cuartel in pursuit of Zorro. As Tornado races through the pueblo, he stumbles and falls. As Zorro lays helpless on the ground, the commandante's lasso snares the Fox. He pulls Zorro back to the cuartel as Sgt. Garcia captures Tornado. Zorro frees himself from the lasso and escapes.

The commandante plans to use Tornado as bait to capture Zorro. He will hold an auction and when someone bids for the black stallion, he will wring information from the bidder, who must be an accomplice of Zorro. Don Diego has a plan of his own. While in the tavern, Diego loans Garcia money so he can bid on Tornado. However, Garcia is the only bidder. He buys Tornado, ruining the commandante's plan.

In the hope of luring Zorro, Tornado is kept corralled in the plaza. That night with Roberto standing guard, Bernardo tries to get Tornado's attention. Roberto sees this and turns his whip on Diego's servant. During the whipping, a fire starts and Tornado tramples Roberto. Hearing the commotion, Diego rushes out of the inn. In the confusion, he quickly changes to Zorro, rescues Tornado and rides off into the night as the lancers watch helplessly.

Author's Notes

The real surprise of "Zorro Springs a Trap" is the somewhat shocking opening — Zorro being wheeled out by lancers in a crudely constructed cage and put on display in the plaza. Although it quickly becomes apparent that this is an imposter, it's still an effective attention-grabbing device. Even with this initial scene, the general light tone which was inaugurated in the previous episode continues here. Given the comedic backgrounds of director Barton and writer Lew Foster, it's easy to see why.

Although Barton worked with Abbott and Costello, the pacing involving Sgt. Garcia and the commandante is more like that of Laurel and Hardy. This may be Foster's influence; he worked for the Hal Roach Studios, the home of Laurel and Hardy. One scene has Garcia showing the newly built hangman's scaffolding to the commandante. As the commandante is standing over the trap door, Garcia accidentally pulls the lever, plunging the commandante to the ground. There is a role reversal here with Garcia adopting the Stan Laurel persona and the commandante portraying the exasperation of Oliver Hardy.

Another bit of verbal comedy more in the style of Abbott and Costello, but without the rapid-fire delivery, is Cpl. Reyes' bidding on Zorro's captured horse, Tornado. Reyes is surreptitiously bidding for Garcia who is conducting the auction. Garcia has given the Corporal precise instructions to bid only after someone else does. Unfortunately, every time Garcia shouts the current bid, the Corporal raises him one. It's an amusing bit handled in a low-key fashion.

Easily the most thrilling aspect of "Zorro Springs a Trap" is Zorro's near-capture. When Tornado stumbles and Zorro is thrown to the ground, it's really the first time in the series that Zorro is put in this type of danger. As in "The Ghost of the Mission" when Zorro fails in his effort to bring food to Nacho Torres, it makes the danger seem a bit more real. However, it's the type of development that can't occur too often or else the character would become too ordinary.

The most visually spectacular stunt of the series occurs when Zorro (Buddy Van Horn) swings by rope from the balcony of the tavern and smashes into the burning corral to rescue Tornado. With Zorro on his back, the stallion leaps over the burning fence and rides off into the night. This was another of those rare night shoots, which makes the scene so much more effective than the day-for-night process.

Occurring just prior to the corral stunt is one of the more violent scenes of the series. When Roberto the lancer begins whipping Bernardo, Tornado attempts to rescue him. Roberto then turns his anger towards the horse, which nearly stomps the lancer to death. Because of the tight rein on violence, Barton was not able to show the actual stomping. However, showing only the horse rearing up and coming down with the lancer screaming and the camera shaking is probably more effective.

Behind the Scenes

> Dave Kashner doubles for George Keymas in the bullwhip scenes.... Don Diamond [Cpl. Reyes] remarked that Charles Barton was "my favorite director, a little short man who knew his comedy."

EPISODE 22
"The Unmasking of Zorro"

Filmed: November 11, 15, 18–21, 25–27, 29, December 2, 1957; *Air Date*: March 6, 1958; *Director*: Charles Barton; *Writer*: N.B. Stone, Jr.; *Cast*: Vinton Hayworth (Magistrado), Anthony Caruso (Ortega), George Lewis (Don Alejandro), Sandy Livingston (Rosarita).

Thus far, all of Capitan Ortega's efforts to demoralize the people of Los Angeles have been unsuccessful. Time is running out. The Magistrado has received a communiqué from the Eagle who grows impatient. Ortega must make good on his plans or suffer the consequences.

That same morning, as Diego and Rosarita are strolling through the plaza, Bernardo sees a strange sight: When the commandante spots Rosarita, he quickly ducks behind the well in the center of the plaza. Bernardo follows the commandante to the Magistrado's office where he hears a frightening conversation. It seems that because Rosarita was a passenger on the ship which brought the commandante to California, she alone knows the true identity of the commandante. The Magistrado and Capitan Ortega, whose real name is Sancho Fernandez, agree that there is only one thing to do: Rosarita must be eliminated. Bernardo races back to the plaza looking for Diego, but he is nowhere to be found. Bernardo takes off on foot for the de la Vega hacienda in a race against time.

As darkness approaches, Fernandez arrives at the hacienda of Rosarita's uncle. The servants have retired for the evening and Rosarita's aunt and uncle are out. The young woman sees a man in the shadows and as he steps forward to introduce himself, she is relieved to see her sailing companion Señor Fernandez. When Fernandez grabs the woman, Zorro leaps from atop the patio wall. The two men engage in a swordfight. Zorro disarms the imposter but, through a stroke of luck, Ortega escapes and heads back to the pueblo with Zorro close behind.

Realizing that his masquerade as the commandante is over and his days as an agent of the Eagle are numbered, he enters the Magistrado's office and steals his gold. Zorro arrives and pursues Ortega to the roof. The two men struggle and Zorro is unmasked. Zorro forces Ortega off the roof and he falls to his death. Another agent of the Eagle is defeated and the secret of Zorro's identity is still safe.

Author's Notes

"The Unmasking of Zorro" created a bit of a problem for the creative forces behind the series. Head writer Lowell Hawley comments, "There was a lot of discussion regarding Zorro being unmasked. It was a big decision including Walt, Bill Anderson and myself." The usual problem in a situation such as this is how will the antagonist who performed the unmasking be dealt with? Surely the hero can't commit outright murder but somehow the perpetrator must be killed in order to preserve the hero's secret. To solve this problem, writer N.B. Stone, Jr., has Zorro commit a kind of *benign* murder. During their struggle on the rooftop, Zorro walks toward the commandante. As the commandante edges backward he simply runs out of roof and falls to his death. In a sense, Zorro's hands are still clean because he never laid a glove on his enemy. The action for the scene was filmed in two different segments. The master shots were filmed atop the Magistrado's house on the back lot using doubles Buddy Van Horn and Lou Roberson. The close-ups were completed on a soundstage mock-up of the rooftop with Guy Williams and Anthony Caruso.

The fencing scene between Zorro and Ortega is exciting with Caruso once again doing most of his own fencing (fencing double Victor Paul stood in for some of the more athletic moves). Most of the fencing moves are saber-style with only a few foil point moves employed. While it's not technically as difficult as some of the later swordplay, the two adversaries employ all of the set, jumping from atop a wall, leaping over tables and moving in and out of the hacienda pillars, which helps make it exciting.

Behind the Scenes

> The sets for the patio and sala of Rosarita's uncle's hacienda are actually the de la Vega hacienda sets slightly redecorated.... In the two episodes in which Sandy Livingston appeared, her character's name was pronounced Rosalita by both Diego and Don Alejandro. However, the ending credits list her as Rosarita.

EPISODE 23
"The Secret of the Sierra"

Filmed: December 20, 1957; January 2, 3, 6–8, 1958; *Air Date*: March 13, 1958; *Director-Writer*: Norman Foster; *Cast*: Vinton Hayworth (Magistrado), George Lewis (Don Alejandro), Rodolfo Acosta (Perico), Rudolfo Hoyos (Cuevas), Laurie Carroll (Marya), Inez Palance (Gypsy Witch).

In the marketplace, a gypsy girl tries to pay for her supplies with gold nuggets. The merchant thinks it is fool's gold and refuses to accept it. Don Diego overhears and offers to pay for the girl's purchase. The girl gives him the gold nuggets in exchange. Perico, a scarred prospector from Mexico, observes the transaction and asks to examine a nugget. He proclaims that it is of no value but Diego thinks otherwise. The prospector is another agent of the Eagle and he reports to the Magistrado that it is indeed gold. The Magistrado proclaims that it would be of great value to the Eagle's cause to find the source of the gold. Perico and his companion Cuevas agree.

Don Alejandro examines the nugget and tells Diego that if word of the gold got out, the land would be overrun by prospectors and ne'er-do-wells, all stricken with gold fever. Diego also realizes that the Magistrado is dangerous enough without the power of gold behind him. Diego and Bernardo set out to find the gypsy girl. Armed with vague directions, they locate the home of the gypsy girl's grandmother, who is a witch. In exchange for information and some so-called magic (exploding) pellets, Diego gives the woman a few gold coins. He learns that the gypsy girl received the gold nuggets from an Indian woman whom she had helped; that two men, one with a scar, arrived earlier looking for help with a sick child. Her granddaughter went with the men to help.

Diego and Bernardo trail the two men and the gypsy girl into the mountains. Perico forces the girl to reveal the location of the area where she came upon the Indian woman. After some searching, they locate digging tools and finally the hidden opening of the Indian mine. As they fill their sacks with gold, the girl escapes. Cuevas gives chase and is about to shoot the girl as Zorro appears and disarms him. Zorro then enters the mine and confronts Perico. A knife fight ensues.

Meanwhile, Bernardo is captured by the mining Indians and Cuevas is killed by an arrow in the back as he tries to escape with the sack of gold. As Zorro is grappling with Perico, he is unmasked. Zorro disarms the bandit and knocks him unconscious as the Indians enter with Bernardo. To keep their gold mine a secret, they must kill all who have discovered it. Taking a cue form Zorro, Bernardo tosses one of the witch's pellets into the fire, causing a blinding flash. Bernardo and Zorro race out followed closely by Perico. The Indians regroup and head up the mountain. They cause an avalanche which buries Perico while Zorro and Bernardo save themselves by taking refuge under an overhanging boulder. Zorro exclaims to Bernardo, "It will be some time before gold is discovered in California."

Author's Notes

The next series of four episodes marks the welcome return of Norman Foster (he directed all four and wrote three of the subsequent segments). These are the best group of episodes within the Eagle series and each has at least one thing which shows why Foster was the consummate Zorro director.

"The Secret of the Sierra" is interesting if for no other reason than Zorro is unmasked again. Why the series would schedule two such segments back to back is unclear. However, once again the dilemma is how to deal with the villain who unmasked Zorro. When Perico is crushed in an avalanche, Zorro's hands once again remain clean. Furthermore, it is assumed that the Indians who see Zorro unmasked simply do not care. They are presumably an isolated tribe, living in the Sierras, far enough away from Los Angeles so as not to cause a problem.

Foster relies upon his *film noir* experience, and the atmosphere he creates is at times a spooky one. When Diego and Bernardo visit the gypsy witch, her house is a soundstage set which gives it an eerie, fantasy appearance. Peter Ellenshaw provides some equally frightening matte work in the form of a mountain that has the look of a buffalo skull. All of this coupled with Bernardo's worried look, jumpy demeanor and an appropriate William Lava score make for some Halloween-type scares.

The episode was filmed amidst the rocky terrain of Chatsworth's Bell Ranch. Robert Foster, Norman's then-11-year-old son, who was on his first and only *Zorro* location shoot, recalls a near calamity; "There were these three enormous mountains with truck-size boulders on top of them. I was downhill and there was a slope and my father was behind the camera. The tripod was there and he said, 'All ready for action,' and I just imagined what would happen. I just saw the boulders come down off the mountain and there was a complete path going right into my father. It seemed obvious to me but no one else had thought of this. I said 'Daddy,' and he said, 'Yes, can't you see I'm directing this scene?' Again I said, 'Daddy, that's not gonna work, that's gonna kill you.' He said, 'No, the engineers figured the whole thing out.' I said, 'What if they're wrong?' So he looked at me, thought a bit and said, 'Okay, let's build a girder and seven foot tall cage with bars and a platform with a

A Zorro comic book giveaway.

camera on top and I'll get up on the platform.' They spent about an hour doing it. They pushed the boulders down and exactly what I'd imagined would happen did and he would've been killed. The boulders ran into the bar and in that episode you can see the camera shaking—they fell with such force, they bent the bars!"

The Fred Cavens—choreographed action sequence which has Zorro involved in

Robert Foster, son of director Norman, finds himself flanked by two Zorros, Guy Williams (*left*) and Buddy Van Horn. They were on location filming "The Secret of the Sierra" (courtesy Robert Foster).

a knife fight with one of the bandits is excellent. Adding to the excitement is the fact that Zorro and his opponent are evenly matched and Zorro is actually wounded during the struggle. The scene is all the more effective because no doubles were used. The only minor drawback is the inevitable cutaway to other peripheral scenes during the action. However in this case, it seems warranted in order to explain impending developments.

Behind the Scenes

For the first time, Zorro appears in action without his cape.... Additional matte work by Peter Ellenshaw includes some mountainous landscape made to look more dangerous.... Part of the avalanche sequence was achieved using miniatures.... Actors Hoyos and Acosta were friends of Norman Foster from his days in Mexico. He tried to use them whenever possible.

EPISODE 24
"The New Commandante"

Filmed: December 2–6, 9, 11, 13 & 18–20, 1957; *Air Date*: March 20, 1958; *Director-Writer*: Norman Foster; *Cast*: Peter Adams (Capitan Toledano), Suzanne Lloyd (Raquel Toledano), Vinton Hayworth (Magistrado), Anthony George (Peralta), Lance Fuller (Alarcon), Armand Alzamora (Figueroa).

When the Magistrado learns that Sgt. Garcia is escorting a new commandante to Los Angeles, he goes to great lengths to make sure the new capitan finds a very unhappy cuartel. He instructs one of his agents, the lancer Figueroa, to put something in the soldiers' food to spoil it. He wants the commandante to find nothing but trouble when he takes over.

After a long and arduous journey, Capitan Toledano and his wife arrive. He is in no mood for the situation he finds at the cuartel. The prisoners, who have also received bad rations, are ready to riot. Toledano orders them strung up by their hands in front of the cuartel. The Magistrado is pleased with the progress of his plan.

That evening, as the capitan and his wife relax in the tavern, he begins to have second thoughts about his treatment of the prisoners. He is ready to have them released when he notices a young don flirting with his wife from across the room. Angry, he decides to let the prisoners stay where they are. At that moment, Zorro appears on the upper stairway and warns the new commandante to use fairness in his dealings with the people. The capitan and his lancers give chase but they are no match for Zorro, who releases the prisoners in front of the cuartel before he disappears.

As time passes, Capitan Toledano proves himself to be a decent man and restores morale to the troops. This is the worst possible development for the Magistrado. He realizes that for the Eagle's plan to succeed they must gain control of the Army, and for that to happen they must eliminate Capitan Toledano. Realizing that the capitan is a very jealous husband, the Magistrado schemes to have Peralta, the young don who flirted with Señora Toledano in the tavern, serenade the young wife. The Magistrado hopes that Peralta, an excellent swordsman, will engage the jealous capitan and kill him.

Don Diego, a friend of Peralta's, learns of the scheme and dons the disguise of Zorro. He makes his way to the back of the tavern and chases the young man out from under the Señora's window. When Toledano learns a young señor is serenading his wife, he looks for the man, sword in hand. As a result of Zorro's double cross, it is Sgt. Garcia the capitan finds under his wife's window. The amused Toledano realizes that they have both been duped. The pair returns to the tavern for a nightcap. Peralta, realizing that there is a 1500 peso reward for Zorro, goes back in search of the masked bandit and engages Zorro in a duel. Although young don is very good, he is no match for Zorro. The Magistrado, who has been keeping an eye on events, arrives with the lancers. They chase Zorro through the pueblo but he escapes into the night.

Author's Notes

"The New Commandante" begins the next series of three episodes. It's a big-budget affair and an excellent example of the show at its best. It includes a dance number, two songs, a witty plot which contains some double- and triple-crosses, a chase through the tavern and cuartel, a large cast of extras and some excellent sword-play. The Zorro-Peralta duel is the best fencing scene up to this point in the series. The moves are fast and numerous between Guy Williams and Victor Paul (doubling for Anthony George). At one point there are 14 moves in a single fencing phrase, ending with Zorro (Williams) leaping atop a brick oven and disarming Peralta.

The chase which begins in the tavern has Zorro (Buddy Van Horn) swing on a chandelier, run up the stairs, leap out a window onto a passing hay wagon, run across the cuartel and up the barracks stairs, swinging onto the stable roof and leaping over the cuartel wall onto the waiting Tornado. In a cost-saving measure, a bit of the chase scene through the cuartel was lifted from "Monastario Sets a Trap." (The top of actor Britt Lomond's head is visible during the sequence.) Obviously Lomond (Capitan Monastario) was long gone from the series by this time.

One minor mistake in this episode concerns the day-for-night shooting employed when Zorro has apprehended Peralta behind the tavern. One camera shot right in the middle of the sequence has the look of a bright sunny day, which it no doubt was when this was shot. However, the scene is supposedly occurring at night and all of the other scenes in the sequence are filmed in the murky day-for-night style.

One of the more intriguing gaffes occurs when Zorro leaps from a rooftop onto the back of Tornado. As he rides away, a hand that was holding the horse can be seen disappearing behind a wall. This would end up as a piece of stock footage to be used often. Stuntman Tap Canutt recounted the unseen difficulties in performing this particular stunt: "When you do this sort of stunt, you just don't want an assistant director yelling quiet on the set because the minute they yell for quiet and you have silence, a horse's ears perk up and nine out of ten times, he'll hear you coming and just as you're in the air he'll move to one side and you'll end up with a pratfall. But all of us hated to run down a wall and jump out to a horse, sometimes covering as much as ten feet when you leap out. For the stunt to work properly, you let your feet hit on both sides of the saddle to take the first impact before you drop to your butt. I would always use blinkers for the horse. I had three different sets and they all had eyes painted on them. They're very soft and fit over the horse's eyes. They come together with two steel loops and a pin is placed between them. You attach fish line to the pin and you pull the line over the horse's head between the ears and attach it to the reins which were set up high on the horse's neck. The minute you hit the saddle, you grab the reins which pulls the fish line which pulls the little pin out and the blinkers flop off and you ride away. You can't ride off on a horse that's blindfolded, because he'll go crazy!"

Behind the Scenes

> The hay wagon fire sequence was filmed at night.... One song is performed: "Zorro's Serenade" by Norman Foster and George Bruns.

EPISODE 25

"The Fox and the Coyote"

Filmed: December 9, 11–13 & 16–20, 1957; *Air Date*: March 27, 1958; *Director-Writer*: Norman Foster; *Cast*: Vinton Hayworth (Magistrado), George Lewis (Don Alejandro), Peter Adams (Capitan Toledano), Lance Fuller (Alarcon), Leonard Strong (Blind Man), Armand Alzamora (Figueroa).

The Magistrado is hatching another money-making scheme for the Eagle's cause. He tells the rancheros about a horse race which all may enter, including the lancers. A substantial purse will be given to the winner. The Magistrado also encourages the rancheros to bet on their favorite horse. This race will serve a dual purpose for the Magistrado: Not only does he stand a good chance of winning the purse because the Eagle is supplying them with the California champion race horse, but he will also be able to steal gunpowder from a relatively deserted cuartel for a large supply of weapons he has purchased. Don Diego suspects something, so Zorro investigates. A secret meeting of the Magistrado and his henchmen is held and Zorro learns of the plan to steal the gunpowder.

The next day, Diego gives Bernardo a note of warning for the commandante. Bernardo carefully plants the note on Garcia, who promptly loses it. When Capitan Toledano, Garcia and most of the lancers show up for the race, Diego realizes something has gone wrong. After the contest begins, a late entry appears—Zorro. He leads the commandante and his lancers across the countryside and back to the cuartel, arriving just in time to prevent two of the Magistrado's men from escaping with a wagonload of gunpowder.

Author's Notes

The main action of "The Fox and the Coyote" is the obstacle course horse race near the conclusion that by and large is very exciting. Occasionally the spell is broken when a close-up of an actor, such as Henry Calvin, reveals that he is obviously not riding a horse. But the master shots of the race, which were filmed at Albertson's Ranch, were well done.

Another scene, one which contains very little action, is the most memorable. It has Zorro quietly following the beggar–blind man through the plaza in order to discover the location of the Eagle's brood. As the blind man walks slowly to his rendezvous, he nervously glances over his shoulder and Zorro darts quickly into the shadows. It's filmed perfectly by Foster, as he uses light and shadows to create a heightened feeling of suspense. At one point, Zorro, who has ducked into an alleyway by the church, is in danger of being discovered as the result of a barking dog. With the blind man coming from one direction and the Magistrado coming from the other and their shadows looming large in the alleyway, it seems there is no escape for Zorro. Foster's use of lighting and shadow goes all the way back to his days as a B-film director of such fare as *Charlie Chan* and *Mr. Moto*. It works very effectively here.

Behind the Scenes

> A children's song performed in this episode, "The Fox and the Coyote," appeared on the Disney album *Songs About Zorro and Other TV Heroes* where it was credited to Norman Foster and George Bruns. The credit at the end of this episode goes to Gil George and Joe Dubin. The song was a paraphrase on "Arroz Con Leche."

EPISODE 26
"Adios Señor Magistrado"

Filmed: December 2, 4, 9–11, 13 & 16–20, 1957; *Air Date*: April 3, 1958; *Director*: Norman Foster; *Writer*: Bob Wehling; *Cast*: Vinton Hayworth (Magistrado), George Lewis (Don Alejandro), Peter Adams (Capitan Toledano), Lance Fuller (Alarcon), Leonard Strong (Blind Man), Armand Alzamora (Figueroa).

Capitan Toledano questions the two men who tried to steal the gunpowder but they keep their silence. Toledano confiscates the eagle feathers they are carrying. He is sure it is a code that he must break to get to the bottom of the plot against the people. Figueroa, the lancer in the Eagle's employ, passes word to the Magistrado that Toledano is getting suspicious. The Magistrado orders Figueroa to let the two men escape.

That night, Sgt. Garcia, in an effort to avoid a creditor who has stationed himself in front of the cuartel, tries to scale the back wall of the fortress. In the process, he recaptures the two prisoners who are trying to escape. The next day, word spreads that the two prisoners have died as a result of suicide by poison. Diego, who received this news from his father's doctor, is very suspicious.

That evening, Zorro pays a visit to the commandante. Before he can talk to Toledano, he is interrupted by the lancer Figueroa, who has some wine for the capitan. Zorro suspects it contains some of the same poison that killed the two prisoners. As he is about to make Figueroa confess, the lancers burst in and Figueroa escapes. After a brief scuffle, Zorro escapes, tracks down Figueroa and imprisons him in his secret cave.

The Magistrado calls a meeting of the rancheros and the commandante to discuss the incident with the prisoners. It is really a trap to frame the commandante. Zorro arrives unexpectedly with Figueroa in tow. He promptly forces the lancer to confess the Magistrado's part in all that has occurred in Los Angeles. The Magistrado pulls out his pistol and shoots Figueroa. A fierce sword fight follows with Zorro and Toledano fighting side by side. The Magistrado is killed and Zorro prevails to continue his fight against the Eagle.

Author's Notes

"Adios Señor Magistrado" was Norman Foster's swan song on *Zorro* and one of his best episodes. It was distinctive because it was one of the few stories that featured two separate appearances by Zorro. The typical formula on the series was to set up the plot for the first 20 minutes and then have Zorro appear sometime in the remaining five minutes. Any deviation from the usual course is always welcome.

The climactic duel (Zorro and the commandante) is one of the more technically complicated and elaborately filmed in the series. At two minutes in length, it is almost a minute and a half longer than the average fencing scene. The scene has the commandante (doubled by Buddy Van Horn) relegated to the background dueling on the stairs and Zorro fencing two villains (doubles Victor Paul and Albert Cavens) in the main action. Foster films some of the fencing with camera angles set low, looking up at the participants, which conveys the chaos and really puts the viewer in the thick of things. This is also the first instance of Zorro not just disarming an opponent but slashing him in the midsection presumably with intent to kill. Unfortunately Peter Adams (Capitan Toledano) appears to be very ill at ease in the fencing close-ups. He looks like a man who has never seen a sword before.

There is one scene which may have been something of a mistake. Zorro and Bernardo are observed together by Zorro's prisoner, Figueroa. He was a soldier who has spent enough time around the pueblo to know that Bernardo is Don Diego's manservant and also smart enough to put two and two together. Although Figueroa was later killed by the Magistrado, Zorro could not have known that would happen. It's interesting to note that in the original version of the script, the prisoner is blindfolded.

Behind the Scenes

There is another scene in which Zorro finds himself in a situation where he is forced to imitate someone's voice. (He did it last in "A Fair Trial.") In this case it is Capitan Toledano. It's a great imitation but unfortunately it's not Guy Williams. They simply used Peter Adams' own voice.... Fencer Al Cavens, who was also an actor, has a few very brief lines — his first since the premiere episode when he played the capitan of the ship that brought Diego back to California.... The bulldog stunt was shot at Albertson's Ranch.... There are a few brief scenes actually shot at night.... Vinton Hayworth went on to co-star as Gen. Schaeffer on TV's *I Dream of Jeannie* in the 1960s.

Following this episode, Norman Foster went on to direct Disney's *The Nine Lives of Elfego Baca*, which his son Robert remembers as something of a dud around the Foster house. It may also have been viewed in similar fashion at the Disney studios. Up until *Baca*, Foster had been something of a golden boy at the studio, what with his great success on *Davy Crockett* and *Zorro*. After *Baca*, Foster went on to direct Disney's *Hans Brinker, Or the Silver Skates* and the live action segments of *Von Drake in Spain* in 1962. He then left the studio and continued to work in both television and films.

8

The Eagle's Brood

Episode Guide, Part 2

EPISODE 27
"The Eagle's Brood"

Filmed: January 9, 10, 13–15 & 21, 1958; *Air Date*: April 10, 1958; *Director*: Charles Barton; *Writer*: Lowell Hawley; *Cast*: Peter Adams (Capitan Toledano), Suzanne Lloyd (Raquel Toledano), Michael Pate (Quintana), Peter Mamakos (Fuentes), Charles Korvin (Señor Varga), Don Diamond (Cpl. Reyes).

The plans of the Eagle are going well in all parts of California except Los Angeles, where Zorro has been able to thwart the Eagle's men at every turn. In an effort to sow the seeds of discontent, Señors Quintana and Fuentes are sent by the Eagle to Los Angeles.

Meanwhile, Capitan Toledano is transferred to San Diego while his wife stays in Los Angeles. Before leaving, he receives word that gunpowder stolen from one of the presidios may be on its way to Los Angeles. Toledano orders Garcia, who is once again in charge, to keep his eye out for the missing gunpowder.

Quintana and Fuentes arrive in the pueblo posing as the new owners of the inn. Garcia wastes no time trying to ingratiate himself to the newcomers. The possibility of a free meal and wine is always foremost in the Sergeant's mind.

A courier arrives with a message for the commandante. Señora Toledano accepts the message and inexplicably replaces the letter with one of her own. She then passes it on to the temporary commandante — Garcia. Don Diego is visiting with Garcia as he reads the letters. It seems the gunpowder has been recovered. Diego is suspicious, noticing that the color of the ink in the letter is different from that of the envelope. This is not what Garcia wants to hear so it is left to Zorro to keep a watchful eye on the road to Los Angeles.

As Bernardo and Zorro wait outside of Los Angeles, a wagonload of hay escorted by an armed Fuentes can be seen heading for Los Angeles. Zorro investigates. After disarming Fuentes, he finds what he is looking for under the hay — the missing gunpowder. Just then, Garcia and a group of lancers appear in the distance and Zorro is forced to ride off. Garcia is led to believe that it is a wagonload of wine and so he escorts his "friend" Fuentes and his precious cargo back to Los Angeles.

Zorro and Bernardo arrive at the pueblo in time to see the kegs being loaded

112

into the wine cellar. Zorro makes his way into the cellar, overcomes one of the guards and passes the kegs of gunpowder out the window to Bernardo as they come down the ramp. Zorro now has the gunpowder and Quintana has the wine. Once again the Fox has outsmarted the Eagle.

Author's Note

The next arc of four episodes in the Eagle saga are directed and written by Charles Barton and Lowell Hawley, respectively. After the fast pace and serious nature of the Foster episodes, the tone lightens up and things move a little more leisurely. In "The Eagle's Brood," the Eagle, played by long-time screen villain Charles Korvin, makes his first appearance. Korvin recalled that the "work was pretty much the same as other studios but it was enjoyable working with that particular company of actors. It was a fun show. Guy Williams and I got along very well together. I thought he was very good for that role. He was also one of the most charming men, great fun to be with. He and I used to cook together." Korvin also supplied the voice of the Red Baron in the Lufthansa Airlines commercials in the 1970s.

Michael Pate, also a veteran heavy, played one of the Eagle's henchmen. Pate remembered, "I was simply trying to play my expected type of villain (not too heavy, not too light). In those days I used to do two dozen or more TV shows a year. The *Zorro* episodes weren't necessarily memorable except that I took my young son Christopher onto the set one day and both Guy and Henry Calvin were very kind to the youngster and later sent signed photographs to him."

This is not one of Zorro's more exciting adventures, as there was no swordplay and very little action in general. Writer Lowell Hawley expressed the feeling that "once in a while we wanted to have Zorro use his wits and intelligence rather than constantly resort to swordplay to defeat the villains." The studio must have realized they had a less than exciting tale on their hands when they put together the coming attraction clip for this episode. It contains a piece of fencing footage from the second episode of the series, "Zorro's Secret Passage."

The "action" of the episode included Zorro loading barrels of gunpowder from a wine cellar onto an ox cart with Bernardo's help. That, coupled with an earlier scene of Zorro intercepting the gunpowder and using his whip to disarm one of the heavies, is the extent of the excitement. The odd aspect of the wine cellar scene is that stunt man Buddy Van Horn doubles for Guy Williams. When a stuntman stands in for a star, it is usually because there is some danger involved. It appears that the only peril here was the risk of lower back injury.

Behind the Scenes

This episode introduces a new outfit for Don Diego. It consists of the typical Spanish-style jacket and pants. However, the tie, shirt, hat and gloves, are all black. There is a reason for this which will become evident in the next episode....

The location work was filmed on the lower flat of the Berry Ranch.... Character actor X Brands, who went on to play Jock Mahoney's sidekick in *Yancy Derringer,* has a small part as a courier.... Carl Pitti doubles as Zorro for the bullwhip sequence.

Episode 28

"Zorro by Proxy"

Filmed: January 8–10, 13–16, 21 & 22, 1958; *Air Date*: April 17, 1958; *Director*: Charles Barton; *Writer*: Lowell Hawley; *Cast*: Suzanne Lloyd (Señora Toledano), Michael Pate (Quintana), Peter Mamakos (Fuentes), Don Diamond (Cpl. Reyes).

Señora Toledano makes her way to the inn and presents Quintana with an eagle's feather. Shocked to learn that the wife of the commandante is involved in the Eagle's plot, he reluctantly agrees to take orders directly from her. Quintana explains that the gunpowder they stole is missing and they suspect Zorro. Señora Toledana gives the men 24 hours to find the gunpowder. She also enlists the help of Sgt. Garcia in the search.

As Zorro and Bernardo are hiding the gunpowder outside of Los Angeles, the Sergeant and his men appear on the horizon. Zorro sends Tornado in the soldiers' direction in an effort to lead them away. However, in a stroke of luck, Sgt. Garcia captures the black stallion and heads back to the pueblo with his prize.

Diego arrives in Los Angeles to check on Tornado and to question Señora Toledano about the letter she received in which the ink was different. She thinks that Diego is getting close to the truth and begins to formulate a plan with Quintana and Fuentes to get rid of him. The Señora believes that if they falsely accuse Diego of being Zorro and jail him, the real Zorro will try to rescue him. They will then capture him and get their gunpowder back. Garcia, knowing nothing of the gunpowder, agrees to go along with the scheme if it means the capture of Zorro.

The plan is carried out and Diego is imprisoned, and to escape he must use all his cunning. As Tornado fetches the sleeping Garcia's cell keys, Diego fashions a crude Zorro costume out of his cell blanket in an effort to fool the Sergeant. Before Zorro escapes, he tells Garcia where he can find the stolen gunpowder, making the Sergeant a hero for the day.

Author's Notes

"Zorro by Proxy" is a sluggish entry not helped terribly by Charles Barton's too light-hearted direction. If Barton has a failing, it's his tendency to take a serious situation and remove the element of danger. In an early scene, Zorro and Bernardo are in the process of hiding the kegs of gunpowder they have taken from the Eagle's henchmen. Sgt. Garcia and his soldiers are hot on their trail so Zorro sends Tornado to lead Garcia on a wild goose chase. As Zorro observes the situation, he is chuckling at the Sergeant's predicament. Even though Zorro is something of a devil-may-care character, if he's not taking the potentially dangerous situation seriously, it diminishes the jeopardy and the excitement.

Sometimes the series did not play things for what they were worth. There is a scene where Diego visits Garcia and comes into contact with the captured Tornado. When the stallion recognizes his master, he comes to him. Incredibly, Diego openly gives hand signals to the horse, waving him away. Some of the Eagle's men see this and begin to suspect that the young don is more than he seems. Believe it or not, this was handled with a little more sense and style in the Dell Comics adaptation of the story. In issue #960, Diego is seen giving hand signals to Tornado but he is doing it surreptitiously. His tight situation is humorous yet it is handled in a realistic manner.

The reason for Diego's new outfit (mostly black, introduced in the previous episode) was to set up the climax here when Diego is jailed and forced to make his own Zorro costume. When one already has a black hat, black shirt and black gloves, it makes it a bit easier to impersonate Zorro.

Behind the Scenes

> The outdoor shots of Zorro hiding the gunpowder were filmed using the set built for the *Andy Burnett* mini series located on the back lot.

EPISODE 29
"Quintana Makes a Choice"

Filmed: January 17, 20–24, 1958; *Air Date*: April 24, 1958; *Director*: Charles Barton; *Writer*: Lowell Hawley; *Cast*: Suzanne Lloyd (Señora Toledano), Michael Pate (Quintana), Peter Mamakos (Fuentes), Don Diamond (Cpl. Reyes).

While attempting to shoot a bear that has wandered into the cuartel, the lancer's muskets misfire. Sgt. Garcia discovers that the gunpowder is missing and charcoal has been substituted in its place. The Sergeant discusses the problem with Don Diego, who suggests questioning everyone in the cuartel. The last person Garcia interrogates is Señora Toledano, who does not appreciate the sergeant's questioning. The Señora, Quintana and Fuentes decide they must get rid of the fat sergeant.

In an attempt to locate the gunpowder, Zorro searches the wine cellar. Señora Toledano hears a noise coming from the cellar and she gets the drop on him. He quickly disarms the Señora and is about to learn of Garcia's fate when she begins screaming for help. Zorro escapes to the cuartel where, with the point of his sword, he is able to extract information from Cpl. Reyes about Garcia's dilemma. It seems Quintana and Fuentes have duped Garcia into believing they can return the gunpowder and take him on a rendezvous into the countryside. Unaware that he is about to be killed, Garcia waits for the gunpowder atop a boulder beside the road. As Fuentes takes aim at the sergeant, Zorro appears and foils their plan. In the confusion, Quintana mistakenly kills Fuentes and Zorro knocks the interfering Garcia unconscious. Quintana escapes.

Author's Notes

"Quintana Makes a Choice" is another bland Barton episode bogged down with the director's style of broad humor. The comedy involving Sgt. Garcia and Cpl. Reyes is bearable at best. This segment has a low-budget feel to it in that the plaza area is almost deserted. A tavern scene with Diego and Garcia includes only those two characters. This is in marked contrast to the previous Norman-Foster directed episodes in which these areas were teeming with activity. Perhaps to compensate for the less lavish look of the plaza scenes, the climax is shot on location at the upper flat of the Berry Ranch. The action includes a scene where Zorro is forced to use a broken tree limb to disarm the heavy. It is not one of his finer moments.

Behind the Scenes

Once again the coming attractions for this episode contain scenes which do not appear. These include a chase segment on horseback taken from "The Fox and the Coyote" and a stock shot of Zorro riding to the top of a hill and rearing Tornado.

EPISODE 30
"Zorro Lights a Fuse"

Filmed: January 23, 24 & 27–30, 1958; *Air Date*: May 1, 1958; *Director*: Charles Barton; *Writer*: Lowell Hawley; *Cast*: Suzanne Lloyd (Señora Toledano), Michael Pate (Quintant), Don Diamond (Cpl. Reyes), Ted de Corsica (Espinosa), Keith Richard & Mike Steele (Henchmen).

Señora Toledano receives word that she and her husband are to return to Spain. This obviously disturbs her as the ambitious Señora has big plans for her husband when the Eagle's forces take over California.

Meanwhile, Diego is determined to somehow convince Sgt. Garcia that Señora Toledano and Quintana are a danger to him. He decides to tell Garcia's fortune using cards and obliquely alert the sergeant to the danger around him.

Later that day, Señora Toledano meets with the Eagle's agents and tells them about the distribution of the gunpowder. More importantly, she informs them that in two days all of the presidios will be attacked simultaneously. Once again, the elimination of Sgt. Garcia is called for as his suspicions grow. The Señora's plan is to send Garcia on a wild goose chase to meet her husband on the road outside Los Angeles.

As Diego and Bernardo observe the situation from the plaza, Garcia leaves the cuartel. Quintana and another man prepare to follow but suddenly Garcia sees a gold cup standing alone in the market and abruptly returns to the cuartel. The cup standing alone was a death warning from Diego when he told Garcia's fortune.

Señora Toledano learns of Garcia's return and fears that the masquerade is up. That evening as she is packing to leave Los Angeles and join her husband, Quintana visits her. She tells him she has second thoughts about her involvement with the

Eagle. Quintana forces her to a winery outside of town. They rendezvous with a group of the Eagle's agents and they decide that the Señora's usefulness has ended. As they are about to kill her, Zorro strikes. A struggle ensues and Zorro and the Señora take refuge in the gunpowder room. As Quintana and company are about to break in, Zorro threatens to blow up the building. They back down and charge outside as Garcia and his lancers ride up and place them under arrest. Before Zorro escapes, he informs the sergeant that Señora Toledano was brought there against her will and wants only to join her husband and return to Spain.

Author's Notes

This series of four episodes concludes with "Zorro Lights a Fuse," the best of this lackluster group as a result of its dramatic climax. There is also some light comedy between Garcia and Cpl. Reyes but this time it doesn't interfere with the more serious tone of the plot. The one unbelievable aspect of the story occurs when Señora Toledano, who is part of the Eagle's plot, suddenly realizes that what she is doing is wrong. Her sudden remorse rings false.

The episode is salvaged by one of the more dramatic moments of the series. As Zorro is about to close in on the Eagle's men, he sends Tornado off with his cape wrapped around his saddle horn. It's a sign to Bernardo that help is needed. As he ties the cape he says to Tornado, "This is it, boy, the whole future of California is at stake right here. Go get help. Go to Bernardo!" The climax filmed inside the winery is exciting as Barton uses light and shadows to create a conspiratorial atmosphere that heightens the mood.

A few notes regarding the set: The interior of the winery was actually the interior of the tavern redecorated. The exterior of the San Gabriel Winery (as it is called in this episode) was located at the end of the Zorro set on the back lot. It was at the right angle of Zorro Street and Western Street. It can be seen under various names in *Elfego Baca* and *Texas John Slaughter*.

EPISODE 31

"The Man with the Whip"

Filmed: January 31, February 3–6 & 19, 1958; *Air Date*: May 8, 1958; *Director*: Charles Lamont; *Writer*: N.B. Stone, Jr. *Cast*: Kent Taylor (Carlos Murietta), Jack Kruschen (José Mordante), Myrna Fahey (Maria), Steve Stevens (Don Rudolfo).

A new agent of the Eagle arrives in Los Angeles. He is Carlos Murietta and his first order of business is to join up with José Mordante, owner of the local tannery. The two men meet in Murietta's room at the Inn where they identify their allegiance to their mutual cause with eagle feathers. Murietta explains that to gain money for the Eagle's cause he has plundered the churches of Argentina for a fortune in gems. Chief among his prizes is the Cross of the Andes. Half of the gems are hidden in a box of boots to be delivered to the tannery and the rest will arrive with Murietta's brother, Pedro.

At the tavern, Don Diego sips wine while observing Don Rudolfo, a young man who is smitten with Maria, the barmaid. Murietta and Mordante enter the tavern and immediately Maria catches the eye of Murietta. As Murietta's flirtations with Maria become aggressive, Don Rudolfo becomes enraged and attempts to step in. One thing leads to another and Rudolfo challenges Murietta to a duel to be held the following morning. As Diego is a witness to the scene, Rudolfo asks him to be his second. Diego agrees and proposes a fencing lesson for the inexperienced youth at the de la Vega hacienda. After a brief lesson from Bernardo, it is painfully clear that Rudolfo stands little chance against the experienced Murietta. There is only one course of action for Diego—his alter ego must step in and deal with Murietta.

That evening, Zorro enters Murietta's room and confronts the bully. The two men cross swords and their duel rages throughout the tavern. In the process, Murietta loses his hat in which his eagle feather is hidden. Zorro retrieves it and learns more about his adversary than he anticipated. While disarming his foe, Zorro cuts Murietta's hand, forcing him to call of his duel with Rudolfo. Another battle is won in Zorro's war with the Eagle.

Author's Notes

Charles Lamont made his debut as a *Zorro* director with the next four episodes. Although all the action was filmed on the back lot and the look is sparse with a bare minimum of extras, these episodes are some of the best of the series.

"The Man with the Whip" is Kent Taylor, perhaps best known to television fans as the star of the *Boston Blackie* TV series. Taylor brings a kind of world-weary soldier of fortune attitude to the role and he's very good.

As is often the case, the high point is the fencing; this is one of Fred Caven's best-choreographed duels of the series. With Taylor being doubled by Al Cavens, the swordplay begins in a darkened candlelit bedroom at the inn. With shadows on the wall, it progresses into the hallway, down the stairs and into the main tavern area. The action moves quickly with William Lava providing an exciting score (using some of the same musical selections that appeared in the premiere episode). There's also some great theatrics as Zorro disarms his foe and sends his blade sailing across the room into the tavern wall where it sticks.

Steve Stevens got the part of Don Rudolfo because Charlie Lamont remembered him from the *Annette* serial he directed for *The Mickey Mouse Club*. Stevens almost lost the role when he showed up at the studio and appeared to Lamont to have grown too tall. It seems that Stevens, believing the part required an actor of a certain stature had put lifts in his shoes. When Lamont told him they wanted a shorter actor, Stevens quickly stepped out of his shoes and got the part.

Stevens recalled his preparation for the role. "I had not really seen the script yet but for three and a half months they had me take fencing lessons from Fred Cavens and I got to be pretty good. Then I get the script and I find out that I really didn't need to learn any of that stuff. I was disappointed because I thought I was going to be a swashbuckler. Actually, I had only one small fencing scene and the irony was I was supposed to be inept but that's how thorough the studio was."

Stevens describes one time he was lucky to be working with a director who had a sense of humor. "There is a scene where I smack Kent Taylor across the face with a glove and challenge him to a duel. Because his back was to the camera, no one could see his nose twitching, which cracked me up. So I yelled 'cut.' There was dead silence on the set. I thought, 'Oh my God, no actor ever yells cut.' So Charlie Lamont walks up to me and takes off my hat and takes my glove and puts the hat on his head and takes me by the hand and walks me over to his chair and sits me down and then goes back and stands next to Guy Williams and Kent Taylor and looks over at me and says, 'Whenever you're ready, Mr. Director.' It broke the tension and he did it with a lot of fun and warmth. I'll always remember that."

Of his co-star, Guy Williams, Stevens observed, "Out of all the actors I worked with, Guy was the most charming and caring actor anybody could work with. When you came on the set he'd make you feel at home. He reminded me of someone who would have fit in very well with the Hollywood of the '20s and '30s."

Behind the Scenes

> Nestor Paiva returns as the innkeeper and Myrna Fahey also reprises her role as Maria the waitress, a role she last played in episode #16, "Slaves of the Eagle...." There is a song from Don Diego, "Quién Sabe" by Tom Adair and Buddy Baker. Although Williams took guitar lessons from Vicente Gomez, it's clear, judging by his hand movements, that he's a little off tempo, while trying to fake it. Bill Lee dubs his voice.... Dave Kashner is the whip double for Kent Taylor.

EPISODE 32
"The Cross of the Andes"

Filmed: January 31, February 4–7, 10–12, 14, 17–20 & 24, 1958; *Air Date*: May 15, 1958; *Director*: Charles Lamont; *Writer*: N.B. Stone, Jr.; *Cast*: Kent Taylor (Carlos Murietta), Jack Kruschen (José Mordante), Mary Wickes (Dolores Bastinado), Don Diamond (Cpl. Reyes), Bobby Crawford (Pogo).

Dolores Bastinado and her brother Pogo arrive from San Pedro with a shipment of boots for Carlos Murietta to be delivered to the tannery. Sgt. Garcia meets the Señorita and becomes very interested when he learns she owns a large hacienda. He does his best to impress her because he would like nothing better than to retire from the Army and become a wealthy haciendado.

Later that morning, when Don Diego learns that an old man named Pasquale has been mistreated by José Mordante, the tannery owner, he rides to the tannery and lodges a protest. Diego gets nowhere with his objections but he does notice the box of boots from Argentina that Señorita Bastinado has delivered.

When darkness covers the Pueblo, Diego decides to search Murietta's room as

Zorro while Bernardo is sent to the tannery to investigate. During his search, Zorro discovers the Cross of the Andes, a priceless artifact. As he continues searching, Murietta enters but Zorro disposes of him.

At the tannery, Bernardo discovers a false bottom in the box of boots. As he uncovers a fortune in gems, he is knocked unconscious by Mordante, who then hides the gems in the tannery well. He is about to toss Bernardo into the well when Zorro enters. In the ensuing struggle, Mordante is killed. While Zorro and Bernardo search the now empty boot box, they are interrupted by an unidentified rider and quickly make their escape. They will have to find the jewels another day.

Author's Notes

"The Cross of the Andes" is another good episode with a different type of action climax. There are some funny moments as well, particularly when Sgt. Garcia tries to woo Señorita Bastinado. When the sergeant is having lunch with the señorita, he makes a point of how important the virtue of honesty is to him. All the while, he is lying about his military record and his rank. When Cpl. Reyes blows the Sergeant's cover over a debt that Garcia owes him, the two soldiers engage in a simple, verbal comedy routine over who owes whom what. There's also an amusing song and dance number that takes place when Garcia tries to teach Reyes how to dance. Long-time movie heavy Richard Reeves makes a cameo appearance as the sentry who discovers the two dancing together. His double take is very funny.

The quarterstave action between Zorro and Mordante is well choreographed by Fred Cavens, who also doubles as Mordante. The struggle moves throughout the tannery with Zorro nearly being backed into the tannery well. Guy Williams handles his own portion of the quarterstave combat with the same skill and style that he exhibits in his sword work. The climax of the fight features one of the more violent scenes in the series. During the action, Mordante is hurled backward into a spike jutting from a post where he is impaled and then hangs limp. The quarterstave bout is another example of how the writers tried to feature Zorro in some action without using his sword. With the exception of "The Secret of the Sierra" knife fight it was the only time that an alternate type of action was as exciting as the swordplay.

The original draft of the quarterstave scene was a little different from what finally aired. It had Mordante breaking Zorro's sword with a pickaxe and exclaiming:

> [To Bernardo]: You serve two masters, eh, my silent friend? Or are the two one and the same? [To Zorro]: And so ends your career as Zorro ... [mock bow] Don Diego De la Vega.

This script must have been changed at the last minute, because the *TV Guide* synopsis referred to the unmasking of Zorro, as did the previous week's coming attraction.

Peter Ellenshaw provides some of his excellent matte work, creating the entire exterior and surrounding area of Mordante's tannery. Ellenshaw's matte paintings seem to work perfectly on a series like *Zorro*. They look realistic yet at the same time have a kind of fantasy appearance that might be found in a comic book.

As in "The Eagle's Brood," Buddy Van Horn seems to be doubling Guy Williams for no apparent reason. When Zorro is searching the room of Murietta (which basically consists of coming through a window, walking across the room, walking through a doorway and searching some drawers), Van Horn doubles about one-half the "action." In conjunction with this scene there is also a very interesting special effect when Zorro signals to Bernardo by waving a lighted candle and making the sign of the Z with the flame. It's done very stylishly with animation.

Behind the Scenes

> Bobby Crawford is the brother of *The Rifleman*'s Johnny Crawford.... A brief
> song "1,2,3 Glide" (uncredited), is performed by Henry Calvin.

EPISODE 33

"The Deadly Bolas"

Filmed: February 10–14, 17–21, 24, March 26 & 27, 1958; *Air Date*: May 22, 1958; *Director*: Charles Lamont; *Writer*: N.B. Stone, Jr; *Cast*: Kent Taylor (Carlos Murietta), Mary Wickes (Dolores Bastinado), Don Diamond (Cpl. Reyes), Paul Picerni (Pedro Murietta), Martin Garralaga (Padre Lucien).

To get a positive identification of the Cross of the Andes, Diego rides to the mission to check with the Padre to see if it has indeed been stolen. The Padre confirms Diego's suspicions and adds that the South American churches have been plundered of a fortune in jewels. Because he doesn't know the location of the stolen gems, Diego realizes that he must wait for Carlos Murietta to make the first move.

When Diego arrives back at the de la Vega hacienda, he finds Sgt. Garcia. In typical Garcia fashion, he is beating around the bush attempting to convince Diego to sponsor a party for Señorita Bastinado. Diego agrees to help and the party is set for that evening. The sole purpose of the affair is for Sgt. Garcia to ingratiate himself with the señorita and her large hacienda.

That evening, as Diego and Bernardo sit in the tavern and await the guest of honor, they overhear Señor Murietta's conversation with Garcia. Murietta is complaining of the break-in at the tannery the previous night. Upon hearing this, Diego decides to leave the party to search the tannery once again. Garcia pleads with him to stay. Diego relents and sends Bernardo in the disguise of Zorro to investigate.

Pedro Murietta, Carlos' brother, arrives in Los Angeles with the remainder of the stolen gems. Carlos relates his misfortune concerning his missing jewels. They decide to leave and search the tannery thoroughly. Diego notices their movement and decides it is time for the real Zorro to step in.

When the two brothers arrive at the tannery, they catch Bernardo red-handed and try to make him talk, thinking he is the real Zorro. Just then the real Fox strikes and disarms both men after a flurry of swordplay. The two agents of the Eagle are defeated but the gems are still missing.

Author's Notes

"The Deadly Bolas" opens with an excellent example of creative cost cutting. By combining stock footage from "Presenting Señor Zorro" and "The Secret of the Sierra," Diego and Bernado are seen riding through the countryside toward the mission. When they arrive, the exterior of the mission is actually just one of the small corners of the back lot *Zorro* set. Through the use of stock footage, the studio saved money by not having to go on location for this episode.

However, there are times when stock footage is employed less successfully. The footage in question occurs after Bernardo puts on Zorro's disguise in the secret room. The next scene is a piece of stock film that was used many times in the series: Buddy Van Horn as Zorro mounting Tornado and heading out of the secret cave and riding across the plains. The basic reason this fails is because Van Horn was physically much different in appearance from Gene Sheldon (Bernardo). Also, anybody who had watched the series with any consistency would have known this footage to signify that the real Zorro was riding. This was a cost-saving device that simply did not work.

Bernardo gets a chance to operate on his own when he dons the disguise of Zorro and searches Señor Mordante's tannery. This is the second time in the series that Bernardo is called upon to impersonate the Fox and it's in situations like this that Bernardo's value as the "sidekick" is apparent. He is an integral part of the team. He's not as involved in the physical aspect of defeating the villains as Robin is to Batman or Tonto to the Lone Ranger, but he's always there when Zorro needs him, whether it's covertly delivering a message or confusing those who would try to discover Diego's secret identity.

The episode concludes with another fast-moving fencing scene where Zorro duels both the Murietta brothers at once. They are doubled by Fred and Al Cavens. The art of fencing two people simultaneously is not easy, as the hero must keep both his adversaries occupied. Williams carries it off well although he and Al Cavens engage in the bulk of the swordplay.

Behind the Scenes

Carlos Murietta's brother, called Pedro in the episode, is listed as "Pietro" in the credits.... The song that Diego is playing on his guitar at Garcia's party is the one he sang in "The Man with the Whip," "Quién Sabe".... Paul Picerni went on to co-star in *The Untouchables* with Robert Stack.... Dave Kashner handles the bullwhip and bolas for the Murietta brothers.

EPISODE 34
"The Well of Death"

Filmed: February 10, 11, 13, 14 & 17–20, 1958; *Air Date*: May 29, 1958; *Director*: Charles Lamont; *Writer*: N.B. Stone, Jr.; *Cast*: Kent Taylor (Carlos Murietta), Mary Wickes

(Dolores Bastinado), Paul Picerni (Pedro Murietta), Bobby Crawford (Pogo), Don Diamond (Cpl. Reyes), Martin Garralaga (Padre Lucien).

The Murietta brothers hatch a plot to recover their missing gems. They will hide their next shipment of valuables in the tannery with the hope that Zorro will attempt to steal them. They will then capture Zorro and force him to reveal the whereabouts of the missing valuables. Meanwhile, Pogo Bastinado arrives in Los Angeles with the new box of boots (containing the hidden gems) for the Mariettas. Pogo informs the brothers of his delivery and they decide to accompany the boy to the tannery.

Searching the tannery at that moment is Don Diego, who believes that the gems must still be there. Bernardo, who is acting as lookout, sees the Muriettas approaching with their wagon and rides to warn Diego. The two men take refuge by the side of the road and spot the box of boots. Diego guesses it's another shipment of stolen gems and decides to let Sgt. Garcia play the role of hero to put him into the good graces of Dolores Bastinado.

Back at the tannery, the box of boots accidentally breaks apart and the jewels scatter for Pogo to see. Realizing the boy may reveal their secret; the Muriettas tie him up and put him in a closet. Acting upon Diego's information, Garcia arrives to investigate and stumbles upon the jewels. As the brothers attempt to push Garcia into the well, Zorro arrives and he and the sergeant fight side by side. During the melee, Pogo frees himself but falls into the well. He prevents certain death by grabbing onto a rope. At the end of the rope is the original cache of stolen gems. When the dust finally clears, one Murietta is dead but the other gets the drop on Garcia and Zorro. He escapes with the jewels only to be captured by Zorro and put into the sergeant's custody. Garcia is also given the glory of returning the plundered valuables to the church.

Author's Notes

"The Well of Death" rounds out director Lamont's quintet of episodes and it's the weakest in the set. The first problem occurs as a result of the coming attractions for this segment. There is a scene in which Pogo falls into a well away from the outstretched hands of Sgt. Garcia. Garcia's expression seems to indicate that the boy has fallen to his death. However, Pogo yells and has saved himself by grabbing onto a rope hanging in the well. Because the coming attraction showed the entire scene, the suspense is dissipated rather than heightened. Disney, sensitive to the fact that the audience for the show was largely made up of children, didn't want to use the possible death of a child as a lure to watch the show.

Sgt. Garcia is allowed to show some intelligence (with the help of Don Diego) for the first time. He puts enough clues together to question the Murietta brothers regarding the suspicious activity at the tannery. It's rather out of character for the sergeant but a refreshing change.

Garcia and Zorro also have their first opportunity to fight side by side. Unfortunately the fencing action is awkward and half-hearted as the two heroes and the Murietta brothers attempt to conduct swordplay in the small tannery. Zorro is actually relegated to the background as Garcia's sword work takes center stage. For once it's Garcia who get to be the hero.

A curious and underwritten aspect of the script is Carlos Murietta's reaction to his brother's death. Even though Carlos is trying to escape, he shows no emotion whatsoever regarding his brother's demise. Adventure series like *Zorro* are not too big on emotional sensitivity but judging from the friendly greeting the two brothers gave one another in "The Deadly Bolos," it seems somewhat inconsistent that no sorrow was exhibited.

The climax has Zorro (Buddy Van Horn) chasing Carlos on horseback and leaping on top of him and knocking him from the saddle (a bulldog stunt). Van Horn stated that his kind of stunt was not something you could rehearse. "You get somebody that knows how to work with you and you go do it. It's a timing thing; you've got to prepare a spot, soften the ground and know where the camera is and hit your marks at the right time. When possible you try to do them on a slope so you're rolling away from things." The entire chase, which appeared to cover a rather large area, was actually filmed on the back lot on the relatively small woodland set. With the help of a few timely edits, it comes off successfully.

The majority of these four episodes, even the few scenes that take place outside the tannery, were shot mostly on a soundstage. This is fairly unusual for the series because most scenes that were supposed to take place outdoors were filmed outdoors, with the exception of the de la Vega patio which was a permanent Soundstage 3 set.

The final scene has a jealous Garcia chasing Cpl. Reyes through the quartel. Garcia is angry because it seems that Señorita Bastinado prefers the corporal to him. The sight of Garcia slowly walking towards a terrified Reyes is very funny and reminiscent of the Laurel and Hardy comedies.

Behind the Scenes

> Once again Fred and Al Cavens doubled for the Murietta Brothers.... Kent Taylor followed this appearance by starring in his own series, "Rough Riders," in 1958 and '59.

EPISODE 35

"The Tightening Noose"

Filmed: February 24, 26–27, March 4–7, 11, 24, 26 & 27, 1958; *Air Date*: June 5, 1958; *Director*: Charles Barton; *Writers*: Bob Wehling, Lowell Hawley; *Cast*: Charles Korvin (José de Varga/The Eagle), Jay Novello (Juan Greco), Jonathan Hole (Don Alfredo), George Lewis (Don Alejandro), Don Diamond (Cpl. Reyes).

Don Diego and Don Alejandro are trying to convince a neighbor, Don Alfredo, to sign an oath. This pledge concerns a standing army made up of 50 other dons who stand ready to defend California in case of attack from within or without. Don Alfredo reluctantly signs and Don Alejandro heads for Monterey to obtain the governor's approval. Don Diego places the list of dons in the library for safekeeping.

Later that same day, Diego receives word form Sgt. Garcia that José Sebastian de Varga, the new Administrado, will soon arrive in Los Angeles; he will stay at the de la Vega hacienda while his house in the pueblo is readied. Diego becomes extremely upset and literally chases Garcia from the house. Bernardo has overheard the entire exchange and calms Diego, explaining that while Varga is there they can keep an eye on him. Since they suspect him to be an agent of the Eagle, this will be to their advantage.

When Varga and his man Juan Greco arrive, Diego greets them with respect and good cheer which confuses Garcia, who recalled Diego's earlier reaction. After dinner the two visitors enter the library, leaving Varga's satchel on a chair in the sala. Diego and Bernardo head for the secret passage to listen in. It seems that Varga knows of the oath and is searching the library for the list of dons who signed it. Diego retrieves the satchel and finds almost what he expects— eagle feathers. But they are *not* clipped.

As the two men's search intensifies, Diego decides to let Zorro step in. Just as Greco comes upon a loose stone on the fireplace, Zorro enters from the secret passage, snatches the list from Greco and ties the two men up. Zorro then steps out of the library into the sala and right into Sgt. Garcia's path. The sergeant yells for help and the lancers appear and chase Zorro through the hacienda. Zorro makes his way to Diego's room where he quickly throws off his costume and puts on the dressing gown of Diego. As the lancers break in, Diego yells and points out the window as a caped figure rides away in the distance. Once the rider is out of range, the mask is removed to reveal Bernardo.

The next day, when Varga and Greco are in Los Angeles, Diego comes across a piece of evidence which proves that his pompous houseguest Señor Varga is in fact the Eagle. A showdown between the two men is imminent.

Author's Notes

"The Tightening Noose" is the beginning of the end of the Eagle saga as Charles Barton returns to direct the last five episodes of the first season. For the first time the secret passage's entrances into the sala and the library are used. Since most of the action in these final episodes takes place in and around the hacienda, they come in handy. The secret passage entrance into the sala is through a silverware cabinet. In the library, it's through a large bookcase that slides open.

There is an exciting stunt by Buddy Van Horn as Zorro when he crashes through a window from the sala onto the patio. This is part of the hair-raising chase through the hacienda which includes both Guy Williams and Van Horn. Barton does a good job keeping Zorro just one step ahead of the soldiers as he makes his way to Diego's rooms. It's another situation where it seems impossible for Zorro to escape. Yet, when he strips off his costume and points to the black garbed figure riding in the distance, it all seems to come together very plausibly.

Behind the Scenes

A stock shot of Zorro rearing his horse by a hillside, which is used in the coming attractions for "The Tightening Noose," is nowhere to be seen in the episode.

EPISODE 36
"The Sergeant Regrets"

Filmed: March 21, 24–27, 1958; *Air Date*: June 12, 1958; *Director*: Charles Barton; *Writers*: Lowell Hawley, Bob Wehling; *Cast*: Charles Korvin (Señor Varga/The Eagle), Herschel Bernardi (Manuel Hernandez), Ralph Clanton (George Brighton), Jonathan Hole (Don Alfredo), Don Diamond (Cpl. Reyes), Sid Cassel (Juan).

Señor Varga and one of his agents, Señor Hernandez, desperately try to learn the names of the men who signed the oath. They question Don Diego but get nowhere. While they are interrogating Diego, a stranger named George Brighton arrives. It is obvious that Brighton represents a country that wants to help finance the Eagle's cause. However, Brighton registers his uneasiness regarding the current situation in California.

Varga is now more desperate than ever to find the list. As Diego listens from the secret passage behind the library wall, Varga dupes Juan, a de la Vega servant, into alerting all the dons who signed the oath. He instructs Juan to tell them they must attend a secret meeting to be held by Don Alejandro that evening. Diego hears this and races up to his room and quickly writes a note to the dons about the impending trap. Since Diego is being watched by lancers and is not allowed to move freely throughout the house, he summons Sgt. Garcia to give the note to Juan.

As Garcia makes his way to the patio, he is sidetracked by a leg of lamb. When Diego learns that Garcia has failed, it is left to Zorro to warn the rancheros. Don Alfredo, who was not warned in time, arrives for the meeting and falls into the hands of Varga and Hernandez, who attempt to force him to talk. Zorro, realizing that Alfredo is in danger, returns to the hacienda and frees him from Varga's clutches. While Zorro binds and gags the Eagle, Hernandez chases down the escaping Don Alfredo. This time Garcia comes to the rescue and in the ensuing struggle Hernandez falls on his own knife. Zorro observes what has happened and forgives his fat friend for failing in his role as a messenger.

Author's Notes

"The Sergeant Regrets" opens in a very promising fashion — a fencing match between Señor Varga and one of the lancers. This scene helps to establish Varga as an expert fencer and whets the appetite for the inevitable showdown with Zorro.

Another facet of Varga's personality is revealed in this episode: He is extremely excitable and high-strung — not particularly cunning or cool under pressure. This would be in keeping with the "Mussolini" model laid out by Lowell Hawley. This behavior also makes one wonder how a character so easily shook could find himself in a position to take over the Spanish provinces. On the other hand, it does play heavily to the "mad dictator," Mussolini influence.

There's more comedy than usual between Garcia and Reyes with the accent on subtle. One scene involves a discussion of the merits of a leg of mutton while the other concerns Reyes' desire to stand guard inside the hacienda as opposed to outside. As Garcia sits under a shade tree and sips a glass of wine, he explains to the corporal the overall hardships of being a soldier.

When the characters of a TV series suddenly act differently toward one another, it's a bit of a surprise. This happens when Diego asks Garcia to deliver a message for him. When Garcia fails in his task, Diego becomes enraged at Garcia in a way he never has before. He rips Garcia up one side and down the other. One can't help but feel sympathy for the befuddled sergeant. However, it seems that after 36 episodes, he had it coming. As with all television series there must be redemption for a continuing character and Garcia doesn't fail a second time. When Zorro tells him, "You're a good man, sergeant," it's Diego's way of apologizing.

Behind the Scenes

> Character actor Herschel Bernardi [TV's, *Arnie*, Broadway's *Fiddler on the Roof*] appears uncredited.... In the opening fencing scene, Al Cavens doubles for Varga and Victor Paul doubles for the lancer.

EPISODE 37

"The Eagle Leaves the Nest"

Filmed: February 24, 28, March 3–7, 11, 12 & 26, 1958; *Air Date*: June 19, 1958; *Director*: Charles Barton; *Writers*: Lowell Hawley, Bob Wehling; *Cast*: Charles Korvin (Señor Varga/The Eagle) Jay Novello (Juan Greco), Don Diamond (Cpl. Reyes).

While Varga speaks to his aide, Greco, Don Diego stands in the secret passage listening. To his dismay, Diego hears Varga making plans to stay at the de la Vega hacienda permanently. When Diego returns to his room, Bernardo gives him a letter from his father that has just arrived. He learns that Don Alejandro's visit to Monterey has been a success and he will return in a few days. Diego is disturbed by the news because he knows that his father will fight Varga to the death to get him out of his house. He also knows he must devise a plan to rid the hacienda of Señor Varga immediately.

As Diego and Bernardo brainstorm, they are interrupted by shouts coming from the patio. They observe a shaken, frightened Varga, who appears to be afraid to be alone. When the guards show themselves, Varga is greatly relieved. Diego has seen enough. He has found his houseguest's Achilles heel. Diego's first chore is to find a way to get Garcia and the lancers away from the hacienda. It's relatively simple as Diego plays on Garcia's greed. He tells the sergeant to think of the great tavern he could buy with the reward money for capturing Zorro. With that seed planted, Diego proceeds to inform Señor Varga of his plans to leave for Los Angeles that evening. "Sometimes," he tells Varga, "it is too lonely at the hacienda." Varga nervously agrees.

When night approaches, Zorro takes over. He overpowers a few of the guards and leaves them tied up in the stable. He then proceeds to lead the greedy Garcia and company on a wild goose chase. Once the sergeant and the lancers are far enough away, Zorro returns to exploit Señor Varga's fear. With the help of Bernardo's noise-maker, a piano that seems to play by itself and candle flames that extinguish for no reason, the Eagle decides to leave the nest for the safety of Los Angeles.

Author's Notes

"The Eagle Leaves the Nest" is probably the most unusual episode in the series. It's really a psychological drama in which there is almost no violence at all. To show Varga's fear, both the music of William Lava and the camera angles chosen by Charles Barton are very effective. The scene on the patio is shot from Diego's point of view. He is looking down at the hysterical Varga from his balcony. As Varga screams and runs back and forth on the patio, he presents a man out of control. Barton uses a crane shot with a wide-angle lens which exposes the loneliness and terror of Varga's situation. When this similar scene is replayed near the end of the episode, an echo is added to his screaming voice which increases his feeling of isolation. The entire atmosphere of this episode is different from any other.

Behind the Scenes

At one point, there is a song playing on a music box. The tune is "The Fox and the Coyote" from an earlier episode of the same name.

EPISODE 38
"Bernardo Faces Death"

Filmed: February 25, 26, March 10–13, 20–21, 1958; *Air Date*: June 26, 1958; *Director*: Charles Barton; *Writers*: Lowell Hawley, Bob Wehling; *Cast*: Charles Korvin (Señor Varga/The Eagle), Jay Novello (Juan Greco), George Lewis (Don Alejandro), Henry Rowland (Count Kolinko), Don Diamond (Cpl. Reyes); Richard Benedict (Blacksmith).

Not realizing that Señor Varga has moved to the pueblo, Count Kolinko, a bearded ambassador, arrives at the de la Vega hacienda to meet with him. Don Diego recognizes the man from his days at the University in Spain and immediately tries to probe him for information. It seems that the Count believes Diego is working with the Eagle and is only too eager to trade information with him. As Diego is about to learn something of importance, the newly returned Alejandro interrupts and the Count becomes wise to Diego's game.

Diego decides to ride into Los Angeles so that he and Bernardo can keep an eye on the comings and goings at Señor Varga's new home. They see men unloading crates—some large, some small. When no one is looking, Bernardo grabs a pot and as he and Diego study it they drop it and discover a cannonball inside. At this point, it's time for Zorro to take over. When the Fox makes his way into Varga's home, he overhears a conversation between Varga, Kolinko and Greco. Kolinko expresses his government's concern over the current situation in California and Greco explains that while they were bringing a cannon into the pueblo via a cart, a wheel broke.

Zorro carefully searches the hacienda and finds a room full of weapons—enough to furnish a revolt. Greco spies Zorro and a fight ensues between Zorro and a few of Varga's men. Zorro escapes and he and Bernardo go in search of the cannon. Remembering the conversation he overheard, Zorro heads for the blacksmith's shop—the logical place where a broken wheel could be repaired.

When they arrive, they find a blacksmith hard at work on the wheel. Zorro shows himself, and the smithy runs away. Zorro decides to blow up the cannon so no one can use it. As he and Bernardo prepare to set the fuse, Bernardo becomes trapped behind the cart when Zorro's back is turned. Inadvertently the fuse is lit and Zorro struggles to set his friend free. He releases Bernardo just in time as the cannon blows. The force of the explosion throws Bernardo out the window.

The blacksmith returns with Señor Varga and Greco, who find only a ripped piece of cape and a part of a sword. Varga believes that the destruction of the cannon for the life of Zorro is a fair exchange. When the three men leave, Bernardo returns to search for Zorro, who he finds shaken but alive. Zorro plans to make his presence known to the Eagle again soon.

Author's Notes

"Bernardo Faces Death" contains what may be the single most exciting scene in the entire series. It's a perfect blending of action and music. It occurs when Zorro and Bernardo are preparing to blow up the cannon. When Bernardo becomes pinned between an ox-cart and ceiling support and the ignited gunpowder trail is heading for the loaded cannon, it's a race against time that they barely win. The stunt that has Bernardo being blown out the window has a look to it that is unforgettable, comical but dangerous at the same time.

This entire scene is unusual because much of their predicament is Zorro's fault. He chases the blacksmith out before he has a chance to repair the ox-cart wheel. If the ox-cart was repaired, then he and Bernardo could move the cannon rather than blow it up. And when Bernardo becomes trapped, it is Zorro who accidentally drops the ember onto the gunpowder which almost kills the two men.

All of this is very reminiscent of the Republic serials, but the writers missed their chance for a real cliffhanger. Rather than let Zorro's apparent death end the episode, it's learned that both he and Bernardo are alive before the teleplay concludes. However, it does give Zorro a chance to cut a burning Z into the door of the barn with a hot poker. It's an intriguing special effect done partially by animating Zorro's arm and hand holding a hot poker over an actual burning Z.

Behind the Scenes

> Stuntman Hal Needham, who appears as one of the Eagle's henchmen, became a director in the mid–1970's handling a number of Burt Reynolds films.... Lou Roberson doubles Bernardo for the explosion that sends him flying out the barn window.

EPISODE 39
"Day of Decision"

Filmed: March 13, 14, 17–21 & 24–27, 1958; *Air Date*: July 3, 1958; *Director*: Charles Barton; *Writers*: Bob Wehling, Lowell Hawley; *Cast*: Charles Korvin (Señor Varga/The Eagle), Jay Novello (Greco), Henry Rowland (Count Kolinko), George Lewis (Don Alejandro), Don Diamond (Cpl. Reyes).

In Los Angeles, Bernardo observes some troubling sights: Most of the lancers leave the pueblo with Sgt. Garcia as Señor Varga places the statue of an eagle in the window of his house. One by one as passersby spy the statue, they enter the house. Bernardo peers through a side gate and watches as men with muskets go through military exercises. He returns to the de la Vega hacienda and explains to Deigo what he has seen. As Diego is about to relay this information to his father, several of Varga's men burst in and take them to his hacienda where they are held captive. Varga's army gathers and storms the cuartel, overcoming the remaining soldiers. When Sgt. Garcia returns alone, he too is imprisoned with the de la Vegas and Bernardo.

Count Kolinko informs Señor Varga that he will be receiving no money for his cause until Don Alejandro's standing army of rancheros is disposed of. Varga becomes enraged. When he tries to strike a deal with Alejandro, he is turned down. However, Diego agrees to get the list of dons at the de la Vega hacienda in return for his freedom. Greco and one of Varga's men accompany Diego to the hacienda where Diego quickly disposes of them. When the battered Greco returns with news of what happened, Kolinko fears that Varga will never gain the control of California that he promised. When Kolinko decides to withdraw his promise of money, Varga becomes so angry that he fires a bullet into the Count's back and kills him.

Unbeknownst to Varga, Zorro has arrived and frees his father and friends, who promptly grab muskets and hold off Varga's men from inside the hacienda. Just as all appears lost, the army of dons arrives to fend off Varga's army. Finally Zorro stands face to face with Varga, the Eagle, sword in hand. After a brief sword fight, Varga yields. While trying to escape, he is shot by his own man, Greco, who has himself been wounded.

Don Alejandro has nothing but compliments for the bravery of Garcia and Bernardo. He also realizes that Diego left so that he could warn the other dons that they were needed. The Republic of California has escaped from the Eagle's clutches.

Author's Notes

The first season ends on an exciting note with "Day of Decision." Although this entire episode was filmed on the back lot, it looks as though Disney spared no expense regarding the almost non-stop action.

Everything builds to an exciting climax as an extremely ruthless side of Varga is shown: When one of his financial backers pulls out, Varga shoots him in the back. The viewer can't wait for him to get his comeuppance. The set-up for the scene is excellent — Zorro swings by rope across the cuartel and in the process rips down the flag of the Eagle. He throws the flag to the ground and stands with feet spread apart. As the soundtrack swells, he whips his cape over his arm, draws his sword and faces off against his archenemy. Unfortunately, the sword fight is a disappointment. It is neither a particularly well-staged or well-filmed fencing sequence. There is very little emotion. Zorro had struggled long and hard against this villain and there should have been some sign of that, some caustic dialogue between fencing phrases (similar to *The Adventures of Robin* [1938] and the *Mark of Zorro* [1940]) would have been appropriate. From previous episodes it's been made clear that Varga fancies himself a good swordsman. But in the course of their duel, it seems that Zorro is never tested by him. Zorro disarms Varga. If there was ever anyone who deserved the sign of the Z cut on him, it's this villain, but unfortunately it wasn't written into the script.

There is one major inconsistency in "Day of Decision": For all Varga knows, Zorro had been killed in the explosion at the blacksmith's shop in the previous episode. Yet when Zorro appears in the cuartel, Varga registers no surprise. It's as if the preceding incident had never occurred. Still, in all, this was a good episode and a satisfying conclusion to the first season.

Behind the Scenes

> Carl Pitti doubled Zorro's bullwhip scenes in this episode and Al Cavens handled the sword work for Charles Korvin ... Korvin went on to star in his own series in 1959, *Interpol Calling*.... This episode was also known as "The Eagle's Flight...." The remainder of the summer season saw the encore showing of the first 13 episodes of the Eagle Saga.

With shooting completed for the first season on March 27, Guy Williams went to New York for a three-week "working" vacation. He made some appearances at various department stores in connection with *Zorro* merchandising setups. He also appeared at a 7-Up® luncheon to sign autographs and chat with company executives. He then submitted to numerous interviews with some of the local TV columnists.

At this point it was clear that *Zorro* could be referred to as a success. Specifically, it was performing well in its time period, 8:00 P.M.* Its competition on CBS was rather weak with *Harbourmaster* starring Barry Sullivan, a show which was replaced

---

*In some areas it ran anywhere from 7:00 P.M. to 10:30 P.M. Thursday night.

at mid-season by *Richard Diamond, Private Detective*. The real competition was on NBC with the long-running *You Bet Your Life* featuring the inimitable Grouch Marx. *Zorro* started strongly against Groucho and closed the gap between the two shows at mid-season. They ran neck-and-neck throughout the winter and spring and finished the TV year in a virtual tie. When the 1958–59 season began, it was clear that Groucho's rapier-like wit was no match of *Zorro*'s cold steel and the comedian moved to 10:00 P.M. on Thursdays. *Richard Diamond* took a temporary vacation.

Being on ABC was something of a disadvantage for *Zorro* because of the young network's fewer affiliates, 149 versus 200 for CBS and approximately 180 for NBC. This made it difficult for ABC to come up with ratings winners. In some parts of the country, the two network shows opposite *Zorro* ran uncontested. In the 1957–58 season, ABC had only three shows in the top 20, all of which happened to be Westerns.

The other obstacle facing *Zorro* was its audience. Because it was primarily geared toward children, it was somewhat limited. Popular series such as *Gunsmoke, Tales of Wells Fargo* and *The Life and Legend of Wyatt Earp* were called "adult" Westerns because of their mature subject matter. Their fans also tended to be older than that of *Zorro* and less distracted by whatever new fad might come along. The drawback of *Zorro*'s young audience was the fickle nature of it. What it loves today, it may not care about tomorrow.

In the face of its network's shortcomings, *Zorro* still performed very well (finishing #31 overall), pulling in approximately 30 million viewers. Specifically, it scored an average rating of 24.8 which translates to about 10 million households. The Arbitron figure was higher at 27.9 which is approximately 11.5 million households. Although *Zorro* did not finish among the top 20 shows, it had very high visibility and even people who didn't watch the show became aware of the masked hero.

The popularity of the show was growing. When *Zorro* went on the air in October, the Disney Studios received 342 fan letters. By the following June, they were getting over 5,000 fan letters a month. In announcing an early renewal of its sponsorship for a second season, 7-Up® stated: "The fact that we have agreed to an extensive renewal of our contract ought to indicate quickly how we feel about *Zorro* as an advertising purchase."[1]

When Walt Disney saw the early *Zorro* rushes, he said, "I don't know if this new *Zorro* character will be a hit. It's just like going to bat: You close your eyes and swing. Then you hope and pray."[2] He needn't have worried. *Zorro* was catching on with kids nationwide and with the confidence of their sponsors to bolster them; the Disney Studio was looking forward to a big second season.

9

The Second Season
Welcome to Monterey (Episode Guide)

At the start of the 1958–59 television season, *Zorro* had a new crop of heroes to contend with for the hearts and minds of the youngsters and their parent's pocketbooks. Such stalwart good guys as Bat Masterson, Josh Randall (*Wanted — Dead or Alive*), Dan Troop (*Lawman*), Bill Longley (*The Texan*), Yancy Derringer, Steve Canyon, Lucas McCain (*The Rifleman*) et al. were hoping to unseat *Zorro* as the kids' new number one favorite. With that in mind, the Disney Studio felt that they couldn't stand pat and they went against the old axiom: "If it ain't broke, don't fix it." Although most of the changes were cosmetic and designed to keep the regular audience interested, there was one major alteration: the addition of some romance for Don Diego/Zorro.

Actress Jolene Brand joined the show as Anna Maria Verdugo, Zorro's love interest. This was an obvious attempt to broaden the series' appeal — specifically, to bring more teenagers and adults (especially women) into the show's audience. Brand, who came to acting after a series of successful beauty pageants, was working at Warner Bros. when "I was told they were looking for a girl to play the love interest for Zorro and that's when I went out to Disney to interview. The interview was like all the others, it scares the hell out of you. The fear helps you a little bit, it gets the adrenalin running so you're not a dead head at the interview. We sat around and chatted with the casting people and after that my agent sent over some film work that I had done. I also filmed a screen test with Guy. By the third call -back I met Bill Anderson and it was a go." Brand beat out 12 other young women for the role.

Brand recalled both Guy Williams and Walt Disney with affection. "Guy was a very sweet man. He made me feel comfortable. Walt could pop up anywhere. He would roam around that studio like it was his own back yard and we were his little Munchkins. I was always sort of stunned to see him, he was always going somewhere." Summing up her experience on nine episodes at the studio, she commented, "Working at Disney was special. Everybody there was a happy camper. Even the guard at the front gate was smiling."

Another modification was in the general format of the show. During the first season, the first 13 episodes dealt with Monastario while the remaining 26 concerned the Eagle. Now, a single theme was handled in anywhere from one to five episodes, but no more. Story editor Lowell Hawley was convinced that the 13-episode unit placed an unnatural restraint on the writer. Many good plots had to be rejected because, while they were exciting for five episodes, they couldn't be stretched for 13. At the time Hawley stated, "Now we play stories for what they're worth. If a writer has enough material for three, four or five episodes, we let it go at that. The result is bound to be faster paced, more varied stories."[1]

This also enabled the series to emphasize different facets such as humor, suspense, romance and sheer adventure within these groups of multiple episodes. However, the main thrust remained action-adventure. This new format also made it possible for the show to sign guest stars such as Cesar Romero, Everett Sloane, Patricia Medina, Jeff York, Richard Anderson and Perry Lopez. They might not have been available for a 13-week run.

Some of the minor tinkering saw Zorro temporarily trading in his sleek black stallion Tornado for a white one. The locale was moved north from Los Angeles to Monterey. The same outdoor *Zorro* set was used, redecorated by Marvin Davis and Hal Gausman. Fish netting and overturned rowboats gave it the look of a coastal fishing village. More trees were added, as was an archway over the narrow road between the tavern and the Magistrado's house. Merchant stands were set up behind the tavern. A matte painting of the pueblo by Peter Ellenshaw, used as an establishing shot at the opening of a number of the Monterey episodes, featured a panoramic view of the ocean and mountains in the background. Lowell Hawley didn't mince words when he commented on the locale switch: "It was pretty much Walt's idea and I felt it was something of a wasted effort. He got tired of the same Los Angeles scenery. I think we should have kept things consistent."

Directors Charles Lamont and Charlie Barton returned, but with Norman Foster gone from the series a directorial void needed to be filled. The studio hired one of the great action directors, William Witney, who in collaboration with John English directed many of the best Republic Pictures serials of the 1930s and 1940s. He also handled Roy Rogers best films of the late '40s and early '50s.

Also brought in to direct in the latter part of the second season was Hollingsworth Morse. Unlike the directors who preceded him, the bulk of Morse's work was spent in television. His career ran the gamut, from the *The Lone Ranger* to *Lassie* and later *Adam-12* and *The Dukes of Hazzard*. In all, approximately 2,000 television episodes bore his name. He directed 19 episodes of *Zorro* — more than any one else. Witney and Morse were two good additions to the series but Norman Foster's directorial style and enthusiasm for the characters would be missed.

The budget, at $2,725,000, was $473,000 less than the first season. It should be pointed out that the bulk of the difference in budget between the two seasons went to the construction of sets, the purchasing of props and the making of costumes for the premiere season. Producer Bill Anderson stated, "Walt never screamed about the budget but we did try to bring the show in a bit and pull the budget down. We certainly weren't getting from ABC what we were spending in the first year."

In this case, "bringing the show in a bit" meant less location shooting and more soundstage and back lot shooting. Although there was still a fair amount of location work, there would be no more episodes filmed entirely on location such as "Zorro

Rides to the Mission" and "The Ghost of the Mission." The series also resorted, albeit briefly, to the dubious practice of filming outdoor scenes on a soundstage. The back lot woodland area was also used a great deal more than in the previous season. This was a relatively small plot of land located on the Alameda berm consisting of large trees, long grass, shrubs, papier maché boulders and a small pond. All of this worked to give the impression that the action was taking place in the wilderness.

The basic "nuts and bolts" of the show, however, remained the same. There was still plenty of action as well as the occasional comedy and music. To someone watching the show in the 1950's or to the millions of kids who tuned in each week, it probably seemed like business as usual.

EPISODE 40

"Welcome to Monterey"

Filmed: June 16–19 & 23–27, 1958; *Air Date*: October 9, 1958; *Director*: William Witney; *Writer*: Lowell Hawley; *Cast*: Eduard Franz (Don Gregorio Verdugo), Jolene Brand (Anna Maria Verdugo), Carlos Romero (Serrano), Joseph Conway (Palomares), Lee Van Cleef (Castillo), Wolfe Barzell (Innkeeper).

Diego and Bernardo have traveled north to Monterey where they promptly take rooms at the inn. As Diego is about to settle in and relax, there is a knock at the door. Two armed bandits burst in and demand all of Diego's valuables. They take his watch and some pesos. However they want more — 17,000 pesos more. Before the situation comes to a head, the innkeeper interrupts the robbery and the bandits escape.

In the afternoon, Diego and Bernardo travel to the Verdugo hacienda where Diego meets Don Gregorio Verdugo, his beautiful daughter Anna Maria and a representative from Santa Cruz, Romero Serrano. Because California is being blockaded by foreign powers, Diego is there as Los Angeles' representative and as a potential investor in Verdugo's plan to bring a shipload of supplies to California. He is concerned that the bandits who robbed him knew the exact amount he was bringing to Monterey, something that only Verdugo could have known. Diego makes it clear that while he is not accusing Verdugo of anything, he is simply ensuring that an honest effort is being made with a reasonable chance of success. Angry words are exchanged between Anna Maria and Diego, leaving Diego's relationship with Verdugo precarious at best.

That evening, as Bernardo passes time in the tavern, he sees two men at the bar, one of whom seems to be holding Diego's stolen watch. When the two men leave, Bernardo follows. Diego returns to the tavern and is quickly taken aside by one of the men that Bernardo followed. Diego is informed that his servant is being held for a ransom of 17,000 pesos. Diego refuses to pay without proof that they hold Bernardo. He is told to stay in his room until proof is brought back.

As the messenger rides out he is followed by Zorro. The man arrives at the hideout where Bernardo is being guarded by his compadre. He takes Bernado's hat for proof and rides back to Monterey. Zorro makes his way into the guarded house and, after a struggle with the outlaw, knocks him unconscious. As Zorro unties Bernardo, a figure at the window fires a shot at Zorro but Bernardo pushes his friend out of the way. Zorro races outside with musket in hand and puts a bullet into the shoulder of the fleeing bandit. Zorro and his faithful servant head back to Monterey unaware of the adventures that will follow.

Author's Notes

Besides the introduction of the love interest Anna Maria, this episode is also notable for a particularly sadistic moment involving a robbery. The scene features the formidable screen villain Lee Van Cleef as a bandit and his attempt to rob Don Diego. When Diego hands over his leather purse filled with coins, the outlaw is not pleased. He proceeds to beat Diego with his purse, repeatedly smacking him across the face as his cohort holds a pistol to Bernardo's head. This is one of the few real violent moments in the entire run of the series mainly due to Van Cleef's convincing performance and director William Witney's flair for violent action.

The interplay between Diego and Bernardo also changes with this episode and remains altered for the remainder of the series. In an effort to inject more humor, the exchanges between the two men have an edge to them; there is more teasing involved. To illustrate the point, when Diego meets Anna Maria for the first time, Bernardo looks at her as she is walking away and then looks at Diego with a mischievous smile. He then twiddles his fingers at Diego as if to ask if there will be any romance. An annoyed Diego looks back at him and says, "No there will not be any [*and then twiddles his fingers imitating Bernardo*]. Out!" It's a funny scene and a different facet of the relationship from the first season.

The Don Diego character is also shifting further and further away from McCulley's original Diego as evidenced by an encounter which has him quietly threatening one of the bandits who has kidnapped Bernardo. It's a physical threat and it's rare to see Diego involved in this sort of the action, but it shows the Zorro side of his personality taking over. It also illustrates how strongly he feels about Bernardo.

When Zorro makes his first appearance in the new season, it is Buddy Van Horn who is leaping over the balcony and across the rooftops. It is also Van Horn who runs across the backs of three saddled horses and leaps onto the back of his own horse (the saddle almost slipping off). To show how some things never change, a similar stunt was preformed by Joe Yrigoyen in the Roy Rogers, Witney-directed *In Old Amarillo* (1951). Zorro is also forced to ride Diego's horse since Tornado is back in Los Angeles. Incidentally, the unanswered question involving Tornado is, who was caring for the horse while his master and Bernardo were in Monterey? Perhaps it is the old Indian shepherd who raised the colt when Diego was at the University in Spain (as mentioned in "Presenting Señor Zorro")

As expected from a Witney-directed episode, the action scenes are very good. While the fencing between Guy Williams and Lee Van Cleef is brief (it takes place in a cramped cabin set) the action surrounding it is very inventive. The excitement begins with a vicious struggle between Zorro (Buddy Van Horn) and Castillo (Van Cleef). At one point Zorro slides over a tabletop and tackles Castillo. This particular maneuver looks awkward and leaves Zorro in a vulnerable position. It's the only weak link in the sequence. More impressive is the stunt that occurs at the conclusion of the duel. Van Horn jumps up onto the edge of a table, forcing the opposite end up into Van Cleef's double's face, knocking him unconscious.

Also appearing in this episode was veteran character actor Carlos Romero. Romero loved working at the Disney studio. "When I did *Zorro* I felt I was in hog heaven because the actors were treated so well. Your dressing room was actually a living area; the whole tenor of the studio was delightful and they had the best commissary in Hollywood. You worked at Disney and you were happy as a hog because you knew you were going to get good food. I used to say if I could have any wish in the world it would be doing a Western at Disney for the rest of my life. It was a marvelous place to work."

Behind the Scenes

There were two small changes at the show's opening and one at the end. Guy Williams was now announced as the show's star, and the silhouette of the fox on the wall was eliminated. And as the credits rolled at the end of the episode, the lettering had been changed from plain block lettering to a pseudo–Gothic style. This was used for the entire second season.... One miscue has Zorro running out of the bandit's cabin with a rifle in his hand preparing to shoot a bandit. Upon close examination it's clear that Zorro is without his sword which he was wearing seconds earlier inside of the cabin.... Lowell Hawley receives his first screen credit as story editor with this episode.... An actor named Henry Delgado also tried out for the part of Romero Serrano. Delgado later changed his name to Darrow and went on to fame on *The High Chaparral*. Joseph Conway, who plays the part of Palomares, auditioned for the Romero role as well.... The interior of the Verdugo home is the de la Vega hacienda redressed.... This is the only episode in which Henry Calvin does not appear.

EPISODE 41

"Zorro Rides Alone"

Filmed: June 5, 17–20, 25, 30, July 2 & 9, 1958; *Air Date*: October 15, 1958; *Director*: William Witney; *Writer*: Gene L. Coon; *Cast*: Eduard Franz (Verdugo), Jolene Brand (Anna Maria), Ken Lynch (Pablo), Joseph Conway (Palomares), Don Diamond (Cpl. Reyes), Wolfe Barzell (Innkeeper).

A courier, bringing money for the Verdugo cause, is shot and robbed by bandits. The wounded man makes his way to Monterey where Diego learns what has happened. Bernardo and Diego then ride to the Verdugo hacienda to tell Señor Verdugo of the courier's fate. As they arrive, they see Señor Verdugo with his arm in a sling talking to Palomares, one of the men who were involved in Bernardo's kidnapping the night before. Diego's suspicions about Señor Verdugo are beginning to grow.

After Palomares leaves, Diego relates to Verdugo what has happened to the courier but Verdugo already knows. It seems that all couriers trying to get into Monterey have been attacked. When Diego inquires about Verdugo's arm, he is told it is an old war wound. As a test of Verdugo's honesty, Diego gives him misinformation about his plan for transport of the de la Vega money from Los Angeles. As Diego relates his scheme, he is overheard by Pablo, the Verdugo servant.

Sgt. Garcia and Cpl. Reyes have been entrusted with the safe conduct of the money. To make sure that they stick to the plan, Zorro follows closely behind. True to form, the sergeant takes a detour and, when Zorro tries to stop him, Garcia and Cpl. Reyes take refuge in an abandoned way station. Pablo, Palomares and two other bandits are waiting for them. Cpl. Reyes is wounded in a brief struggle. Pablo decides the two soldiers must be eliminated and forces them to dig their own graves.

Zorro arrives and, after failing to get Garcia's attention, overpowers the bandit guarding them. Before Zorro and Garcia can enter the way station to face the bandits, Señor Verdugo arrives and enters the station. When Verdugo realizes that he has been duped by Pablo, he draws his sword and engages the bandits. Zorro and Garcia enter the fray. Pablo escapes but Palomares, a man Verdugo unwittingly hired to protect Garcia, is killed.

Author's Notes

"Zorro Rides Alone" suffers from some belabored comedy, miscasting and obvious use of doubles. The comedy, which for the most part involves Garcia and Reyes, is lackluster and tired. Don Diamond had been instructed to play his character low-key but he appears to be sleepwalking in this episode. The byplay between the two becomes annoying.

The miscasting concerns character actor Ken Lynch as an Indian. In the 1950s, Native Americans were seldom cast as Indians. More often than not Caucasian actors were chosen to play these roles. Lynch, an Irish New Yorker, seemed more at home playing tough gangsters or cops. In his black wig and makeup-enhanced tan, he seems more ridiculous than villainous.

The action finale is directed in the old Republic serial style: a wide master shot with action occurring in every corner of the screen. With Eduard Franz being doubled by Al Cavens and Victor Paul standing in for Joseph Conway, that part of the scene works well. It's when Zorro enters the fray that things begin to unravel. Because Buddy Van Horn moves too close to the camera, the use of a double is obvious. Also, when Zorro uses his sword against a villain who wields a chair, it seems silly. Likewise, as Zorro attempts to jump out a window in pursuit of the escaping bandits and stumbles over Garcia, it's totally out of character. The entire scene lacks the Zorro style that the series established in the first season. An earlier scene has Zorro chasing Garcia and Reyes on the roadway trying to warn them of trouble ahead. They believe he is after the money they are carrying and race off. It would seem that by this time Garcia would have some clue as to Zorro's motives and character. It's the kind of reaction that makes Garcia seem stupid rather than just a lovable buffoon.

There is, however, one scene that is fun to watch. It is when Garcia and Reyes have been captured by the bandits and are being forced to dig their own graves. As

Garcia digs, Zorro tries to get the Sergeant's attention without alerting the guard. Zorro goes through various pantomimes, essentially playing a game of charades with Garcia. Zorro's frustration with the thick-headed Garcia is very amusing. Technically, the scene is shot in an interesting manner: Garcia and Reyes are filmed on an exterior location while the shots involving Zorro are filmed on a soundstage.

Behind the Scenes

> Writer Gene L. Coon went on to write for *Star Trek* and to produce *The Wild Wild West*.... The end credits list a song by Tom Adair and Buddy Baker. However there is no song in this episode.... The way station used in this episode was actually the rear of the cabin that appeared in "Welcome to Monterey." It's located at the Berry Ranch.

EPISODE 42

"Horse of Another Color"

Filmed: June 17, 18, 26, 27, 30, July 1–3, 7, 10, 14 & 15, 1958; *Air Date*: October 23, 1958; *Director*: William Witney; *Writer*: Robert Bloomfield; *Cast*: Eduard Franz (Verdugo), Jolene Brand (Anna Maria), Carlos Romero (Romero), Ken Lynch (Pablo), Michael Forest (Anastacio), Wolfe Barzell (Innkeeper), Don Diamond (Cpl. Reyes), Robert Richards (Lieut. Santos).

A solider astride a white stallion is chased down and shot by Pablo and his horde of bandits. The soldier's papers reveal that he is Lieut. Santos from San Francisco. Anastacio, one of Pablo's men, dons the soldier uniform and, papers in hand, heads for Monterey.

At the Verdugo hacienda, Diego, convinced of Verdugo's honesty, agrees to turn over his 17,000 pesos to him. Romero and Anna Maria arrive with "Lieut. Santos" (Anastacio), who tells Verdugo that a ship will be docking in San Francisco that they can take to Spain to purchase their supplies. It is a change in plans but, after checking Santo's papers, Verdugo agrees to leave that afternoon. Anna Maria, who will accompany her father, apologizes to Diego for the difficulties they have had between them. Diego is more that willing to accept the apology.

That afternoon, Señor Verdugo, Anna Maria, Anastacio and Romero, who will join them for part of the journey, ride out for San Francisco. Diego, whose business is now finished, returns to Los Angeles with Bernardo.

During their travels, Diego and Bernardo come upon a riderless white stallion who seems to want them to follow. Diego obliges and discovers the body of the soldier the bandits left for dead. His voice, barely a whisper, tells Diego that he is Lieut. Santos. Diego immediately realizes that the Verdugos are in danger as Santos slips into a permanent sleep. Astride Phantom, the Lieutenant's stallion, Zorro races against time.

At the Verdugos' campsite, Anastacio carefully signals to Pablo and his band, who quickly overpower Verdugo and Romero. Before the bandits can complete their plan, Zorro strikes and they scatter. After a furious sword fight with Anastacio, the imposter tries to escape but is unnecessarily cut down by Romero. As Anna Maria thanks Zorro, he steals a kiss from the willing señorita and rides off into the night as the travelers return to Monterey.

Author's Notes

An alternate title for "Horse of Another Color" could have been *The Kiss*: It was a bit of a milestone in the series because it was Zorro's first screen embrace and kiss. Jolene Brand remembered the particular scene with amusement: "The kiss was an uproar. The executives were very concerned. The kiss could not be a real kiss—they wanted a kiss but not to show too much. Guy had to be very masculine and virile but not too much. I had to have passion that was restrained. Incidentally, he was the first man I every kissed that had a mustache; and a mask for that matter. Everybody had his own idea of how Guy should act and how I should act. And all I could think was that Guy is a married man and I'm married, too." The five-second Zorro kiss was filmed for two hours. Cameras recorded it from eight different angles on the back lot as nervous executives looked on.[2] What ends up on the screen is just the very end of the kiss, a "Disney-ized" version of passion. Better than the kiss is the mischievous look on Zorro's face when Anna Maria asks, "How can I thank you?" The expression on Guy Williams' face implies more than the kiss delivers.

The other mini-milestone in the segment concerns the title; for the first time Zorro rides a horse other than Tornado. During the next 11 episodes Zorro finds himself astride a white horse called Phantom. Judging from Don Diego's comment, "He was like trying to catch the wind—I don't think I could have caught him even with Tornado," the chief attribute of the animal becomes obvious. Story editor Lowell Hawley intimated that the rumor around the studio was that the real reason the horse made it onto the show was because it belonged to Walt Disney. The truth of the matter is the horse belonged to horse trainer Glen Randall, Sr. Phantom was actually King, who also stood in as Capitan Monastario's mount in the first season. Coincidentally, a white horse was used by Zorro in the Bill Witney-John English-directed serial *Zorro's Fighting Legion.*

Buddy Van Horn doubles for Michael Forest in his first extensive fencing scene of the series. Van Horn and Guy Williams work well together to produce some fast-moving and exciting swordplay. One note of fashion: While Williams is fencing, his sword arm is not through the cape's arm slit.

Behind the Scenes

An unusual close-up is used, a very tight shot of Zorro's eyes. This same shot is used in the following episode ... Carl Pitti once again handles Zorro's whip.

EPISODE 43

"The Señorita Makes a Choice"

Filmed: June 18, 27, 30, & July 7–10, 1958; *Air Date:* October 30, 1958; *Director:* William Witney; *Writer:* Robert Bloomfield; *Cast:* Eduard Franz (Verdugo), Jolene Brand (Anna Maria Verdugo), Carlos Romero (Romero), Dan Blocker (Blacksmith), Ken Lynch Pablo), Al Ruscio (Bandit), Don Diamond (Cpl. Reyes).

Anna Maria Verdugo arrives home to find the inside of her hacienda torn apart. As she looks around in confusion, she is confronted by Pablo with gun in hand. He tells her they are holding her father prisoner and it will take all the money he has collected for the supply ship to free him. Anna Maria protests that she doesn't know where her father has hidden the money but Pablo doesn't believe her. They are interrupted when Diego and Bernardo arrive. Before they enter, Pablo warns her to say nothing or her father will suffer.

When Diego sees what has happened, he sends Bernardo into town to bring a military guard to watch the house. Anna Maria reluctantly reveals to Diego what has happened. He tells her not to pay the ransom until the kidnappers prove that her father is alive and well.

Later that day, a ransom note arrives, but because of Pablo's warning, Anna Maria refuses to reveal the contents to anyone. That evening she frantically searches for her father's hidden chest of money. She accidentally discovers it concealed behind a bookcase. She summons Sgt. Garcia and gives him the money with instructions to turn it over to her father's kidnappers. Long after Garcia has left, Zorro enters Anna Maria's room and tries to persuade her to reveal the contents of the ransom note she received. She gives in and tells Zorro what she has done. The Fox races off in pursuit of Garcia. He finds the sergeant up to his neck in trouble and arrives just in time to save his fat friend and his ransom from the banditos. The bandits also do him the favor of revealing the whereabouts of Señor Verdugo.

Zorro rides for the blacksmith's shop in Monterey and finds Pablo and a burly blacksmith holding Señor Verdugo prisoner. They are preparing to leave the heavily guarded pueblo disguised as monks. Before they can make their getaway, Zorro appears but in the ensuing struggle Pablo escapes with his prisoner. Zorro himself barely avoids the blacksmith and his lackeys. Zorro then returns the ransom to Anna Maria and gives her hope that her father will be rescued soon.

Author's Notes

"The Señorita Makes a Choice" is a rather lackluster script but William Witney makes the best of the situation. There is the usual dash of comedy, the best of which is supplied by Bernardo. He comes to Garcia's office with a note from Diego asking for the Army's help in protecting Anna Maria at the Verdugo hacienda (bandits have turned everything upside down looking for money) then, proceeds to destroy Garcia's office in an effort to drive his point home. The entire scene is played for laughs and achieves its goal thanks to Henry Calvin and Gene Sheldon, an actor whom Witney called a comic genius.

One of the episode's weak links is a plot point which strains credibility. It's the sort of thing that happens quite often in television series. It concerns Anna Maria's discovery of the loot her father has collected to purchase supplies for the rancheros. At her wit's end, she sits at her father's desk with her hand on a book. Somehow this leads her to look at the bookshelf where the money is hidden. It's a tremendous leap of logic that really stretches the imagination.

There is a minor miscue in a scene that is supposed to be taking place at night. Filmed on a soundstage, Zorro enters a blacksmith's shop; when he opens the door it's clearly daylight outside. This episode did employ the day-for-night process, something that William Witney did not care for. He remembered complaining to Bill Anderson, "You spend a lot of money for the stunt work and with all this day-for-night shooting you can't see it."

The next-to-last scene of the episode is a very ominous one: Zorro is hiding from the blacksmith and his two cohorts in the plaza. He finds himself lying under a slightly elevated, overturned boat, and a hair's breadth away stands the blacksmith, his sledge hammer swaying back and forth.

Behind the Scenes

> Playing the uncredited part of the blacksmith is Dan Blocker, who one year later would star as Hoss on *Bonanza*.

EPISODE 44
"Rendezvous at Sundown"

Filmed: July 10, 11, 14–16 & 22, 1958; *Air Date*: November 6, 1958; *Director*: William Witney; *Writer*: Gene L. Coon; *Cast*: Eduard Franz (Verdugo), Jolene Brand (Anna Maria Verdugo), Ken Lynch (Pablo), Carlos Romero (Romero), George Lewis (Don Alejandro), Don Diamond (Cpl. Reyes).

Anna Maria has received another communiqué from the kidnapper. If she wants proof that her father is still alive, she will have to come to them. Diego is against the idea but Romero feels it's the only way to get her father back. In the midst of their disagreement, Diego receives word that his father has arrived in Monterey and wishes to see him. After Diego leaves, Romero convinces Anna Maria to meet with the kidnappers. Garcia and Reyes, who are guarding her, decide to come along for protection.

When Diego and his father return to the Verdugo hacienda, they find everyone gone. Diego leaves his father at the hacienda under the pretense that he is going out in search of the group. Privately, he tells Bernardo that if the money is still in the house, then someone will have to come back for it. When they do, Zorro will be waiting.

Following instructions, Anna Maria, Romero and company arrive at the church ruins. They are quickly surrounded by Pablo and his cohorts. Señor Verdugo is still alive but unless he returns to his hacienda and brings the money back, his daughter will be harmed. Romero accompanies Verdugo home, where they find Don Alejandro. After the two old friends embrace, Alejandro recognizes Romero as the ne'er-do-well son of another old acquaintance, someone who has stayed one step ahead of the authorities and gambled away his inheritance. Alejandro convinces Verdugo to send the Army and not to trust Romero. At this point, Romero, who is in league with the kidnappers, drops his masquerade and knocks Alejandro unconscious. He threatens Verdugo and demands the money. Zorro leaps through a window and crosses swords with the traitor. Zorro disarms Romero and sets about to devise a plan to rescue Anna Maria.

Two riders, Romero and Verdugo, who is still in his monk robes with a cowl obscuring his features, enter the church ruins. As they dismount, the cowled figure puts a pistol to Romero's head and reveals himself to be Zorro. It is a standoff until Pablo shoots and kills Romero. When the smoke finally clears, the kidnappers have been captured and the Verdugos are safe.

The following day, before the Verdugos leave on their mission to purchase supplies for California, Anna Maria hands Diego a note which is meant for Zorro. She makes him promise not to read it. As the coach fades from view, Diego and Bernardo race up to his room. Diego quickly dons his Zorro costume and then and only then does he read the note from his love.

Author's Notes

Zorro fares a bit better in "Rendezvous at Sundown," the conclusion of this series of episodes. This segment contained more of what William Witney specialized in — action. An excellent fencing scene between Zorro and Romero highlights this teleplay. Although Al Cavens doubles for Carlos Romero (Romero), the latter was actually a capable fencer who had trained at the Faulkner studios early in his acting career. However, in a situation such as this, it was more economical (not to mention safer) to have Guy Williams work with an expert like Al Cavens. Williams had been fencing with Cavens since the series began and the routines could be learned more quickly by two swordsmen familiar with each other's abilities. Incidentally, if the viewer looks closely, Zorro can be seen fencing without wearing his sword scabbard. The scene takes place inside the hacienda sala which is crowded with furniture, and Williams was able to move with more dexterity minus the scabbard. It was the only time in the series this was done.

One year earlier, a similar fencing scene was filmed for the second episode of the series, "Zorro's Secret Passage." The improvement in Guy Williams' ability as a fencer cannot be exaggerated and becomes all the move obvious because of the similarity of the sets used. Both take place in the crowded sala of a hacienda. In "Zorro's Secret Passage" all of the fencing phrases are of the very basic sabre style; they're very deliberate. There is also an economy of foot movement. In "Rendezvous at Sundown" the entire room is used, the moves are very quick and more complex. The difference is truly night and day.

The conclusion is the type of scene this series excels in — light comedy with tongue in cheek. The setup has Anna Maria giving Don Diego a note to be passed on to Zorro. She knows that it's unnecessary but she asks Diego not to read it. Of course he agrees. Diego and Bernardo run up to his room and, without exchanging any words, Diego makes the sign of the Z. With a look of confusion Bernardo scurries about the room grabbing various pieces of Zorro's costume from their respective hiding places. Shirt and pants from under the mattress, hat and cape from atop the armoire and finally the sword from behind the curtain. Zorro now stands in Diego's place as Bernardo opens the window for the Fox's exit. Instead Zorro picks up Anna Maria's letter, opens it with his sword and remarks, "You don't think I'd let Don Diego read this, do you?" As he reads the letter, a broad smile breaks out on his face as he keeps a perturbed Bernardo at sword's length.

Behind the Scenes

> George Lewis makes his first appearance of the season in this episode, giving it a more familiar feeling and making one yearn for a return to Los Angeles. One also has to wonder who's taking care of de la Vega business with both Don Alejandro and Don Diego in Monterey.... Legendary stunt men Tom Steele and Dale Van Sickel, old friends of Bill Witney's from his days at Republic Pictures, put in an appearance as two of the bandidos. Also appearing as a stunt double was Hal Needham.... One problem surrounding this episode concerns the coming attraction for it. Although one may have suspected Romero was up to no good, his villainy is revealed in the preview for this episode. This is not the first time a coming attraction has given away more than it should.... The mission ruins used for this episode were on the Disney back lot and were built especially for the Monterey episodes.... Carlos Romero went on to co-star with Joel McCrea in *Wichita Town* [1959], a series that lasted one year.

EPISODE 45
"The New Order"

Filmed: May 20–23, 26–28, 1958 & June 2, 10 & 18, 1958; *Air Date*: November 13, 1958; *Director*: Charles Barton; *Writer*: Bob Wehling; *Cast*: Barbara Luna (Theresa), Perry Lopez (Joaquin Castenada), Ric Roman (Capitan Briones), Frank Wilcox (Rico), Don Diamond (Cpl. Reyes).

While still in Monterey, Sgt. Garcia and Cpl. Reyes have the unpleasant task of informing the merchants that they must close down their stands in the plaza. Theresa, who owns a tamale stand, is so angered that she attacks the sergeant. Garcia is rescued by his friend Don Diego, who learns that Señor Rico, the acting governor, is behind the new law. Diego decides to go talk to Rico. Before this can happen, Capitan Briones and his "Especiales" (the scum of the garrison) begin to tear apart the stands. Theresa's hot-headed boyfriend, Joaquin Castenada, arrives on the scene. To keep Joaquin from getting in trouble, Diego has Bernardo knock him over the head. Briones arrests Theresa for attacking his soldiers.

Diego arrives at the garrison and speaks with Señor Rico, but it is to no avail. Rico is intent on following a strict law-and-order policy. Before he leaves, Diego pays Theresa's bail.

Later that day, Joaquin has a run-in with the "Especiales" and is arrested. During another visit to the garrison Diego learns that Briones plans to whip Joaquin the following morning. He fears that if this happens, Joaquin will fight and give the soldiers an excuse to kill him. Zorro is Joaquin's only hope.

As darkness falls, Zorro overpowers the two soldiers guarding Joaquin and frees him. Hearing the commotion, Briones comes outside with pistol in hand and takes aim at the escaping Zorro. Using a fallen soldier's rifle, Joaquin shoots first and wounds the captain, returning the favor to Zorro. Zorro then takes his grateful friend up into the hills where he'll be safe for the time being.

Author's Notes

"The New Order" returns Zorro to some familiar thematic turf. As in the first 13, the military is once again punishing the citizens with a tyrannical rule. A rival to Zorro is also introduced with Joaquin Castenada. Like Zorro, Castenada is fighting against injustice, although he is somewhat less successful. Zorro seems to spend most of his time snaring the hot-headed rebel from the jaws of the military.

A Disney favorite and comedy specialist, Charles Barton returns to steer the next four episodes, still based in Monterey. This segment includes the physical comedy that is the director's trademark. Along those lines it features Theresa's attacks on Garcia as well as a running gag between Theresa, Diego and Bernardo: Theresa leaps into Diego's arms and smothers him with kisses at every opportunity, and the humor results form the disapproving, stone-faced look that Bernardo gives Diego.

Barbara Luna plays the part of Theresa as a "fiery" Latina who by today's standards is a bit of a stereotype. Luna, however, is so good in the role and seems to be having so much fun that any negativity would be nitpicking. She was called upon to engage in physical action in a number of scenes throughout this series of episodes. This usually included a scuffle with the military. Luna complained, "All that braid and belts and buttons. I never struck one of those actors with out coming away with welts and bruises. I had to go home and soak for hours in the tub."

Behind the Scenes

For this episode, set decorator Hal Gausman made the inside of the cuartel to look like the market square in Monterey. Gausman does a very convincing job as there are very few telltale signs that give away the actual location.... This set of four episodes were actually filmed before the previous Bill Witney episodes. This is unusual as the episodes were usually aired in roughly the same order they were filmed.... In the original script for this episode, there were actually two military villains, one doing acting Governor Rico's bidding and one who was head of the garrison soldiers. Before filming began, these characters were combined into the person of Capitan Briones.... The song "Tamales" [Tom Adair–Buddy Baker] was suggested in the script as "a little refrain reminiscent of "Pickle in the Middle" as applied to tamales."

EPISODE 46
"An Eye for an Eye"

Filmed: May 26–29, & June 2, 18 & 24, 1958; *Air Date*: November 20, 1958; *Director*: Charles Barton; *Writer*: Bob Wehling; *Cast*: Barbra Luna (Theresa), Perry Lopez (Joaquin Castenada), Ric Roman (Capitan Briones), Frank Wilcox (Rico), Don Diamond (Cpl. Reyes), George Lewis (Don Alejandro).

Wanted posters are going up all over Monterey: 1,000 pesos for the capture of Joaquin Castenada. Joaquin is taking his place alongside Zorro as a defender of the people and a thorn in the side of the military.

Don Alejandro, fed up with Señor Rico's activities, is going off in search of the governor, who is believed to be vacationing in Santa Barbara. He instructs Diego to try to contact Joaquin in an effort to get him to tone down his activity against the Army. That night while Joaquin and some of his men are painting some anti–Rico signs near the garrison, the soldiers shoot and kill one of his band, a 14-year-old boy.

The next day, Joaquin sends a message to Rico, telling him that he will kill two soldiers in retaliation. However, Rico and Capitan Briones devise a plan. They will allow him to kill Garcia and Reyes and this will give them the excuse they need to kill Joaquin.

In an effort to locate Joaquin, Diego and Bernardo follow Theresa to his camp. Once there, Diego tries in vain to convince Joaquin to curtail his efforts. Joaquin will not hear of it; he wants revenge. Diego learns that Garcia and Reyes will be on patrol that night. He realizes that only Zorro can protect them from Joaquin.

As the two soldiers patrol, Zorro keeps an eye on them, quietly disposing of one of Joaquin's men. While doing this, Zorro overhears Capitan Briones and the "Especiales" plot to move upon Joaquin only after he has killed Garcia and Reyes. Zorro grabs Joaquin as he is about to fire upon Garcia and Reyes and proves to him that he was walking into a trap. Joaquin is not in a grateful mood. Already he is plotting his next move against Rico.

Author's Notes

"An Eye for an Eye" is an example of what producer Bill Anderson referred to as "bringing the show in a bit." Although extras don't add much of an expense to a television budget, there are very few of them here; the tavern is deserted, as is the plaza. There is very little atmosphere. It gives the episode a cheap look. Joaquin is supposed to have a large band of followers but he never has more that two or three men around him. What little action occurs is handled by Diego as he tries to locate

Joaquin. There really isn't much for Zorro to do when he appears at the end of the episode and with no sword play he's rather inactive.

There is one interesting scene which shows a new side to Garcia. As Theresa is being pursued by some lancers, Don Diego allows her to take refuge under his table at the inn. The soldiers come through with Garcia trailing and they see no sign of the woman. After the lancers leave, a brief conversation takes place between Diego and Garcia.

> GARCIA: This is a very pleasant inn, don't you think, Don Diego?
> DIEGO: Yes, very pleasant, sergeant.
> GARCIA: But the one in Los Angeles has much larger tablecloths, eh?

It's clear that Garcia knows that Theresa is hiding under the table but his subtlety and intelligence is very out of character. However it is refreshing because it's not only what Garcia says but also the ways he says it, very nonchalantly. It also leads one to believe that there is much more to Henry Calvin as an actor.

Behind the Scenes

Two days after this episode aired, *Zorro* creator Johnston McCulley died at age 75. Although McCulley did not contribute directly to the Disney series, he was a frequent visitor to the Disney lot. He was very impressed with the *Zorro* set and enjoyed sitting there for long periods of time reminiscing about past *Zorro* productions. McCulley and Guy Williams became fast friends, often discussing *Zorro* and the Disney treatment of it between takes. The author admired the fact that Williams handled his own fencing and overall seemed very impressed with the series.

EPISODE 47

"Zorro and the Flag of Truce"

Filmed: June 2, 4–6, 9, 10, 12, 13, 18 & 24, 1958; *Air Date*: November 27, 1958; *Director*: Charles Barton; *Writer*: Bob Wehling; *Cast*: Barbara Luna (Theresa), Perry Lopez (Joaquin Castenada), Ric Roman (Capitan Briones), Frank Wilcox Rico), John Litel (Governor), George Lewis (Don Alejandro), Don Diamond (Cpl. Reyes).

As Rico is bearing down on the peons to learn the whereabouts of Joaquin Castenada, Don Alejandro is returning with the governor. Rico explains to the governor what has happened in his absence. His version is less than accurate but the governor believes him and they attempt to come up with a plan to deal with Joaquin. That night, Joaquin attempts to blow up Rico's quarters but he is thwarted at the last minute by Zorro. As Joaquin is making his escape he runs into Garcia and Reyes, but again he is saved by his masked guardian angel.

Don Alejandro and Diego meet with the governor and Rico to discuss Joaquin Castenada. The governor wants Joaquin to come into town under a flag of truce so they can discuss their differences. All agree this is a good plan — especially Rico, who privately believes this will be a chance for Briones and his "Especiales" to kill Joaquin.

For the next few days Sgt. Garcia passes the word throughout the pueblo of the governor's offer to Joaquin but he gets nowhere. In an attempt to locate the bandit, the "Especiales" take Theresa into custody. Bernardo relays this news to Diego, who promptly takes the matter up with Señor Rico. To obtain Theresa's release, Diego guarantees that Joaquin will come into Monterey. Diego learns from Theresa the location of Joaquin's new campsite, and he and his father visit Joaquin. They attempt to convince Joaquin to come into town; he agrees. Diego decides that Zorro had best keep an eye on the situation. An ambush is set by Rico and Capitan Briones but Zorro prevents Joaquin's murder and whisks him out of town. Rico reports to the governor that Joaquin and his band opened fire on the soldiers, a far cry from the truth. The governor decrees that law and order will be restored to Monterey. He wants Zorro and Joaquin dead or alive!

Author's Notes

"Zorro and the Flag of Truce" starts off in unusual fashion as Zorro makes a rare appearance at the episode's opening, rescuing a peon from a whipping. Interestingly, there are five separate appearances by Zorro and in four of them Guy Williams is being doubled by either Buddy Van Horn for riding purposes or Carl Pitti because of his expertise with a bullwhip. When Williams does appear as Zorro, it is for a humorous duel between himself and Garcia and Reyes. As one would expect, it's a brief encounter and the literal *end*-result has Garcia wearing a Z where he has never worn one before.

At one point there is a strange comment by the governor when he speaks as though he has never heard of Zorro. Although Monterey is approximately 450 miles from Los Angeles, it seems that some news of the bandit would have traveled up to his city. As a matter of fact, in "Double Trouble for Zorro" the swordsman Martinez states "his fame has spread even to Monterey."

There are a number of amusing bits involving Bernardo, one of which has him playing chess with himself. The other has Bernardo attempting to describe Theresa's arrest to Diego. As always it's played for laughs with apropos accompaniment by William Lava. Lava once again uses his musical sound effects to punctuate Bernardo's mime.

There is still more evidence of Don Diego moving further away from the character created by Johnston McCulley. No longer the ineffectual fop, he mediates a truce between Joaquin Castenada and the governor. Don Alejandro even tells his son how proud he is of him. Head writer Lowell Hawley believed that "Diego can not be on TV quite what McCulley made him in print. You see him on screen so much of the time that he if he were always silly and foppish, viewers would tire of him."

Behind the Scenes

Veteran character John Litel, the governor, may best be known as the father of *Henry Aldrich* in the movie series of the same name.

EPISODE 48

"Ambush"

Filmed: May 19, June 5, 6, 9–13 & 24 & July 23, 1958; *Air Date*: December 4, 1958; *Director*: Charles Barton; *Writer*: Lowell Hawley; *Cast*: Barbara Luna (Theresa), Perry Lopez (Joaquin Castenada), Ric Roman (Capitan Briones), Frank Wilcox (Rico), John Litel (Governor), Don Diamond (Cpl. Reyes).

Diego and Bernardo ride into Joaquin's camp where they find an angry outlaw. He believes that Diego betrayed him and if not for Zorro he would have been ambushed and killed. Diego tries to explain that it was Rico, not the governor or himself, who deceived him. Joaquin will not hear of it and chains Diego and Bernardo. Joaquin has learned that tomorrow is the Governor's Saint's Day and Rico will accompany the governor to church. Joaquin will lie in wait along their route and settle his score with them. Before he rides into town, Joaquin frees Diego and Bernardo.

Joaquin positions himself in the plaza but he is captured by Sgt. Garcia and Cpl. Reyes while on their evening patrol. As Theresa watches and then tries to prevent his capture, she too is taken into custody. Rico now has a plan that will help him become governor. He will force Joaquin to kill the governor — and if he refuses, Theresa, will be killed. The outlaw has no choice.

Diego learns what has happened and in the dead of night Zorro arrives at the garrison. He comes upon Capitan Briones, from whom he forces the truth. Early the next morning, as the governor is on his way to church, Zorro prevents Joaquin from killing him. Zorro then shackles both men, giving each the other's key. They will have to settle their differences or remain in chains. Zorro now heads back to the garrison to rescue Theresa.

By this time Rico and Briones suspect that something has gone wrong and are preparing a hasty exit as Zorro arrives. Briones and Zorro cross swords with the usual result. The governor arrives with Joaquin, Garcia and company. As Rico tries to escape, the governor shoots him down. Theresa is released from jail, Joaquin is pardoned, the food stands are repaired and all's well in Monterey once again.

Behind the Scenes

Character heavy Dick Reeves makes his second appearance in the series, once again playing a lancer. As before, his appearance amounts to no more that a "bit." In this teleplay he is drenched with water and then knocked unconscious by Zorro.... This quartet of episodes end as they began with Theresa, Garcia and Reyes standing around her market stand, laughing and singing about the attributes of tamales. It is a very standard television "all's well that ends well" wrap-up.

EPISODE 49

"The Practical Joker"

Filmed: July 21–25, 29 & 31, 1958; *Air Date*: December 14, 1958; *Director*: Charles Lamont; Writer: Bob Wehling; *Cast*: Jolene Brand (Anna Maria), Richard Anderson (Ricardo Del Amo), Don Diamond (Cpl. Reyes).

While walking through the Monterey pueblo, Diego is accosted from behind by a man with a knife. He quickly disarms his assailant and finds that it is an old friend, Ricardo Del Amo, who has just arrived from San Francisco. Ricardo has a reputation as something of a joker and a ladies' man. He goes into great detail describing a woman that he met on the stage from San Francisco. He is planning on serenading the woman that evening and asks Diego to come along. Diego reluctantly agrees and is practically speechless when the object of Ricardo's affection turns out to be Anna Maria Verdugo. Ricardo is surprised when he learns that Diego knows his new acquaintance.

Anna Maria explains to Diego that she decided not to accompany her father to Spain and is temporarily staying at her uncle's house. Diego and Ricardo spend most of the evening vying for Anna Maria's attention and the trio decides to go riding in the morning.

Later that evening, Sgt. Garcia comes to Diego's room with some disturbing news: He is under arrest for horse stealing. Diego is shocked and demands to see his accuser face to face. When they arrive at the garrison, no one is there, so Diego is forced to stay in jail overnight.

The next morning, when Diego learns that the complaint against him was signed by Julius Caesar, he realizes that Ricardo must be up to his old practical jokes again. When Ricardo and Anna Maria arrive at the garrison, Ricardo laughingly confesses and Diego is freed. Sgt. Garcia admonishes Ricardo for wasting his time.

As Garcia and Cpl. Reyes prepare to deliver the payrolls to the southern presidio, Ricardo accidentally overhears two men plotting to steal the money. He tries to warn Garcia but given his reputation the Sergeant does not believe him. Before Diego leaves to go riding with Anna Maria and Ricardo, Bernardo convinces him that perhaps Zorro should keep an eye on the sergeant and the payroll. Ricardo and Anna Maria ride on ahead and come across Garcia and Reyes, who have indeed just been robbed. Zorro rides upon the scene and with help from Ricardo captures the bandits and recovers the money. This time the joke is on Ricardo when Zorro rides off with Anna Maria.

Author's Notes

Charles Lamont, who directed an excellent series of episodes in the first season, returns to take charge of the next four. The practical joker in the title of this episode is Ricardo Del Amo, portrayed by Richard Anderson. Over the years Anderson appeared on hundreds of television shows and a number of movies. Among his more prestigious films are *Scaramouche* and *Paths of Glory*. Unfortunately, he seems somewhat miscast in the role of Ricardo. He attempts no Spanish accent and seems slightly out of place. He also doesn't have the impishness or twinkle in the eye to pull off this role. While playing his jokes on other people, he seems more of a dullard and you have to wonder what Anna Maria would see in this character, especially compared to Don Diego. What saves this first episode is the script of Bob Wehling. It's very witty and the byplay between Williams and Anderson is genuinely funny in spots. Williams is especially good delivering his lines with tongue firmly in cheek.

When the episode opens with Diego being accosted at knifepoint, it's a great attention-grabber although it runs counter to the light tone of this episode and the three that follow. Part of that light tone and one of the funnier scenes concerns Bernardo trying to smuggle a file, hidden in a sausage, into Diego's jail cell. Even better is when Bernardo, unaware that Diego has been released, arrives dressed as Zorro and armed to the teeth to free his master. Diego frantically waves him off before anyone can see him.

The action, which has Zorro and Ricardo capturing some bandits, was filmed at the Rowland V. Lee Ranch. The stunt involved was a "bulldog" which has the rider of one moving horse leaping onto the rider of another horse and knocking him to the ground. As usual, Buddy Van Horn doubled for Williams and Tap Canutt stood in for Richard Anderson.

Behind the Scenes

> A duet is performed between Diego and Ricardo, "Fly Gaviota," by Tom Adair and Buddy Baker.

EPISODE 50

"The Flaming Arrow"

Filmed: July 16–18, 21–23, 25, August 5 & 6, 1958; *Air Date*: December 18, 1958; *Director*: Charles Lamont; *Writer*: Robert Bloomfield; *Cast*: Jolene Brand (Anna Maria), Richard Anderson (Ricardo Del Amo), Whit Bissell (Commandante), Yvette Dugay (Milana), Don Diamond (Cpl. Reyes).

It seems that Ricardo Del Amo cannot resist his penchant for practical jokes and as a result he gets off on the wrong foot with the new commandante. (While Ricardo was attempting to play a joke on Diego, the commandante got caught in the crossfire.) It will take 200 pesos to keep Ricardo out of jail. He reluctantly pays. Later that day, while involved in a game of jousting to impress Anna Maria and her cousin Milana, Ricardo again runs afoul of the commandante when a joke meant for Diego backfires onto the hapless commandante. The commandante is humiliated and is determined to do whatever it takes to deal with Señor Del Amo.

Ricardo decides to make himself scarce. However, he still seems not to have learned his lesson. Annoyed that Anna Maria seems smitten with Zorro, he confides in Diego that he has sent a love letter to Milana and signed it Zorro. That night, dressed as Zorro, Ricardo plans to serenade Milana, make Anna Maria jealous and cure her of her infatuation with the legendary Fox. Diego decides that this is the perfect opportunity to play a joke of his own on his adversary. He informs his friend Sgt. Garcia of the evening's events.

The serenade takes place as planned and Garcia promptly arrests Ricardo to teach him a lesson. However the joke goes awry. The commandante, still smarting from the humiliation of Ricardo's joke, plans to hang Ricardo whether he is Zorro or not. Both Garcia and Diego try to convince the commandante otherwise but it is to no avail. It is left to Zorro to save Ricardo, which he does just in time while making the commandante admit his mistake. Before he makes his exit, Zorro takes the opportunity to dunk Ricardo the joker in a water trough for all to see.

Author's Notes

"The Flaming Arrow" is superior to "The Practical Joker" because it has something that can save any *Zorro* adventure — an exciting fencing scene. Long-time character actor Whit Bissell joins the cast, briefly, portraying the new and overly vain commandante. A particularly funny scene has Ricardo, once again playing a joke, spraying the commandante with soot. The sight of the commandante's enraged face totally blackened is very funny. When Diego turns the tables and has Ricardo arrested for playing Zorro, it's poetic justice to see Ricardo finally get a taste of his own medicine.

When Zorro rescues Ricardo from the vindictive commandante, he must out duel doubles Al Cavens and Victor Paul. The scene is set up well as Zorro descends the steps of scaffolding, throws his cape over his forearm and draws his sword. As the duel rages across the courtyard, most of the action is filmed from up high looking down in a master shot which shows the speed and the footwork of the participants. After he has disarmed his foes, Zorro then dunks his rival Ricardo in a water trough for Anna Maria to see — a very satisfying conclusion.

One incongruity in this episode has Diego and Anna Maria being put in the custody of an armed guard. The next scene has Zorro arriving to save Ricardo. How Diego slips out to transform himself into his alter ego is never clear but it should probably be chalked up to typical unexplained television phenomena.

Behind the Scenes

One song is performed by Richard Anderson [dubbed by Bill Lee], "Sweet Señorita" by Tom Adair and George Bruns.

EPISODE 51

"Zorro Fights a Duel"

Filmed: July 22, 28–31, August 4 & 6, 1958; *Air Date*: December 25, 1958; *Director*: Charles Lamont; *Writer*: Bob Wehling; *Cast*: Jolene Brand (Anna Maria), Richard Anderson

(Ricardo Del Amo), George Lewis (Don Alejandro), Don Diamond (Cpl. Reyes), Fred Cavens (Monsieur Gerard).

Ricardo arrives at Anna Maria's house (where Diego is visiting) with a box of chocolates in hand. When Anna Maria opens the box she finds a piece of wood with a Z carved in it. Both Diego and Anna Maria find this very funny but Ricardo seems to have lost his sense of humor. He feels that Zorro is a coward because he hides behind a mask. This obviously irritates Diego. Ricardo decides that he must finally take action to thwart his masked rival. He puts up posters around the pueblo challenging Zorro to a duel. When Garcia sees a poster, he explains to Cpl. Reyes that this is their chance to capture Zorro. If they stay close to Ricardo, he will lead them to Zorro. Two suspicious-looking characters overhear Garcia and decide to do the same.

At the inn, Don Alejandro voices his opinion on the matter of a duel. He feels that Zorro is a caballero and must therefore take up the challenge. Anna Maria also wants to see Zorro accept the challenge to teach Ricardo a lesson. Unfortunately for Diego, she wants him to accompany her to the duel. Later that evening, Garcia reveals his plan to Diego and asks his help in capturing Zorro. Diego cannot help but laugh about his dilemma.

With the aid of Bernardo, Diego and Monsieur Gerard, a fencing master, Ricardo prepares for his duel with Zorro by working out with whip, pistol and sword. He proves to be an expert in all three. Diego realizes he will have his work cut out for him.

Early the next morning, Zorro sends a message to Ricardo and they meet at the mission ruins. They face each other and, as they are spied upon by the suspicious men from the pueblo, Zorro disarms Ricardo after some extended swordplay. Both men then turn on Zorro's would-be captors and run them off. There will be no reward collected for Zorro this day.

Author's Notes

"Zorro Fights a Duel" would have been a perfect conclusion to the *Practical Joker* series because by defeating Ricardo in the duel, Zorro essentially ends whatever rivalry there is between the two. However, there is one more segment to follow which wraps up the romantic triangle.

This is another well-written episode by Bob Wehling, who implements a number of twists and some good comedy such as when Diego becomes indirectly involved in the duel and finds himself in a bit of a pickle. Not only is he expected to be Ricardo's second, Anna Maria wants him to escort her to the duel and Garcia wants his help to capture Zorro. Diego is so overwhelmed by the situation he can only laugh.

There is a fair amount of physical comedy as well. As Ricardo prepares for his duel, he leaves nothing to chance, practicing with pistol, whip and sword. Diego wants Bernardo, an expert with the whip, to teach Ricardo a bit of a lesson. However, it's Ricardo, being doubled by Carl Pitti, who gives the lesson by first removing Bernardo's pocket watch, then removing his feet from the ground, leaving him with a sore posterior. All of this activity was filmed around the lake at the beautiful Rowland Lee Ranch.

An episode titled "Zorro Fights a Duel" should contain an exciting fencing scene; however, the sword work here does have its problems. With Buddy Van Horn standing in for Richard Anderson, the Fred Cavens- choreographed swordplay is a bit deliberate and there doesn't seem to be enough of it. Three are too many stops and starts so the action never builds any momentum. There is also some shameful cost-cutting when the same fencing phrase is reused, separated by a few seconds of cut-away activity. However, the setting for the scene at the mission ruins on the back lot is perfect and makes the action more palatable.

Behind the Scenes

> Fred Cavens has his first speaking role in the series playing the part of, fittingly enough, a fencing master. Cavens, who had done some acting in his long film career, had worked solely as a fencing choreographer on *Zorro*, only occasionally appearing on camera, doubling a villain.... At the inn "Zorro's Serenade" plays on a guitar in the background.

EPISODE 52
"Amnesty for Zorro"

Filmed: July 25, 30–31 & August 4–7, 1958; *Air Date*: January 1, 1959; *Director*: Charles Lamont; *Writers*: Bob Wehling & Lowell Hawley; *Cast*: Jolene Brand (Anna Maria), Richard Anderson (Ricardo Del Amo), George Lewis (Don Alejandro), Don Diamond (Cpl. Reyes), I. Stanford Jolley (Messenger), Nacho Galindo (Nacho).

As Sgt. Garcia and Cpl. Reyes share a bottle of wine, an injured man stumbles into the tavern with news for Don Diego: The Indians in Los Angeles have burned the de la Vega hacienda to the ground. Clearly shaken, Diego relays the news to Don Alejandro and the two prepare to return to Los Angeles. Before leaving, Diego stops at Anna Maria's house and bids her farewell. While exiting her hacienda, he sees Ricardo talking with the injured messenger from Los Angeles. Anna Maria points out that the man actually arrived one day ago from San Francisco. Diego deduces that the fire is another of Ricardo's practical jokes. Diego angrily confronts Ricardo, who apologizes for not realizing that Don Alejandro would have been affected by his childish prank.

After Diego leaves, Ricardo explains that it is he who has been summoned home to San Francisco. He simply didn't want Diego to be without competition for Anna Maria's affection, hence the deception. Anna Maria tells Ricardo that it is Zorro who has her full attention. Ricardo exclaims that if Zorro can prove he is the man for her, he would bow out. This gives him an idea and he goes to the governor with an amnesty plan for Zorro. The governor agrees that if Zorro gives himself up he will be given a full pardon. Posters go up all over Monterey informing the people of the governor's decision.

Many people have different opinions as to what Zorro will do. Don Alejandro believes Zorro will not give up, that he will continue to fight for the oppressed. Ricardo believes and hopes that Zorro will stay away. Anna Maria, whose opinion is most important to Diego, hopes and prays that Zorro will arrive at the hour of the Angelus to reveal his identity and express his love to her. It is her opinion that makes up Diego's mind.

Diego enters his secret barn where he keeps his white stallion and costume. As he opens the door, he is knocked unconscious. He awakes to find a sword at this throat held by a man dressed in his costume with a black hood covering his features. He creates a diversion and struggles to overcome his captor, eventually disarming him. He rips off the hood to find ... Don Alejandro. It seems his father has known his secret for some time. Alejandro believes that it is important for all of California that he remains Zorro. Diego reluctantly agrees.

As the hour of the Angelus passes, the crowd in the plaza begins to disperse and the governor withdraws the offer of amnesty. Just then, Zorro rides up and whisks Anna Maria away. They ride to the mission ruins where Zorro explains why, for the moment, he must hide his true identity. With the lancers in the distance, the pair embrace, then Zorro races off.

Author's Notes

"Amnesty for Zorro" is a landmark because at the end of the segment someone other than Bernardo will share Diego's secret. This is also an uncommon episode because it involved a certain amount of introspection on Diego's part regarding his secret identity. At one point Diego asks his father, "This Zorro, whoever he is, don't you think he has the right to live his own life?" It's a revelation because this sort of subject matter was never really broached in the earlier episodes.

Diego's soul-searching, along with the introduction of Zorro's romantic interest Anna Maria, was another attempt to add some depth to the show. Head writer Lowell Hawley believed that viewers were interested in the dual nature of the Don Diego/Zorro role. He felt that "they wanted to see both characters as three-dimensional people complete with human emotions, problems and triumphs." Unfortunately, the dual identity dilemma was never fully explored and was taken up in only one subsequent teleplay.

When Diego is climactically confronted by a hooded figure in Zorro's costume, it truly is shocking. When his adversary turns out to be his father, who feels that his son should not give up his role because the people need him, the scene is heartfelt. When Diego asks his father how long he has know, his father replies, "For a long time, a very long time."

It's interesting to look back over episodes to see some indication of when Alejandro may have begun to suspect there was more to his son than met the eye. During "The Luckiest Swordsman Alive," in an effort to slip out and ride as Zorro, Diego pretends that he has broken a guitar string. After Diego leaves, Alejandro examines the guitar and finds it intact. He glances off with a look that indicates that he is beginning

Television's Zorro, GUY WILLIAMS, Rides Back Into Action   PART 4

Inside in Color: Preview of Dramas Coming Up on Channel 9's Play of the Week

to suspect what the viewer already knows. The guitar incident is the only time that Don Alejandro gives any outward appearance that he may sense that things are not as they seem. This may explain Alejandro's change in attitude toward Diego in subsequent episodes. Curiously, the elder don's discovery in this episode has no impact at all on the storylines of future adventures.

Of course, this episode is not without comedy which is supplied in the form of a song extolling the virtues of the sergeant, sung by Sgt. Garcia with snide retorts contributed by Cpl. Reyes.

This segment marks the final appearance of Jolene Brand as Anna Maria Verdugo, who was good in her role but was less than a hit with the kids who watched the show. She laughingly remarked, "I wound up the villain of the whole show. I was hired to be the love interest but the little kids hated [Zorro] having a girlfriend. The kissing scene we had was the kiss of death for me. My agent told me I was in trouble." Brand went on to co-star in the sitcom *Guestwood Ho!* in the 1960–61 television season. She also worked as a regular on *The Ernie Kovacs Show*.

Richard Anderson, who continued to be one of the busiest actors in Hollywood, remembered Guy Williams as "a very simple kind of person — he didn't lead you to believe that he was pretentious in any way. He was very methodical in how he approached the sword work and acting. I think he looked upon it as a business and he went through the motions and gave people a good show. He was also very tired, he was in almost every shot. It was a heavy workload."

Behind the Scenes

> The black hood that Don Alejandro wears to disguise himself from his son is very similar to the illustrations of Zorro in the Johnston McCulley pulp novels.... There is one other song performed in this episode, Anna Maria's "Mi Caballo, My Zorro." Both this song and the one sung by Garcia ["The Sergeant's Theme"] were written by Tom Adair and Buddy Baker.... The coming attraction for the episode uses the "iris in, iris out" camera effect. It was the only time it was utilized during the run of the series.

10

Return to Los Angeles

Episode Guide, Part 1

EPISODE 53
"The Runaways"

Filmed: August 21, 22, 25–28 & September 8, 1958; *Air Date*: January 8, 1959; *Director*: William Witney; *Writer*: Robert Bloomfield; *Cast*: Tom Pittman (Romaldo), Gloria Castillo (Buena), John Hoyt (Yorba), Arthur Batanides (Lazaro), Mack Williams (Padre).

In Los Angeles, the de la Vegas' indentured servant Buena wants to marry Señor Yorba's indentured servant Romaldo. She presents her written permission to the padre. But Romaldo has nothing for the priest and therefore they cannot be married. Romaldo explains that Señor Yorba has declared that he may not marry until his two-year term is up. He tells her that he has actually run away to be with her. It is at this moment that Señor Yorba and his head vaquero, Lazaro, ride into the pueblo in search of the runaway servant. Yorba explains the situation to Garcia, who joins in the search, but the young peon escapes.

Diego and Bernardo arrive and the padre explains to them what has happened. Diego goes looking for the pair and arrives in time to rescue Buena from the jealous Lazaro. Señor Yorba enters the scene and explains to Diego that he believes that Buena and Romaldo would marry and then run off into the hills, reneging on their pacts as indentured servants. When Diego asks Yorba where he got such an idea, Lazaro looks very suspicious.

Romaldo comes to the de la Vega hacienda that night with the intention of running off with Buena. Diego and Buena are able to convince him to return to Señor Yorba and work out his indentured term. The next day he meets with his master, who is not sympathetic, and adds another year to his term. After Yorba leaves, Lazaro begins to beat Romaldo. The two men struggle and Romaldo escapes.

Hoping to lure Romaldo back, Lazaro tricks Buena into coming with him by telling her that Romaldo has been injured. When Diego learns what has happened, he feels that Zorro must step in. Yorba learns of Lazaro's action and berates him. At this point Lazaro's jealous rage simmers to the surface and he threatens to kill both Yorba and Buena. Just then Zorro arrives but Lazaro escapes. Zorro tracks him down and returns him to Yorba to deal with. Yorba then returns Romaldo to his original two-year term, and after that he can marry Buena.

Author's Notes

"The Runaways" is really the first one-shot (self-contained) episode of the series and it marks a welcome return to Los Angeles. Director William Witney also returns to handle a story whose theme is indentured servitude, something that was common practice in Spanish California. This was a rather touchy subject for the series to tackle because, although it was part of the fabric of its time, it certainly was foreign to modern America. It was also part of the series' attempt to tackle more adult subject matters. Don Diego's role here is largely one of counselor. Much of the tedious affair is taken up with his efforts to find a way for the two lovers to marry.

Once again, Witney is saddled with a script that, while different, is short on action. When Zorro finally does show up, a chase ensues on horseback with Zorro (Buddy Van Horn) finally tackling Lazaro (stuntman Lou Roberson) after sliding down a hill. The stunt, while performed well, looks unwieldy, similar in its awkwardness to a stunt performed in the Witney-directed "Welcome to Monterey."

John Hoyt, the veteran character actor who plays the master of Romaldo, is stuck in a rather thankless role. He comes across as a pompous and unyielding character. By the episode's end, he tries to be more sympathetic but it really doesn't work.

On the sets of television series, practical jokes are played to relieve the boredom; Gene Sheldon was one of Bill Witney's favorite targets. "Gene was very funny. Every time there was a shot of his eye looking through the peephole from the secret passage, he was wary as hell because he couldn't see and he knew he was going to get some water in his eye. The last time we pulled it on him, I fooled him by sneaking around behind him while the camera was running. I got him in the back of the head," Witney laughingly recalled.

Behind the Scenes

> A simple stunt has Zorro [Buddy Van Horn] leaping onto Tornado from a corral fence and nearly losing the saddle in the process.... One tragic note regarding this episode: Tom Pittman, the young actor who played the part of Romaldo, was killed in a car accident before the episode aired.

Episode 54

"The Iron Box"

Filmed: August 27–29, September 2, 3 & 8, 1958; *Air Date*: January 15, 1959; *Director*: William Witney; *Writer*: Bob Wehling; Cast: Harold J. Stone (Salvio), Mark Damon (Eugenio), Tige Andrews (Nava), Rebecca Welles (Moneta), Jerry Oddo (Crispin).

Diego and Bernardo arrive in Los Angeles with tax money for Sgt. Garcia. After collecting Diego's taxes, the sergeant takes Diego to see Salvio the blacksmith and his son Eugenio. Salvio has designed a great iron box into which the pueblo's tax money will be placed. As a precaution, Garcia's plan is to send the key for the box that evening to the governor in Monterey and then send the impregnable box.

After his work is done, Eugenio ignores his father's disapproval and meets his girlfriend Moneta in the tavern. (Salvio thinks the woman is too old for his son.) However, there are more sinister forces at work. Moneta is in league with two men who want to steal the contents of the iron box. Their plan is to force Eugenio to make an impression of the key. Before they can approach him with their scheme, he innocently tells them that the key has already been sent to Monterey. The bandits attempt to devise a new plan.

A ceremony is held to send off the giant box, during which Garcia inadvertently closes the lock before placing it on the box. Salvio must forge a temporary key to open it. Much to Garcia's relief, it works. The two bandits attempt to grab the temporary key as the crowd departs but Bernardo is already in the process of melting it down.

In the plaza, Moneta asks Eugenio to take her for a moonlight ride in the country that evening. This is the beginning of the bandits' alternate plan. As the iron box is en route to the governor, the bandits attack the convoy protecting it. A few lancers are killed and the box ends up at the bottom of a canyon.

That evening, during his ride with Moneta, Eugenio is taken prisoner by the bandits, who try to force him to open the lock. He tells them that only his father can do it. The bandits ride into Los Angeles and deceive Salvio into coming with them. However, Diego and Bernardo observe what is happening and Bernardo recognizes the two men as the ones who tried to take the key at the ceremony. Sensing trouble, Diego steps aside and lets Zorro take over.

At the bandits campsite, an attempt is made to force Salvio to open the lock. They are about to torture Eugenio when Zorro strikes. With the help of the blacksmith and a hot poker, Zorro subdues the bandits. He has saved the tax money and the blacksmith and his son have forged a better relationship.

Author's Notes

"The Iron Box" is another one-shot episode, that opens with a rather unusual camera shot. The scene begins in the plaza, as Diego and Bernardo ride into the shot from camera left; the camera pans and follows them to the cuartel. The point of view is from a balcony across the plaza from the cuartel where the two men who later turn out to be bandits are sitting. In past episodes most shots of the plaza area were taken from eye level so this is probably the first time the cuartel is seen from this perspective. Another scene which takes place at the blacksmith's shop is shot from a crane to obtain an aerial view. Camera angles of this type help to make the sets seem more spacious. They also add variety and give a fresh feel to a back lot that has been photographed a great deal.

The iron box was designed by William Witney himself. Actually made from wood, not iron, Walt Disney was so impressed with it that he put it on display at Disneyland. Witney laughingly recalled how Disney timidly asked him if it would be all right to display the box and Witney replied, "Hell, Walt, it's your studio, you can do anything you want."

In this episode, Witney had a chance to show off his expertise as an action director with a great chase along the mountainous roads of the Berry Ranch. This scene was very reminiscent of the director's days with Republic Pictures when he shot a couple of stunts like this a week. The scene involving the theft of the iron box was accomplished in one shot. Witney said, "The box went down once. [Production manager Roy Wade] was so mad at me because he had to retrieve it. It was the last shot of the day and when I turned that s.o.b. loose it kept going. Roy cussed me up one side and down the other because he was going to be there until eight o'clock that night trying to get it back up."

Zorro's arrival on the scene is one of the most dramatic and inventive. From the inside of a covered wagon he cuts a large Z and then leaps through the ripped canvas. The action that follows is a variation on the usual fencing, substituting hot-tipped pokers for swords. Like "The Cross of the Andes" where the action included a quarterstave-style fight, the action here works very well. The scene, filmed on a sound stage, takes place at the bandit's campsite after dark. It's very exciting as Zorro takes wide, hard swipes with this poker as his cape swishes about.

There is a minor set change, as the inside of the tavern has been re-modeled. The bar has been moved to the left of the front door as one enters and the tables and fireplace have been shifted to the right, opposite the bar.

Behind the Scenes

> Al Cavens and Victor Paul doubled the two bandits and Eric Alden stunted as Salvio, the blacksmith, for the fencing action.... Tige Andrews [Nava] went on to fame as Capt. Greer on TV's *The Mod Squad*.

EPISODE 55
"The Gay Caballero"

Filmed: September 17–19, 22–24, October 1 & 8, 1958; *Air Date*: January 22, 1959; *Director*: Hollingsworth Morse; *Writer*: Lowell Hawley; *Cast*: Cesar Romero (Estevan de la Cruz), Patricia Medina (Margarita), Nestor Paiva (Innkeeper), Howard Wendell (Don Marcos), Don Diamond (Cpl. Reyes), George Lewis (Don Alejandro).

A stranger arrives in Los Angeles on the stage from Santa Barbara. Sgt. Garcia meets the stage and learns that the man's name is Estevan de la Cruz and he has arrived in Los Angeles in search of his fortune. Garcia questions the man about a pouch he is holding and finds that it is filled with sparkling jewels. De la Cruz is looking for a place to stay; a hacienda would suit him. He has heard of the de la Vega rancho, so why not there? He exclaims he may even take it over. Garcia tries to dissuade the stranger but it is no use.

When they arrive at the hacienda, they learn that Don Alejandro and Diego are out but will be back shortly. De la Cruz takes the time to rearrange the furniture. The de la Vegas return and after a brief conversation on the patio with Garcia, an enraged Alejandro races in with sword in hand. The two men meet and embrace. The stranger is none other than Don Alejandro's brother-in-law (Diego's uncle) Estevan.

From a conversation between Alejandro and Diego it becomes apparent that Estevan is a bit of a ne'er-do-well, a con man. Estevan persuades Alejandro to hold a party for him, welcoming him to California.

At the fiesta that evening, Estevan shows his jewels to a new acquaintance, Don Marco. This is observed by two suspicious-looking strangers. Alejandro also sees what has transpired and confides to Diego that he is worried that Estevan may be trying to sell jewels that are not genuine. To get a closer look, Diego has Bernardo try to "steal" the jewels but he is unsuccessful. In the process, he spills wine on Estevan's jacket.

Estevan goes to his room to change while Diego is donning his Zorro disguise. But before Zorro can grab the jewels, the two strangers beat him to it. They knock Estevan unconscious and make off with the pouch. As Zorro enters the room, Estevan comes to and begins screaming. Zorro races outside where he encounters the two bandits. As he is about to capture them, Garcia and some lancers step in. Zorro is able to expose the two as thieves by using his bullwhip to snare the pouch from the bandits' pocket. Zorro rides off with the jewels hoping to keep Estevan out of mischief.

Author's Notes

"The Gay Caballero" marks the directorial debut of Hollingsworth Morse on *Zorro* and begins the next series of four episodes. Morse, who was a veteran of television, liked to work fast, perhaps a little too fast, as assistant director Ron Miller remembered with amusement. "Everything in series work is measured by the number of pages you can film each day. This is how the budget is determined and if you didn't do a certain amount of pages you were fired. Holly did 16½ pages in one day and all in the sala of the de la Vega hacienda. All of sudden it was said from upstairs, 'Everything is a master shot or two shots. Where are the close-ups?' Right then and there Holly said, 'Okay, if that's the way they want to play the game, then that's the way we'll play the game.' And he never averaged more than five and one-half or six pages per day."

This episode inaugurates another minor change in the series. According to Disney Studio publicity releases at the time, "*Zorro* episodes will open with new action and impact, specifically designed to retain viewer interest at the highest possible peak. Action film clips taken directly from the ensuing episode will replace the familiar theme and film footage." With the *Zorro* theme song retired, the episodes now opened with a stock shot of Zorro's sword cutting a Z over a surface (wanted poster, music sheet, barn door, canvas cover, etc.) and then a teaser (brief clip) from that night's episode was shown. This was followed by announcer Dick Tufeld exclaiming,

"*The Walt Disney Studios Present Zorro*," with the *Zorro* logo appearing on the screen. The clip of Zorro standing in the shadows and slashing a Z in the air followed, then a commercial and then the episode. Lou Debney, production coordinator of the show, felt that this "new" opening would quickly emphasize many of *Zorro's* strong new points to a wide range of viewers. "Viewers who have considered *Zorro* a pure adventure series will now see teaser film clips in each program, curtain raisers from episodes stressing romance, humor and high drama. Particular attention will be given the adult audience which now will be apprised of the highly adult sequences of that evening's adventure."[1] Loosely translated: Let's get more adults to watch the show. To this end, the teasers usually stressed the dramatic aspects of the particular episode rather than the adventure. The idea of a teaser shown at the opening of a dramatic TV series was fairly common practice in the late 1950s and early '60s. The studio was merely following a trend in an effort to get older viewers interested. Making the episodes slightly more adult-oriented was the strategy behind bringing Cesar Romero onto the show. Romero was well-known to parents who grew up in the '30s and '40s and with his Latin heritage was a perfect choice for the show. The episodes were written specifically for him and he was excellent in his role as Uncle Estevan, brother-in-law to Don Alejandro. He even received co-billing with Guy Williams at the opening of each episode. Romero was a breath of fresh air after the somewhat repetitious Monterey episodes.

"The Gay Caballero" begins with a humorous song, "Viva El Vino," sung by Sgt. Garcia and Cpl. Reyes. Cesar Romero also has a chance to show off some of the dance steps he used early in his career when he engages a barmaid in a quick whirl around the tavern.

Don Diego's mother, who is something of a mystery finally, is mentioned when an exasperated Alejandro (referencing his skepticism about Estevan's character) exclaims, "Diego, your mother was a wonderful woman. But as for the rest of the family, *ha!*"

Behind the Scenes

> The exterior of the rear of the tavern doubles for the rear of the de la Vega hacienda.... Veteran stuntman Dick Crockett plays a bandit who robs Uncle Estevan.... Nestor Paiva, who plays the innkeeper returns to the series for his first appearance in the second season.... The song "Viva El Vino" was written by Tom Adair and Buddy Baker.... The *Zorro* theme song with vocals will henceforth only be heard sporadically over the episode ending credits.

EPISODE 56

"Tornado Is Missing"

Filmed: September 15–18, 22, 23, 26 & October 7, 1958; *Air Date*: January 29, 1959; *Director*: Hollingsworth Morse; *Writer*: Bob Wehling; *Cast*: Cesar Romero (Esteven de la Cruz), George Lewis (Don Alejando), Don Diamond (Cpl. Reyes), Patricia Medina (Margarita).

As Diego and his father discuss Uncle Estevan's lack of ambition, Sgt. Garcia arrives. The sergeant is collecting donations for the charity horse race. Alejandro generously gives the sergeant 500 pesos. When Estevan gets wind of the race, he decides he must enter.

That afternoon, Diego receives some distressing news from Bernardo: Tornado is missing. While Diego, Alejandro and Bernardo go in search of the black horse, Estevan is in the process of trying to improve Diego's love life, extolling Diego's romantic qualities to Margarita, Don Marcos' daughter. As Estevan returns from Margarita's, he comes upon a black stallion. Estevan captures the horse and hides him in the old winery outside the pueblo. He returns to Los Angeles and tries to purchase oats on credit but the shopkeeper will have none of it. As luck would have it, Garcia and Cpl. Reyes happen by and Estevan is able to coax the money out of the sergeant by telling him that he will share his wager earnings with him. Estevan appears to have a horse that cannot lose.

Estevan takes Garcia and Reyes to see his prize stallion and they immediately recognize the horse as Zorro's. For Estevan this is icing on the cake. Not only will he win the race but he will follow Tornado back to Zorro and collect the reward for his capture.

That evening, after leaving Garcia and Reyes to guard Tornado, Estevan returns to the de la Vega hacienda. He lets slip to Diego that he is in possession of a powerful black stallion. Figuring that he has Tornado, Diego decides to let Zorro follow his uncle back to the horse. Once at the winery, the Fox has no trouble outwitting the hapless trio. Zorro rescues Tornado and for Estevan all bets are off.

Author's Notes

"Tornado Is Missing" is a relatively actionless affair but it's still fun because of the dialogue of Bob Wehling and the performance of Cesar Romero. Most of the humor results from the contrasting personalities of Don Estevan and Don Alejandro. Estevan is a bit of a devil-may-care rogue, somewhat irresponsible and a bit of a con man. Alejandro is just the opposite and Estevan spends most of his time trying to get the best of his brother-in-law. Diego takes the part of an amused bystander. At one point, Estevan refers to the wine Alejandro is serving as "not even good vinegar" and Alejandro becomes apoplectic. The comedy is derived from the fact that Estevan appears to be oblivious to how upset he is making his brother-in-law, who is being restrained by Diego.

Don Alejandro is not Estevan's only target. Sgt. Garcia and Corporal Reyes come in for their share as Estevan tries to interest them in one his schemes.

ESTEVAN: I'm going to let you in on something. Can he be trusted? [*Looking at Cpl. Reyes*]
GARCIA: [*Proudly*] I would trust Cpl. Reyes with my life.
ESTEVAN: This is a matter of money.
GARCIA: Corporal, talk to the storekeeper.

Another one of those scenes that this show does so well has Zorro quietly sneaking into the winery where the captured Tornado is being hidden. What makes it fun is that he slips in right in back of Garcia, Reyes and Estevan, who are standing not more than five feet from him but whose backs are turned.

Behind the Scenes

> Carl Pitti, who performed all the whip stunts in the second season, takes another turn in this episode as Zorro removes a mallet from Estevan's hand using a bullwhip.... The locations scenes are shot at Albertson's Ranch.... Jack Lilley doubles for Cesar Romero during the winery action.

EPISODE 57

"Zorro vs. Cupid"

Filmed: September 24–26, 30, October 1, 3 & 6–8, 1958; *Air Date:* February 5, 1959; *Director:* Hollingsworth Morse; *Writer:* Bob Wehling; *Cast:* Cesar Romero (Estevan), Howard Wendell (Don Marcos), Patricia Medina (Margarita), Don Diamond (Cpl. Reyes), George Lewis (Don Alejandro).

Both Diego and Alejandro are concerned: It seems that Estevan is now courting Margarita. Alejandro is afraid that his brother-in-law will seek his fortune through her. To keep an eye on the situation, Diego drops in on his uncle and watches him pour on the charm, singing and dancing to woo Margarita.

Don Marcos, Margarita's father, tells Estevan of the large dowry that Margarita will receive when she marries. It is at this moment that Estevan announces that he has asked Margarita to marry him and she has accepted. A look of concern comes over Diego's face.

During a ride later that day, Alejandro accuses Estevan of marrying Margarita for her money. This accusation just rolls off Estevan's back. Alejandro says that Zorro may ride against him because Zorro always rides against a thief. And he does just that when it becomes dark. Zorro pays a visit to Estevan and the two cross swords, much to Estevan's regret. Before Zorro leaves, he tells Estevan the climate would be better for him in Spain.

The next day, when Estevan tries to deliver flowers to Margarita, Zorro intercepts him and Estevan ends up in a lake. The beleaguered Romeo goes to Sgt. Garcia for help. Together they devise a plan to capture Zorro. As part of their scheme they convince Cpl. Reyes to dress up like Margarita. It seems that Estevan will take a well-publicized late night ride with someone who looks like his fiancée.

As expected, Zorro arrives—and also as expected the trap fails miserably. This time Garcia, Reyes and Estevan end up in the lake. As Zorro rides off, his laughter echoes in the night.

Author's Notes

In "Zorro vs. Cupid" the action kicks into a higher gear and the result is one of the best episodes of the second season. There are actually two separate fencing scenes, which is unusual, as well as other action in the form of a horse chase. The first duel is top-notch with Zorro facing off against Uncle Estevan (doubled by Buddy Van Horn). It takes place in the small confines of Estevan's bedroom but the action flows smoothly and the two adversaries make the most of their tight situation. The second duel is not quite so serious as Zorro is merely toying with his uncle. Estevan ends up all wet after being tossed into a lake for the second time by his masked nephew.

Comedy is not to be overlooked as Cpl. Reyes is forced to disguise himself as a señorita, going so far as to wear a dress but refusing to shave his moustache. The climax has Garcia being surrounded by three skunks preventing him from coming to Estevan's rescue. Both he and Reyes end up by being sprayed by the animals and they make a mad dash for the lake to join Uncle Estevan. Writer Bob Wehling added his own helpful hint regarding the skunks; in his script, in parentheses at the mention of the skunks he wrote, "preferably deodorized."

Behind the Scenes

> Music and dance is supplied courtesy of Cesar Romero. Although he is dubbed [by Bill Lee] in the song, "Mi Amor" [Tom Adair-Buddy Baker], he handles the dance steps without any help.... One curious note has the "deaf" Bernardo accompanying Estevan on guitar.... The lake scenes were shot at the Rowland Lee Ranch. Other location scenes were filmed at Albertson's Ranch.... Both of Zorro's fencing scenes are performed without his cape.... Margarita's patio is the de la Vega patio redecorated.

EPISODE 58
"The Legend of Zorro"

Filmed: September 25, 26, 29, October 2, 3, 6 & 8, 1958; *Air Date*: February 12, 1959; *Director*: Hollingsworth Morse; *Writer*: Lowell Hawley; *Cast*: Cesar Romero (Estevan), Howard Wendell (Don Marcos), Patricia Medina (Margarita), Don Diamond (Cpl. Reyes), George Lewis (Don Alejandro).

Margarita comes to the de la Vega hacienda to visit her fiancée Estevan who romances her with songs of love at the piano. Diego and Alejandro doubt Estevan's sincerity.

Alejandro wants Estevan to prove his love for Margarita and he makes Estevan an offer: He will give him land and cattle and if he can make a go of it, it will prove that he is ready to settle down. Estevan agrees. Alejandro and Estevan ride out to visit the piece of land and Estevan is visibly disappointed. It is an arid, dusty landscape. Somehow Estevan cannot picture himself and Margarita sharing marital bliss is such a place. That evening, during a conversation with Diego, Uncle Estevan makes it clear that he has no intention of taking Alejandro up on his offer. He says there is no sense to it; when he marries Margarita, he will be rich. Diego tries to plant the idea in his head that Zorro will find out. Diego explains, "You can't get away from Zorro." Estevan scoffs. Over the next few days a series of incidents, with Zs appearing in strange places, brings Estevan to the brink of defeat. He tells Diego that after he bids farewell to Margarita, he is heading back to Spain.

At midnight, Margarita's father Don Marcos arrives at the de la Vega hacienda in a harried state: Margarita is missing. Diego suspects his uncle so Zorro rides in pursuit of the rogue and his fiancée. He chases down the pair and crosses swords with Estevan. Zorro disarms him and makes off with Margarita. They ride to the mission where Zorro attempts to change the woman's mind regarding her future husband.

Estevan arrives just as Zorro is leaving. Estevan tries to hurry his fiancée into the church but she tells him that because of a legal stipulation she will receive no money if she marries a non–Californiano. She is testing Estevan's sincerity and he fails miserably. For her own good they should not get married, he tells her. He must go and fight for Spain—anything not to get married. As Estevan rides off into the night, from high on a hilltop Zorro waves farewell to Margarita.

Author's Notes

"The Legend of Zorro" is the final installment in the "Adventures of Uncle Estevan." The plot deals with the concept of Zorro as a supernatural being. In this regard, it owes a debt to the pulp stories where Zorro was often presented in this manner. In this story, Diego plants this idea in his uncle's head that "Zorro finds things out and no one knows how. You think you're alone the way we are here and then you find out that Zorro was there all the time." Zorro attempts to put a scare into Estevan in a number of creative ways: Candles on the floor in the sign of the Z, a Z burned into his lunchtime tortillas and, the most outrageous of all, after an afternoon nap, Diego's favorite uncle wakes up with a Z painted on his forehead. It's all done with a sense of real fun which makes it effective.

The conclusion contains another excellent fencing scene with Buddy Van Horn once again standing in for Cesar Romero. As in the previous episode, the duel is light–hearted at least from Zorro's point of view, as he has no interest in harming his uncle. At one point a laughing Zorro even out-fences Estevan while sitting on a log.

One false note is the reaction of Margarita when she learns that Estevan really only wanted to marry her for her money; she seemed to be in love with him but when she learns of his insincerity she laughs off the whole matter.

Overall "Adventures of Uncle Estevan" was a delightful group of episodes, possibly the best of the second season. They were genuinely funny with singing and dancing as well as exceptional fencing and the estimable talents of Cesar Romero. Hollingsworth Morse did a fine job with some first rate Lowell Hawley-Bob Wehling scripts. The quality of the four episodes was such that the studio considered packaging them for release abroad.

Behind the Scenes

The location work was filmed at Albertson's Ranch complete with a matte shot of San Juan Capistrano Mission by Peter Ellenshaw.... A previously unseen exit from the secret passage is used when Zorro enters a guest bedroom through an armoire.

EPISODE 59
"Spark of Revenge"

Filmed: September 3–5, 8, 11 & 12, 1958; *Air Date*: February 19, 1959; *Director*: William Witney; *Writer*: Lowell Hawley; *Cast*: Robert Vaughn (Miguel Roverto), Neil Hamilton (Don Hilario), Richard Devon and Mark Sheeler (Alviso Brothers), John Zaremba (Magistrado).

As a severe drought spreads across Southern California, Miguel Roverto races along the King's Highway with two men in pursuit. In his wagon he carries a large barrel of water. The two vaqueros chasing him are in the employ of Don Hilario, upon whose land Miguel has trespassed for the water. Miguel is captured and beaten, his water confiscated. The vaqueros warn him to stay off Don Hilario's land.

Don Hilario reports to Sgt. Garcia what has happened. Garcia persuades the don not to press charges against Miguel; however, Don Hilario says he will shoot Miguel on sight if he trespasses again. Foolishly, Miguel makes another attempt and once again he is stopped by Don Hilario and his men. This time they smash his barrels and take his rifle. Before more damage can be done, Sgt. Garcia and his lancers arrive.

That night at the de la Vega hacienda, Diego talks to Bernardo of the drought. As he looks off in the distance he sees a fire burning. He and Bernardo race off to help only to find that it is Miguel's house and it has already burned to the ground. Miguel bitterly blames Don Hilario—with one barrel of water, he could have prevented the fire from spreading.

The next day at the tavern, Miguel has words with Don Hilario and threatens him for all to hear. Diego tries to calm the situation and offers Miguel money to help him rebuild. He refuses the offer. A few days later, Diego learns from Sgt. Garcia that Miguel has been accused of burning down Don Hilario's hacienda. When Diego goes to the Magistrado's office to speak on Miguel's behalf, he learns that Don Hilario was killed in the fire and the charge is now murder. Diego believes that Miguel is innocent but he learns that Miguel has escaped from the lancers who were bringing him in. Diego feels he has done all he can do, now it's Zorro's turn.

Zorro pursues the fugitive through the countryside. After capturing Miguel and talking to him, he thinks that Don Hilario's two vaqueros may have had something to do with the don's death. Zorro rides ahead to what is left of Don Hilario's hacienda. There he finds the two vaqueros preparing to escape and overhears them admit to killing their employer. Zorro steps in and after a dangerous hand-to-hand struggle is able to subdue the two with the help of Miguel. As Zorro is about to take his leave, the heavens open up and rain begins to fall. Perhaps Miguel's troubles are finally over.

Author's Notes

"Spark of Revenge" marks William Witney's last directorial chore of the second season. Like "The Iron Box" before it, "Spark of Revenge" contains the kind of action that Witney is noted for: Horse and buckboard chases, fistfights and the often-used bulldog stunt. All are on display in this segment. The problem with the action scene that takes place inside the barn is that it's very obvious that Guy Williams is being doubled. As good as Buddy Van Horn was at his job, sometimes the illusion is shattered by certain shots. The action in question is a brief fistfight between Zorro and a vaquero. It is out of character for Zorro to engage in this kind of physical action. In the past, the few times that Zorro has been involved in hand-to-hand combat he usually strikes his foe with the back of his hand, more of a slap than a punch. Williams usually performed these scenes himself and they have a certain style to it that fits the character. When Van Horn throws a punch, as he does in this episode, it seems out of place, too much like a Western. His body movements weren't like Williams' and in scenes such as these the differences become obvious.

The theme of "Spark of Revenge" (the drought in California and how it affects the land owners) is interesting and the scene where it finally does begin to rain is very dramatic. As the thunder cracks and the rain begins to fall, Miguel falls to his knees and holds his open hands to the darkened heavens. Zorro looks up as the lightning flashes against his face, pats Miguel's shoulder and then rides off into the night.

Behind the Scenes

> The exterior action footage was shot at Berry Ranch.... John Zaremba, who played the Magistrado went on to co-star in *The Time Tunnel* and then later became commercial spokesman for Hills Bros. Coffee. Robert Vaughn, who was a year away from his big break in *The Magnificent Seven*, turned up as a co-star in one of the biggest shows in the '60s, *The Man from U.N.C.L.E.*.... Buddy Van Horn doubles one of the vaqueros for the chase along El Camino Real.... The exterior of Don Hilario's hacienda is actually the winery on the back lot.... Neil Hamilton went on to portray his most memorable role, that of Commissioner Gordon on the *Batman* TV series.

The next three episodes return Hollingsworth Morse as director and are most notable for the facts surrounding their creation rather than the stories themselves. They were written especially for Annette Funicello, who had enjoyed great popularity as a Mouseketeer. Next to Fess Parker, she was Disney's biggest live star and was receiving 1,000 fan letters a week in 1958. Annette recalled the circumstances of her appearances on *Zorro*. "For my sixteenth birthday, Walt Disney knew that I was crazy in love with Guy Williams. He came to me one day with a script and he said, 'How would you like to appear in a *Zorro*?' And I said, 'You're kidding, me?' And he said, 'Now that you're all grown up here's your script.' It was such a thrill for me that Mr. Disney would think of such a wonderful birthday present. They had a big surprise party for me when the show was finished filming. It was one of the nicest experiences of my life."[2]

Annette stands by her hero (courtesy of Walt Disney Productions).

Episode 60

"The Missing Father"

Filmed: October 20–24, 27–30 & November 3–7, 1958; *Air Date*: February 26, 1959; *Director*: Hollingsworth Morse; *Writer*: Bob Wehling; *Cast*: Annette Funicello (Anita Cabrillo), Carlos Rivas (Ruiz), George Lewis (Don Alejandro), Arthur Space (Gonzales), Wendell Holmes (Storekeeper), Penny Stanton (Cresencia), Don Diamond (Cpl. Reyes).

Anita Cabrillo has just arrived in Los Angeles from Spain for a surprise meeting with her father. Anita begins to inquire as to her father's whereabouts, and it seems nobody has heard of him. Sgt. Garcia attempts to help but it is fruitless. Because the girl is underage and seems to have nobody to care for her, Garcia must send her back to Spain. Don Diego, who has been observing the situation, steps in and agrees to let Anita stay at the de la Vega hacienda until her father can be found.

As Anita prepares for bed, a mysterious figure appears at the window. Her terrified scream brings Diego, Alejandro and Bernardo. When Diego investigates, he finds nothing. It seems that now Alejandro is beginning to doubt Anita's story but Diego, ever the optimist, is determined to help her find her father. The next day Diego and Alejandro pore over documents in Garcia's office hoping to find some mention of Don Miguel Cabrillo. Diego questions Gonzales, the mail handler and horse tender, who also is no help. However, believing that Anita's life may be in danger, Diego lets Zorro keep an eye on her.

That evening, Anita leaves on horseback and rides into the mountains with Zorro trailing. Following instructions from a note, she dismounts and heads off on foot. Zorro keeps a discreet distance. Anita meets with the mysterious stranger, his face hidden by a large sombrero and serape. He warns her to go back to Spain or face the consequences. Zorro's arrival frightens the girl and the stranger, who dashes off. Zorro gives chase but abandons his prey as he hears Anita scream. Her horse has been frightened by a rattlesnake and takes off at breakneck speed with her aboard. The horse is no match for Tornado as Zorro saves the frightened girl and returns her to the de la Vega hacienda. The girl is contrite and apologizes to Don Alejandro but she is still determined to find her father.

Author's Notes

"The Missing Father" is short on action but does manage to impose a rather ominous mood by way of a mysterious character who is seen mostly in shadow. There is one scene in which Anita is combing her hair by an open window and two hands come up as if to grab her. She sees them and screams. It's well-done and would probably seem rather frightening to the younger audience. The comedy comes in the form of Bernardo trying to cheer up a crying Anita. He trips and falls and then does a dance number pretending that one leg is shorter than the other. It's actually an old vaudeville routine that Gene Sheldon did a few years later in *Babes in Toyland*.

Hollingsworth Morse creates a lonely, eerie atmosphere for all the scenes filmed at Vasquez Rocks. They were shot using the day-for-night process, and there is the constant sound of howling wind on the soundtrack and echoes added to voices, which intensifies the feeling of isolation. There is also some impressive matte work by Peter Ellenshaw to augment the Vasquez landscape. The mattes give the impression that the entire area is perched on the edge of a cliff. In reality, while there are many round boulders and large, sharp slanted rocks, there is no cliff.

Behind the Scenes

> Valley Kean, who doubled Jolene Brand in the Monterey episodes, stands in for Annette in the riding scenes at Vasquez.... A total of four days was spent filming at Vasquez Rocks.

EPISODE 61
"Please Believe Me"

Filmed: October 20–23, 29–31, & November 3–6, 1958; *Air Date*: March 5, 1959; *Director*: Hollingsworth Morse; *Writer*: Lowell Hawley; *Cast*: Annette Funicello (Anita Cabrillo), Carlos Rivas (Ruiz), George Lewis (Don Alejandro), Arthur Space (Gonzales), Wendell Holmes (Storekeeper), Penny Stanton (Cresencia), Greigh Phillips (José).

In an attempt to find Anita Cabrillo's father, Diego takes her into Los Angeles and makes some inquiries. He again questions the mail handler Gonzales, who says he can remember no mail leaving Los Angeles addressed to Cabrillo. Diego's questioning prods Anita's memory and she tells him that she has all the letters her father wrote to her. They return to the hacienda, where she searches her trunk for them and finds nothing. At this point Don Alejandro begins to doubt Anita's story even more and decides it is time to send her back to Spain.

Realizing this will be her last chance to find her father, Anita goes to see Ruiz, a vaquero Diego has recently hired. She offers him money if he will take her to the Mission of San Fernando to see the padre who came over from Spain with her. She believes that he will help corroborate her story. Ruiz agrees and brings his compadre along. When they begin to travel in an out-of-the-way direction, Anita suspects their motives and breaks away. While being pursued, she tumbles over a cliff onto a ledge.

At the de la Vega hacienda, Anita's disappearance has been noticed so Diego makes a quick change to Zorro and begins tracking her. He arrives in time to disarm the two vaqueros, who escape as he rescues Anita with the help of his rope and Tornado. When he returns her to the hacienda, he discovers that she is a headstrong young woman and still very much determined to find her father.

Author's Notes

"Please Believe Me" is almost interchangeable with "The Missing Father." Both conclusions were filmed at Vasquez Rocks although this episode provides a little more

An outtake photograph from the AC sparkplug ad. It was taken at Vasquez Rocks during the filming of the Annette episodes (courtesy of Toni Anderson).

action and excitement than the previous installment. One scene at Vasquez gives the impression that Anita is perched on the edge of a cliff with a sharp, pointed peak up above her. Once again this is almost entirely created by the matte work of Peter Ellen-shaw. The only part of the landscape that really exists in this scene is the pointed rock up above Anita.

There is one song performed by Anita, "Lonely Guitar," which was written by head Mouseketeer Jimmie Dodd. The song was actually recorded as a single in 1958 to cash in on Annette's popularity. Interestingly, during the coming attractions for this episode there is a scene of Anita singing this song and (unbeknownst to her) a pair of hands are reaching for her as if to strangle her. However, this scene did not appear in the episode.

The scene leading to the climax makes little sense. It occurs when Anita hires two vaqueros to take her to the Mission of San Fernando and along the way they try to kill her. Since she has already offered to give them all the money she has for their services, why would they try to kill her?

Behind the Scene

> Charles Horvath, a stuntman turned actor, stands in for Carlos Rivas when a judo-style flip is required. Horvath appears in a later *Zorro* episode, "Señor China Boy," as the main heavy ... Carl Pitti cracks Zorro's bullwhip.

EPISODE 62

"The Brooch"

Filmed: October 22–24, 27, 28, 31 & November 3–7, 1958; *Air Date*: March 12, 1959; *Director*: Hollingsworth Morse; *Writer*: Bob Wehling; *Cast*: Annette Funicello (Anita Cabrillo), Carlos Rivas (Ruiz), George Lewis (Don Alejandro), Arthur Space (Gonzales), Wendell Holmes (Storekeeper), Penny Stanton (Cresencia), Greigh Phillips (José).

Gonzalez the stable master arrives at the de la Vega hacienda to pick up Anita's trunk for her trip back to Spain. As he waits outside, he overhears Diego and his father argue the merits of the decision. As Anita prepares to leave, Alejandro notices the brooch she is wearing and inquires about it. She claims her father sent it to her. Alejandro recognizes it as a brooch that belonged to his wife. When she passed away he donated it to the church to auction it off. The brooch seems to substantiate Anita's story. Her father must be somewhere in Los Angeles. It is decided that she will be allowed to remain.

Diego and Alejandro ride into Los Angeles to check the church files and see if there is any record of who purchased the brooch. The trio, now joined by Sgt. Garcia, find the record book, but the page they are looking for is gone.

The former de la Vega vaqueros, Ruiz and José, are searching through Gonzales' room looking for money. Instead they find the Cabrillo letters. After browsing through them, Ruiz concludes that Gonzales must be Anita's father. When the stable master returns, they knock him unconscious and devise a plot. They will hold him for ransom, believing that Anita will pay for his safe return. While playing a hunch, Diego and Alejandro go to Gonzales' room. There, on the floor, they find the missing page to the church record book.

Back at the de la Vega hacienda, a young boy brings a note for Anita. She is instructed to come to a special meeting place and to bring money. She slips out from under Bernardo's watchful eye and rides into the country. When she arrives at the meeting place, she is met by Ruiz and José and for the first time in many years she meets her father. Ruiz, however, double-crosses her — he takes the money and intends to kill both of them. Anita is armed with a small pistol and she and her father escape. As they hide, Gonzales explains that he was afraid she would be ashamed of him, which is why he tried to scare her back to Spain. As the two thieves close in, Zorro arrives and pursues Ruiz, who in an effort to escape falls to his death. Gonzales takes care of José with a bullet in the arm.

The next day, Diego and company bid farewell to Don Miguel Cabrillo and his proud daughter as they return to Spain.

Author's Notes

"The Brooch" plays out the arc of "Annette" episodes and once again the similarities between the three episodes cannot be ignored. They probably could have been edited into a very tight one-hour show which would have eliminated some of the obvious padding. However, writers Lowell Hawley and Bob Wehling were very generous to Annette's character, Anita. Any editing may have left a number of her scenes on the cutting room floor. These episodes were really a showcase for Annette and, given her popularity, it was easy to see why.

The climax takes place at Vasquez again, with a few selected action scenes being filmed on the Disney back lot. When the action does finally come, it is exciting, as Zorro must fend off Rivas, who is wielding long pieces of burning wood. When the villain falls to his death into a deep crevice, it's one that's been created by matte artist Peter Ellenshaw.

There is a perplexing bit of business at the conclusion. In an effort to devise a "happily ever after" finale, Gonzales, Anita's father, mysteriously goes from poor stable master to the well-dressed Don Miguel with no explanation whatsoever. Although she says otherwise earlier in the episode, it seems that for Anita to be happy her father must be a don.

All in all these episodes were more moody than exciting and were hindered somewhat by Annette's lack of dramatic acting experience. However, it is fun to see a pop icon in her prime.

EPISODE 63

"Zorro and the Mountain Man"

Filmed: November 7, 10–13, 18, 19, 21, 24, 25, December 16, 23, 1958, & January 19, 1959 *Air Date*: March 19, 1959; *Director*: Charles Barton; *Writer*: N.B. Stone, Jr.; *Cast*: Jeff York (Joe Crane), Jonathan Harris (Don Carlos), Jean Willes (Carlotta), Paul Richards (Hernando), Don Diamond (Cpl. Reyes), Robert Swan (Pedro).

While traveling to Los Angeles, mountain man Joe Crane happens upon Bernardo, whose carriage has lost a wheel. Using his prodigious strength, Crane lifts the carriage, puts the wheel back on and sends Bernardo on his way. As Crane enters Los Angeles he is noticed by Don Carlos and his head vaquero. Don Carlos makes it clear to his man that he hates foreigners.

At the tavern, as Crane is questioned by Sgt. Garcia, Don Diego arrives with Bernardo. He introduces himself to Crane and thanks him for helping his manservant. Garcia tells Crane that because he is an "Americano" and has entered California without a permit, he must be jailed. Diego tries to intercede but Garcia will not be deterred. Before Crane is led off to jail, he steals a kiss from Carlotta the waitress. Don Carlos arrives in time to see this "affront to Spanish womanhood" and attacks Crane for what he considers an insulting action. Crane easily manhandles Don Carlos and in doing so has created an enemy for life. As the mountain man is led off to jail, Diego overhears Don Carlos plan to kill Crane and make this an example to all foreigners.

As darkness descends, Zorro obtains the cell keys form a sleeping Garcia. He sets Crane free and engages an awakened Garcia in a swift sword fight. The sergeant is left trying to hold his pants up and Joe Crane has been freed before Don Carlos and his men can kill him.

Author's Notes

"Zorro and the Mountain Man" begins the next series of three episodes and, after the rather serious tone of the "Annette" series, the emphasis is definitely on comedy. These episodes are somewhat similar to the *Annette* segments in that one teleplay is barely distinguishable from another. The plot line, which has Crane trying to recover his furs and avoid the wrath of Don Carlos, wears thin quickly.

What saves the episode is the comedy which is placed upon the broad and able shoulders of Disney veteran Jeff York. York, whose real name was Granville Schofield, began his career in the 1930s. He started out doing theater work as well as amateur and professional boxing and then went on to success as *Li'l Abner.* He signed an exclusive contract with Disney in the 1950s and appeared as Mike Fink in *Davy Crockett and the River Pirates.* He popped up in other Disney vehicles such as *Westward Ho the Wagons!, The Great Locomotive Chase, Johnny Tremain, Old Yeller* and *Savage Sam.*

The character of Joe Crane the mountain man was actually introduced on *The Saga of Andy Burnett,* a series which appeared on the Disneyland TV show in 1957. With long shaggy hair and beard, York is perfect for the part as he announces to Sgt. Garcia just who he is: "Joe Crane stands in front of you as big as life and twice as nasty. I was born in a grizzly den and raised on buffalo milk. I'm blood brother to the west wind and full cousin to the hoooowling wolf. I'm so mean I'll fight a rattlesnake and give him first bite! I'm king of all mountain men." Crane also had his own theme song, written by Gil George, George Bruns and N.B. Stone, Jr., extolling the virtues of the mountain man.

There is one duel in this episode between Zorro and Sgt. Garcia and as always when Garcia is involved it's played more for comedy. Zorro cuts both of the sergeant's suspenders, leaving him more occupied with his pants than the sword fight at hand. Part of this scene employs a camera angle shot from straight overhead looking down, giving the viewer a unique perspective.

The villain in this piece is Jonathan Harris, who co-starred with Guy Williams on TV's *Lost in Space* in the mid–1960s. Harris recently commented that although the two men worked on the science fiction show for three years together, Harris' appearance on *Zorro* was never mentioned. In the course of the episode, the Joe Crane character had a chance to do to Harris' character what *Lost in Space* fans probably wanted to do for years—smack Harris in the jaw.

The conclusion in Zorro's secret room is entertaining in the Disney style. As Zorro removes his mask by candlelight, he tells Bernardo to remind him to send Sgt. Garcia a new pair of suspenders. Having said this, he takes his sword and slashes the candle from the table and laughs as the screen goes dark.

Behind the Scenes

> This was Charles Barton's last episode on *Zorro*. He went on to direct *The Shaggy Dog* [1959] and *Toby Tyler* [1960] for Disney.

EPISODE 64
"The Hound of the Sierras"

Filmed: November 12–14, 17, 18, 21, 25, 26 & 28, 1958; *Air Date*: March 26, 1959; *Director*: Hollingsworth Morse; *Writer*: N.B. Stone, Jr.; *Cast*: Jeff York (Joe Crane), Jonathan Harris (Don Carlos), Jean Willes (Carlotta), Paul Richards (Hernando), Lloyd Corrigan (Sancho), Don Diamond (Cpl. Reyes).

After having been rescued by Zorro the night before, Joe Crane makes his way to the house of Carlotta's father. Crane has remained near the pueblo so he can retrieve his furs which Sgt. Garcia has confiscated.

After a futile night of searching for the mountain man, the good sergeant has returned to the pueblo. There he is berated by Don Carlos for his failed efforts. Diego, who is sitting on the tavern patio, overhears Don Carlos' plan to track Crane with his vicious wolfhound. Don Carlos' aide Hernando tells him that Crane's rifle is in the tavern and would give the wolfhound the mountain man's scent. Diego rushes inside and quickly handles the musket, replacing Crane's scent with his own, thereby confusing the wolf. For the moment, Don Carlos is foiled.

Later that day, after attempting to track the mountain man again, Sgt. Garcia returns with Crane's hat. While Garcia and his men are drinking, Hernando takes the hat so their hound can use it to track Crane. Diego, also in the tavern, observes what has happened. Meanwhile, Joe Crane has returned to the pueblo to retrieve his furs.

The wolf catches the scent but it is the animal that is trapped by Crane. However, Don Carlos and his men capture him. As they are about to hang him, Zorro once again intercedes and it is Don Carlos who ends up bound and hanging. Crane escapes once again but he is still determined to retrieve his furs.

Author's Notes

In an unusual move, director Charles Barton did not complete this trio of "Mountain Man" episodes. At the time they were shot, November 1959, Barton was also involved with *The Shaggy Dog* for Disney. Because of Barton's busy schedule, Hollingsworth Morse was brought in to direct the remaining two.

Most of the comedy in "The Hound of the Sierras" concerns Joe Crane and his windbag ways. One scene has Crane hiding from Garcia in a large barrel full of rainwater. The camera is able to show Crane underwater making some hilarious faces as he tries to hold his breath. Sgt. Garcia also gets off a good line when discussing Zorro's identity with Diego: "He is a man and he lives somewhere near here."

There is an excellent duel between Zorro and Hernando (Al Cavens doubling) with Williams and Cavens employing a number of new fencing combinations which add to the excitement. During the swordplay, a screaming Don Carlos hangs overhead suspended by a rope, adding a light touch to the affair.

Behind the Scenes

There is a Peter Ellenshaw matte of Don Carlos' hacienda (exterior) ... "A Soldier's Sweetheart" by Gil George and George Bruns is sung by Henry Calvin.

EPISODE 65

"Manhunt"

Filmed: November 11, 13, 18–20, 28 & December 1, 1958; *Air Date*: April 2, 1959; *Director*: Hollingsworth Morse; *Writer*: N.B. Stone, Jr.; *Cast*: Jeff York (Joe Crane), Jonathan Harris (Don Carlos), Jean Willes (Carlotta), Paul Richards (Hernando), Lloyd Corrigan (Sancho), Don Diamond (Cpl. Reyes), Robert Swan (Pedro).

After having been saved by Zorro the night before, Joe Crane makes his way back to Carlotta's house. He refuses to leave Los Angeles without his furs. Back at the pueblo, Don Carlos also refuses to give up and is hatching a new plan to capture the mountain man.

Diego is still looking for Crane and, playing a hunch, visits Carlotta. After much prodding, Crane reluctantly shows himself and Diego makes him an offer: He will buy the furs from Sgt. Garcia, give them back to Crane and send him on his way. Crane agrees and Diego returns to the pueblo and visits with Garcia only to find out he is too late — Don Carlos has already purchased the furs. Diego rides to Don Carlos' hacienda and makes him a generous offer but he is turned down. Diego realizes that Don Carlos is using the furs as bait to trap Crane.

Growing impatient for Diego to return, Crane bids Carlotta farewell and heads for the pueblo. He comes upon a sleeping Garcia and, with knife in hand, awakens him and finds out that his enemy now owns his furs. He locks Garcia and the other lancers in the cuartel jail and heads off to deal with the waiting Don Carlos. Diego and Bernardo arrive at the cuartel and learn of the mountain man's plan. It is time for Zorro to put an end to Don Carlos' treachery.

Zorro arrives ahead of Crane and disposes of two of Don Carlos' men. The mountain man makes his way to the hacienda and quickly handles Don Carlos. So, with the help of Zorro, Joe Crane regains his furs and finally heads back to his beloved mountains.

Author's Notes

"Manhunt" concludes the "Mountain Man" series and it's very similar to the two that preceded it — Jeff York comedy, back lot filming, very few extras and over-acting by Jonathan Harris. One only has to look at Jeff York to start laughing. He's big, comical and not afraid to ham it up a bit. At the conclusion there is a hilarious scene where Crane must stare down a wolf. He not only accomplishes this with some very outrageous facial expressions but with a series of howls, growls and yips he befriends the animal and the pair head off into the hills together. At one point, Crane sports willow branches on his moccasins to throw off trackers. They must be seen to be believed. Later he says to Garcia, "I'm so hoppin' mad I could bite myself." Needless to say, York was born to play this and all the other similar parts he played at the Disney Studio.

There is a very interesting piece of editing utilized when Zorro climbs up on a rooftop and is about to overcome one of Don Carlos' unsuspecting henchmen. It is a close-up shot of Zorro and, as he turns his back to the camera, his cape fills the screen. It is here that the edit is made with just a slight jump to make it noticeable. As Zorro moves toward the villain, he grabs him and appears to tie him up although the viewer doesn't see what has transpired until Zorro steps away. The reason for the edit is so that the scene can be stopped and the actor playing the villain could be tied up. If this scene had been shot in one take, it would have been difficult time-wise for Guy Williams to bind and gag the villain and have the end result look convincing.

The conclusion of this tale has Zorro actually stabbing one of the rifle-wielding villains in the stomach. It was only the second time in the series that Zorro would presumably kill someone intentionally. (Viewers don't actually see the man die, but it is assumed that he does.)

Behind the Scenes

Jeff York went on to star in his own series with Roger Moore, *The Alaskans*, in 1959. He appeared only occasionally after that series went off the air, retiring for personal reasons in 1966.

11

Return to Los Angeles
Episode Guide, Part 2

EPISODE 66
"The Man from Spain"

Filmed: December 1–3, 8, 9, 12 & 17, 1958; *Air Date*: April 9, 1959; *Director*: Hollingsworth Morse; *Writer*: Robert Bloomfield; *Cast*: Everett Sloane (Andres Basilio), Robert J. Wilke (Capitan Mendoza); George Lewis (Don Alejandro); Gloria Talbott (Moneta), Nestor Paiva (Innkeeper); Don Diamond (Cpl. Reyes).

Sgt. Garcia is in the tavern with all his friends celebrating his birthday. As Diego blindfolds the sergeant in anticipation of his piñata, in walk two strangers. One is a tall military man, the other a short, well-dressed aristocrat. The taller man is Capitan Mendoza and the other introduces himself as Andres Basilio, the king's emissary. Both are newly arrived from Spain. Reminding all that Spain is at war with England, France and the Netherlands, Señor Basilio quickly puts an end to the celebration.

Basilio's main purpose in Los Angeles seems to be to help raise money for Spain's war effort. To do so, he seeks the help of Don Alejandro, who agrees to assist in the sale of royal bonds. Basilio also has his man Mendoza begin to coerce the merchants to contribute a large share of their profits.

That evening, when everyone is asleep, Sgt. Garcia goes in search of his birthday gifts, which were confiscated by Basilio and last seen in the tavern. Unfortunately for the sergeant, he surprises Capitan Mendoza who is sampling the wine. He doesn't see Mendoza, who knocks a wine rack over onto the fat sergeant. The innkeeper catches Garcia in the act and Basilio puts Garcia in the stocks as an example.

In the dead of night Zorro arrives on the scene and, after a furious sword fight, disarms Basilio and Mendoza. He then replaces Garcia in the stocks with the arrogant newcomer whom he proceeds to humiliate in front of the entire pueblo. He forces Basilio to sing a birthday song to Garcia. Zorro then returns Garcia his piñata, wishes him a happy birthday and disappears into the night.

Author's Notes

"The Man from Spain" begins the next series of four episodes, all directed by Hollingsworth Morse. They are more serious in content following the broad humor of the Jeff York episodes. The "man" in the title is the very talented and prestigious actor Everett Sloane. Sloane's career was all-encompassing: radio (one of Orson Welles' Mercury Playhouse Theatre players), theater, movies and, grudgingly, television. Like many actors of his generation he saw television only as a way to make a living. It was difficult for a man who co-starred in such films as *Citizen Kane* and *The Lady from Shanghai* to work in what he considered "a sea of mediocrity." Nonetheless, Sloane was very good in these episodes. He overplayed things a bit but that's what the role called for — a bit of mustache-twirling villainy. Like Cesar Romero, the addition of Sloane was part of the continuing Disney effort to add more adults to the show's audience.

Sloane's henchman in these episodes was Robert J. Wilke. Next to Lee Van Cleef, there probable wasn't a better villain in movies or television in the 1950s and '60s. But Wilke, who seemed to be born with a sneer on his face, is somewhat restrained here and not up to his usual villainous standards. He seems a bit out of place; he doesn't attempt an accent and looks extremely uncomfortable with a sword at his side instead of a six-shooter.

There is a very good sword fight involving Zorro and two adversaries with Buddy Van Horn standing in for Wilke and Victor Paul doubling for Everett Sloane. The choreography here is excellent as Zorro keeps both men busy without missing a beat. The fencing shows Guy Williams at the peak of his abilities. After Zorro disarms his opponents, he has the opportunity to force Basilio to sing a birthday song to Garcia. The sergeant's discomfort is very amusing as he realizes that he will have to live with Basilio after Zorro is gone and would probably have preferred to have not quite so much help from his masked friend.

Behind the Scenes

> Sgt. Garcia performs one song for his birthday, "Happiest Day of the Year" by Lowell Hawley and George Bruns.

EPISODE 67

"Treasure for the King"

Filmed: December 1, 3, 4, 9, 12, 15 & 17–19, 1958; *Air Date*: April 16, 1959; *Director*: Hollingsworth Morse; *Writer*: Maury Hill; *Cast*: Everett Sloane (Andres Basilio), Gloria Talbott (Moneta); Robert J. Wilke (Capitan Mendoza), Edgar Barrier (Don Cornelio), George Lewis (Don Alejandro), Don Diamond (Cpl. Reyes).

Diego visits the office of Señor Basilio and learns that the sale of royal bonds does not go well. However, he brings good news: Don Cornelio has invited Basilio for dinner and wants to discuss the purchase of a large supply of royal bonds. After Don Cornelio's purchase, others follow his example and the money and valuables begin to pour in. It seems that now Basilio's negative view of Los Angeles is rapidly changing. He decides not to return to Spain and, more important, he decides to keep the treasures for himself.

Later that day, Basilio crosses paths with Diego and tells him of his new out-look on Los Angeles and also of his desire to purchase a hacienda. This arouses Diego's curiosity regarding Basilio's newfound wealth.

Back at his office, Basilio shows Capitan Mendoza a device he has concocted: an exploding chest that will sink the ship that is supposed to take the treasure back to Spain. All will think the valuables went down with the ship. However, the real treasure will remain with Basilio.

The chests are loaded aboard a wagon and are taken on their way to the port at San Pedro where they will begin their long journey to Spain. Diego, whose suspicions about Basilio are increasing, decides to investigate. While Bernardo keeps a guard occupied, Diego enters Basilio's empty office. In a closet he finds three locked chests. "If they are locked, they must contain something valuable — the treasure Basilio has collected, perhaps. If so, what was in the chests Basilio has sent to San Pedro?" won-ders Diego. It is time for Zorro to act.

Zorro and Bernardo race after the caravan carrying the dummy chests heading for Spain. When the lancers see Zorro, they separate from the caravan and chase after him; however, it is a black-caped Bernardo they're chasing. The real Zorro gallops after the wagon containing the chests. As the lancer leaps from the driver's seat, Zorro jumps aboard and brings the wagon to a halt. But the loaded caisson breaks away and hurtles into a canyon, exploding in mid-air.

That evening Señor Basilio receives word from the ship's captain that the treas-ure is safely on board. Slipping into the closet to examine the real treasure chests, he opens one to discover — rocks. He frantically opens the other two to discover the same. There is also another similarity: All three chests have a Z carved into the lid of the chests. Outfoxed again.

Author's Notes

"Treasure for the King" is a difficult episode to enjoy because it is littered with inconsistencies and loose ends. Normally these type of half-baked plots can be over-looked but here it begs to be examined. The first question that comes to mind is, why does Zorro chase after the coach? If the real valuables are in Basilio's closet, what's the point? Also, what would make Basilio believe that the chests would make it to the port of San Pedro without blowing up first (which is exactly what happens)? If the motion of the sea would set off the booby trap, wouldn't a rough country road have the same effect? Perhaps the most unbelievable development of all is how Zorro gets the three treasure chests out of Basilio's closet and to the port of San Pedro and then replaces them with three chests full of rocks and place them back in Basilio's closet before nightfall. Of course, Zorro is capable of extraordinary things, but this is truly a miracle.

While Basilio's booby trap device may be ill-conceived, there is an amusing Rube Goldberg quality to it. It works like this: The trunk is split into two halves; on one side is a loaded flint lock pistol whose trigger is bound by a leather thong. The thong in turn is tied to a cup which is held in mid-air by the leather. Up above the cup is a water bucket that will slowly fill the cup (as a result of the jostling of the waves). As the cup is filled, it will put pressure on the leather thong tied to the trigger. Once the trigger is pulled, the spark from the gun will ignite the gunpowder in the other half of the box, causing a huge explosion.

The action climax has Zorro (Buddy Van Horn) chasing, then leaping onto a moving buckboard. This is a transfer stunt that was standard for its time but it's still very exciting. Stuntman Jerry Brown drives the wagon and then leaps off before Zorro jumps aboard.

Behind the Scenes

> The chase scene was filmed at the Berry Ranch where a similar action sequence for "The Iron Box" was shot.... The interior of Don Cornelio's hacienda is the de la Vega hacienda slightly redecorated.... Edgar Barrier also played a don in the first season ["Monastario Sets a Trap"].

EPISODE 68
"Exposing the Tyrant"

Filmed: December 4, 5, 8, 12 & 15–17, 1958; *Air Date*: April 23, 1959; *Director*: Hollingsworth Morse; *Writers*: Bob Wehling and Maury Hill; *Cast*: Everett Sloane (Basilio), Gloria Talbott (Moneta), Robert J. Wilke (Capitan Mendoza), Edgar Barrier (Don Cornelio), George Lewis (Don Alejandro), Don Diamond (Cpl. Reyes).

With his thirst for money and power increasing, Señor Basilio is devising a plan, and he will use Sgt. Garcia as his pawn. He tells the gullible sergeant that he should think about retirement and that the government will give land to a soldier when he retires. Garcia's eyes grow as large as his stomach. "Don Demetrio Lopez Garcia" sounds good to him. Basilio has his eye on the rancho of Don Cornelio Esperon and, if he can convict the don of treason, then by law he will have the right to confiscate his land. He will then give the land to Garcia, who will hold it until the uproar over what has happened dies down. Then nothing will be easier than taking it from Garcia. He will use the sergeant as his scapegoat.

Putting his plan into action during a social visit to Don Cornelio's hacienda, Señor Basilio prods Garcia to examine some of Cornelio's beautiful possessions. The items come from countries with which Spain is at war, so Basilio charges Don Cornelio of trading with the enemy. Diego, who is present, protests that this is an absurd law but it is to no avail and Cornelio is arrested. In front of all present, Basilio turns the land and all it contains over to Garcia for his good work in exposing this treason. The sergeant is clearly embarrassed.

The next day, Basilio informs Garcia that he must testify against Don Cornelio at the inquest or risk being charged with not doing his duty and be hung. If he reveals any of their conversation, the punishment will be equally severe. That night Zorro pays a visit to Garcia and puts his own threat to the sergeant. However, not being able to reveal the threat of Basilio puts Garcia in an impossible position.

At the inquest, the honesty of Garcia shines through despite visions of a hangman's noose and the sign of the Z dancing before him. Basilio is livid as Zorro leaps from the balcony and puts his blade to the tyrant's throat. After Zorro takes inventory of Basilio's coat, vest and watch, it becomes clear that Don Cornelio is not the only one who has been "trading with the enemy." At the point of Zorro's sword, Basilio declares Don Cornelio innocent. After a brief scuffle, Zorro is gone as quickly as he came.

Author's Note

"Exposing the Tyrant" brings Zorro closer to a showdown with Señor Basilio. Writer Maury Hill, who contributed two scripts to the series, recalled some of the plusses and minuses of writing for a formula series like *Zorro*. "In a way it made it easier because you knew what you could do and what you couldn't do. At the same time it was a little bit difficult because you had to stay within a certain formula. You just went according to the usual standards of the period."

The climax of this episode is well-done as once again Zorro is found humiliating Basilio, this time by methodically cutting away various pieces of the tyrant's clothing in front of a large gathering. The tone and attitude of this scene has been used in countless swashbucklers over the years. Often the hero must humble his adversary, usually with comedic overtones, before thoroughly defeating him.

There is a scene near the midpoint of the episode that is perplexing regarding the use of stunt doubles: Garcia is sitting dejectedly in his room on his bed as Zorro steals through the window and draws his sword. This particular scene is a master shot. The camera then cuts to a two-shot with Zorro holding his sword on Garcia's back. For a reason that is not entirely clear, Buddy Van Horn is doubling Guy Williams in the master shot as Zorro comes through the window. When the scene cuts to the two-shot it is Williams as Zorro. The only bit of "action" was the entry through the window which looked to be about four feet off the ground. Van Horn also doubles Williams leaving the room, once again through the window. This kind of baffling stunt doubling has happened in other episodes and, when questioned, Buddy Van Horn has no real explanation for it.

Behind the Scenes

An instrumental version of "Lonely Guitar," introduced by Annette in an earlier episode, can be heard playing in the background in the tavern.... There is a simple but effective special effect as Bernardo shines the mark of the Z on a wall using a mirror with a Z carved into it.... The matte drawing used for the exterior of Don Cornelio's hacienda was used for the Verdugo home in the Monterey episodes.

Episode 69

"Zorro Takes a Dare"

Filmed: December 10, 11, 15, 17, 22 & 23, 1958; *Air Date*: April 30, 1959; *Director*: Hollingsworth Morse; *Writer*: Robert Bloomfield; *Cast*: Everett Sloane (Basilio), Gloria Talbott (Moneta), Robert J. Wilke (Capitan Mendoza), Edgar Barrier (Don Cornelio), George Lewis (Don Alejandro), Don Diamond (Cpl. Reyes).

After all the humiliation he has suffered, Señor Basilio is more determined than ever to capture Zorro. There will be no leaves for the soldiers until the masked bandit is dead or behind bars. To this end, Basilio plans to use Garcia as bait to capture the Fox. A rope is tied around the sergeant's ample waist and he is hung over the cuartel entrance. Basilio dares Zorro to free him. Diego has been keeping a close eye on the situation and, although he knows it's a trap, Zorro must ride to help his friend.

With the help of Bernardo, Zorro makes his way into the cuartel and sets a snare to catch Basilio and free his friend. Bernardo races to Basilio's office and describes how he has just seen Zorro. Basilio races out and in his haste he steps into Zorro's trap and his leg catches in the rope snare. As Garcia comes down, Basilio goes up. Zorro and Bernardo are gone in a flash.

After Basilio is freed, he begins to link Bernardo with Zorro, and actually thinks for a moment that Bernardo may *be* Zorro. Basilio, Capitan Mendoza and the lancers gallop to the de la Vega hacienda to question Diego's mute servant. As Don Alejandro and Don Cornelio celebrate the news of Zorro's deed, the soldiers break in and demand Bernardo. Mendoza knocks Don Alejandro to the ground as they chase Bernardo. He escapes into the secret passage just as Zorro returns. He describes what has happened and Zorro makes his way through the passageway and into the sala. He is able to get his sword to the back of Basilio. As the soldiers rush Zorro, he escapes to another part of the house.

While the lancers comb the hacienda, Basilio searches Diego's room for clues and accidentally discovers the secret room. He enters but hears footsteps approaching. Basilio hides by the side of the door and with the pommel of his sword knocks the intruder unconscious. He has captured Zorro! Basilio removes his enemy's mask to find ... Don Diego. Basilio is beside himself with joy. He dons the cape, mask and hat of Zorro and runs from the room shouting for Capitan Mendoza. The capitan sees him and fires his pistol, killing the masked figure immediately.

Don Alejandro rushes to see what has happened and is greatly relieved to find Basilio, not his son behind the mask. Alejandro accuses Mendoza of murder but the capitan swears it was an accident. Alejandro declares that it will be for the king to decide. Another tyrant has been foiled by Zorro.

Author's Notes

The coming attraction for "Zorro Takes a Dare" makes it almost impossible for anyone to miss this episode. In a hushed tone, announcer Dick Tufeld exclaims, "Ladies and gentlemen, you are about to witness the most dangerous moment in the adventurous life of Zorro. Zorro unmasked! You'll be stunned. Thrilled by the amazing revelation and dramatic tenseness next week when Zorro takes a dare. Don't miss it!" During Tufeld's narration, a scene from the episode plays across the screen: Basilio, hiding in the secret room, knocks Zorro unconscious and unmasks him. Many questions come to mind: How did Basilio find Zorro's secret passage? What will happen to Zorro? What will happen to Basilio? All of those questions are answered in what is a relatively plausible script by Robert Bloomfield.

This is another instance where Zorro really uses ingenuity rather than physical expertise. It's especially amusing when he catches Basilio in a rope snare and the tyrant is yanked off the ground upside down screaming as Garcia is lowered slowly to earth. Basilio is freed by Cpl. Reyes, who takes his cries to "get me down" literally and cuts the rope suspending Basilio, who lands on his head. The reaction shot of Garcia and Mendoza wincing at the sight adds a comical exclamation point.

The scene of Basilio accidentally discovering Diego's secret room is the most suspenseful of the series. As he pokes around the fireplace mantle, viewers can only hold their breath. Basilio finally stumbles upon the hidden button and the panel opens as a whoosh of air blows through. Only in "Zorro's Ride into Terror" did anyone really come close to discovering the secret passage. It's a true violation of Zorro's secret. A brief scene, also well-done, has Bernardo closing the secret door a split second before lancers enter Diego's room.

All that really remains is to see how Basilio will be handled. As in the two other unmasking episodes, Zorro cannot have blood on his hands, so with a neat twist, Basilio is killed by his own henchman. Alejandro's relief when the imposter's mask is removed lends a realistic air to the scene.

Behind the Scenes

> Dick Crockett doubles for Everett Sloane.... A piece of stock footage that has Zorro galloping across the screen mistakenly had the negative reversed. This is evident because his sword is being worn on the wrong side. It was used in "Zorro vs. Cupio."

EPISODE 70

"An Affair of Honor"

Filmed: February 11–13, 16 & 17, 1959; *Air Date*: May 7, 1959; *Director*: Hollingsworth Morse; *Writer*: Lewis R. Foster; *Cast*: Tony Russo (Avila), Booth Colman (Pineda), George Lewis (Don Alejandro), Don Diamond (Cpl. Reyes), Nestor Paiva (Innkeeper).

Señor Avila, a professional swordsman, has come to Los Angeles and he is taking on all comers. He has already defeated two opponents and his aide, Pineda, has collected his winnings. Included in the small group of onlookers is Don Diego and Sgt. Garcia. Avila challenges Diego, who begs off saying he does not fight. However, when the swordsman learns that Diego's family is the wealthiest in Southern California, he plots to coerce Diego into a duel.

When the crowd enters the tavern, Avila spies Don Alejandro, who is playing cards with some friends. He tries to enter the game but Alejandro rebuffs him. A scuffle ensues and Avila strikes Alejandro. Diego comes to his aid and knocks Avila across a table. Avila then challenges Diego to a duel, to take place the next day. It seems the swordsman's plan is working.

That evening, Diego asks his father what to do about Avila — to fight with all his ability and risk his identity or to fight clumsily and risk death. Alejandro thinks Zorro should step in but Diego disagrees. There is a knock at the door. It is Avila's second, Pineda. He says that Avila is willing to accept money to spare Diego's life. Alejandro and Diego remove him bodily from the hacienda. Diego now agrees that Zorro should ride.

Fearing for his friend's life, Garcia and Reyes arrive at the hacienda. With a tale of a lame horse, Garcia coaxes Diego outside as some lancers knock him unconscious and lock him in the woodshed. The sergeant believes that he is saving his friend's life. The next morning, Bernardo reports to Alejandro that Diego is nowhere to be found. They ride to the cuartel to report Diego's disappearance to Garcia, who plays innocent. When Alejandro leaves the office, Bernardo overhears Garcia discussing Diego's imprisonment in the woodshed.

As his son's second, Alejandro must duel Avila. Diego's father fights valiantly, but he is no match for the master swordsman. Zorro arrives just in time to give Avila a fencing lesson and to make a promise: "If I ever see you again, señor, I'll kill you."

Author's Notes

First-season director Lewis R. Foster pens only his second *Zorro* script with "An Affair of Honor." He was something of a triple threat at the studio, directing and co-writing *Tonka* as well as scripting some *Swamp Fox* episodes. He also co-wrote the latter's theme song.

This is a good story that further puts to rest the image of Diego as a fop. In doing so, it shows a more human side of Diego when, in his anger, he forgets himself and strikes Avila. As a result of this action, Diego does a little rare soul-searching as he speaks of the confusion of a dual identity: "The trouble is, Father, I don't know when to act like myself or what's expected of me. I don't know any more." It would have been interesting to see the series delve into this a little bit more deeply but the studio was aware that this might be a little too introspective for *Zorro's* young audience.

Looking back over 70 *Zorro* episodes, it is intriguing to speculate on why and how the Diego character changed. After the first 13 episodes Diego seemed to believe that he had deceived people so thoroughly that he could relax and begin living his life closer to his own personality. In this episode Avila makes various derogatory comments aimed at Diego: "Ah, yes, I seemed to have heard of your reputation," he exclaims. "The young one is soft, I doubt he would fight to protect the family honor." These slanders would have most likely been based upon Diego's actions in the early stages of the series when his behavior was less than heroic. Since that time, Diego's only obvious shortcoming was the fact that he would not carry a sword. In terms of

Diego's evolution, he became something of a detective, investigating situations and gathering clues until it was time for Zorro to swing into action. Regardless of the situation, Diego always kept himself on the periphery if not right in the middle of anything dangerous in the pueblo. His actions were not exactly those of a fop but rather someone who was benignly involved.

The swordplay which is largely filmed in master shots is some of the best of the second season. There are the inevitable cutaways and close-ups but it doesn't bog down the action too much. Because Zorro does not wear his cape, and the duel happens during the daytime, all his movements can be seen clearly. The coup de grâce has Avila landing in a fountain as Zorro stands over him. Tony Russo (wearing phony whiskers as Avila), who guest-starred in the first season playing a similar character, was a competent fencer, but for the usual reasons of time, safety and budget, Buddy Van Horn doubled him in the long shots which comprise most of the duel.

A nice dramatic touch has Zorro putting two cuts on Avila as payback for the two cuts Avila put on Don Alejandro. These were shot close-up and done by the special effects department, which did a similar job when Zorro cut his mark on the clothing of various villains.

Behind the Scenes

> Al and Fred Cavens play two townspeople who accept Avila's challenge. Fred Cavens also doubles for George Lewis in his big sword fight.... Tap Canutt, who did some stunt work in the first season, doubles as Zorro in the non-fencing scenes while Van Horn was busy standing in for Tony Russo.... This was the last episode filmed for the series. The last day of filming was February 17, 1959.... All of the fencing action which was supposed to be taking place out behind the tavern was filmed on a soundstage in an area of the tavern heretofore unseen.

EPISODE 71

"The Sergeant Sees Red"

Filmed: October 7, 1958, January 30 & February 2–4, 1959; *Air Date*: May 14, 1959; *Director*: Harmon Jones; *Writers*: Robert J. Shaw and Bob Wehling; *Cast*: Richard Reeves (Carlos), Joseph Calleia (Padre Simeon), Don Diamond (Cpl. Reyes).

Padre Simeon has just returned home to California from Spain. With Sgt. Garcia as his escort, the two men arrive in Los Angeles to find it almost deserted. Almost, except for Cpl. Reyes, who is camping outside the cuartel gates. It seems all of the lancers, except for Reyes have contracted measles. Most of the pueblo is under quarantine.

Don Diego rides into Los Angeles to view the treasure that Padre Simeon has brought back with him from Spain — a priceless silver chalice. The padre proudly shows it to Diego and to Carlos, the padre's orderly. Then Diego and the padre leave to deliver supplies to those who are ill. Carlos, after some thought, makes a decision:

He will steal the chalice. When the padre returns that evening, Carlos locks him in a closet and puts a quarantine sign on the door. This will give him a two-week head start, the length of time for the quarantine.

A few hours pass and Diego and Bernardo return to help the padre deliver food. When they see the quarantine sign, Diego becomes suspicious. He concludes that the newly returned padre could not have contracted measles so quickly. They investigate and find the imprisoned padre. When Diego learns that Carlos is the culprit, Zorro must act. He tracks Carlos to a smithy where he is about to melt down the treasure. Zorro wants only to talk but Carlos attacks him. A desperate struggle takes place but Zorro is finally able to reason with his foe. He allows Carlos to return the chalice to Padre Simeon. Carlos does so and he remembers what Zorro told him: "You will always have two consciences, yours and me."

Author's Notes

"The Sergeant Sees Red" is a one-shot episode and the *Zorro* debut of director Harmon Jones. Jones was a Canadian who had directed such films as *The Pride of St. Louis*, *The Kid from Left Field* and *Target Zero*. This episode has very much the same feel as a Charles Barton or Charles Lamont episode — not too much style, just a capable, no-frills affair. It is very low-budget as everything, except for one brief scene, is filmed on the back lot. As a result of a clever plot device (a measles epidemic) no extras were needed.

Robert Shaw, who co-wrote this episode with Bob Wehling and went on to create such shows as *Hawaiian Eye* and *Medical Center*, didn't really consider himself a *Zorro*-type writer. "I hated the show and didn't know a damn thing about it. As I recall, there was an accent on early California missions and I didn't know a damn thing about them and couldn't care less. I like to write about people in bed and Zorro never went to bed with anybody." Shaw, who compared working at the Disney Studio to being at summer camp, recalled his first and only meeting with Walt Disney. "I was sitting in my office on 'Dopey' Drive the first morning and the door burst open and it was Walt Disney. And naturally you know who he is; you've seen his picture. So I stood up and saluted and so forth and he said, 'Bob, I'm Walt. There are no last names at Disneyland.' And I said 'Oh?' And he said, 'What is it you do? Now let me think a minute, oh, you're going to write for *Zorro*.' And I said, 'Yes, sir,' and he said, 'It's Walt, Bob.' And I said, 'Yes,' and then he turned around and started out the door, turned back and said, 'Well, just remember we're in the picture business, not words.'" Shaw who was at the studio for eight weeks, wrote only this episode and would leave for what turned out to be greener pastures.

Joseph Calleia, who plays Padre Simeon (another in a long line of priests passing through Los Angeles), had portrayed a similar role in a 1955 Disney film, *The Littlest Outlaw*. Calleia was a film veteran and was probably best known in Hollywood for his roles as, ironically, gangsters and priests. He also appeared in another Disney film, 1958's *The Light in the Forest*.

Richard Reeves (Carlos) was another long-time screen tough guy in both gangster films and the occasional Western. He had appeared in two earlier episodes of *Zorro* performing bits. The role is something of a departure for him because he's not really a heavy but rather someone who made a mistake, paid for it and re-entered society. At the end of the episode, with Zorro's help, he redeems himself. Not being remotely a Latin-type, Reeves seems somewhat miscast, not unlike Ken Lynch from the Monterey episodes.

The high point of this episode is the action climax that takes place inside the blacksmith's shop and is perfectly choreographed by Buddy Van Horn. Working with Jack Perkins who is doubling Richard Reeves, Van Horn makes full use of the interior set as shelves come crashing down around them. All of the action seems very Zorro-like and in keeping with the character. No punches are thrown as in "Spark of Revenge" and with carefully integrated close-ups of Guy Williams and Reeves it all comes together convincingly.

Behind the Scenes

> The "Red" in the episode title refers to measles spots.... Many years earlier, Joseph Calleia played a Zorro-like bandit in *My Little Chickadee* [1940].

EPISODE 72

"Invitation to Death"

Filmed: January 5–9, 20, 23 & 26, 1959; *Air Date*: May 21, 1959; *Director*: Hollingsworth Morse; *Writer*: Lowell Hawley; *Cast*: Joan Evans (Leonar), George N. Neise (Capitan Arrellano), John Litel (Governor), Douglas Kennedy (Manuel), George Lewis (Don Alejandro), Don Diamond (Cpl. Reyes), Ramsey Hill (Doctor).

En route to Los Angeles, the governor's carriage overturns and he is injured. He is brought to the nearby de la Vega hacienda until the doctor arrives. After the governor is examined, it's determined that he will recover but it would be best if he wasn't moved. He will be staying with the de la Vegas for some time.

Capitan Arrellano, the governor's aide, believes that the mishap was a deliberate attempt on the governor's life by a group calling themselves the Rebatos, an organization opposed to California's alliance with Spain. Don Alejandro and Diego become very concerned when they hear this. The governor appoints Capitan Arrellano acting governor for the purpose of attending an important meeting in Los Angeles.

At the gathering are many of the pueblo's dons. After the capitan's speech, Don Alejandro is first in line to take the oath of allegiance to Spain in hopes of encouraging the others to follow his lead. Manuel Larios from San Luis Rey approaches the capitan and plants a seed of treachery in his mind: "Would you not become the governor if the actual governor were to die?" he asks. Although the capitan shrugs him off, there is something in his eye that contradicts his action.

The next day, the governor chastises the capitan regarding his jealous behavior toward Diego and his (the governor's) daughter, Leonar. The governor realizes the capitan is a man of many weaknesses and when he is well enough they will discuss the possibility of sending the capitan back to Spain.

The capitan, with Larios' remarks fresh in his mind, decides to act. He removes the guards, leaving the governor unprotected. When Bernardo observes what has happened, he tells Diego, who realizes that the governor may be best protected by Zorro. The Rebatos make their move as three armed men enter the sala where the governor is sleeping. With the help of Bernardo, Zorro disarms them but they escape. The governor is safe for the moment.

The next morning, Alejandro and Diego put some hard questions to the capitan concerning his removal of the guards. As long as the governor is a guest, it is a situation that bears watching.

Author's Notes

The next set of four episodes, all directed by Hollingsworth Morse, begins with "Invitation to Death." Joan Evans, who was brought in to play the governor's daughter, recalled with fondness her experience on the show, "I went in to meet Holly Morse, Bill Anderson and Walt Disney and they all said, 'Wonderful. Would you like to do our show?' And I said, 'Sure.' I didn't have to audition, they thought I was just right."

Evans continued, "In those days, Disney's product was the most prestigious in television and it was the best working experience. I felt as though I had died and gone to Heaven. They treated you like a dream. The pace was very comfortable, five days to do a half-hour show when most studios did them in only three. They paid well; I made $1,000 a week which was very good. We also got into Disneyland for free for the duration of the filming [*laughs*]. "I remember writing a letter to Walt after appearing on the show saying that it had been such a wonderful experience and that now I was somebody important in the eyes of my four-year-old because I had been on *Zorro*."

Evans remembered Guy Williams: "I was crazy about Guy, he was a real flirt. He also bitched and complained a bit because like most actors he was having contract problems. I wanted to say, 'Please, you're in Heaven here.' I always thought that we were all so lucky to be actors so that we didn't have to work real jobs." Of director Morse, Evans concluded, "Holly was a clever man, a journeyman director who could put a show together at a comfortable pace. He wasn't much into telling an actor what to do." George N. Neise, who played the evil capitan was, according to Evans, "very much an old school actor, he was rather grand like John Barrymore. Overacting slightly but in a fun way."

Of the four episodes, "Invitation to Death" is probably the least exciting but it is filled with political intrigue and an exciting climax as Zorro and Bernardo rescue the governor just in time. Speaking of Bernardo, he assists in a lot of the action with Zorro in the "Rebatos" series. This is truly a case of Zorro not being able to do what he does without Bernardo's help.

Behind the Scenes

John Litel returns to play the part of the governor. Interestingly, the governor's name is never given. He is only referred to as "governor" or "your Excellency...." These four episodes are all filmed on Sound Stage #3 with only a few brief exterior back lot scenes.

EPISODE 73

"The Capitan Regrets"

Filmed: January 13–16, 19, 20, 22, 23 & 26, 1959; *Air Date*: May 28, 1959; *Director*: Hollingsworth Morse; *Writer*: Lowell Hawley; *Cast*: Joan Evans (Leonar), George N Neise (Capitan Arrellano), John Litel (Governor), Myron Healey (Gabriel Luna), George Lewis (Don Alejandro), Don Diamond (Cpl. Reyes).

As the governor is recovering from his injuries at the de la Vega hacienda, Capitan Arrellano has assumed his duties. The capitan receives a visitor named Gabriel Luna. In an oblique manner, Luna attempts to talk him into betraying the governor. Arrellano angrily rebuffs his suggestions and sends the man on his way.

Arrellano seems to be wildly confused. On the one hand he would love to become governor; on the other he respects no man more than the governor. When he learns that the governor believes he is well enough to assume his duties, he attempts to get Leonar, the governor's daughter, to sign a letter of incompetency. This would merely be a formality to allow the governor more time to recover., Leonar seems to doubt Arrellano's motives and refuses.

The next day, the governor is up and around and makes it clear to Arrellano that when they return to Monterey, he will be relieved of his duties because of his erratic behavior. Realizing his chance to become governor is slipping away, the capitan goes to the pueblo to visit the Rebatos. They agree to kill the governor but only with Arrellano's help.

That night at the de la Vega hacienda, the capitan adds a sleeping potion to the wine he has offered to the governor's guards, Garcia and Reyes. Bernardo observes what has happened and summons Diego. While Diego dons the disguise of Zorro, Bernardo waylays two of the Rebatos near the stables. Zorro dispenses with one Rebato and engages the capitan in a brisk fencing lesson. However the capitan gets his sword on the unconscious Garcia and threatens to run him through. Zorro is forced to give up his sword. Bernardo comes to the rescue with a perfectly aimed potted plant from above. The capitan will be asleep for some time. Once again the governor's life has been spared.

Author's Notes

"The Capitan Regrets" is virtually indistinguishable from the previous episode except for the fact that it does contain an excellent sword fight between Zorro and Capitan Arrellano (with Buddy Van Horn doubling for George Neise) which takes place on the patio. Simultaneously, Bernardo is getting the better of two of the capitan's henchmen. This was a side of Bernardo that had not been seen too much before, a man of action. In the past, Bernardo has used his pretense of deafness as a way to gather information for Diego. Occasionally he would dress up as Zorro to help Diego out of a tight spot, but here he was handling two heavies trying to kill the governor. After he takes care of the situation at hand, he arrives just in time to rescue Zorro. It's a real *tour de force* for Zorro's right hand man.

In an uncharacteristic display of irritation, Zorro chides his friend for waiting to the last minute to save him, saying, "That was a little too close for comfort. Next time don't sit around twiddling your thumbs. What happened to you, my friend?"

A self-satisfied Bernardo motions his master around to the back of the hacienda where his own struggle took place. Zorro makes up for his presumption when, in the final scene as Diego, he proposes a toast. "This Zorro, we all seem to take him so much for granted. He seems to be the friend to everyone. Somewhere there must be a man who is a friend to Zorro. I propose a toast to him." As Diego makes the proclamation he sneaks a glance at his friend, whose ready smile and overflowing glass tells Diego that all is forgiven.

One of the unnerving aspects of these four episodes is the Capitan Arrellano character as played by George Niese. In one scene he is pledging his allegiance to the governor, proclaiming that he would give his life for him and that he's "the finest man I know." In the next scene he is ready to allow him to be killed. The script tries to convey the fact that Arrellano is a troubled character, which should explain his confusion and duplicity. However, with Niese's interpretation of the character, he merely comes off as inconsistent and indecisive.

There is a bit of sleight of hand by film editor Cotton Warburton concerning the duel between Zorro and the capitan. One fencing phrase is actually used three times. It is accomplished this way: A fencing phrase is shot in the master format where both Zorro and the capitan are in full view. A few frames of the film are then enlarged so that it becomes a close-up of Zorro. The entire phrase is actually used three times — once as the master shot and twice as close-ups of Zorro. Depending upon how one looks at it, this is either creative cost-cutting or an obvious cheapening of production values.

Behind the Scenes

> Myron Healey, a long-time screen villain, makes an uncredited appearance as, of all things, a villain. He was on the Disney lot at the time working on the *Swamp Fox* show for *Walt Disney Presents*…. Diego sings a song [dubbed by Bill Lee], "Mi Corazon, My Love," written by Tom Adair and Joe Dubin…. One set change has the exterior rear of the de la Vega hacienda being shot on a sound-stage. In previous episodes, the rear of the tavern, an exterior located on the back lot, doubled for the hacienda.

Episode 74

"Masquerade for Murder"

Filmed: January 9, 14, 15, 19–23 & 26, 1959; *Air Date*: June 4, 1959, *Director*: Hollingsworth Morse; *Writer*: Bob Wehling; *Cast*: Joan Evans (Leonar), George N. Neise

(Capitan Arrellano), John Litel (Governor), George Lewis (Don Alejandro), Don Diamond (Cpl. Reyes), Don Haggerty (Carmelo [Assassin], Martin Vargas and Pepita Funez (Flamenco Dancers).

A messenger arrives at the de la Vega hacienda for Capitan Arrellano. When the man enters the study, the temporary headquarters of the capitan, Diego and Bernardo listen in. They learn that the stranger is a hired assassin. When and where he will strike is not yet determined. Diego, Bernardo and Alejandro makes plans to keep a close watch on the governor.

The governor is in a depressed state, so a fiesta is planned. That afternoon, Leonar informs Diego that Capitan Arrellano has suggested they instead hold a costume ball. All agree it would be a fine idea — all except Diego, who realizes that the assassin's face will be hidden, making it difficult to identify him.

There is a large crowd at the fiesta. The governor is dressed as Nero, Leonar as Cleopatra and Alejandro as a hooded executioner, a costume he found on his bed. He assumed Diego put it there. Midway through the party, Arrellano orders Garcia to relay a message to Alejandro: He is to meet Diego, at the stables. Bernardo passes this information to Diego, who eventually breaks away from the festivities.

Alejandro waits at the stables as another executioner sneaks up behind him. As the assassin raises his deadly scimitar, Zorro shouts a warning. He barely misses Alejandro as Zorro races to the rescue. After a short scuffle, the assassin escapes but Zorro has saved his father's life.

Author's Notes

"Masquerade for Murder" has one initial problem: The teaser reveals too much. Granted, the idea is to hook viewers but this scene shows the entire action sequence. The studio may have felt that it was time to mix things up a bit considering almost all of the previous teasers were basically dramatic in theme.

The action in question is good and a little different as Zorro takes on a hooded executioner armed with a large scimitar who breaks Zorro's sword in two. Zorro is forced to improvise and continues to fight with a piece of broken bench. Throughout most of this action sequence, Buddy Van Horn stands in for Guy Williams with the exception of the very brief fencing segment. The man in the hood is Al Cavens.

The comedy, as always, involved Garcia and Reyes and their attempt to find a comfortable spot for the governor on the patio as he recuperates. As the governor is carried about on his "throne," one spot is too sunny, one too dusty, one has no breeze, one has too much shade, until they finally end up where they started — the perfect spot. Another brief bit of humor has both the governor and Garcia showing up at the masquerade party both dressed as the Roman Emperor Nero.

The conclusion finds Garcia mistaking Zorro for just another partygoer:

GARCIA: Just a moment, Don Alejandro. I do not believe I have met your friend who is dressed just like Zorro.
ALEJANDRO: My friend? Why, I thought he was your friend.

GARCIA: My friend? He was with you. It couldn't be!

With this Zorro leaps over the wall and rides off into the night.

EPISODE 75
"Long Live the Governor"

Filmed: January 8–13, 15, 19, 20, 23 & 26, 1959; *Air Date*: June 11, 1959; *Director*: Hollingsworth Morse; *Writer*: Bob Wehling; *Cast*: Joan Evans (Leonar), George N. Neise (Capitan Arrellano), John Litel (Governor), George Lewis (Don Alejandro), Don Diamond (Cpl. Reyes), Douglas Kennedy (Manuel Larios).

At the de la Vega hacienda, Capitan Arrellano receives visitor Manuel Larios, the Rebato whom the capitan has met before. Larios believes it is in the best interests of his organization if the governor were no longer alive. Arrellano realizes that Larios is right and that time is growing short. The governor plans to remove the capitan's name from the order of succession when he is well enough to return to Monterey. If they are to kill the governor, it must be soon.

Behind the walls of the library, Diego and Alejandro stand in the secret passage listening carefully to every word. Don Alejandro wants to make matters come to a head by gathering dons and taking on the Rebatos. Diego, fearing that some of those very same dons may themselves be members of the Rebatos, suggests they play a waiting game until all of the scoundrels have exposed themselves. Alejandro reluctantly agrees.

Later that day, the capitan begins to put his plan into action. Systematically he temporarily eliminates everyone who would stand between him and the governor. He has Don Alejandro sent out on government business; the soldiers are quietly ordered back to the pueblo; and Diego is off gathering rice for the governor's dinner — or so Capitan Arrellano thinks. The only ones who stand between the Rebatos and the governor are his daughter Leonar, Bernardo and, of course, Zorro.

At the hacienda, it is naptime for His Excellency. As his favorite tune plays from his music box, he falls fast asleep. Members of the Rebatos quietly gather at the hacienda and a showdown grows closer. Now Zorro puts his plan into action. The first order of business is to get the governor to safety. Bernardo gets the governor, bed and all, into the secret passage, all the while keeping the music box playing to make sure he remains asleep.

As the Rebatos and Arrellano make their way through the hacienda searching for their prey, Zorro beings to eliminate them one by one. As he does so, each victim's sword is stuck in the sala ceiling. Finally, five swords hang and only Zorro and the capitan are left to face one another. Their swords clash with Zorro finally driving the point of his blade through the capitan, killing him. All the while, Bernardo has done his job keeping the governor unconscious and finally returning him to the library where he is none the wiser.

Author's Notes

"Long Live the Governor" is the conclusion to the "Rebatos" series and there are a number of standout scenes. The entire sequence which has Zorro eliminating the Rebatos and Bernardo trying to keep the governor asleep via his music box is very well put together. The excitement of the physical action involving Zorro coupled with the tension of Bernardo's dilemma (when he loses the key to the music box) work well together. The idea of having Zorro stick the swords of those he has eliminated into the sala ceiling adds a touch of drama.

One curious aspect of these four episodes is Diego's general attitude toward Bernardo. He seems to be constantly aggravated with this friend. Bernardo was a great deal of help to Zorro, even saving his life at one point, so there seemed to be little reason for Diego's irritation. Although there was a general change this season in the interplay between the two, in an effort to emphasize the comedy the writers seemed to have gone to extremes and missed the more subtle possibilities.

The sword fight between Zorro and Capitan Arrellano (Buddy Van Horn) is well-staged and unusual in the sense that, for the first and only time in the series, Zorro kills someone deliberately. In two previous episodes, Zorro has slashed opponents in the stomach and while the viewer can only assume their fate, no such doubt lingers here. Using a feinting move, Zorro quickly dispatches the capitan with a lunge to the gut and the capitan falls dead at Zorro's feet. It's a shocking moment.

There are two errors in this segment. One has Zorro in the secret passage behind the library running down the spiral staircase to get to the sala. Since the sala and the library were on the same floor, no such trip was necessary. The second mistake concerns a piece of footage taken from "The Capitan Regrets" and used during the fencing sequence of this episode. For the shot in question the camera angle is from over Zorro's shoulder looking at the capitan as they duel. Only Zorro's arm is actually visible but the reason this piece is inappropriate is because Zorro's cape can be seen. However, in the fencing scene in "Long Live the Governor," Zorro is not wearing his cape.

This is the last of the continuing series of episodes for *Zorro*. The one problem with these series of three and four episodes beginning with the "Joaquin Castenda" stories on through "Annette," "The Man from Spain," "The Practical Joker" and "The Mountain Man," is that there is a pattern of repetition. They are all heavily padded affairs with unrelated comedy bits, songs and so forth, which leaves a viewer wondering, "Haven't I seen this before?" This is one of the problems with series television. Even as early as the late 1950s, most plots and themes had already been used in every conceivable format (Western, detective, straight drama). *Zorro* had to try to find an inventive way to divert viewers from a plot they had seen dozens of times before. They usually accomplished this by padding the episode with a song, a comedy routine or a bit of romantic byplay. Any of these scenes could have been edited out and the plot would not have been affected one bit. However, it was these very scenes that made *Zorro* a unique series. And what Guy Williams referred to as a "Disney thing."*

Guy Williams interview with Mike Clark, 1986. Published in Starlog, January 1987.

Episode 76

"The Fortune Teller"

Filmed: January 27–30 & February 4, 1959; *Air Date*: June 18, 1959; *Director*: Harmon Jones; *Writer*: Robert Bloomfield; *Cast*: Roxane Bernard (Lupita), Alex Gerry (Don Sebastian), Paul Dubov (Gustavo), Kay Kuter (Hernando), Don Diamond (Cpl. Reyes), George Lewis (Don Alejandro).

At the tavern, Diego and a business associate of his father's, Don Sebastian Portes, are enjoying the dancing of Lupita and her two musical associates. Don Sebastian is being held over in Los Angeles because the stagecoach upon which his money (1500 pesos) was to be transported is being repaired. Sgt. Garcia arrives with the disappointing news that the damage to the coach is more serious than expected so the repair will take much longer. After some discussion, Don Sebastian decides to entrust Garcia with his money. The sergeant will put it aboard the stage when it is repaired, much to the concern of Diego and Don Alejandro. Diego decides that he will stay in town to keep an eye on the sergeant and Don Sebastian's money.

All of this is overheard by Gustavo and Hernando, the traveling musicians. They immediately report the news to Lupita, who quickly devises a plan to separate Sgt. Garcia from his loot. By this time, Garcia has returned to the cuartel with Diego to place the money in a strongbox. The sergeant returns to the tavern but Diego decides to stay closer to the money.

Back at the tavern, Lupita catches the eye of Garcia and offers to tell his fortune using her cards. When the death card, the king of cups, comes up, Garcia becomes very nervous and Lupita tells him that the last person he would suspect is plotting to kill him. Obviously, this is part of a plot by Lupita so that she and her friends can get Garcia alone and take his money.

The worried sergeant returns to the cuartel and obligingly does what the cards have told him to do— he sends Cpl. Reyes and the lancers to the mission and then locks Bernardo and then Diego outside the cuartel. Seeing what has happened, Lupita and her friends move in. They climb the cuartel wall, subdue Garcia and then proceed to locate the strongbox. Diego, who has been keeping a close eye on the situation from outside the cuartel, decides to let Zorro step in. The Fox arrives as the trio are trying to escape. He quickly dispatches Hernando and after an extended swordfight disarms Gustavo. All three are put in a jail cell.

Author's Notes

"The Fortune Teller" is a one-shot episode, one of the least inspired of the series. Part of the plot is taken from an earlier and much better episode, "Zorro Lights a Fuse." The plot device in question involves using playing cards to dupe the gullible Sgt. Garcia. In this episode it is a gypsy girl who deceives Garcia; in the earlier one it was Diego. Both used the "cup" card, specifically the king of cups, a symbol of danger and death. The viewer's patience is stretched to the limit, as Garcia actually believes that Reyes and Diego might want to kill him for the money he is guarding. It's unbelievable and really doesn't work.

The two villains in this piece are very ineffective in both appearance and manner. One tall and thin, the other short and pudgy, they take on all the villainy and danger of Mutt and Jeff. This aspect makes the sword fight that ensues all the more of a dichotomy. On the one hand, it's really a very well-staged, exciting duel as Zorro races across the cuartel to face the villain, Gustavo (doubled by Al Cavens). On the other hand, it shouldn't take more than a quick fencing combination for Zorro to dispatch his adversary. The sword fight goes on too long. To add insult to injury, duelist Zorro trips backward over a wagon hitch. This has *never* happened before. It's the sort of thing that has always happened to those foolish enough to cross swords with Zorro. If this *faux pas* were ever to occur, it would be more appropriate to use it when Zorro faces a master swordsman such as Avila in "An Affair of Honor" or Ricardo Del Amo in "Zorro Fights a Duel." But certainly not against someone who looks as ineffective as Gustavo.

Behind the Scenes

> Buddy Van Horn doubles for Guy Williams for the backward trip over the wagon hitch.... An instrumental of "Lonely Guitar" plays in the background at the tavern.

EPISODE 77

"Señor China Boy"

Filmed: September 9–12, 15 & February 17, 1959; *Air Date*: June 25, 1959; *Director*: Charles Lamont; *Writer*: David Lang; *Cast*: James Hong (Prince), Charles Horvath (John Vinson), Richard Deacon (Padre Ignacio), Oliver Blake (Tomas Gregorio), Don Diamond (Cpl. Reyes).

Merchant Tomas Gregorio has returned to Los Angeles with a wagonload of goods he has picked up at the harbor in San Pedro. As he begins to unload his cargo at his warehouse, he hears an intruder in his wagon. Frantic, he runs to Sgt. Garcia who, with Cpl. Reyes, searches the wagon but finds nothing. Then, with noises coming from the warehouse, the pair begin a clumsy search which ends with the capture of their quarry, a frightened Chinese boy who speaks no English. Garcia has no choice but to take the boy into custody.

Diego, who is in town with Bernardo, arrives at the cuartel to lend a helping hand to the sergeant. Speaking various languages, Diego attempts to communicate with the boy but the results are disappointing. Bernardo, using sign language, has better luck and they learn that the boy was a prisoner aboard a ship and has escaped overboard. He attempts to explain more by writing on a piece of paper which Diego keeps in hopes of translating later. Garcia must now place the boy in jail as a result of his breaking into the warehouse and entering the pueblo without permission.

Diego sends Bernardo with the boy's message to Padre Ignacio in hopes that he will have better luck.

The following day, a stranger arrives at the cuartel looking for a Chinese boy. The man explains to Sgt. Garcia that he is John Vinson, first mate of the *Burma Queen* out of Shanghai. He also claims that the boy is a murderer. Although Garcia cannot believe it, he has no other choice but to return the boy to Vinson. As the pair ride off, Bernardo, who was leaving Padre Ignacio's quarters, observes and rides off to report to Diego.

Bernardo gives Diego some startling information he obtained from Padre Ignacio: The boy is actually a prince who was kidnapped by Vinson and held for ransom. Diego realizes that he must move quickly and, as Zorro, he rides off in pursuit of Vinson and his prisoner. The pair have a head start as they race for the San Pedro harbor but they are no match for Tornado. At the crest of a hill, Zorro cuts off Vinson and demands he let the boy go. The sailor refuses, a struggle takes place and Vinson falls to his death at the bottom of a canyon. The prince has been saved and Sgt. Garcia and his lancers arrive in time to return him to Los Angeles. As goodbyes are made, the sergeant places the prince aboard a stagecoach which is the first leg of his journey back to China.

Author's Notes

"Señor China Boy" is a decent effort and Charles Lamont's last directorial chore for *Zorro*. A lot of stock footage is used but the show gets off the back lot for the first time since "Treasure for the King" with a climax shot at the "Garden of the Gods" section of Iverson's Ranch. The action at Iverson's includes a sword fight of sorts between Zorro and the villain, Capt. Vinson. (Actually, the captain uses a broken tree limb in lieu of a sword but it's well choreographed by Fred Cavens). There is a disjointed piece of editing after the captain is disarmed. As Zorro replaces his sword in its scabbard, the camera cuts back to the captain, who begins to make a move toward him. In the very next shot the two men are rolling on the ground struggling. It has a jump cut quality to it, with a frame or two of action missing.

True to form, director Lamont engages in some broad physical comedy as Reyes and Garcia search a warehouse looking for the Chinese boy. They run into one another, there are falling boxes and at one point Garcia's suspenders get caught on a nail. Of course, he thinks that someone has grabbed him from behind.

A number of character actors are in attendance. A very young James Hong (who is still active today) portrays the Chinese prince. Charles Horvath was a veteran screen bad guy usually playing the muscle to somebody else's brains. At the time Richard Deacon, who was best known as Fred Rutherford (a role he was playing at the time) on *Leave It to Beaver*, portrays yet another new padre in Los Angeles. Also on hand in smaller roles are Oliver Blake, a long-time screen comedian, and Kermit Maynard, a B-Western actor and brother of Ken Maynard. Maynard has the non-speaking role of a lancer.

Writer David Lang, who like Robert Shaw ("The Sergeant Sees Red") before him wrote only one *Zorro* episode, recalled his brief stay at the Disney Studio. "I knew the show very well because as a kid I grew up with the Fairbanks version of Zorro. As a boy I just lived by Zorro. When my agent called with the offer, I grabbed it." Lang's tenure at the studio was brief because "everything went through Walt and he was very particular. He nitpicked a thing to death. He wanted to be sure that everything was the way he wanted it. However, when you're working on a formula series like *Zorro*, you can only take so much and I didn't want to go through the abuse so I got out."

Behind the Scenes

> A bit of footage that was shot very early in the series [but never used] surfaces here. It features Diego in his secret room donning his Zorro costume. If the viewer looks carefully, it is obvious that the Don Diego clothes that hang on a peg behind Diego are different from those he entered the room wearing.... *Leave It to Beaver*, in which Richard Deacon was a semi-regular, was the lead-in show for *Zorro* in this season. Deacon would go on to portray Mel Cooley on TVs *The Dick Van Dyke Show*.

Episode 78
"Finders Keepers"

Filmed: February 5, 6, 9–11, 16 & 17, 1959; *Air Date*: July 2, 1959; *Director*: Hollingsworth Morse; *Writers*: Lowell Hawley and Bob Wehling; *Cast*: Fintan Meyler (Celesta Villagran), Richard Garland (Lopez), Rudolfo Hoyos (Montez), Don Diamond (Cpl. Reyes), George Lewis (Don Alejandro).

A coach is carrying a señorita and her servant along a country road. The señorita nervously eyes the money pouch she is carrying. From around a bend, a masked bandit steps out and fires his pistol at the coach. A short time later, Bernardo happens along and notices a shiny jeweled brooch in the brush along the side of the road. As he stops, picks it up and wraps it in his handkerchief, he notices an overturned coach. He then hears the moans of the injured señorita. He picks the woman up attempting to help, but as she regains full consciousness she begins screaming. Just then Sgt. Garcia and Cpl. Reyes come upon the scene and the señorita accuses Bernardo of trying to kill her.

At the cuartel, Diego attempts to defend his servant against the charges. The señorita agrees that perhaps she acted hastily and wrongfully accused the good Samaritan. Bernardo is released much to his relief and the señorita apologizes. As he takes out his handkerchief to mop his brow, the jeweled brooch falls to the ground. Bernardo is in trouble again.

Garcia, Diego and some lancers return to the scene of the crime where Bernardo reenacts what has happened. Don Alejandro and Cpl. Reyes arrive with news of recent developments. Alejandro explains that, according to the doctor, the señorita was not shot as previously thought but rather struck on the head from behind. Now the suspicion falls on Montez, her servant, who was traveling with her and has now disappeared. Diego deduces that Montez committed the crime with an accomplice and is probably miles away. "Not so," says Cpl. Reyes, who has news that the wounded Montez is in Sgt. Garcia's office.

Back at the cuartel, Montez tells a convoluted tale of having his arm broken by the shot from the bandit's pistol and then in a dazed state going to get help and being assisted by a stranger named Lopez. During the time he was missing, he claims to have been searching the hills for the señorita, unaware that she had been taken to Los Angeles. Montez also says he saw the bandit's face and can identify him. Diego, who believes none of the man's tale, challenges him to pick Bernardo out of a line-up of similar physical types. Montez reluctantly agrees.

In the tavern, Bernardo is lined up with five other men. The stranger Lopez is also in attendance and, when he believes no one is looking, he signals to Montez the whereabouts of Bernardo in the line-up. Diego and Alejandro observe what has happened. When the finger of guilt is pointed at Bernardo, Diego realizes that only Zorro can save his friend from the hangman's noose.

That evening, Zorro makes his way into the tavern and locks both Garcia and Reyes in the storeroom. He then proceeds to confront Montez and Lopez. He forces the truth from them for Garcia to hear and a terrific sword fight ensues. After subduing Lopez, Zorro places Montez in the custody of Sgt. Garcia. Now Montez is more than ready to confess his part in the crime.

Author's Notes

"Finders Keepers," the last episode of the second season, is a simple and predictable tale of right and wrong filmed entirely on the back lot. In watching this teleplay, it is impossible not to notice how the scope of the series had changed. When *Zorro* began, the entire first season dealt with Zorro's struggle against tyranny, which came in the form of Capitan Monastario and the Eagle. The second season saw the stories become a little more personal in nature and this episode along with other one-shot episodes such as "The Sergeant Sees Red," "The Fortune Teller," "The Runaways" and "The Iron Box," are good examples of that. These are all very standard television dramas, long on exposition and short on action. At this point *Zorro* had the look of a series that was becoming a victim of its own formula. In "Finders Keepers," most of the activity dealing with Diego's attempts to prove Bernardo's innocence is labored. The viewer knows that Diego's manservant did nothing wrong. It's only a question of when Zorro will arrive to prove it.

When Zorro does appear, a rough-and-tumble sword fight commences complete with leaps over bars, swings on chandeliers, bodies flying over tables and falling down stairs. Buddy Van Horn doubles as the villain Lopez and Tap Canutt stands in as Zorro for the non-fencing action. At different points during the excitement, Tap Canutt loses his sword scabbard and rips his pants. There is a slightly altered fencing style employed in this episode, similar to that in "Long Live the Governor." It's much more stunt-oriented than previous fencing bouts and there is more physical contact between Zorro and his adversary. This is something that was avoided before.

All things considered, "Finders Keepers" is not one of Zorro's better adventures. And it is certainly not the best way for the series to go out. But it could have been worse; it could have been "Zorro's Romance."

Behind the Scenes

Rudolfo Hoyos appeared in the first season's "The Secret of the Sierra." For a tumble-down-the-stairs, Jack Perkins doubles for Hoyos.... Like "Señor China Boy," there is a bad continuity jump: While involved in a sword fight, Zorro is wearing his cape and seconds later it has disappeared without a trace.

The following episodes were repeated during the summer of 1959:

July 9	"The Runaways"
July 16	"The Missing Father"
July 23	"Please Believe Me"
July 30	"The Brooch"
August 6	"Zorro and the Mountain Man"
August 13	"The Hound of the Sierras"
August 20	"Manhunt"
August 27	"The Iron Box"
September 3	"The Gay Caballero"
September 10	"Tornado is Missing"
September 17	"Zorro vs. Cupid"
September 24	"The Legend of Zorro"
September 26	"Spark of Revenge"

"Spark of Revenge" was shown on Monday night because ABC owed its affiliates an extra show as the result of a preemption earlier in the summer.

12

Zorro Merchandise

> The merchandise really comes from the show itself; it springs from the series. If you go in with the idea of "I'm going to merchandise this and that, "then you're dead." Vince Jefferds [Vice President of Merchandising] was a very bright guy and he was alert to what was happening. He started to work with *Zorro* as soon as he saw what the show was going to look like.
>
> Producer Bill Anderson, 1991

> I had a problem there because of Fess Parker. They wanted to make sure that what Fess Parker got away with, Guy Williams never would. We had to fight for the little bit that we got.
>
> Guy Williams, 1986

Probably at no other time in television history have there been as many popular kids heroes as there were in the 1950s. A child turning the dial in 1957 could choose from Wyatt Earp, Cheyenne, Paladin, Jim Hardie, Matt Dillion, Jim Bowie, Vint Bonner, Robin Hood, Sgt. Preston, Maverick, etc. Not to mention holdovers from the early 50's: Roy Rogers, Gene Autry, Hopalong Cassidy, the Lone Ranger, Superman, Wild Bill Hickok, the Cisco Kid and Sky King. Zorro had to compete with all these heroes and in doing so, he emerged as the number one fad of the 1957—58 television season. But fads by their very definition are fleeting and Disney was prepared to make the most of the economic opportunities with his newest TV sensation. *Zorro* was the biggest thing to hit the airwaves since *Davy Crockett* three years earlier and the studio was determined not to get caught off guard as they had been with the popularity of Crockett.

Kids were the target audience and they loved *Zorro* as evidenced by the sign of the Z which was turning up everywhere from shop windows to sidewalks to dirty cars to the covers of schoolbooks. Inglewood, California, and Bryan, Texas, held "Zorro Days." Bellingham, Washington, went even further and declared "Zorro Week." The activities included Zorro games, storytelling sessions and craft classes which had children making Zorro masks and swords. The week wound up with a costume parade. Other examples of "Zorromania" included:

- An allergist in Stockton, California, became the rage of the town by making his skin test scratches in the form of the Z.

Vince Jefferds (right), Vice-President of Disney Merchandising, and Guy Williams look over the new Zorro toys about to hit the stores (courtesy of Walt Disney Productions).

- A disc jockey in Cleveland, Ohio, parachuted into Lake Erie to plug the Chordettes' *Zorro* single. Once on-shore, he handed out free copies to the crowd that had gathered.
- When *Zorro* switched affiliates in West Virginia, station publicists had Zs painted all over the sidewalks of the local communities. When it came time to clean up, the station sent young women in Zorro costumes to do the job. Both campaigns generated big publicity.
- In Newport News, Virginia, the high school band kicked off the football season by performing themes of popular TV programs. The band formed the sign of the Z across the field and blasted out the *Zorro* theme.
- Gene Barry, TV's *Bat Masterson,* was taken down a peg or two when he took his son to see Santa Claus. The boy told Santa the gift he wanted most was ... a Zorro costume.
- It was poetic justice of sorts when Guy Williams, the man responsible for thousands of Zs appearing on the woodwork, walls and fences throughout the country, awoke one morning to find a huge Z scratched into the side of his convertible.[1]

All of this speaks to the tremendous interest in Zorro which translates into merchandise. There were over 70 companies licensed to market Zorro merchandise and over 420 products with the Walt Disney Copyright on them. Manufacturers began to ship Zorro items to the stores in the spring of 1958. Everything from anklets to wallets was covered. Any conceivable piece of children's clothing was carried including jeans, shirts, T-shirts, sweatshirts, pajamas, boots, slippers, belts and suspenders. The clothes were fine, but what the kids really wanted were toys and some of the more popular items that could be found in department stores were:

Zorro Sword — Empire Plastics Corp.: The blade was made of a flexible black plastic, the hand guard was a soft yellow or red plastic. The aspect of this item that worried parents was the replaceable chalk tip. The sign of the Z began showing up everywhere around the house. The sword also came with a Lone Ranger–style black plastic mask.

Zorro Whip — M. Shimmel Sons: This was almost as frightening to parents as the sword, which meant that the kids loved it. The item also included a lariat, a ring and a Lone Ranger–style mask. The packaging was eye-catching with a big red Z and a photo of Guy Williams.

Zorro Viewmaster Sawyer: The images were taken from the premiere episode, "Presenting Senor Zorro." The cover of the Viewmaster packet was a color photo of Zorro on a rearing Tornado with sword raised in the air. The face is in shadow but it's most likely Buddy Van Horn. When this was reissued in 1965, the cover was a much better shot of Guy Williams as Zorro, close-up with sword drawn in front of the cuartel. These slides afforded fans a chance to see how beautiful the series would have looked in color.

Topps Trading Cards were very popular, as were most trading cards at that time. The Zorro set of 88 was based upon the first 13 episodes which featured Capitan Monastario. They were also in color. Some were genuine color photographs while others were painted. Some faces were changed, such as the lawyer, Piña, who was given a large mustache, and Benito, whose mustache was removed.

Horse and Rider from Marx was a very detailed item. The Zorro figure stood almost seven inches high and had a removable mask, hat, cape, sword and whip. Tornado had a bridle and a removable saddle. Although the face did not really resemble Guy Williams very closely, it was a detailed figure right down to the string that was used to hold his hat on. It was very similar to the Hartland cowboy figures that were popular at the time. The box that it came in was also very colorful and nicely illustrated.

Halloween Costume by Ben Cooper, Inc., was very typical of the Halloween costumes that are still popular today. Looking nothing like Zorro's actual costume, it had a plastic red sash and had Zorro written on the torso. Some came with a plastic molded Zorro facemask which also did not look like Guy Williams. Others had a separate hat and Lone Ranger-style mask. For Halloween in 1958, a spokesman for Ben Cooper, Inc., stated, "Zorro is the hottest character I've seen in 30 years in the business. We're outselling all other costumes three to one."

Dell Comics had beautiful color cover photographs of Guy Williams as Zorro. One cover even featured Annette with her hero. There were 15 comics in all and they

Courtesy of Tomart's Disneyana.

first appeared in 1957 and ran until 1961. The first three issues followed the first 13 episodes of the series very closely, even taking dialogue directly from the show. The highly regarded Alex Toth, who drew these issues and a few others, felt the studio's tight grip on the comics hindered his creativity a bit. As Toth became less interested in handling the series for Dell, his artwork seemed to diminish proportionally. Toth drew seven issues in all. Warren Tufts, who followed Toth, drew three issues. His renderings of the characters looked like the actors who portrayed them, whereas Toth's Zorro seemed to bear a strong resemblance to Errol Flynn and his other characters were more caricatures. Doug Wildey, who would later create *Jonny Quest*, handled two issues of all-original stories. At times his artwork was uncannily close in resemblance to the television characters. For the final two issues, John Ustler took over the artwork. The popularity of the show was such that Dell continued to publish comics even after the series had been cancelled. The last issue hit the newsstands in November 1961. Nine issues were reprinted between 1965 and 1967 by Gold Key Comics to coincide with the syndication of the series.

Marx Zorro Playset was a very popular item for Christmas 1958. In keeping with the excellent quality of all Marx playsets, it consisted of 80 pieces: Zorro, Tornado, Don Diego, Don Alejandro, Bernardo, Garcia, the commandante, 32 soldiers, eight horses, cannons, palm trees, the entire cuartel (made of steel) and Zorro's molded plastic secret cave. There were at least three different versions of the playset. The price was a whopping $5.79.

A *Whitman Hardcover Book* came out in 1958 and was well-written by Steve Frazee. Based upon the first 13 episodes, it also contained a few illustrations by Henry Luhrs. Aimed primarily at the preteen set, it had a very nice cover illustration by Bill Edwards which featured Zorro jumping over the cuartel wall with sword drawn. This item was also reissued in the mid–60s.

Little Golden Books: There were two of them and both were adapted by Charles Spain Verral. The first, simply titled *Walt Disney's Zorro,* was based upon the first 13 episodes and drawn by John Steel. Some of his drawings were taken directly from still photos and the resemblance to the series actors was fairly close. Not so with the second book, *Zorro and the Secret Plan.* Drawn by Hamilton Greene, the illustrations are quite beautiful. Although they in no way bear much of a resemblance to Guy Williams and company, Greene had taken the bold step of drawing the characters to look like what they were ... Latin. These two books were also reissued in the–mid–'60s with their covers slightly altered. A large hardcover Golden Book, also published in 1958, was an expanded version of the first Golden Book. Also illustrated by John Steel, it was adapted by Irving Werstein. It was reissued in 1965 as a large softcover book with a slightly different cover.

Whitman Coloring Books: There were two, one with artwork by Tony Sgroi, and the second by the very busy John Steel and Tony Pawlo. The first was once again based loosely upon the first 13 episodes, the second was an original story. As with most coloring books, the tales were very simple. Both were reissued in 1965. The first book was slimmed down and tracing paper was added. The second remained virtually the same.

Puzzles — Jaymar/Whitman: They came boxed and in frame trays. They were in color and the Whitman puzzles had some excellent photographs of Zorro and the commandante in posed fencing positions at the Mission San Luis Rey.

Zorro Lunch Box by Aladdin was very popular and featured two paintings of Zorro. On one side, the standard Zorro trademark pose: Zorro on a rearing horse with a sword in the air. The other side depicts Zorro knocking Sgt. Garcia into a well. The thermos has Zorro facing off against the commandante and another lancer.

Zorro Hats produced by Benay — Albee Novelty Company came in three different types: felt, wool and plastic; a Lone Ranger-style mask was also supplied. A white cardboard placard with the Zorro trademark sat atop the brim.

Zorro Wristwatch by U.S. Time Corp. had a black wristband and black watch face and came wrapped around a miniature Zorro hat.

TV Guide: Guy Williams appeared on the cover of the April 26, 1958, issue. The article inside had a one-and-a-half page biography of Williams and an interesting color photograph of Williams and Britt Lomond (Monastario) with their swords locked in combat. It was voted one of the top 45 covers of all time in 1998. The August 13, 1958, issue of *Life* magazine also had a multi-page spread on the series and the fad it created. Another issue of *Life*, March 1, 1959, contained a full-page color ad featuring Guy Williams as Zorro for AC Sparkplugs. There were also numerous stories on Guy Williams in many of the movie magazines of that period.

Zorro Records: Two LPs were released as well as a number of 45s. The first of the albums was *Four Adventures of Zorro* from Disneyland records, based upon the first 13 episodes with voices supplied by Guy Williams, Henry Calvin and Jan Arvan. Britt Lomond (the commandante) was replaced by Phil Ross. Head Mouseketeer Jimmie Dodd provided the voice of Padre Felipe. The four adventures were *Presenting Senor Zorro*, *Zorro Frees the Indians*, *Zorro and the Ghost* and *Zorro's Daring Rescue*. With music provided by William Lava and stories adapted by Bob Thomas and George Sherman, the record was an exciting abbreviation of the initial *Zorro* segments. Listed as a "record book," the LP also contained a few pages of text and artwork which summarized the stories.

The second album was *Songs About Zorro and Other TV Heroes*. It contained various Henry Calvin vocals as well as the *Zorro* theme. The other songs were mostly Disney-related ("Andy Burnett," "Davy Crockett," "Mike Fink," etc.) with "Cheyenne" and "The Sheriff of Cochise" thrown in for good measure. Various singles were also released; most of them culled from the albums. Annette Funicello released "Lonely Guitar," which she performed on the show. For the teenagers, the Chordettes, a female quartet, registered a top 20 hit with the *Zorro* theme (Cadence label). The ladies got into the spirit of things by going so far as to appear in Zorro garb on such dance shows as *American Bandstand*.

Zorro Puppet: The Zorro hand puppet by the Gund Manufacturing Co. consisted of a removable cape, hat and mask. It was well-made with gold trim on the chest and a red tie for the Don Diego character. The face of the puppet looked more like Tyrone Power than Guy Williams. This was reissued in a much cheaper version in 1965.

Postcard: All who wrote to the studio requesting an autograph received a postcard with a photo of Guy Williams as Don Diego on the front and "Thanks for writing, Guy Williams. *Z*" on the back. The second postcard had a photo of Zorro in the center with a smaller photo of Sgt. Garcia and Bernardo at either end. An autograph was below each photo.

Walt Disney Magazine: Published in the late 1950s and available by subscription only, it contained mostly short stories based upon Disney-related characters. A few issues had *Zorro* stories with some nice photos in black-and-white and color.

Zorro Writing Tablet (Western Tablet & Stationery): These were to be used by kids in school to draw or make notes on. There were at least four different covers; three were artists' renditions, one was a photograph. One cover was a reward poster for Zorro with his face. Another had the Zorro trademark figure, while another had a close-up of Zorro's face with a mask that could be cut out and worn. The photo cover was a publicity still shot early in the series, taken in the cuartel, of an angry-looking, sword-wielding Zorro.

Zorro Oil Painting by Numbers (Hassenfeld Brothers, Inc.) was a popular item that contained various scenes of Zorro which could be painted according to the artist's taste.

Although it proved to be extremely profitable (anywhere from 11 million to 20 million dollars worth), *Zorro* didn't have quite the financial punch of *Davy Crockett.* However, it wouldn't be until the *Batman* craze of the mid–1960s that the kids would have something to get really excited about again on television.

13

"Adiós, Señor Zorro"

Filming for the second season of *Zorro* wrapped on February 17, 1959. Everybody was optimistic about the chances for a third season because the series was once again performing respectably and winning its time period with an overall 23.5 rating for the season. *Zorro* garnered a 40 percent audience share while its CBS competition *December Bride* captured 37 percent and *The Ed Wynn Show* on NBC pulled in 22 percent. (*Wynn* was actually canceled and replaced by *Steve Canyon* in mid-season.)

All of the principals went on vacation and were scheduled to return to the studio to begin filming another *Zorro* season in July. Guy Williams was especially excited as he was set to return to the studio in March to begin work on a film called *Gold*. He felt this would give him a chance to break away from his *Zorro* role and show some versatility. He knew *Zorro* would not last forever. *Gold,* which would recount the 1849 gold rush, was scripted by *Zorro* head writer Lowell Hawley. *Gold* was also to feature two other Disney stars, Robert Loggia (*Elfego Baca*) and Tom Tryon (*Texas John Slaughter*).

However, trouble began to brew behind the scenes between the Disney Studio and ABC. There was a conflict developing over who actually owned *Walt Disney Presents, The Mickey Mouse Club* and *Zorro*. Walt Disney also complained that he was being put in a creative bind with his *Walt Disney Presents* series. "I gave ABC their first full-hour Western series with my *Davy Crockett* shows and soon the network was flooded with other Westerns. They made so much money for ABC that before long I found myself in a strait-jacket. I no longer had the freedom of action that I enjoyed in the first three years. They kept insisting that I do more and more Westerns and my show became loaded with *Elfego Baca, The Swamp Fox* and *Texas John Slaughter*. I found myself competing with *Maverick, Wyatt Earp* and every other Western myth. When I came up with a fresh idea in another field, the network executives would say 'no.' Just to give you some notion of what they turned down, one of the rejects was *The Shaggy Dog.* We made a theater movie out of it and it grossed $9 million."[1]

Since 1954, the studio had been producing high-quality children's programs, the popularity of which enabled ABC, the new network on the block, to compete with CBS and NBC. But Disney was paying a price for the top-notch production they were putting on the small screen: The studio was operating in the red. However, they were never really in television to make money but rather to help finance and advertise Disneyland and their movies. (One of the ways Disney did eventually make money from television was to combine episodes of their TV shows and release them theatrically in foreign markets.) But now, not only were they hampering creativity but also ABC no longer wanted to pay the amount of money they had been paying for Disney product, specifically *Zorro*. They felt that they could make more money with series they owned rather than ones purchased from outside producers.

Bill Anderson explained the conflict from the Disney perspective: "The network and the sponsors wanted out of *Zorro*, especially the sponsors. They considered it to be a kid's show and although the ratings were high, they felt they weren't reaching the audience they wanted to reach. Both the network and sponsors wanted a more adult show in that time period. They came to us about doing a Western in place of *Zorro* but almost half the shows we were doing for *Walt Disney Presents* were Westerns already. We would've gone ahead with another year of *Zorro* if they wanted to. Even though we were having trouble with price, Walt knew that the series had great value down the line in syndication. But we were so busy at that time and ABC was scrambling to find a sponsor so we just said 'Forget it.'"

Anderson added, "ABC did talk about cheapening the show but if you didn't have the action, what the hell did you have? We weren't interested in doing a cheap show. It was not our interest at that time to have a continuing series anyway. I think Walt would've been happy just to do the original 13 that we did back in '57 and then call it quits. Our emphasis was more on the anthology-type series."

The bottom line was that *Zorro* was costing much more to produce than ABC was willing to pay. Disney himself was becoming somewhat disenchanted with *Zorro*. It was no longer a challenge and it lacked the variety of the anthology series. Now he felt he had no choice and in effect he canceled the show himself. Guy Williams stated simply, "Walt took the show away from ABC, away from himself and away from me."[2] The formal obituary appeared in *Daily Variety*, May 20, 1959: "*ABC Says Tag Too High So Disney Kills Zorro*: Walt Disney will discontinue production of his *Zorro* series following the inability of the studio and ABC to get together on a price for the show. Disney had submitted a final price of $49,500 per episode on the series. ABC felt the tag too high arguing that it is essentially a fringe time property with audience potential not large enough to justify costs. ABC has had difficulty in selling it and had scheduled it only on a tentative basis." It was one of the few shows in the history of television canceled with a 40 percent audience share. Williams received more bad news when his feature film, *Gold*, was put on hold as the result of a writers' strike.

According to Bill Cotter's research for his book *The Wonderful World of Disney Television*, "On July 2, 1959, Disney filed a lawsuit against ABC, asking the court to invalidate the contracts between the two companies under provisions of the federal anti-trust laws." Roy Disney summed up the Studio's position, saying, "Several weeks ago the ABC network advised us and announced publicly that they would not televise *Zorro* or *The Mickey Mouse Club* over their network next season, and at the same time they told us we could not offer these programs to any other television outlet. Subsequently, they have interfered with our attempts to offer these programs to any other networks or independent television station. Although we do not dispute ABC's right to discontinue these, or any other programs on their own network, we will certainly fight ABC's maneuvers to suppress these programs from public exhibition over other television stations."

Guy Williams may have been too busy to sit and worry about his misfortune and his studio's impending litigation with ABC because he was traveling all over the country making public appearances as Zorro. He would often be on the road for as long as three weeks at a time, riding in parades and appearing at state fairs, rodeos and shopping centers. The appearances were extremely lucrative for Williams, who made as much as $2,500 per appearance. This was more than he was making in salary. Some of the more exciting shows occurred at Disneyland where Williams would appear with Henry Calvin, Gene Sheldon and Britt Lomond for what was referred to as *Zorro Days*. The first appearance there was in April 1958, followed by shows in May and November 1958, November 1959 and November 1960. The stars would ride in the Disneyland Parade which would take them through the park to Frontierland. A stunt show would ensue, as Zorro (being doubled by Buddy Van Horn) would be chased across the rooftops. The action would culminate in a duel between Zorro (Guy Williams) and Capitan Monastario (Britt Lomond) atop the Mark Twain riverboat. The cast would also appear in the Magnolia Park area where Williams and Lomond would cross swords again and Gene Sheldon and Henry Calvin would amuse the crowd with magic and comedy. The cast would usually perform four shows a day.

Britt Lomond recounted a time when he claimed things did not go exactly as planned: "We did a lot of P.A.s together and one of the things we did at Disneyland was to fence atop the Mark Twain. I'm disarmed and fall into the water as part of the act. After Guy defeats me, he comes prancing off the boat and jumps onto his horse and rides off into the night. Well, one of the times we did it, we completed the fencing scene and my double falls off into the water and Guy comes running off the paddle wheeler. Now there were about 25,000 people there and Guy leaps, heroically, up onto his horse and promptly falls off the other side. I kidded him about that for years." Gene Sheldon's wife Peggy, who was at all the Disneyland shows, doesn't recall this incident. She said, "I do remember the horse kept shying away from Guy and he couldn't get up on the horse. If he had fallen off the horse like Britt said, he would have broken his neck. It was a little embarrassing though."

On June 15, Williams appeared on *Kodak Presents Disneyland '59*. This was a live special intended to inform the public of the additions and improvements Disney had made to the park. The *Zorro* cast appeared riding a parade float. Many other Disney stars and celebrities were also on hand. (Zorro would make one final appearance at Disneyland in July of 1962 on another live broadcast for the 13-week Disney summer series *Meet Me at Disneyland*. This was a joint venture with local station KTTV intended to increase attendance at the park. For the *Fun in Frontierland* episode Zorro appeared atop the Golden Horseshoe swordfighting with stuntman Al Cavens. It was Buddy Van Horn behind the mask this time.[3]

At his appearances away from Disneyland, Willliams would travel with Buddy Van Horn and studio publicist John Ormond or production coordinator Louis Debney. Van Horn remarked, "During the hiatus, when Disney would send Guy and me on tour, we'd put on a fencing exhibition. We'd show people how we did it, set up a routine, choreograph it and perform it for the crowd."

Riding down Main Street at Disneyland, 1958.

The P.A.s were great publicity and exciting for adults and kids alike. Sometimes things got out of hand as when Williams served as Grand Marshal of the Portland, Oregon, 1958 Rose Festival Grand Parade. The event was spread over two days and included, among other things, two parades, one of which was especially for Portland's youngsters. It was here that a number of small children broke ranks and pressed in dangerously close to Williams atop his horse. Fortunately no one was injured by the horse's hooves. But because Williams was unfamiliar with the horse he was riding and because it was not shod for pavement, it was reluctantly decided that, for safety reasons, Zorro would be forced to ride in an open convertible for the second parade. Some negative articles appeared in the local papers critical of the decision (a photo of a child atop the same horse added insult to injury). However, the change of plans did not seem to disappoint Zorro's young fans as they cheered themselves hoarse for their idol.[4]

Williams also rode, this time on Tornado, in the Tournament of Roses Parade on New Year's Day in 1958 and '59. Williams' wife Jan recalled that "he left for the parade about three or four in the morning and it was very cold. I remember that he

Buddy Van Horn (*left*) and Guy Williams take a break from fencing practice, 1960 (courtesy of B.V. Horn and A.G. Lane).

was laughing about trying to find a bathroom and then trying to get unwrapped from his costume." Williams jokingly commented, "I rode in the parade until I realized that I couldn't get up at three in the morning any more."

In the summer of 1958, Disney held a family night at the Hollywood Bowl. Most of the *Zorro* cast appeared along with Buddy Van Horn. Van Horn, doubling for Williams as Zorro, descended on a rope from atop the bowl to chase Sgt. Garcia off the stage. Williams then appeared as Zorro in a duel to the near-death with

Buddy Van Horn (*left*) and Guy Williams discuss fencing (courtesy of B.V. Horn and A.G. Lane).

Britt Lomond's Commandante. A spotlight then flashed to the hillside near the Bowl and Zorro (this time, stuntman Dean Smith) rode off astride Tornado into the night.

In an effort to keep the sponsors happy, Williams appeared, along with the rest of the cast, at a number of functions for 7-Up®. At a 7-Up® convention in St. Louis, the stars performed a mini-show and Williams and Lomond engaged in some exciting swordplay. During the course of the series, Williams and Henry Calvin also found time to ride a float in a parade honoring the fiftieth anniversary of General Motors. (G.M. owned AC, the show's other sponsor.)

Because of *Zorro's* cancellation, 20th Century–Fox was considering the purchase of Guy Williams' contract in order to get him to star in *The King Must Die,* an on-again, off-again project at Fox. However, Williams found himself in professional limbo. While there was hope that *Zorro* would be revived, Williams' only activity consisted of doing public appearances for a show that had been canceled. He was still on full salary (which had been raised to placate him) but, his wife Jan said, "He was extremely frustrated. It was really terrible career-wise. He said then that 'this time I should be acting.' The show was at its height and it was going very well. He always felt that it hurt his career." At the time, Williams himself said that he would rather quit show business than spend another year like the one that had just passed (1959). "The fact that I could be doing another series at much more money than I'm getting doesn't bother me as much as the fact that I'm not working. My biggest concern is getting back to work."[5]

Williams is mobbed by fans at the General Motors 50th anniversary celebration, 1959 (courtesy Toni Anderson).

When the actor complained, Walt would simply say, "Guy, sail your boat."[6]

Although his complaints may have had merit, most people would envy the life Williams led in 1959. He was still a hero to millions of kids and making good money. Fans were heaping adulation upon him during his public appearances and in between those appearances Williams would take his boss' advice and leave for weeks at a time to sail aboard his 42-foot ketch *Oceana.* As Williams himself admitted, "I climbed way up on the hog."[7]

As Willliams pondered his professional future, the Disney Studios released a compilation of *Zorro* episodes which were edited into a 90-minute film titled *Zorro the Avenger.* It was seen only in foreign markets, countries where the series had not aired. It opened in Japan and played in Holland, Denmark, France, Italy, Finland, Brazil and Portugal, among others. The studio used the same marketing approach with *Elfego Baca* and *Texas John Slaughter*.

Zorro the Avenger was based upon the Eagle saga of the first season. The predominant episodes featured in the movie were "The Tightening Noose," "The Sergeant Regrets," "The Eagle Leaves the Nest" and "Day of Decision." A few brief scenes from "Bernardo Faces Death" and "The Eagle's Brood" were also used for exposition purposes.

One new scene was filmed for the picture, a conversation between Zorro and Bernardo in the secret room. It addresses an issue that many viewers must have wondered about while watching the Eagle saga: Why didn't Zorro just dispose of the Eagle once he uncovered the villain's identity? Zorro explains to Bernardo that he wants to discover who is behind the Eagle, where he gets his money from, the identities of his followers and when they are preparing to strike.

It may have been a wise move not to release *Zorro the Avenger* in the United States. It was a slow-moving, dull affair with the exception of an opening montage featuring action scenes from "Slaves of the Eagle," "Zorro Fights His Father," "The Iron Box," "Sweet Face of Danger" and "Shadow of Doubt." In the entire 90 minutes there is only one fencing scene. It's difficult to imagine what the studio was thinking of when they

Buddy Van Horn (*left*) and Williams rehearse for a 1960 public appearance (courtesy of B.V. Horn).

put together an adventure film aimed at children with no excitement. (*Zorro the Avenger* finally made it to the U.S. when it aired on the Disney Channel in 1992.)

In October 1959, the Disney Studio announced that it was planning yet another theatrical release of a *Zorro* feature, this time for the domestic market set for June 1960. (The film actually premiered in Japan and Great Britain in 1958.) Like *Zorro the Avenger*, *The Sign of Zorro* was a compilation of episodes edited together into a 91-minute film. The five primary episodes used were "Presenting Senor Zorro," "Monastario Sets a Trap," "Double Trouble for Zorro," "The Luckiest Swordsman Alive" and "The Fall of Monastario." Snippets of "Zorro Saves a Friend," "Zorro's Ride into Terror" and "A Fair Trial" were also in evidence.

Although Norman Foster and Lewis Foster are listed as directors, for the sake of continuity, Charles Barton directed five new scenes, uncredited, in May 1958. These segments were shot when he was directing four new episodes for the start of the second season. The first scene has Zorro displaying his costume for the first time. He also shows Bernardo the secret room in which Bernardo becomes trapped after Zorro leaves. It is a typical physical comedy bit, as he cannot figure out how to get out of the secret room.

Other new inserts included a lancer posting a reward for Zorro and Nacho Torres; Zorro getting Bernardo's help to save his father, who's been shot; Zorro entering the back of the tavern; and Diego discussing with Bernardo a plan to flush out a Zorro imposter. Finally there were two master shots of the ship that brings Diego from Spain which are different from the original episode ("Presenting Señor Zorro").

Composer William Lava wrote some new music for the film but by and large his existing music was simply sweetened and shifted around to accompany different scenes. For the opening credits of the film, Lava added a musical vamp as a prelude to the *Zorro* theme which does add a touch of drama. The traditional theme then follows with various stock shots of Zorro galloping across the countryside as the credits role.

The studio pulled out all the stops in an effort to promote the film. In a 2002 interview, unit publicist John Ormond recounted his days with the traveling *Zorro* road show. "We covered about 18 states throughout the USA, including Hawaii. We also played to Canada in Toronto and Vancouver. When *The Sign of Zorro* premiered in a city or town, we performed a stage show, usually in a movie theater. In our traveling entourage, there were three of us. I was the tour manager and emcee, there was Guy, of course, and we had Buddy Van Horn; he played the villain, who would play out a sword duel with Guy, worked out by our *Zorro* fencing master, Fred Cavens. We really didn't know how we would be received. We needn't have been concerned, as all of the shows were sell-outs everywhere we went. All in all, they were greatly successful. Our audience was always lots of parents with lots of children. It was helped along by the massive school craze of scribing Zs everywhere—parks, shopping malls—any public wall. What we did were pre-movie appearances in the beautiful movie theatres that existed in the 1950s.

"Musicians started playing prelude music to set the mood before we started. I would step up to the microphone and welcome all to the show. Being the storyteller, I would illustrate to the folks that a beautiful senorita has been kidnapped and kept against her wishes at this hacienda. *She must be rescued before it is too late.* I would build up the audience excitement, explaining Zorro was now riding his magnificent horse at great speed and would soon be here. Suddenly, the villain [Van Horn] would

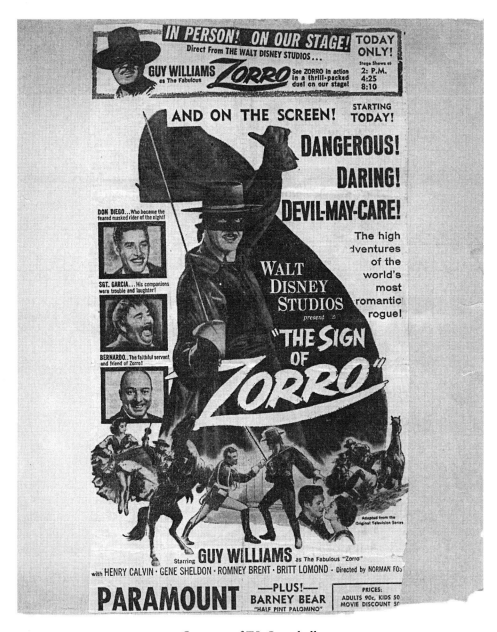

Courtesy of T.J. Campbell.

arrive on his horse and I would ignite the crowd to boo him. The off-stage wranglers quickly removed the horse and I would concern the crowd in a worried voice, the safety of the entrapped senorita would be in jeopardy unless Zorro would arrive soon. Then, after much calling out, Zorro finally arrives on his magnificent horse and the two adversaries would exchange some kind of loud dialogue. They then drew their foils and dueled. I kept hosting and describing each parry and thrust — enticing the crowd to cheer Zorro on to win.

"I would commentate throughout the tense on-stage drama saying lines like 'Ooh, Zorro looks to be in trouble. Can it be that Zorro will be defeated? But wait — our hero is not to be outdone! Using all of his strength and courage, Zorro will surely save the day.' The two would battle the full length of the stage and after a few minutes of flashing blades of a well-choreographed fencing display' finally Zorro would defeat and disarm the villain. Then, victorious, Zorro would parade around the edge of the stage. I exclaimed, 'The great Zorro has done it again.' Guy would throw his cape around and the orchestra would play triumphant music as Guy and Buddy would take their bows exiting the stage, waving to the audience.

"Besides horses being hired, we didn't carry or use any props for our shows. Sometimes the theater owner might have a backdrop or something interesting which would suit the background for us, but usually we had a bare stage — but full of imagination. The shows were always similar in content but, for a change of pace, in Florida I suggested we invite anyone from the audience the opportunity to fence, or 'swordfight' as we called it, with Zorro. We always had two or three 'takers' at each show who wanted to take Guy on. This is a piece of audience participation that worked well at Disneyland whenever Zorro appeared. We took 'all comers' and unfortunately, it sometimes turned to a real jousting match where anything goes. I put a stop to that as it became a little unpredictable and, as you can imagine, in most theaters it wasn't a completely controlled environment. And, by the way, we were using real swords.

"At Disneyland it was a different story because we had a security and screening process—things couldn't get out of hand. Anyway, that shortened our stage show a little, but not too much. After our routine was finished, the film would start screening and we were out of there. In those days, there were no autograph sessions—our mission was to get in and get out as soon as possible. Our shows were usually in theaters, but in the larger cities we played in amphitheaters–huge places. Sometimes we appeared in grand open-air rodeos, which from memory were in Iowa, Fort Smith, Arkansas, and Kansas. We performed on a makeshift stage and the feature film was later shown at a close-by theater.

"I clearly remember the rodeo show we did in Fort Smith. There were more than 7,000 people who turned up to see Zorro. Wearing his black garb, Guy had to ride around a gigantic tent several times (with obstacles and in-house lighting). He wasn't happy with that, as anything could happen. Studios today would never let their star do anything that may cause an accident. I reassured Guy the ride wasn't dangerous and he relented. By the time his ride was over, and upon hearing the huge roar of the crowd, he was immensely happy, and we did our usual routine to that huge crowd.

"There were quite a few places where we entertained *huge* crowds, always consisting of parents with children. We came close to being literally mobbed every now and again. Occasionally some of the crowds got a little out of control but there were no incidents that I can recall. Basically, the children were nearly always behaved and most parents were always responsible. The admission price was about $1 or $2, maybe it was less, it's hard to remember. I believe at some theaters there were some *Zorro* program books or magazines given out as well. Buena Vista (Disney's distribution company) set all the dates, promoting and advertising [that] Zorro would be appearing in person. Although the main reason for our show was to sell and push the merchandise — that wasn't our department. Other people were doing that.

"In some cities we did five or six shows a week. From memory, the cities we toured were St. Louis, Memphis, Nashville, New Orleans, Pensacola, Miami Beach, Atlanta, New York, Washington DC and Oregon. Buena Vista was very happy with us and they got great newspaper reports of our shows going over very well. Because we were moving on from one city to another, we never had a chance to read what was being printed about us. We were dubbed *The Three Musketeers* by the office people of Buena Vista. We had terrific times with that. My code name was Porthos, I think. Well, it was a favorite of mine, and Guy's name was Aramis— it was a lot of fun.

"After a few cities on tour, you can imagine what it was like — Guy used to say to me, 'Well, it's Tuesday, John, what do we do today?' I was in charge of everything. Sometimes there was nothing on our schedule, but that was rare. Buena Vista had us working as much as we possibly could. As soon as we arrived in a new city, we had time to unpack, get our bearings and then get ready to perform. After we finished our week or two weeks there, it was time to move on.

"Guy was always resplendent in costume and there was a lot of *Zorro* costume to wear — he had so much to put on. When he was fully garbed, it was difficult for him to have 100 percent vision as the mask and hat were sight prohibitive. You can imagine how that went over with Guy, waiting in the wings of a darkened theater. That became a sore point for Guy. He was being Zorro day in and day out and he really started to dislike wearing the black suit. But he had a contractual agreement with the studio and I was representing the studio. We once had a bit of an altercation about taking the black mask off. Guy wanted to unmask after every performance but Bill Anderson, our producer, was quite tough on this point, wanting to keep the mystique of Zorro always in a costume. I had to make sure during the shows he remained in full costume, meaning Guy had to exit each presentation wearing all of his Zorro ensemble. I would then wrap up the show on the microphone knowing he was trudging off a little unhappy about it. However, because we were so close, I could see this becoming a *big* issue. Since Walt Disney put me in charge, I decided to give Guy a break on this issue. I told him, 'All right, Guy, you know what Bill Anderson wants. But if you really want to go back out there as yourself, that's fine with me. If you won't say anything, [to Bill Anderson], neither will I!' So in the shows, from then on, after Zorro left, I would vocally wrap up and call back 'Guy Williams!' He would then reappear in normal attire. The people could then see Zorro unmasked — as Guy. I would again announce his name and he would take his final bows. He was happy with that. As a little rebellion, Guy loved having photographs taken with his mask *off*— making sure there were a *lot* of those taken.

"Towards the end of the tour, Guy was really getting more than a little tired of wearing the Zorro attire. Actually, anyone would — doing the same routine continually. To illustrate how disenchanted he was, a businessman approached us with a proposition. He had a daughter attending a school that was not far out from our tour schedule. He wanted Guy to appear at their school and offered him $1000 as a fee. It was a lot of money, we considered the offer, and Guy was in agreement, if that was all he wanted. But then we found he wanted his full pound of flesh. He wanted Guy to appear in the full black costume, and to do a full show for all on the school grounds ... to which Guy responded, '*Not even for $100,000!*'"[8]

In retrospect, *The Sign of Zorro* seemed like an attempt to cash in on a dying fad. However, considering the success the studio had with the theatrical release of the re-edited *Davy Crockett*, it is understandable. *The Sign of Zorro* proved to be a popular feature film. Also jumping on the Zorro bandwagon was Republic Pictures with re-releases of *Zorro Rides Again* (1937) and *Ghost of Zorro* (1949). 20th Century–Fox followed suit with *The Mark of Zorro* (1940).

November 1959 found Disney renewing Guy Williams' contract for one year. One of the stipulations which may have induced the actor to re-sign was his freedom to do work outside the studio. This was one of the few times Disney agreed to this clause although Williams never exercised it while under contract to the studio.

ABC reentered the picture and began to inquire about the possibility of doing more *Zorro* shows. The series, having gone off the air in September 1959, was still very popular as fan mail to both ABC and the Disney Studio was attesting. Since everything was still in place to film the series, Disney agreed and six one-hour specials were planned to be presented on *Walt Disney Presents* during the 1960–61 season.

Filming of the first episode began in May 1960 with most of the original cast members. Guest stars Gilbert Roland and Rita Moreno helped round out the cast. Following completion of the first pair of hour-long episodes, "El Bandido" and "Adiós El Cuchillo," Guy Williams hit the road again for a seven-day, 11-city tour to promote *The Sign of Zorro*. The film premiered in El Paso, Texas, chosen because of its close proximity to Mexico and its large Latin population. Greeted by over 1000 fans wearing promotional Zorro masks at International Airport, Williams and Van Horn performed three fencing shows on the Plaza Theater stage to the delight of the movie audience. *The Sign of Zorro* helped to keep the character out before the public without costing the studio much money.

Williams returned to film two more one-hour *Zorro* specials, completing his run as Zorro with the studio. Although press releases touted six specials, only four were filmed and they performed very well in the ratings, beating the competition and attracting more viewers than almost any other segment on *Walt Disney Presents* in the 1960–61 season.

After putting away his mask, Williams reflected on the role that made him famous. "The show has been a great experience but Zorro is a role I both love and hate. It wasn't what I prepared for as an actor. I'm not worried about being typed as Zorro because the whole thing has had so many pleasant aspects to it. Besides, such typecasting buys a lot of groceries...."[9] Williams went on to say, "It was sad to leave the Disney Studios; even my son loved the show. I made good friends at Disney, which has a very good atmosphere; it's a friendly place to work. I'd like to work for Walt again if another good character came up."[10] Williams did complain about the limited range of the role, describing it as being "nothing more than a comic strip." In the end, *Zorro's* production coordinator Lou Debney concluded, "Guy was happy to get in and happy to get out."[11]

Following the final *Zorro* special ("Auld Acquaintance," completed in November 1960), Guy Williams found time for a few more public appearances in between sailing jaunts. He finally left Zorro behind and headed for England to play Miles Hendon in *The Prince and the Pauper* for Disney. Trading on Williams' image, Hendon was a swashbuckling soldier of fortune who actually wasn't that far removed from Zorro. But at least no mask was required.

Gene Sheldon and Henry Calvin also kept quite busy during this time. In between filming the *Zorro* specials, the pair co-starred in *Toby Tyler* (1960) and *Babes in Toyland* (1961) for Disney. Fans of *Zorro* had the chance to hear Sheldon speak in *Toby Tyler* and then saw the two portray ersatz Laurel and Hardy types in *Babes in Toyland*.

During this period, Walt Disney settled his lawsuit with ABC. According to the agreement, "Disney would be able to take *Walt Disney Presents* to another network. Disney would buy out ABC's one-third interest in Disneyland for $7,500,000. The purchase from ABC in 1960 gave Walt Disney Production total ownership in Disneyland."[12] Walt immediately signed with NBC, for whom he would produce *Walt Disney's Wonderful World of Color* beginning with the 1961–62 season. This sounded the final death knell for *Zorro*. The show was too expensive to produce and, despite the impressive ratings of the one-hour specials, the momentum built during the first two seasons on ABC was dissipating. Besides, *Zorro* was black-and-white and Disney was moving into the future to the all-color network.

Guy Williams completed filming *The Prince and the Pauper*, which aired in three parts on Disney's new show, then left the studio for good and worked as a freelancer starring in *Damon and Pythias* (1962) and *Captain Sindbad* (1963) for MGM. In the

Williams in the movie ***Damon and Pythias***, 1962 (courtesy of K. Gregory).

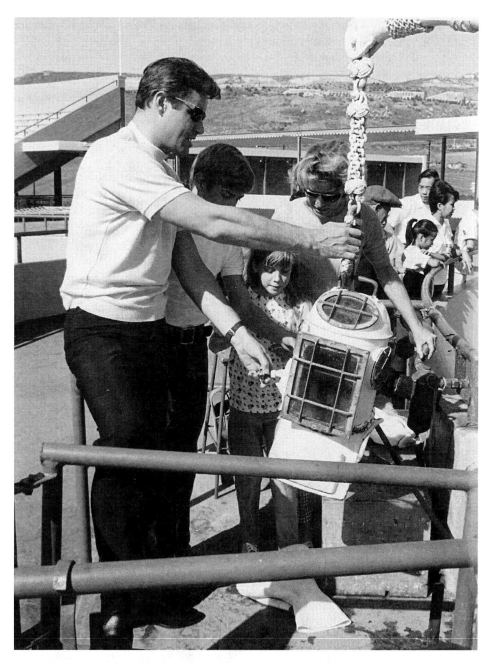

A 1967 trip to Marineland with the family.

first film, Williams plays Damon, a rogue who learns the value of friendship. This was a role that had a little more depth than Zorro and Williams was very good in it, playing the part to the hilt. Curiously, all of the swordplay was left to co-star Don Burnett. With *Captain Sindbad*, Williams was more or less back on familiar ground as the legendary sea captain. A children's action-fantasy, filled with special effects, it

The Williams family in 1969 (*left to right*): Guy, Jan and Steve. Daughter Toni is in front.

was a popular matinee entry. The sword work in this film was a far cry from the standard set by Fred Cavens, perhaps because Williams refused to perform any of his own fencing unless he was paid extra. The production refused, and Williams declined to handle his sword in anything other than the close-ups.

Both films were shot in Europe and the main reason Williams agreed to do them was because of the trips involved. According to Williams, "Traveling in Europe was a big plus, especially with the family. In the meantime my agent didn't know where I was and I was missing opportunities. But the trip was worth it."[13] Jan Williams added, "It was a great experience, a great education for the kids. Guy was Italian and we were based in Rome. One of the last times I saw him, he said that he regretted leaving Europe and returning to the States." In a mid–1960s interview, Williams referred to the two films as his most enjoyable professional experiences.

Back in the U.S., Williams appeared on the top-rated *Bonanza* for five episodes as a Cartwright cousin in the 1963–64 season. It was not a pleasant experience for him since he was used by the producers as a pawn to keep Pernell Roberts (the actor playing the oldest Cartwright son, who wanted to exit the show) in line. "I realized I was being used and I didn't get any help from the other actors, because if Roberts left, they would take up his slack. The whole session was very negative for me," explained Williams.[14]

In 1965, the *Zorro* series was sold into syndication to 43 stations around the country and enjoyed a mini-revival. Much of the merchandise, in a slightly cheapened form, was re-issued to the delight of a new generation of kids. The show ran for two years and was seen as something of a cousin to the popular *Batman* TV series which premiered in January 1966.

Williams moved on to 20th Century–Fox where he starred from 1965 to 1968 in the diminishing role of John Robinson in the *Lost in Space* television series. (In some cities, Williams competed with himself as the syndicated *Zorro* ran head to head against his new series.) It was a disappointing experience for the actor, who found himself playing a quintessential Irwin Allen hero that was humorless, bland and two-dimensional, a role totally unsuited to the image Williams had created for himself. While he got on well with cast and crew, he was unhappy with the change in the show's concept and the fact that his part was becoming little more than a walk-on each week. It was mainly his ample paycheck which kept him there. "It didn't have for me the feeling that I got out of *Zorro* because there was nothing of an extreme nature to do. We stood around machines that were going click-click-click and stared at various alien monsters. I got less out of it as a performer than I did with *Zorro*. It wasn't one of my bright moments,"[15] Williams lamented.

14

From Frontierland

The Return of the Fox:
Episode Guide for Walt Disney Presents

"El Bandido"

Filmed: May 9–May 26, 1960; *Air Date*: October 30, 1960; *Director*: William Witney; *Writer*: Bob Wehling; *Cast*: Gilbert Roland (El Cuchillo), Rita Moreno (Chulita), Vito Scotti (Chato), George Lewis (Don Alejandro), Bern Hoffman, Rodolfo Acosta, and Rudolfo Hoyos (Bandits), Nestor Paiva (Innkeeper),

The legendary bandit El Cuchillo and his men have been driven out of Mexico. After narrowly escaping capture, Cuchillo decides they should stay in California until things cool off south of the border. As they head for Los Angeles, Chato, one of the Cuchillo's men, seems a bit concerned that they may cross paths with Zorro. Cuchillo says that Zorro will not show his face while they are in Los Angeles.

Meanwhile, Sgt. Garcia has a heavy burden to bear. He and his lancers are in charge of guarding a warehouse full of hides. This is just the sort of information that El Cuchillo is interested in.

As Cuchillo and his men carefully make their way into Los Angeles, Diego and Sgt. Garcia meet this charming bandit. When Cuchillo offers to have Garcia and Diego as his guests at the tavern, Garcia falls completely under the stranger's spell. As the three men chat, Garcia innocently blurts out some interesting information to Cuchillo: The Sergeant must place a valuable silver service worth 5,000 pesos aboard a coach heading for Santa Barbara. However, the coach is not coming into Los Angeles; he must go and meet it. Cuchillo now realizes he has made some very nice friends. However, Diego has his suspicions about El Cuchillo and he thinks that perhaps Zorro should keep an eye on the sergeant.

Zorro follows the tracks of Garcia and his men. When he comes upon them, they are tied up and Cuchillo and his men are making off with the silver. Cuchillo leaves two of his men behind to handle Zorro. But it is Zorro who handles them. Zorro moves in on Cuchillo, telling him, "As a stranger to California you're entitled to one warning and this is it ... take your men, Cuchillo, and leave California." Nobody tells Cuchillo what to do and the two adversaries cross swords. The duel rages back and forth and, as Garcia and his lancers arrive, it finally ends in a draw. It's not a bad night's work for Sgt. Garcia, though; he has captured three bandits and saved the valuable silver service.

In the pueblo, Garcia has the three captured bandits help carry the ever-increasing supply of furs into the warehouse. Diego takes Garcia aside and tries to subtly clue him in regarding the identity of the masked bandit who attempted to steal the silver service the night before. Garcia, astute as always, is having none of it. Unless Diego told Garcia directly that it was El Cuchillo, the sergeant would never have a clue. The two friends head for the tavern and once again they encounter Cuchillo and once again Garcia says too much: He mentions that a ship will be arriving from the East with 20,000 American dollars to pay for the hides. This is reason enough for Cuchillo and his bandits to remain in Los Angeles.

That evening at the de la Vega hacienda, a group of unwelcome guests pay a call: Cuchillo and his men along with Chulita, a waitress at the tavern, want to spend a little time at the hacienda. Alejandro is not amused but Diego calms him in an effort to learn what the bandit is up to. As Chulita dances for them, Cuchillo sends his men out on the patio. Two of them return to Los Angeles with plans to rob the innkeeper. Bernardo, who has observed the men planning their robbery, relays this information to Diego after the intruders have left. Diego now realizes that Cuchillo merely used the de la Vegas as an alibi while his men, who were supposedly on the patio, were robbing the inn. Diego calms his own anger long enough to decide to let Zorro get even for him.

He follows the bandits out to the countryside where they are now involved in a bit of sport. Cuchillo is racing his men for the money they have stolen and he gives them a head start to boot. Unbeknownst to the outlaws, Zorro cuts ahead of them and positions himself above the trail in a tree. With lasso in hand, the masked man is able to snare the last rider, Chato. As the bandit dangles helplessly, Zorro plucks the stolen money pouch from his belt. Chato's screams bring Cuchillo, who engages Zorro in another duel. After disarming the bandit, Zorro puts another Z on Cuchillo's vest, to match the last one he put there. Before Cuchillo's men return, Zorro rides off with the stolen money and a little bit of Cuchillo's pride.

Author's Notes

This is the first of the four one-hour episodes that appeared on *Walt Disney Presents* in 1960–61. The "El Cuchillo" episodes were actually written for the pending third season of *Zorro*. They were completed and turned in by Bob Wehling on March 2, 1959. When the show was sold into syndication, these one-hour specials were edited into 30-minute episodes to fit the format of the original series.

The one very special aspect of these episodes is the introduction by Walt Disney himself. Disney gives a brief sketch of the Zorro character to reacquaint the viewers (the show had been off the air for one year) and does the same for El Cuchillo. He goes so far as to momentarily don Zorro's mask and make the sign of the Z with Zorro's sword. It's all great fun.

Director William Witney is in top form as a fast-paced horse chase opens the episode. In the eight teleplays that Witney directed for the original series, he was somewhat hampered by dull, actionless scripts. Here, with an excellent script by Bob

Wehling, his work harkens back to his best days at Republic. There are a number of inventive and exciting stunts all through these episodes, very similar to the kind of action Witney handled in the serials.

Perhaps the most surprising aspect of Witney's return is the fact that he came back at all. His initial experience at the studio was a very unhappy one. Witney, who was used to directing at the brisk pace endemic to Republic, found the more leisurely pace of some Disney crew members to be intolerable. It also caused the always-prompt director to fall behind schedule. His main conflict was with the director of photography, Gordon Avil, who was replaced by Lucien Ballard for these two one-hour segments. Witney recalled, "Ballard was a good cameraman. They knew I didn't like the other guy [Avil]. I told them. I'm not one of those bashful people." Perhaps for the good of all concerned, Gordon Avil was on location filming the Disney feature *Ten Who Dared* when these new *Zorro* segments were shot.

Regarding his return to the Disney Studio, Witney said, "I wanted to show everybody that I could make pictures on schedule. I had a terrible time there before, I was unhappy with the whole situation. I like Bill Anderson, he was a peach of a guy, it wasn't his fault. I love Amigo [Gilbert Roland], and the little girl [Rita Moreno] was a doll. We had a good cast; everything worked out fine."

El Cuchillo, as portrayed by Gilbert Roland, is every bit a match for Zorro. He's witty, charming and dangerous—the first really intimidating villain Zorro has faced since Lee Van Cleef's Castillo in "Welcome to Monterey." Roland was one of the Latin heartthrobs of the '30s and '40s and he was perfect for the part. With his trademark "Ai Chihuahua" exclamation and a cigar dangling from his lips, the character was not unlike his *Cisco Kid* portrayal in the mid–1940s.

Diego makes his first appearance fencing with Bernardo on the de la Vega patio. Unbeknownst to Diego, Garcia has entered through the front gate and is amazed at Diego's ability with the sword. Bernardo tries to warn his friend by making a motion with his hand that depicts Garcia's ample girth. Diego misreads the gesture and laughingly replies, "A chest protector won't help you now, Bernardo." When Diego realizes what is happening, he is able to explain his way out of the predicament. It is all done with a great sense of style and fun. From Diego's uneasiness to Garcia's befuddlement, it is these dual identity scenes which are often among the best of the series.

There are also two excellent sword fights with Al Cavens doubling for Gilbert Roland. The first match ends in a draw while the second is more decisive with Cuchillo being disarmed. The one running gag that accompanies the duel is Zorro's habit of cutting Zs into Cuchillo's vest, even after he has them mended. It's an extra touch that adds to the rivalry between the two men. A more unusual feature of the sword duels is the almost dream-like inserts that are used. They are close-ups of Zorro reading a line of dialogue with backgrounds that don't match the scene that they are in. They seem so out of place and unrealistic that it's almost as if they were meant to be that way. Nothing like it every appeared in other episodes.

Behind the Scenes

Don Diamond, who portrayed Cpl. Reyes in the series, does not appear in any of the four one-hour episodes.... All of the location work for this episode was filmed at Disney's Golden Oak Ranch.... A chasm that Cuchillo's horse leaps is a Peter Ellenshaw matte drawing.... There was a noticeable weight loss by Henry Calvin in these episodes. So much so that he had to be padded.... Rudolpho Hoyos and Rodolpho Acosta had both appeared in earlier *Zorro* episodes.... Legendary stunt man David Sharpe has a small role as one of the bandits.... Fashion note: There is no white piping on the cuff of Zorro's gauntlets.... The de le Vega patio, which was set up on Soundstage #3 for the entire run of the regular series, could now be found outside on the back lot. Because the show had been out of production for a year, Soundstage #3 was no longer its permanent home as other features were now being filmed there. Since the patio was supposed to be outdoors anyway, the effect was much more authentic. The only problem was when somebody opened the patio gate; the pueblo could be seen. The de la Vegas were supposed to live out in the country.... Louis Debney, production coordinator for the *Zorro* series, was now the associate producer.... The Plaza landscape area has been augmented by the addition of some large trees.... During a tavern scene, "Zorro's Serenade" and "Quien Sabe," songs from the first season, can be heard in the background.... Al Cavens doubles as Bernardo for a brief fencing scene with Diego.

"Adiós El Cuchillo"

Filmed: May 9–May 26, 1960; *Air Date*: November 6, 1960; *Director*: William Witney; *Writer*: Bob Wehling; *Cast*: Gilbert Roland (El Cuchillo), Rita Moreno (Chulita), Vito Scotti (Chato), George Lewis (Don Alejandro), Bern Hoffman, Rodolfo Acosta and Rudolfo Hoyos (Bandits), Nestor Paiva (Innkeeper).

After crossing paths with Zorro, Cuchillo and his men are in need of money. Under cover of darkness, they enter the pueblo and split up, each group in search of their own loot. Unfortunately for them, Zorro has followed their trail. One by one, with the aid of Bernardo, Zorro deals with the bandits until he comes to Cuchillo, who has just had the Zs that Zorro cut into his vest repaired by Chato. Just to spite the head bandit, Zorro undoes all of Chato's work with a quick cut of Cuchillo's own knife. Zorro then runs off into the night as Garcia and his lancers return to the pueblo.

The following morning, Diego and Bernardo arrive in the pueblo. Diego heads for the tavern as he sends Bernardo to fetch Sgt. Garcia. As always, Cuchillo and his men are found relaxing at the cantina and the head bandit is sketching the beautiful Chulita. Diego greets Cuchillo, who then begins to question him about Zorro. As the interrogation continues, Cuchillo begins to sketch Diego and the young don is becoming more agitated and uncomfortable. Bernardo enters and sees that Cuchillo's sketch of Diego is now wearing a hat and mask. As he carefully signals the situation to Diego, Sgt. Garcia enters the tavern. Cuchillo informs the sergeant that he may be interested in his artwork. Bernardo moves quickly to spill a large platter of food on the bandit's masterpiece. In doing to, he accidentally splatters some of the mess on Carancho, one of Cuchillo's men. He becomes enraged and wants to kill Bernardo.

Diego steps in to protect his friend and engages Carancho in a desperate struggle that finds them tumbling over tables and leaping over the bar. He eventually subdues the bandit.

Diego, Bernardo and Sgt. Garcia make their way over to the sergeant's office so Diego can clean up. Again Diego attempts to convince the doubting Garcia that there may be more bandits involved than the three Garcia has in his jail and Cuchillo may be one of them. The innkeeper suddenly barges into the office exclaiming that he has been robbed by Cuchillo and his men. The sergeant gathers his lancers and goes in pursuit of the fleeing bandits.

Diego assesses the situation and realizes that Cuchillo may intend to make his way back to release his jailed friends. That is exactly what the bandit has in mind. He and his companions split into two groups with Garcia and his men chasing one group while Cuchillo and his band head back to Los Angeles. Zorro is waiting for them. After he disposes of the bandits trying to rush the cuartel, he and Cuchillo once again cross swords. And once again, they are interrupted by the returning Garcia. The two adversaries head off in separate directions knowing they will meet again.

The next morning finds Diego and Don Alejandro on the patio of their hacienda contending with unwelcome visitors — El Cuchillo and his men. Bernardo, who sees the bandits approaching and tries in vain to warn Diego, makes his way into the secret passage before he is discovered. Cuchillo informs the de la Vegas that he and his men will be staying with them until the ship arriving from Boston with the $20,000 arrives. Cuchillo also tells the pair that they may come and go as they want as long as one of them stays in a chair under guard in the sala. If there is any trouble, the one in the chair will be shot.

As Alejandro takes first turn in the chair, Sgt. Garcia arrives with some very interesting news for the de la Vegas: The ship has arrived early from Boston and Garcia and his men are on their way to pick up the money. After the sergeant leaves, Cuchillo decides he must make a move. With Diego and Alejandro tied up, he leaves Chato to dispose of them. Luckily for the captives, Bernardo, who was spying on the situation from the secret passage, is able to get the drop on Chato. He frees Diego and Alejandro so that Diego can turn the situation over to Zorro. Alejandro rides off to gather the dons.

Cuchillo and his band spot Garica and his lancers returning from the harbor with the money. They give chase but Garcia and company ride off and decide to make a stand at the country bridge. Zorro arrives just in time to leap aboard the money wagon which was hijacked by one of the bandits. The two men struggle with Zorro prevailing. Cuchillo, seeing what has happened, rides off in pursuit of the wagon. At that moment, the dons arrive to assist the lancers in the capture of the remaining bandits.

As Zorro guides the wagon through the plaza into the cuartel, he is pursued by El Cuchillo and soon the two men are matching cold steel. As the contest moves across the cuartel, up the barracks stairs to the top floor balcony, Zorro knows Cuchillo means business. As the pair nears the edge of the balcony, Zorro loses his balance and crashes through the hand railing, but regains his composure long enough to knock Cuchillo unconscious.

The next morning, Sgt. Garcia prepares to transport his prisoner Cuchillo back to Mexico. The other bandits have already been sent ahead. Diego, Alejandro and Bernardo have come to see the bandit leader off. They talk briefly and then Garcia and company lead them away. Immediately Diego spies Chulita, who with bag packed seems to be waiting for someone. That someone is Cuchillo, who comes racing in to grab her, preceded by the very same lancers who just rode off with him, bound atop their horses.

Diego decides then and there to fix his friend one last time. As Cuchillo and his love make their way into the countryside, a long lariat snakes out and wraps itself around the two. Zorro, at the other end of the lariat, instructs Cuchillo to ride slowly around a large boulder. He obeys only to find a priest ready to perform a marriage ceremony. At first Cuchillo protests but realizes that perhaps it would be for the best. A married bandit doesn't have much time to be a bandit. It seems as though Zorro, with a little help from Cupid, has won the final round.

Author's Notes

The best part of this episode is the Bob Wehling dialogue that creates a very subtle tension between Diego and Cuchillo as they engage in a verbal game of cat and mouse. In this scene, Cuchillo interrogates Diego as he begins to sketch a portrait of the young don that looks more and more like Zorro.

CUCHILLO: Diego, how long have you been in Los Angeles?
DIEGO: Well, except for six years in Spain, all my life. Why?
CUCHILLO: Then you must know everyone in Los Angeles, eh?
DIEGO: A great many but not everyone, why?
CUCHILLO: I'm interested in one man ... Zorro.
DIEGO: Zorro?
CUCHILLO: You know, the bandido. If you can call him that.
DIEGO: That's what he's been called.
CUCHILLO: You must have thought about it one time or another — have you any idea who he is?
DIEGO: Now what makes you think that I would know who Zorro is?
CUCHILLO: Zorro must have another identity. He can't hide behind a mask all the time.
DIEGO: (Becoming aggravated) You're right, he can't.
CUCHILLO: Well, who is he?
DIEGO: You seem to be very concerned. May I ask why?
CUCHILLO: I don't think Los Angeles is big enough for Zorro and El Cuchillo.

In one of their final confrontations, Cuchillo questions a captive Diego one more time.

CUCHILLO: Well, Diego, I'm sorry the ship is a week early.
DIEGO: I'm sorry too.

CUCHILLO: I could have enjoyed our little visit. We could have talked about a lot of things. You might even remember who Zorro was.

DIEGO: I believe we discussed that yesterday.

CUCHILLO: It wasn't much of a discussion. You answered each of my questions with one of your own ... I wish I had time to find out why.

Diego has never before had to deal with anyone like El Cuchillo, an adversary who is not really a complete villain. In some ways, Cuchillo is much like Zorro: an excellent swordsman, a fine horseman, a bit of a rascal and someone who will not back down from a confrontation. Cuchillo even suspects that Diego and Zorro are one and the same. This is a twist that is missing from most other *Zorro* episodes, the possibility that Diego's secret will be uncovered. It is a plot device that can't be overused or it would lose its effectiveness. When it does occur, it adds an extra dimension that makes the shallowness of the simpler plots seem obvious.

Another development of note is a rare episode opening appearance by Zorro, a pleasant surprise. Prior to this, it occurred in "Monastario Sets a Trap," "Zorro by Proxy" and "Zorro and the Flag of Truce" Here it is a very well-done series of scenes in which Zorro and Bernardo eliminate the bandits one by one. It's an excellent blending of light comedy and action.

Regarding the action, there are two duels and one incident of hand-to-hand combat and all three have a flaw or two. The worst of the group is the scuffle between Diego and Carancho, a bandit. Although within the context of the story Diego is attempting not to reveal his secret identity, it is a very clumsy and poorly staged fight. Buddy Van Horn is obviously doubling for Guy Williams in everything except the extreme close-ups and it hurts the scene.

The first sword fight is the better of the two. Part of it includes an inventive scene which has Zorro and Cuchillo dueling inside a small canvas hut which they eventually cut to shreds. The one negative is a very brief piece of film taken from the fencing scene in "The Fortune Teller." It fits in adequately with the original footage but it seems to be a rather blatant cost-saving measure. The second and final duel of the episode suffers somewhat from poor editing which affects the continuity. Parts of it are very good, but it has a choppy feel to it. It seems as if some of the fencing phrases could have been reshot to provide a more fluid feel. The original script has the duel ending with Zorro disarming El Cuchillo and backing him into a cell at the cuartel. William Witney changed this and added an elaborate stunt to finish things off.

Behind the Scenes

Rita Moreno went on to win the 1961 Best Supporting Actress Oscar for *West Side Story*.... Once again the tune being played on guitar in the tavern is "Zorro's Serenade...." In this episode, Diego states that he has been in Spain for six years. However, in the premiere episode "Presenting Señor Zorro," he claims to have been away for only three years.... Once again the location work for this episode was filmed at the Golden Oak Ranch.... Al Cavens handles the sword work for Gilbert Roland.

"The Postponed Wedding"

Filmed: July 22–July 29, 1960; *Air Date*: January 1, 1961; *Director*: James Neilson; *Writers*: Bob Wehling and Roy E. Disney; *Cast*: Annette Funicello (Constancia), Mark Damon (Miguel Serrano), Carlos Romero (Ansar), George Lewis (Don Alejandro).

Diego and Bernardo ride into Los Angeles to meet an old family friend who is arriving aboard the stage from Santa Clara. Simultaneously, two well-dressed young men enter the pueblo and head directly for the inn, seeking rooms. When the stage arrives, Diego welcomes Constancia and is surprised to see that the young girl has grown into a very lovely young lady. As they chat, she seems distracted. She tells Diego that she is tired and would like to rest in the tavern. Upon entry, she sees a familiar face — one of the young men who arrived earlier — and then she asks Diego to get her handkerchief which she left on the stage. It is merely a ploy so that she and the young man, Miguel, could be alone. It seems that they are planning to elope. They make plans to do so that evening at midnight. She will be staying at the de la Vega hacienda and will leave a light burning in the window so he will know which room is hers.

When Diego returns to the tavern, Constancia introduces her friend and immediately Diego begins to quiz the man about his background. The two lovers, who keep their elopement from Diego, bid each other an almost tearful goodbye. Seeing this, Diego invites Miguel to the hacienda that evening where he can visit with Constancia. Miguel arrives after dinner and makes small talk until someone suggests that the two go for a walk on the patio.

Bernardo is sent to Constancia's room to retrieve her shawl and in the process can't resist examining the contents of her very heavy suitcase. He opens it to find it filled with all kinds of valuable coins, jewelry, etc. When the opportunity presents itself, Bernardo conveys this information to Diego and Alejandro. The two men examine the inside of the trunk to find an inscription which indicates that this is the young woman's dowry. They conclude that she is planning to elope with Miguel. Alejandro wants to take the direct approach and put a stop to things right here and now. As always, Diego is the cooler head and proposes that perhaps Zorro stop in and set the lovers' plan back a little.

Later that evening, after Constancia has gone to bed and fallen asleep, Zorro enters her room and removes the light she has burning in the window, to make it harder for Miguel to find her. When Miguel arrives with his companion, the two make several attempts to enter the hacienda but Zorro thwarts them at every turn. They make so much noise that Alejandro awakens and scares them off.

The next morning, Constancia is very angry and disappointed. Because she slept through the night's activities, she believes Miguel did not try to keep his date with her. She demands a horse to go to Los Angeles but Diego wants to go along with her. She prefers to go alone because she is planning to meet Miguel. Diego will not relent, and as Bernardo goes to saddle the horses and Diego goes to speak with his father, Constancia waits. Miguel arrives and attempts to explain the botched elopement to his love, embellishing his tale somewhat saying that he was attacked and robbed by Zorro. Miguel then convinces her that they must try to elope again and she agrees.

Diego returns and, after being told what happened to Miguel, he plays along and concludes that all of this must be reported to Sgt. Garcia.

When they arrive at the pueblo, Diego sends the pair into the tavern to speak with Garcia. Meanwhile, Diego has spotted Miguel's friend, a man who Miguel seldom mentions, riding by in his coach. Diego decides to investigate and walks around to the rear of the tavern where the coach is waiting. As he calls out for the driver, he is struck from behind, dragged off and locked in a shed. Ansar, Miguel's companion, has done his work well. He enters the tavern and signals to Miguel that they are ready for Garcia. Miguel then tells Garcia that Diego wants to speak to him and of course the rotund sergeant complies. His fate is the same as Diego's.

With the help of Ansar, Miguel and Constancia head for the harbor in San Pedro where they will marry aboard ship and head for Mexico. Meanwhile Diego and Garcia have worked to free themselves and Diego is counting on Zorro to be an uninvited guest at the wedding.

Miguel and Constancia board the ship and he proceeds to sweet talk her — all the while planning to make off with her dowry. As Miguel speaks to the ship's captain, Constancia overhears his plan but by now it is too late. He is leaving with her loot and has given the captain orders to toss her overboard. However, Zorro has other plans as he swings into action. He quickly dispatches the first mate, Ansar and the captain, who ends up in the drink. And so does Miguel, thanks to Constancia, who gives him a push with Zorro's sword.

All's well that ends well as Constancia's dowry is saved and Diego, Alejandro and Bernardo see the young woman off the next morning as she returns home, a little wiser but no poorer.

Author's Notes

This is a very simple, romantic, lighthearted affair directed by James Neilson, a former war photographer and a man who spent most of his subsequent career directing for the Disney Studio. Some of his films for Disney included *Moon Pilot, Summer Magic, Bon Voyage* and *The Moon Spinners*, all very light entertainment.

"The Postponed Wedding" is the least exciting of the four one-hour episodes simply because the action sequences are not very good. The first bit of action has Zorro thwarting the attempts of Constancia's suitor when he tries to elope with her. Zorro really doesn't do very much as Miguel and his companion really do themselves in.

The climactic fencing scene between Zorro and the ship's captain is shot too tight. There are too many single-shot close-ups, which gives the action a choppy feel. (Al Cavens, who portrays the sailor, played a similar part in the premiere episode "Presenting Señor Zorro.") The best thing about the scene is the set upon which it takes place, the deck of a ship. It had not been used since that first episode.

Annette Funicello, a Disney favorite, returns and her acting seems somewhat improved. Versatility was never her strong suit, however; she was always more of a personality than an actress. Other Zorro alumni include Mark Damon, who starred in "The Iron Box," and Carlos Romero, who had a continuing role for five episodes at the start of the second season. His role as Damon's accomplice is surprisingly small.

"The Postponed Wedding" marks the first *Zorro* segment that was not scored by William Lava. Lava, who had written the music for all 78 half-hour shows and the first two one-hour specials, had left the studio and was working in feature films by this time. *Hell Bent for Leather* and *Seven Ways from Sundown* were the two films that prevented him from scoring the final two one-hour *Zorro* shows. Buddy Baker, who had joined the Disney Studio in 1954 to assist George Bruns on *Davy Crockett*, took over for the final two *Zorro* episodes. Baker used all of the familiar Lava cues for the main characters but wrote some new music for most of the action scenes. He was familiar with the *Zorro* show as a number of his songs appeared in the series.

Behind the Scenes

Two songs are performed, "Como Esta Usted" and "Amo Que Paso," both written by Robert and Richard Sherman.... Richard Farnsworth, who later became an actor of note [*The Grey Fox* and *The Natural*], was working at the Disney Studio as a stunt man when he appeared in this episode.... Lou Roberson doubles as Miguel.... Ron Miller, who worked as an assistant director on earlier *Zorro* episodes, was moving up in the ranks and took over as associate producer for this segment.

"Auld Acquaintance"

Filmed: November 15–November 23, 1960; *Air Date*: April 2, 1961; *Director*: James Neilson; *Writer*: Bob Wehling; *Cast*: Ricardo Montalban (Ramon Castillo), Ross Martin (Marcos), Suzanne Lloyd (Isabella), Nestor Paiva (Innkeeper).

Two newcomers, Ramon Castillo and his companion Marcos, arrive in Los Angeles. They make their way to the tavern where Sgt. Garcia and his lancers are in the midst of a celebration. Castillo introduces himself to the sergeant and learns that the soldiers will finally receive six months worth of back pay that evening. Castillo and Marco seem very interested in the soldiers' good fortune and they begin to hatch a plot that will help relieve the soldiers of their heavy monetary burden.

As the party continues, Don Alejandro and Bernardo enter the tavern. Bernardo casually makes eye contact with Castillo and the two seem to recognize each other. Bernardo quickly wheels and heads out the door with Castillo in hot pursuit. He grabs Bernardo and begins questioning him regarding Diego's whereabouts. Alejandro breaks the confrontation up and Castillo explains that he is an old friend of Diego's. Ignoring Bernardo's surreptitious objections, Alejandro invites Castillo and his companion to the hacienda.

Upon arrival, Bernardo immediately makes his way to the secret passage in search of Diego. The two men just miss each other but Bernardo uncovers some interesting information as he overhears the conversation between Castillo and Marcos in the guest bedroom. It seems that Diego defeated Castillo for the Royal Competition Trophy in

Spain and now Castillo wants revenge. More important, Bernardo learns of the pair's plan to steal the military payroll.

In the sala, Diego and Alejandro cross paths and Diego learns of Castillo's arrival. Diego explains to his father who the stranger really is. Alejandro expresses concern about Castillo's knowledge of Diego's ability with a sword. He fears that the secret of Zorro could be revealed. They both decide the two guests should leave, by force if necessary. Bernardo catches the pair just in time and tells them what he has learned. Diego decides to change his tactics.

When Castillo and Diego meet, Diego is on his best behavior and even invites his rival to stay for supper. He says he must leave by 9:00 and Diego says that all will be arranged to accommodate him. Castillo still wants to cross swords with Diego, who reluctantly agrees, but they will wait until after supper.

Later that evening, when dinner has been finished, Ramon is ready to avenge his defeat. As the two men are about to cross swords, they allow the distant mission bells to count off the start, 6 ... 7 ... 8 ... 9 ... 10! When the bell rings ten, Ramon realizes that somehow he has been tricked; he is an hour late! He must rush off—he has a date with a military payroll. But so does Zorro.

Castillo and Marcos, masked, make their way into the cuartel as the unsuspecting Garcia is counting the payroll. They relieve the sergeant of his loot and begin to escape when a whip snakes out and removes the money pouch from their grasp. Now Castillo gets his sword fight and the results are the same as they were in Spain. Zorro disarms his rival but now they are both in danger of being captured by the lancers. Castillo and Marcos beat a hasty retreat and Zorro as always escapes, but not before returning the money to Garcia. There may be a problem, though. It seems Castillo, after having matched steel with Zorro, believes that he and Diego are one and the same.

The next morning in the tavern, Ramon fumes over his humiliation the night before. He will not let Diego run him out of Los Angeles. He tries to convince the doubting Marcos that Zorro is Diego. He goes so far as promising his friend that by midnight he will have destroyed Zorro and made both of them rich. When Garcia enters the tavern, Ramon puts his plan into action. He tells Garcia that Diego is Zorro. The sergeant roars with laughter. When Ramon repeats his charge for all to hear, the laughter can be heard in the street. Ramon proposes a bet, 20 to 1 odds, that his accusation is true. Everyone takes him up on his charge and the innkeeper will hold the money.

Later that day, Ramon explains his ground rules for the bet; Garcia and his lancers will surround the inn at 11:00 P.M. and he and Marcos will "pretend" to rob the innkeeper. Zorro will arrive and Garcia will capture him. Ramon will keep all of the wager money because it will be proven that Diego is Zorro and Garcia can keep the reward. All is going according to Ramon's plan until Garcia, who of course can't keep a secret, visits with Diego and asks him point blank if he is Zorro. Diego is visibly shaken but is able to fend off his friend and hatch a plan of his own.

As darkness falls over the cuartel, Diego begins to put his scheme into action. He tells Garcia that he wants to fight side by side with the sergeant in his effort to capture Zorro. After Diego clumsily shows off his inept swordplay, Garcia realizes his friend will be more of a hindrance than help. Diego plants the thought in the sergeant's head that the only way he could be prevented from helping in Zorro's capture would be to lock him up, which is just what Garcia does. Now Diego has his alibi and, with the help of a rope lowered down a chimney by Bernardo, is free to act as Zorro.

Marcos and Ramon are in the tavern carrying out their charade when Zorro shows up. He quickly dispatches of Marcos and then he and Ramon cross blades once again. Zorro is tested but finally disarms his old rival. Before he leaves, just to taunt his friend, Zorro reveals himself for only the frustrated Ramon to see. After the pair is taken into custody and back to Garcia's office, Ramon still swears that he will win the bet because he knows Diego is Zorro. Garcia unlocks the door to his room and slowly, every so slowly, out walks Diego, much to the chagrin of the disbelieving Ramon. The two arguing bandits are led away as Zorro has saved the day and his identity. Meanwhile, Garcia has won his wager and Ramon and Marcos have lost their freedom.

Author's Notes

This final episode in the *Zorro* saga teams Ricardo Montalban and Ross Martin as a pair of ne'er-do-wells and both are excellent in their roles. Montalban is especially good as Castillo, a somewhat bitter and intense man, determined to get even with Don Diego. Martin is definitely the lighter half of the duo, caring only for the loot they can plunder. The two have a good rapport and at times are quite funny together. However, they are not bunglers and are quite serious in their intentions.

The entire plot hinges on Ramon Castillo's belief that Diego is Zorro. Concerning Diego's secret identity, the theme is more intense in this regard than any other episode save for "The Fall of Monastario." Like the El Cuchillo episodes, it makes things so much more interesting when the nature of the conflict becomes personal. Seeing how Diego outsmarts Ramon is plausible and fun in the Disney style.

One of the more shocking moments in the series occurs when the defeated Ramon stands proclaiming that "Don Diego de la Vega is Zorro!" as he stares at the unmasked face of Zorro. However, Zorro is actually taunting Ramon because when the innkeeper, whose back is to Zorro, turns to look at the object of Ramon's scorn, Zorro has disappeared. Not only has Zorro defeated his old adversary, but also he has humiliated him in the process. This scene was used as an effective teaser to open the broadcast.

The two fencing scenes are well-done and exciting with Al Cavens standing in for Ricardo Montalban. There is one major editing mistake during the first meeting between Zorro and Ramon. The fencing scene in question takes place in the cuartel. A master shot shows Zorro and Castillo fencing their way up the steps and onto the front porch of the soldier's barracks. A medium shot then shows almost the exact same scene occurring. They were already on the porch of the barracks in the first shot, but they are shown in the second shot repeating the same action.

The comedy of the episode has Diego trying to convince Garcia of his desire to

(*Left to right*) Production coordinator Lou Debney, actress Suzanne Lloyd and Williams at a wrap party for "Auld Acquaintance," 1960 (courtesy of Suzanne Lloyd).

fight alongside with the sergeant when they come face to face with Zorro. Diego performs some uncoordinated fencing moves in Garcia's office and in the process nearly destroys his furniture. Later, after Ramon and Marcos have been captured, Garcia releases Diego from his living quarters. Diego saunters out of the room with cigar in hand, nonchalantly stating, "Sergeant, I may never speak to you again." The way Williams delivers the line is priceless and the humor of the scene is augmented by the bickering Ramon and Marcos as they are led away.

Behind the Scenes

One song is performed, "Payday" by Robert and Richard Sherman ... Don Diego plays "Mi Amore" on the guitar. This was Cesar Romero's theme from the second season.... Suzanne Lloyd, who plays Isabella, appeared in seven first-season episodes playing the part of Raquel Toledano, the commandante's wife.... At one point Don Alejandro badly mispronounces Ramon Castillo's last name.... Some actual night shooting was done for a scene that takes place on the de la

Vega patio.... Almost every scene of Zorro riding Tornado in these four one-hour episodes was stock footage taken from the original 78 episodes.... There is no credit at the end of this episode for George Lewis or fencing master Fred Cavens.... These four one-hour shows scored a 12 percent higher rating than any other *Disneyland* shows that season.... All four, one-hour shows were repeated during the summer of 1961.

15

Zorro Forever

Guy Williams once said, "You only go through life once. You might as well see all the furniture."[1] That's just what he did: tailored clothes, fast cars, good food, expensive cigars. Ever since he hit it big on *Zorro,* he could afford all these things. He had also invested well so he could afford to sit and wait for the right role to come along. However, the negative effect of the *Lost in Space* experience on Williams was such that he really didn't care whether or not he acted again. He always had a casual yet practical view of his profession. He once remarked, "You hear Hollywood people say, 'I always wanted to be an actor.' But I didn't always want to be an actor. I got into it by the process of elimination, by avoiding the things I didn't want to do. Acting seemed a pleasant compromise between considerable laziness and a comfortable income."[2]

The remainder of the 1960s and early 1970s found Williams involved in endeavors outside of show business. He and his wife Jan put together their own cookbook, complete with a wine list to compliment each meal. The entire family got together and baked "Guy Williams Panforte Bread," which was sold to health food stores. However, much of Williams' time was spent on the telephone buying and selling stocks through his stockbroker, old friend and *Damon and Pythias* co-star, Don Burnett.

On the professional side, Williams would have tolerated doing another series but he was worried about finding himself trapped in a *Lost in Space*–type situation which would make life miserable. During the mid–60s he had become interested in writing and producing but had difficulty making headway. Now with no new series offers forthcoming, Williams was in danger of becoming a primary subject of "Whatever became of...?" questions. His wife Jan remembered, "After the success Guy had with *Zorro* and *Lost in Space,* it was hard for him to get into the smaller parts he was offered on other series. He kept waiting for something big to come along again. Guy was always a bit of a gambler."

In April 1973, after five years of professional limbo, Williams' gamble paid off when he received an unexpected phone call from New York. Leo Gleizer, an Argentine journalist from that country's Channel 13, was imploring Williams to come to New York and from there fly to Buenos Aires. It seems that Channel 13 had been airing reruns of *Zorro* since 1968 with incredible success and they wanted Williams to come to their country as a publicity stunt for their station. The only stipulation was that Williams had to show up with his trademark Zorro mustache intact. He had never

Zorro and son, 1969.

been to South America, thought it would be fun and decided to go, with his newly grown mustache. Williams was so uncertain of what to expect when he got there that he wore a Zorro-style black hat so people would recognize him. He needn't have worried; the airport in Buenos Aires was packed with children and adults, all of whom wanted to meet Zorro. It was like 1957 all over again. Lightning was indeed striking twice.

One of the things that impressed the Channel 13 executives was that the 48-year-old Williams was still in great shape and still very handsome. It was decided to put Williams in costume for an interview and also have him engage in a fencing exhibition. Williams agreed, a costume was hastily put together and a sword was found for him to use. The interview went great, Williams was completely charming. To duel with Williams, Channel 13 enlisted Fernando Lupiz, an Argentine fencing champion. The sword fight went perfectly and thrilled the packed studio. Williams and Lupiz would become great friends.

Williams' first trip to Argentina lasted only two weeks but it would change the rest of his life.

After their big success, Channel 13 invited Williams to return to Argentina in July 1973. Williams was more than happy to oblige and this time his wife Jan accompanied him. Like her husband earlier in the year, Jan was amazed by what she found when they arrived. "We were driving in from the airport and crowds were lining the roads and it's about 30 or 40 miles and there was never an area where there were not people standing there. I wasn't really catching on to what was happening so I asked the person in the car with us and she said, 'Don't you know? They're here to see Guy.' Daughter Toni added laughing, "He never let any of us forget that."

Jan Williams: "I was absolutely stunned at the way he was treated down there. We would go into a restaurant for dinner, one of the huge restaurants, and everyone would stand up and applaud. They had a tremendous armory down there where Guy would do a fencing routine and I remember being taken out before he was finished with the show because they were afraid there was going to be a stampede." Williams' popularity was such that there was even a half-serious "Zorro for President" drive among the populace.

During his second visit, Williams was contacted by Isabelita Peron, wife of Argentine President Juan Peron. Juan had just returned from exile in Spain and had been re-elected. Guy recalled, "She wanted to know if I would do one of her charities. She let it be known to the counsel here that she would give me carte blanche to move around Argentina and do what I wanted in terms of personal appearances if I would do her charity. I said fine."[3] Williams went on to appear on such popular Argentine shows as *Mirtha Legrand*, a kind of talk show where the guests would sit around, eat a lunch of several courses and chat. Comedians Pato Carret,

Alberto Olemedo and Jorge Procel all asked Williams to guest on their respective shows.

Also accompanying Williams during this second visit was his popular comic foil Sgt. Garcia, Henry Calvin. Jan Williams remembered that when Calvin and her husband were filming the *Zorro* series, "Guy used to joke with Henry, 'Just wait. In our old age we'll be doing this together and you'll be thin and I'll be fat.' Well, Guy had put on a little bit of weight and Henry had lost some of his due to illness. They had to put padding in his costume to make him look like the Sgt. Garcia of old." Williams and Calvin remained in Argentina for two weeks appearing on television and doing interviews before returning to the States.

Williams returned once again to Argentina in 1975 and scored a great triumph when he appeared for two months at the Rural Theatre with his new partner, Fernando Lupiz. Williams' segment of the show was relatively short (approximately 15 minutes) but the crowd went wild during his duel to the finish with Lupiz, who was playing the part of Zorro's old adversary, Capitan Monastario. It was during this period that two Argentine producers, Carlos Montero and Enrique Garcia Fuentes, approached Williams and Lupiz with their idea of doing a *Zorro* film, to be shot in Argentina. The script had an older Don Diego living peacefully on his rancho with only his servants, his wife having died during childbirth. Diego's son arrives home from Spain after completing his education at the same university his father attended. Once again the pueblo falls under tyrannical military rule — time for Zorro to return to action. During the course of events, the son discovers his father's secret identity. The finale has an unmasked Zorro killing his antagonist, but in the process he too is seriously wounded. Before he dies, Diego hands over his mask to his son who takes his father's place with the possibility of new adventures to follow. Working titles for the film included *The Son of Zorro, Zorro: Wanted Dead or Alive* and *Zorro, Twenty Years Later.*

With the belief that this *Zorro* film would jump-start his career, Williams decided to make a semi-permanent move to Argentina. He loved the vitality, culture and people of South America so he moved into a furnished apartment in Buenos Aires. Although he would continue to travel back and forth between Southern California and his new residence, his stays in Buenos Aires would last longer and longer. This decision would put a strain on and eventually break his 30-year marriage to Jan.

Carlos Patiño, a local agent who had become aware of Williams' move, had seen some of his personal appearances and had heard rumors of the *Zorro* movie. Patiño felt that a great way for Williams to promote the project would be to appear in the Real Madrid Circus, the biggest circus in South America. The problem was, would Williams, who was by now considered a legend in Argentina, appear in a circus? Patiño asked Fernando Lupiz to convince his friend to do it. Lupiz went to see the show, thought it was first-class quality and conveyed this to Williams along with the fact that it would be financially lucrative for the American actor. Williams agreed to a fee of $5,000 a week and soon found himself the toast of Argentina.

The circus was based in Mar del Plata, a popular summer resort town. The show that Williams put together was similar to the P.A.s he did 20 years earlier. Fernando Lupiz, who appeared as the son of Zorro in the act, said, "The routine was always

Williams greets his Argentine fans, 1978 (courtesy of A. Lisazo).

Williams and Lupiz fencing onstage, 1978 (courtesy of A. Lisazo).

the same: First Guy rode twice around the arena on a black horse, as the Zorro theme played, then he came down and said, 'From Disneyland I bring a big kiss for all Argentine children.' The emcee asked him to reveal his great secret, to tell if he really was Diego de la Vega. Then he took off his mask, and told the children not to tell anybody the secret. The children asked questions, which the emcee read aloud. Usually it was how many Tornados there were, if Bernardo was really mute, etc. Then the emcee said that Guy had come to make a film from Argentina to the world, and that in it there was a 'young Argentine actor and fencing champion.' Then I came in also dressed in black. The man asked the children if they wanted to see us fight. They all screamed, 'Yes!'"

"Then Guy said, 'If you do a good performance with your sword, I will give you my sword and costume and you will be the new Zorro!' We did some passes and my sword fell down. The man asked the children if they would give me another opportunity. They said, 'Yes!' but Guy said, 'One opportunity is enough. We already fought.' The children insisted, and so we started again. This time it was long and after an elaborate routine, he would again disarm me. We always tried to leave my sword hanging from the ceiling or stuck in the floor. There was a spot marked that we tried to hit. Guy would make a joke like, 'I hope you practice for the film.' The whole thing lasted about 40 minutes. By the way, for the sake of authenticity, we used sharp tips on the swords and I was cut four different times on the face and I caught Guy once on the stomach. That's actually not too bad for over a thousand performances." From December 1977 to March 1978 (the Argentine summer season), the circus was seen by more than half a million people. It is still a record that stands for any Argentine summer show to this day.

In 1978, with the help of Patiño, Williams broke away from the circus and traveled the country with Fernando Lupiz performing their *Zorro* show. The group had a successful two-year run but it was beset with problems such as Patiño's poor financial management and the company's practice of doing free shows for publicity, then discovering down the line that people would not pay for what they had already seen for free. The *Zorro* traveling road show shut down in 1980.

Williams pursuing one of his favorite pastimes in the mid–1980s, playing chess on his computer (courtesy of Zorro Productions).

The *Zorro* film, which had always been the primary reason for the live shows, had been re-written several times, once by Williams himself in collaboration with Doris Band and Juan Carlos Torres. The Argentina Film Institute read the script and declared the proposed film in the "national interest" and offered Williams a loan of a half million dollars for his budget. Williams felt that was enough to start with but that the film he envisioned could not be done for less than $2–3 million. Palito Ortega, a sort of jack of all trades (movie director-producer, entertainer and politician), showed some interest in financing the project. In exchange for his support, he seemed to want total control over all aspects of the film. Williams, who had already invested three years of his life into the movie, felt that he knew the character and how to make this type of movie as well as anyone. Williams rejected Ortega's offer and temporarily abandoned the project rather than make a film that would damage the image of Zorro.

Back in the U.S., the Disney Studio re-released *The Sign of Zorro* as a 45-minute "featurette," pairing it with *The Jungle Book*. Throughout the

Williams arrives in Argentina, 1977. Fernando Lupiz helps with the bags (courtesy of A. Lisazo).

years, Disney had considered reviving *Zorro* with new episodes but cost always seemed to be a prohibiting factor. They did look at the possibility of syndicating the old series to a new generation of viewers. However, they ran into several obstacles, not the least of which was opposition from Latino groups who found the series to be objectionable. The fact that the show was in black and white also presented a problem, as did some of the musical numbers, which were felt to be irrelevant to a 1970s audience. The situation proved to be more trouble than it was worth so *Zorro* was put on hold indefinitely.

Although financial backers and producers would come and go, Williams and Lupiz continued to hold out hope that a new film would be produced. They were forever coming up with new ideas for the film and Williams and Lupiz would often keep their skills sharp by going to the Palermo Lakes for a morning of fencing practice. However, by 1980, the Argentine economy was in a downturn and it seemed unlikely that a film would see the light of day. With public appearance requests dwindling, Williams needed to make some money. He was offered $15,000 for an Argentine TV commercial. He held out for $17,000 and got it. The product was Schick Super II razor blade and the concept played on Williams' *Zorro* image with the actor making the sign of the "S" for Schick. However, Williams was unhappy with the dubbing used and he never made another commercial.

During a 1982 trip to the U.S., Williams suffered a brain aneurysm. It took almost six months for his wife Jan to nurse him back to health. When he finally recovered, he received a call from the Walt Disney Studios regarding a series that they had in the offing ... *Zorro and Son*. If they couldn't syndicate the old show, then maybe the public would accept a different approach to the character. Producer Kevin Corcoran explained, "The new show was totally camp. It was completely different from the other series. Disney was in such bad shape that they needed a change and this

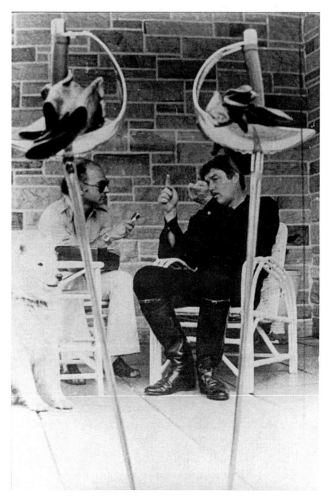

was a good transitional property. Some people may think of it as sacrilegious, but they had to make a change. Not that this was earth-shattering, but at least it was something different. We did talk to Guy Williams but for the approach this new show took he wasn't right for it. He didn't have enough of a comedy background."

Williams remembered things differently. "The concept was slapstick-comedy, but very broad comedy. I had a feeling the concept was more CBS's than Disney's. I would've been willing to do Zorro with a son because playing that part a certain way might be interesting even though there might be some comedy in it. A man in his 50s with a son, still in good shape but not quite able to pull off all the old stunts. It could have its comedy aspects as well as its slightly sad aspects. In a way, it could actually be a bit more realistic depending, of course, on how you handle

Williams (*right*) discusses the finer points of fencing with an Argentine journalist, 1978 (courtesy of A. Lisazo).

Williams (*left*) and Lupiz practice their fencing at the Palermo Gardens, 1978 (courtesy of A. Lisazo).

it. However, when you start out to do very broad stuff, well, then you're lost."[4] In the end, Williams discovered that "CBS was really in charge, not the Disney people. They decided to give *Zorro and Son* the 'cutes' and it was an abortion. It happened because Walt wasn't there. I've seen Walt throw network people off the lot. If he had seen their script, he would have yelled bloody murder."[5]

Henry Darrow eventually won the title role with Paul Regina playing his son and comedian Bill Dana as a talking, Jose Jimenez–like Bernardo. Unlike the original series, the budget was very tight and, because the accent was on comedy, the stunts and swordplay were kept to a minimum. It was filmed using some of the original costumes and the aging back lot *Zorro* set, primarily the cuartel. It died after five episodes in May of 1983. Perhaps the studio should have listened to Guy Williams. (In 1969, the studio actually considered reviving *Zorro* in color with a new star but axed the idea when costs were considered. When the studio decided not to exercise its option to renew the character, the rights reverted to the Gertz estate in 1967.[6])

At the same time that *Zorro and Son* was disappearing on CBS, the Disney Company started its own cable channel and *Zorro* was a staple, airing five days a week. When the Disney Channel premiered in France in 1985, Zorro's popularity there rivalled Argentina's. Williams recalled that "a man came out from Paris to find me in Buenos Aires. We did three days of interviews and photos for a French magazine because *Zorro* was a huge hit there."[7] Merchandise based on the series became very popular with the French children and sold briskly.

Guy Williams with man's best friend in the Argentine countryside, 1978 (courtesy of A. Lisazo).

Clowning around with friend Aracelli Lisazo in Marina del Rey, 1983 (courtesy of A. Lisazo).

Williams returned to Buenos Aires in 1984 and moved into an apartment in the fashionable Recoleta district of the city. He continued to enjoy what he described as a "very pleasant life, as quiet or as loud as I want it to be." Toward the end of the 1980s, he limited his public appearances and would rarely even submit to an interview. His last public act was to file a lawsuit against a magazine that had printed a story about a paternity suit filed against him by a young Argentine actress. Williams vehemently denied the charge and was confident he would win in court. Williams spent more pleasant times having dinner at one of his favorite restaurants, Oviedo's, or having a light breakfast and newspaper at La Biela. Ice cream could be enjoyed at Freddo's and, to work it off, fencing at the Jockey Club.

Williams and his wife Jan attend a charity event at the Beverly Hills Hotel, 1981 (courtesy of K. Gregory).

(*Left to right*) Henry Darrow, Bill Dana and Paul Regina star in the ill-fated *Zorro and Son*, 1983 (courtesy of Zorro Productions).

Publicity photographs used for Disney's 1978 re-release of *The Sign of Zorro* (courtesy of Walt Disney Productions).

He also enjoyed writing, reading, playing chess on his computer, putting some Beethoven or Mozart in his Walkman and talking long strolls around the city he loved. An Argentine friend remarked, "Guy is a man who knows how to live alone."

In May 1989, some of Williams' friends became concerned when they couldn't reach him for a few days. The doorman of his apartment building was also suspicious about the actor's absence and used his passkey to enter Williams' apartment. What he found was something of a horror: Williams' lifeless body lay on the bedroom floor. An autopsy would determine that he had been dead for almost a week, most likely the victim of a brain aneurysm. Fernando Lupiz was called in to identify the body of his longtime friend. It was front-page news in Argentina and reported around the world. Some of the Argentina newspapers tried to sensationalize Williams' death; one headline screamed "La Misteriosa Meurte de El Zorro." When he heard the news, Carlos Souto, an Argentine friend, said, "I think Guy died well, at the right moment. He would not have liked to see himself old or ill. Some months before his death he told me, 'Things are going so well that I think I could die now.'"

For a time, Williams' body rested in the pantheon of the Argentine Association of Actors, which had at first denied Williams the privilege because he was not a native of the country. Two years later, his ashes were sent to his family where they were scattered over the Pacific Ocean and the mountains of California.

Zorro makes his way through a crowd of fans after a 1978 show (courtesy of A. Lisazo).

Zorro and Tornado take a ride through the park, 1978 (courtesy of A. Lisazo).

This photograph was taken in April 1989, two weeks before Guy Williams died (courtesy of Silvia Rojos).

Every generation has its own heroes, its idols to hold onto and never let go. Although others will surely follow, for those of us who grew up in what now seems a million light years away, Guy Williams will always be "the bold renegade who carves a Z with his blade."

Epilogue

Life After Zorro

Guy Williams made only two American television appearances after *Lost in Space*. One was on the game show *Family Feud* for a *Lost in Space* reunion and the other was a brief interview on *Good Morning America*. Both appearances were in 1983. Williams would occasionally appear on television in Argentina. In 2001, he was awarded a star on the Hollywood Walk of Fame.

Appearances by Henry Calvin and Gene Sheldon after *Zorro* were few and far between. Calvin appeared on *The Dick Van Dyke Show* in 1963 performing a Laurel and Hardy sketch with the star. He had a bit part in the prestigious *Ship of Fools* (1965). Calvin also showed up in "Run Buddy Run," "Mannix" and "Petticoat Junction." His last role was in "The Boy and the Turtle" for PBS in 1971. Calvin retired from show business and returned to his native Dallas, where he died in 1975.

The multi-talented Sheldon's post–*Zorro* career was even more sporadic than Calvin's. In 1962 he appeared in *The Golden Horseshoe Revue* for Disney. Later in the 1960s he would occasionally turn up on variety shows such as *The Hollywood Palace* and *The Dean Martin Show* performing his old vaudeville act. Sheldon died of a heart attack in 1982 at the age of 75.

When Britt Lomond completed his run as Capitan Monastario, he appeared in *Tonka* as Gen. Custer and in an episode of Disney's *The Saga of Andy Burnett.* He had a recurring role on *The Life and Legend of Wyatt Earp* series portraying Johnny Ringo. Lomond continued acting throughout the 1960s but became increasingly interested in working behind the camera. He served as an assistant director or production manager on such films as *Midnight Run, Somewhere in Time* and *Airport '79*. Throughout the 1970s Lomond worked as a television production manager at Universal Studios. He now has his own company, LISADA, which estimates prospective film budgets. Lomond also loves bridge and competes in tournaments whenever possible. On his career switch, he stated, "I never regretted leaving acting. I didn't want to be a 60-year-old character actor waiting for the phone to ring."

George J. Lewis played bit parts in such films as *Batman* (1966) and *Indian Paint* (1965), reunited on the latter with his former director, Norman Foster. Lewis retired from acting in the 1970s to work in real estate. Lewis died in 1995, a few days short of his ninety-second birthday.

Buddy Van Horn continued to work in television and film as a stunt man. He eventually became involved with Clint Eastwood as a double and second unit director during the star's post–*Rawhide* career. Van Horn worked his way up to a full-fledged director and handled such Eastwood vehicles as *Any Which Way You Can*, *Pink Cadillac* and *The Dead Pool*. His recent activity includes work in the Eastwood films *The Rookie* (1991), as second unit director; technical consultant on the Oscar–winning *Unforgiven* (1992), and stunt coordinator on *In the Line of Fire* (1993), *Space Cowboys* (2000), *Blood Work* (2002), *Mystic River* (2003), and *Million Dollar Baby* (2004). Van Horn received the Lifetime Achievement Award on the 2002 World Stunt Awards.

Don Diamond was probably the busiest actor of the *Zorro* cast in the ensuing three decades since the show went off the air. The character actor appeared on hundreds of TV shows over the years and was a regular on *F Troop* playing the role of Crazy Cat. He had a bit part in an episode of *Zorro and Son* and was the voice of Sgt. Gonzalez in the *Zorro* cartoon series in 1981. He is now semi-retired, living in Southern California.

Writer-director Norman Foster could be found working in television (*Batman* and *The Green Hornet*) and the films *Indian Paint* (1965), *Merry Wives of Windsor* (1966) and *Brighty of the Grand Canyon* (1967). Foster was reunited as an actor with his old friend Orson Welles in the legendary (and unfinished) *The Other Side of the Wind*. In the film, Foster portrayed an associate of a Welles-like film director played by John Huston. Foster, the most stylistic of all *Zorro* directors, died in 1976.

Producer Bill Anderson stayed on at the studio until his retirement in 1978. He produced many films, among them *Swiss Family Robinson* (1960), *Savage Sam* (1963), *The Moon Spinners* (1964) and *The Happiest Millionaire* (1968). After Walt Disney's death in 1966, Anderson helped run the studio until 1974 when Ron Miller took over. Anderson passed away in 1997.

Writers Lowell Hawley and Bob Wehling took divergent paths. Hawley remained at the studio and wrote such films as *Babes in Toyland*, *Swiss Family Robinson*, *A Tiger Walks* and *In Search of the Castaways*. He retired in the 1970s and passed away in 2003. Bob Wehling, left Disney for financial reasons. Recounting her husband's departure from the business, Anna Wehling remembered that "Bob left because the Writers Guild went on strike in 1959. He needed a job because we had just gotten married and he wouldn't cross the picket line. He took a job teaching drama at California Lutheran College. He missed it, though, and I think his heart was always in it." Bob Wehling died in 1983.

After *Zorro* was canceled, William Lava scored the *Swamp Fox* series for Disney then left the studio. In 1962 he returned to Warner Brothers to help out on their animation shorts and continued to do so on a sporadic basis throughout the '60s. He also composed music for the films *P.T. 109* (1963), *Chamber of Horrors* (1966), *In Enemy Country* (1968) and a number of others. On television he worked on *Bonanza*, coincidentally scoring the episodes that Guy Williams appeared in. Also for TV he wrote the music for *F Troop* (1965–67) and co-composed the theme for *O'Hara of the Treasury* (1971–72). His last film was *Dracula vs. Frankenstein* (1971). Lava died in 1971.

Fencing master Fred Cavens' last work was on the *Zorro* series. The legendary choreographer died in 1962 at the age of 79. Because the swashbuckling genre had all but died out, his son Albert worked only occasionally, appearing on such shows as *Batman* (when a dueling double was needed for the Penguin) and as a dueling coach for Robert Shaw in the 1976 film *Swashbuckler*. He died in 1985.

"In Living Color"

The *Zorro* series, which had been appearing off and on since 1983 on the Disney Channel, returned there in October 1992 airing on a weekly basis. There was something very different about the show. Zorro was still in black but everyone and everything else was in full color. To make the series more palatable to the MTV generation (and looking to the possibility of selling the show to foreign markets), the Disney Company called upon American Film Technologies to colorize *Zorro*. At a cost of approximately $3.2 million for 78 episodes, AFT had used state-of-the-art technology to bring *Zorro* into the 1990s.

Using the Disney archives and their own imagination and discretion, AFT has tried to accurately replicate the original colors as much as possible. For various reasons, some alterations were deemed necessary. Henry Calvin's hair color goes from dark brown to reddish blond. Gene Sheldon's salt and pepper hair is now light brown; the olive green suit which he wore during the entire first season is now medium brown with a bright blue sash. Tornado's saddle is no longer gray but brown. The day-for-night scenes are also not as effective with the colorization process.

To the hardcore *Zorro* fans with access to color photos that provide solid evidence of specific colors, these changes are jarring violations; however, to the casual viewer, these modifications are of little or no consequence. Because of colorization, perhaps the show will reach a wider audience. But in the process, *Zorro* lost some of its 1950s charm that helped make it a classic show. That is a trade-off that the studio seemed willing to make.

Chapter Notes

Chapter 1

1. Bob Kane, *Batman and Me* (Forestville, CA: Eclipse Books,1989), pp. 37–38.
2. Jim Harmon, *The Great Radio Heroes* (New York: Doubleday, 1965), pp. 195–196.
3. Tony Thomas, *The Great Adventure Films* (Secaucus, NJ: Citadel, 1976), p. 5.
4. Keith Keller, *Mickey Mouse Club Scrapbook* (New York: Grosset & Dunlap, 1975), p. 10.
5. Leonard Mosley, *Disney's World* (New York: Stein and Day, 1985), p. 233.
6. "Editor Salutes 7-Up," *Zorro Newsletter,* January 1958, p. 4.
7. Jean-Pierre Coursodon, with Pierre Sauvage, *American Directors Volume I* (New York: McGraw Hill, 1983), p. 136.
8. Guy Williams interview with Ken Meyer, 1983. Published in *TV Collector*, July-August 1989.
9. "Has Zorro Fouled Up Guy Williams?" *TV Radio Life*, July 12, 1958, p. 5.
10. "Four Faces of Love," *Movie Stars Parade,* September 1958, p. 67.
11. "A New Zorro," *TV Life*, April 1958, p. 34.
12. "Meet Henry Calvin," *Zorro Newsletter,* September 1957, p. 3.
13. "Meet Gene Sheldon," *Zorro Newsletter,* September 1957, p. 3.
14. Disney studio publicity, 1957.

Chapter 2

1. David Hartman, *Good Morning America* television interview, September 8, 1983.
2. "Fencing Master Teacher of Stars," *Hollywood Citizen-News*, January 31, 1949, p. 16.
3. Rudy Behlmer, "Swordplay on the Screen," *Films in Review*, June/July 1965, p. 363.
4. "Men Behind the Scenes," *Hollywood Citizen-News*, January 31, 1949, p. 16.
5. "Zorro Foiled His Rival," *TV Guide*, April 26–May 2, 1958, pg. 26
6. Philippe Garnier, "Thirty Years Later We Found Zorro," *Télé Jour*, October 1985, pp. 40 & 42.

7. "Latest Zorro Beats 'em All, Reports Coach," *Zorro Newsletter*, January/February 1959, p. 3.
8. Guy Williams interview with Mike Clark, 1986. Published in *Starlog*, January 1987.
9. Guy Williams interview with Mike Clark, 1986. Published in *Starlog*, January 1987.

Chapter 3

1. "On the Set," *Zorro Newsletter*, August 1957, p. 4.
2. Leonard Mosley, *Disney's World* (New York: Stein & Day, 1985), p. 236.
3. Dave Holland, *From Out of the Past: A Pictorial History of the Lone Ranger*, (Granada Hills, CA: Holland House, 1989), p. 217.

Chapter 4

1. Leonard Maltin, *The Disney Films* (New York: Crown, 1973), p. 20.
2. Guy Williams interview with Mike Clark, 1986. Published in *Starlog*, January 1987.
3. Guy Williams interview with Mike Clark, 1986. Published in *Starlog*, January 1987.
4. Johnston McCulley, "Zorro Frees Some Slaves," *West*, January 1946, p. 94.

Chapter 5

1. "Cast, Crews Plunge Into Past at Historic Mission Filming," *Zorro Newsletter*, September 1957, p. 3.

Chapter 7

1. "Zorro Foiled His Rivals," *TV Guide*, April 26–May 2, 1958, p. 26.

Chapter 8

1. "Program Sound Ad Buy: Thul," *Zorro Newsletter*, March 1958, p. 1.
2. "It's the Molloy, Paul Molloy," *Zorro Newsletter*, March 1958, p. 2.

Chapter 9

1. "Editor Sees New Series Changes," *Zorro Newsletter,* July/August 1958, p. 3.
2. "A Match for Zorro," *TV Guide,* October 4–10, 1958, p. 26.

Chapter 10

1. "New Zorro Opening Potent Drawing Force for Viewer Attention," *Zorro Newsletter,* January/February 1959, p. 1.
2. Annette Funicello television interview, Disney Family Album, 1985.

Chapter 13

1. Leonard Maltin, *The Disney Films* (New York: Crown, 1973), pp. 319–320.
2. Guy Williams interview with Mike Clark, 1986. Published in *Starlog,* January 1987.
3. Bill Cotter, based upon research for *The Wonderul World of Disney Television* (New York, NY: Hyperion, 1997).
4. *Daily Variety,* June 17, 1958.
5. "Out of the Tube," *Daily Variety,* February 3, 1960.
6. Guy Williams interview with Mike Clark, 1986. Published in *Starlog,* January 1987.
7. "When Guy Hisses the Villain — He Means It," *TV Guide,* September 24–30, 1966, p. 26.
8. "Guy Williams: An Inside Story," *Alpha Control,* January–June 2002, #28.
9. "The Return of Zorro," *Chicago Daily Tribune,* "TV Week," October 22, 1960, p. 7.

10. "These Guys Are Lost in Space," *TV Times,* April 1965.
11. "When Guy Hisses the Villain — He Means It," *TV Guide,* September 24–30, 1966, p. 26.
12. Bob Thomas, *Walt Disney: An American Original* (New York: Pocket Books, 1976), p. 30.
13. Mike Clark, "Guy Williams — Relaxed, Retired and Lost in Space," *Starlog Magazine,* January 1987, p. 24.
14. Mike Clark, "Guy Williams — Relaxed, Retired and Lost in Space," *Starlog Magazine,* January 1987, p. 24.
15. Guy Williams interview with Ken Meyer, 1983. Published in *TV Collector,* July-August 1989.

Chapter 15

1. "When Guy Hisses the Villain — He Means It," *TV Guide,* September 24–30, 1966, p. 24.
2. *TV Star Parade,* February 1958, p. 17.
3. Guy Williams interview with Mike Clark, 1986. Published in *Starlog,* January 1987.
4. Guy Williams interview with Ken Meyer, 1983. Published in *TV Collector,* July-August 1989.
5. Mike Clark, "Guy Williams — Relaxed, Retired and Lost in Space," *Starlog Magazine,* January 1987, p. 72.
6. Bill Cotter (based upon research for) The Wonderul World of Disney Television (New York, NY: Hyperion, 1997).
7. Guy Williams interview with Mike Clark, 1986. Published in *Starlog,* January 1987.

Index